Beyond Hindutva

Beyond Hindutva

S.L. VERMA

RAWAT PUBLICATIONS
Jaipur · New Delhi · Bangalore · Mumbai · Hyderabad · Guwahati

ISBN 81-316-0053-X

Published by
Prem Rawat for **Rawat Publications**
Satyam Apts., Sector 3, Jawahar Nagar, Jaipur 302 004 (India)
Phone: 0141 265 1748 / 7006 Fax: 0141 265 1748
E-mail: info@rawatbooks.com
Website: www.rawatbooks.com

New Delhi Office
4858/24, Ansari Road, Daryaganj, New Delhi 110 002
Phone: 011-23263290

Also at Bangalore, Mumbai, Hyderabad and Guwahati

Typeset by Rawat Computers, Jaipur
Printed at Nice Printing Press, New Delhi

Contents

IV
Internal Threats to Hindutva

V
Global Threats to Hindutva

VI
The Remedy of Hindatva (Indianism)

VII
Indian Democracy and Globalization

Preface

This book has been addressed to the people, particularly the Hindus and other big and small communities, presently living in India, that is, Bharat. It makes an appeal to all of them to learn Hindatva, Indianism or Bharatatva based on territorialism (material base and resources) and nationism (emotional attachment and feeling of oneness). Next to them, every one is free to adopt any ideology, faith or religion, form of worship, particular lifestyle, profession or language. With this macro feeling one is free to live a life of his own. Affinity with territory or land of India is enough for the people to work for its growth, security, increase in production and affluence, and its progress in different directions. All these factors can broadly be measured to a certain extent to examine and compare the inadequacies and find out appropriate remedies to remove them. Greater the depth of Indianism (Hindatva), more would it be effective in its progress and advancement, and vice versa.

Still the book is specifically meant for the majority community (now being reduced equal to some large minorities) of the Hindus, who have been the worst sufferers throughout past ages at the hands of their own people. It is due to the claim of their divinity, particularly of the pseudo-Brahmins as a class, and some of the Hindu seers and sages, reformers, founders of new religions and political leaders in general.

As a result of socio-religious and political deprivation of two-third of the Indian people, a large number of Hindus found it better to get rid of this inhuman Hindu system and seek shelter of some egalitarian religion. They eagerly joined Buddhism, Jainism, Sikhism and other religions, which had promised to free them from the frustrating and dreadful Hindu social system. In the Brahmin-Kshatriya ruling classes, in fact, there were no more 'Brahmins' or 'Kshatriyas'. As such, the castrated Hindu masses, along with these pseudo-Brahmins and Kshatriyas, cowed down before the aggressive hordes of Islam and Christianity. Their rule for over one thousand years or so further sealed the fate of Hindus in terms of their diminishing power, unity and number. The Hindus and their remnant culture crystallized in form of 'Hindu Dharma' which provided ample space to the newly settled forces of Islam and Christianity. The latter expanded, dominated the land and converted by force, conviction and persuasion a large chunk of the depressed castes and classes of the Hindus. The number of converts grew to the extent that by 1947, India had to be partitioned despite best efforts of Mahatma Gandhi and the Indian National Congress for Hindu-Muslim unity and independence of India as a whole. The separated parts of the country in the West and East formed Islamic/ Muslim nation of Pakistan. Many areas, which appear as parts of India in the North and North-East, were already occupied by the forces of Christianity. Besides the division of India into Bharat and Pakistan, there are several areas in form of provinces, districts and talukas which were dominated by large non-Hindu communities and political groupings. If this process continues, the Hindus are destined to be reduced as one of the minorities of India. It would put unity, integrity, autonomy and democracy of India in jeopardy.

The Hindus, on failure of their Hinduism, pinned their hopes also in the attempts of a great leader and Mahatma Mohandas Karamchand Gandhi. Gandhi proclaimed to work for the independence of United India and bring about Hindu-Muslim unity. People could realize that goal if they were willing to act on truth and non-violence and eschew untouchability and treat depressed classes and caste at par with them. The Hindus came forward to follow him in large number, but their old evils somehow remained with them. His efforts even within the Indian National Congress proved futile before the claims of the Muslim League under the leadership of

Mohammad Ali Jinnah and the opposition of Dr. B.R. Ambedkar, the sole leader of the depressed classes. Still the Hindus continued to consider Gandhi as the sole remedy for the decadent Hinduism and the only alternative left to them and India as a whole.

During the freedom movement, some of the farsighted and patriotic Hindu leaders discovered and diagnosed some of the main causes of decay and downfall of the Hindus in the lack of their 'organization' and 'nationalism' as its basis. On utter failure of both of the Hindu Dharma and the Hinduism, a new set of ideas and programme of action came into being. It is popularly known as the ideology of 'Hindutva'. It claimed Hindustan for the Hindus, and for those who were willing to respect Hindu heroes and Hindu culture. The influence of the Hindutva ideology grew in several areas on the basis of teaching and training to the Hindus. Its workers voluntarily came forward to render social services and to defend and protect their rightful interests. But, it could neither offer a viable and broad form of 'nationism' nor unite the Hindus at large. The Hindus are badly divided from within and outside. They still stand on the old ground of the 'Hindu Dharma' or the 'Hinduism' or both. The Hindus still live in a dream world that non-Hindus of India would ever bank upon such Hindutva for their support, survival and advancement and be one with them. For them, as offered here, only a new ideology of 'Hindatva' or Indianism stands valid and workable. All should work it out and act on it in proper and effective manner.

The Hindus are advised here, on the basis of their frustrating and suicidal past experience of several centuries, to eschew guidance from orthodox Hindu saints and seers, socio-religious organizations like the Brahmo Samaj, Arya Samaj and Ram Krishna Mission, and misguided fundamentalists of the erstwhile Jan Sangh, Hindu Maha Sabha, VHP (Vishwa Hindu Parishad), Shiv Sena and the like. They should also not repose their faith and confidence in the present pseudo-secular parties—Congress, Socialist, Communist, BSP, BJP and the like. The latter operate at the expense of the Hindus, and are eager to teach *hara-kiri* to the Hindus by reducing them into a group of small minorities. The Hindus, at their own, and in cooperation with all other minorities, should lead them all to carve their own ideology of Hindatva or Indianism. Only then would they become the people of India or Bharat.

I am sure that the suggestions offered in this book would be taken seriously for the betterment and safe future of all concerned.

The book has been divided into seven parts and each part consists of chapters. Part One presents the basic framework of the book and outlines discussion on the Vedic Age and the Hindu Dharma. Part Two is on Hinduism and Hindutva. Part Three deals with attempts to renovate Hindutva and contains five chapters. Parts Four and Five discuss internal and global threats of terrorism to Hindutva. Part Six, explaining Hindatva, suggests some permanent remedies in three chapters. Part Seven is on Indian Democracy and Globalization. As most of the Hindus, and the world at large, still bank upon Gandhi as solution to their present and future problems, Gandhi has been reconsidered in Chapter 11.

The book also confides the non-Hindu communities to avoid entertaining false hopes from the Hindutva forces or from their enemies who look friendly to them. The author would like them to stand firm for compelling the Hindus to fully renovate, restructure and modernize themselves to meet the needs of a viable democracy and nationism. They had to teach the Hindus many good things in the past, but they themselves went astray. Presently, the Hindus are to learn a lot from them. But to do this, the non-Hindu communities also have to reorient themselves on new lines of Hindatva, Indianism or Bharatava. The book is thus meant mainly for those who entertain doubts on Hindutva and wish to go ahead.

I thank Shri Kailash Rawat of Rawat Publications and am indebted to him for bringing out this enlightening book in the present form. Suggestions, comments and analyses are cordially invited.

August 15, 2006 **S.L. Verma**

I

The Basic Framework

1

Introduction

A viable community and its members, in order to live, grow, enjoy and pursue goals of life, have to work in many directions and at several levels.

Collectivities do all this on basis of their understanding of Basic Reality. It is Basic Reality which operates as a Force, and makes and moves Nature. It is also the basic material which appears as living and non-living things. It includes human beings, plants, animals, birds and other things. This Basic Reality may be called as Ultimate, Energy, Life, God, Brahma, Khuda, Allah and the like. In its Ultimate Form it is Unmanifest or one. Some of that Unmanifest or one appears as Manifest or Nature—in form of innumerable living and non-living things.

Man is closely related with Basic Reality. There can be five levels or grounds of such relationships. One can live at first level of Basic Reality, or second level of Unmanifest, or third level of both Unmanifest and Manifest, or fourth level of Manifest with some space to Unmanifest, or fifth level of Manifest pure, direct and simple. Some people while living at Manifest of fifth level can also remain aware that they are also on the ground of Basic Reality. They act and operate using reason, discussion and cooperation with other human beings. In view of the contents of Basic Reality, they find no difference between Manifest and Unmanifest (see Table 1).

Cosmos and all human discourse originate from Basic Reality. Contents of Basic Reality are most important. They may be either (i) abstract, or (ii) empirical, or (iii) both. On the basis of his understanding of these contents man determines the form of cluster of religion, culture and society. In a cluster, form and practice of religion results in social organization, pattern of living, status of priesthood, kinds of worship and relations among followers and non-followers of a religion. Religion along with other factors also generates obedience, state and government, gives details of material conditions and forces of production to sustain them. After their emergence arises the problem of inter-state and inter-community relations and attitude to be developed towards other communities and nationalities. Religion, directly as well as indirectly, indicates preferences for the use of particular instruments, methods and techniques to deal with matters of conflicts and cooperation inside and outside communities. Cluster is totality of all these things.

Clusters relate to various levels. They can be studied on basis of aforesaid stages (see Table 1). Understanding of Basic Reality broadly fructifies in nine forms. In Table 1, these have been captioned as 10 points. All are discussed as clusters operating at five levels.

Contents and Forms of Basic Reality

Religions, socio-political systems, cultures and interrelations among them come out of the understanding of Basic Reality. Relationship between man and Basic Reality generates five broad clusters of human living. Each cluster relates to particular form of belief system or religion, polity and culture. Man can know Basic Reality in five ways. Each way has specific implications when (i) God himself speaks about its own Basic Reality (a) directly to man, or (b) through some Messenger to man or (c) some seer, sage or godman tells his own realization of or about that Basic Reality; (ii) man himself may find every thing made of and moved by that Basic Reality; (iii) he may divide the Basic Reality into Unmanifest and Manifest, and like to live by subordinating the latter to the former; (iv) a man, without believing in Basic Reality, may like to live in a world of sense experience. However, some may like to keep their faith at the level of their conscience; and (v) man sees (a) this world as Reality, or (b) finds

Table 1

Levels of Understanding Basic Reality and their Impact on Religion, Culture and Polity

Areas of action and serial number (points 1-10)	*Levels and description of Reality*	*Area number or point, extent and description of activities*	*Overall impact*	*Challenges and problems*
Background	*Level One:* Basic Reality	Points from 1 to 10 Almighty, God, Nature Brahman itself Operates the cosmos	Bliss and pleasure	nil
1. Forms of Ultimate Reality and its Implications 2. Message to man, ultimate goal, religion and idol worship 3. Social set-up, hierarchy, supremacy of Brahmins and the Individual 4. Role of knowledge, science, technology, tradition and education	*Level Two:* Unmanifest (after a few decades– downgrading to power of priest hood)	Only Points 1 and 2 Theocracy, forced or persuasive conversions, colonialism, crusades, etc.	Spread of religion, Plurality of religions, Spirituality, renunciation, hierarchy, Poverty, Other-worldliness	No-actionism, Neglect of man, Society, State, Invites Aggression Enslavement; Ritualism, plurality of gods, idolatry social hierarchy, degradation of men, conversion
5. Organization of state and government	*Level Three:* Unmanifest and Manifest	Covers Points 1, 2, 3-7 and 9 Theocracy, forced or persuasive (power of priesthood) Conversions, colonialism, material gains, industrialization	Imperialism, expansion of trade 3 commerce, exploitation, vandalism, materialist advancement in science and technology, secularism in temporal matters	Religion of dominated people turns introvert, other-worldly, superstitious, challenges coming from rise of nationalism, demands of independence, rights, rule of law etc.
6. Material conditions livelihood, agriculture, trade and commerce	*Level Three:* rolls down to level four	Enjoyment of power, wealth, sensual pleasures, domination, Theory of Two Swords, but actually there is control of the Sword of Religion over the Secular Sword		

Areas of action and serial number (points 1-10)	*Levels and description of Reality*	*Area number or point, extent and description of activities*	*Overall impact*	*Challenges and problems*
7. Inter-state relation 8. Status of masses awareness, participation and nationism 9. Relations with other religions, races and communities 10. Instruments, and Techniques of Agitation	*Level Four:* Manifest	Relates to Points 3 to 9; Rise of nationalism, democracy, rationalism, individualism, liberalism, spread of education, science and technology, Freedom from all types of religious orthodoxy, faith is limited to conscience of the individual	Covers all human activities, welfare, international world order, regional organizations, law and order	Competition, rivalry, wars, weapons, neglect of morality and religion, atheism
	Level Five: Manifest and Basic Reality	Concerns with Points 3 to 9 in case some people operate as if staying in Basic Reality, cover all the points	Covers all human activities, welfare, international world order, regional organizations, law and order	Co-existence, international peace and cooperation, human rights, world peace and liberalism

no distinction between this world or other world. For him, all these are aspects of Basic Reality.

First three ways relate to the first and second levels. Fourth and fifth ways can be connected respectively with fourth and fifth levels. Third way primarily belongs to temporal and secular world.

Sometimes, time in the knowing of that Basic Reality is also important: whether divine statements on that Basic Reality are made several centuries ago, or in recent past or are being learnt just in present.

Generation of Religions and Implications

First three ways of knowing Basic Reality appear closer to each other, but have different implications for man and his living. God speaking directly to man vouchsafes equality and fraternity. His utterances through Messenger or some Chosen Person leads to orthodoxy meant for selected followers. Visualization of Basic Reality by seers and sages results in plurality of faiths ensuring freedom of religion.

Standing away from these considerations, man at the first level knows, feels, imagines or learns about that Ultimate or Basic Reality as his own origin and source of life. Both Manifest and Unmanifest are two aspects of Basic Reality. One may confine oneself to totality of Basic Reality or its Unmanifest form only. Some other may act at both Unmanifest and Manifest levels. Such person makes no difference between Unmanifest and Manifest. For him secular world or Manifest is part and parcel of Unmanifest or Basic Reality. That way his actions are that of Basic Reality: निष्काम कर्म। Such men of Basic Reality find themselves as part of that Ultimate Reality, Energy or Life. They appear to work as Nature or Prakriti. At that level, man is part of existence-in-action.

At the second level, a man identifies himself with the Unmanifest: ज्ञानयोग। He shuns Manifest or worldly living. He remains lost in meditation (*samadhi*), prayers and salvation. When he acts with that understanding, he is part of that Ultimate or Unmanifest. Few persons are able to live like that. Seers and messengers belonging to level two teach human beings to devote themselves to meditation (ध्यान), prayers and yoga and realize the Unmanifest. They operate the Manifest in an ascetic manner. Their doing and acting has little concern with the material situation. Even when they appear to work upon the Manifest, they continue to live in the Unmanifest. Intelligent people call this stage of living in Basic Reality or operating it as Realization of God, Brahma, Moksha, Nirvana, Kaivalya and the like. Third level is related both to Unmanifest and Manifest, but upholds Unmanifest. But, the third level persons or godmen are super-intelligent. They feel and find the limitations of common man and see him suffering at the hands of worldly arrangement. Ordinary people think and find the Manifest, Nature or Cosmos as the only Reality. Often on behalf of or keeping in view of that existent Basic Reality, they proclaim message of God; or God Himself is told to have spoken to them through some messenger or seer in human language. They often tell what is Ultimate Reality, what is to be seen, what is to be believed, where to go and what to realize and the like. All is declared as Code of Conduct of Man. They appear to be executing the divine mission of taking people from Manifest to Unmanifest. Later on, their statements become source of fanaticism, extremist and terrorism. Their successors, instead of living from Manifest to Unmanifest begin to stay only at the Manifest and enjoy power and control over millions of followers. Their religion stands for Power and Authority. As they happen to utter, speak or write in the name of Almighty or God Himself, no one can verify or oppose their statements. It means whatever they have said must be accepted as true. These messengers of God suo motto restrain their followers from thinking and believing differently from them. Deviants are threatened to be punished by God or His ordained ruler, messenger, son or successor here in this world, and life beyond in heaven or hell. Later, when their devotees or followers grow in large number and organize, form institutions and prescribe rites and rituals, the disbelievers and apostates are physically persecuted, exiled and executed. Non-believers are forcibly converted, persuaded and attracted to their religion. This is done to take those neo-converts on the right path or to God.

But the people usually do not understand niceties of religion or Shastras. They live at fourth level and like to operate only at the Manifest or Temporal Worldly level. Human beings often are confined to and attached with, and find themselves living at the level of Manifest. This Manifest to such people is the only Reality. They think, do and act in accordance with their own understanding of the Manifest world. Understanding of this Manifest suffers from several known and unknown limitations, inadequacies and evils with pains appearing in limitless forms. At the fourth level a person may permitted to nurse his religion or faith to his own internal self or soul. His approach on matters pertaining to Manifest can be public, empirical and collective. It operates on reason, persuasion and compromise. He may stop at the Manifest level. People can live, enjoy and make progress even while remaining at this level. They may not feel any need to hanker after the Unmanifest. Within the givens of fourth level, individuals can be allowed to enjoy faith at their personal level. The fifth level persons are rare. They are free to act in the Manifest. While doing so they can also think that they are working upon Basic Reality. The religion of those who work on Basic Reality is always universal, humane and spiritual. They identify themselves with Basic Reality and do not stand for any particular form of worship or personal God. In practice, they make use of reason, discussion and decision by majority if not consensus. The basis of their acts remains temporal and moral. At heart they, remain detached, but, pursue good of all or common good.

Formation of Social Set-up

Social set-up is built upon what the godmen say about Brahma or Existence. Godmen and their followers, when they stay at first level, act as if they are part of God, Absolute or Ultimate. They act like God or His Nature. They form no society, community or caste. Everyone is a member of their family. They are 'jeevan mukta', yet work ceaselessly for the maintenance of Good Order. They stand away from the formal forms of metaphysics, worship or status. Next to them, another set of godmen stays at the second level. They envision that only Unmanifest or Brahma is the Basic Reality. The followers are taught to treat the world as 'Maya'—Unreal, Nescience or Illusion, and, give up to the maximum possible extent all worldly acts. To them worldly acts bind the soul, cause sin and lead to bondage. Renunciation (*sanyas*), devotion (*bhakti*) and knowledge (*gyan*) are the only permissible ways for them.

Godmen or ideologues at the third level provide for the Manifest part of Basic Reality and regard the rest as Unmanifest, as in the divine theory of Two Swords. They call Manifest world as temporal or secular, and leave its operation to reason and likes of human beings. The Unmanifest or ecclesiastical world is kept under the control of some personal God, religion, church, mosque and priesthood which often controls education, marriage, divorce, worship, morals, rights and duties to keep all believers treading on one particular path. This is done either in name of love or compassion to be expressed through rendering service to the poor, depressed, orphans and outcastes. Faith is told to replace Reason in all walks of life.

Their mentors prescribe detailed directives to followers about family life, marriage, divorce, children, last rites etc. The followers have to earn livelihood, property, give alms to the poor, have fasting, regular prayers, engage in fighting against the enemies and maintain relations with other fellow beings. In order to please God or obtain Heaven, they are taught specific ways of worship and make sacrifice, raise religious structures, keep women under control and the like. They give directions to organize society or community in a particular way: social hierarchy, upper and lower castes, classes, their duties, need of religious guidance to laymen through holy books, priests and Shastras. Some Pope, Khalifa or Guru like successor, one or many, to the Original Messenger of God might be ordained to keep the followers united and multiply on permanent basis. Rites and rituals are prescribed in detail. It is commanded that owing to their sins in past life, some people are born in poor, lower and degraded sections of society. Such people have to suffer exploitation, oppression and ill-treatment as a matter of punishment for their past sins. Women and children are also put along with them. All this is ordained in the name of divine dispensation.

Those who happen to live at fourth level often are modern, competitive, materialistic, acquisitive, democratic and egalitarian. They rule and dominate through ethnicity, colour, wars and diplomacy. The fifth level so far has been found only in the Vedicas of the past. Presently, few persons are able to attain it. At this level, man is supposed to maintain balance between Manifest and Unmanifest, but do stand firmly against all odds and have final victory of life.

State and Governance

People at level one have no concern with or care for matters pertaining to state and government. Those who live in Unmanifest at the second level, tend to neglect state, society, nation and culture treating them as 'Maya' or illusion. Even when some attempt to reinterpret 'Maya' as real, they stand for the Unmanifest. Their Unmanifest leads them to a world of no-action and prefer to have utmost patience, tolerance, non-violence and making all sacrifice for peace and self-realization. But utterances from godmen, at the third level, permit life of Manifest but only under the control and supervision of Unmanifest or religion. They provide for the political and organizational set-up – emphasize need and specific form of government, appointment and anointment of rulers, mobilization and use of armies, relations between the ruler and the ruled, law, taxation, and punishment. They also put emphasis on education, knowledge, discovery, making of science and technology etc. and their use to spread particular form of inter-state relations and make empires, operate succession and merger of states, warfare, diplomacy, development and use of arms, and hold others as prisoners and slaves. They often do so in the name of God and religion, and launch conversion of faith of other people in large number. But they suffer from the over control of religion, which often lags behind and turns out of date and rise of forces of humanity, nationalism, democracy, industry and advancement in science and technology. They are materialist par excellence. In this respect, the fourth level people follow secular ways. The fifth level people are almost free from all such weaknesses and limitations. They are men of detached action pursuing common good.

Material Conditions

First level has no concern with material conditions. Second level godmen speak only of Basic Reality of Unmanifest (Brahma) and find Manifest as Unreal (Maya). Third level preachers also appear to follow them in matters of religion. Both religion and ruler, respectively appearing as Unmanifest and Manifest, claim share in various form of taxes from all these people—farmers, tradesmen, artisans and artists. But, the fourth level men permit common people to look after material production, agriculture, trade, commerce, arts and crafts, and architecture, waterways and other material conditions. These people, in secular areas, happen to keep away from the teachings or influence of godmen and their powerful followers. They deal with Manifest or temporal/secular world, as it appears to them. They cannot be prompted or pressurized by the fears, threats and greed of godmen like heaven or hell. They keep a vigilant eye over the persons doing wrong, anti-state, unsocial, inhuman things, and take rightful and effective action. Only the fifth level man acts as if Basic Reality itself is operating Nature. However, they act in cooperation with each other, preferring use of reason, morality and utility.

Status of Masses and Awareness

Godmen and religions connected only with Basic Reality or Unmanifest, i.e., levels one and two, leave no scope for the rights of individuals and groups, awareness of the masses in worldly matters, spread of nationalism, participation in social, economic and political affairs, or organizing people for the realization of material goals. The people and masses are supposed to do only their duties, meditate or perform formal religious rites and rituals. They happen to have high regard for those who neglect family life and remain satisfied with whatever they get from begging, alms or directly from Nature. They grow into orthodoxy and fundamentalism.

Religions, operating at third level, are concerned both with Unmanifest and Manifest, permit organization of religion, state, nation, particular form of governance, doing propaganda even indoctrination, making of favourable public opinion, use of press and media, and IT, but attempt these to allow only under the directives of Shastras, religion, or priestly hierarchy.

Fourth level elite are concerned only the Manifest or Temporal World. They have freedom to operate all these means, institutions and devices, using reason, persuasion, election and compromise. They may use personal faith as means to temporal ends. Fifth level men are available only as ideals who have identified their self with Ultimate Self operating in close cooperation with all.

Inter-state Relations and Consideration Towards Other Communities

As regards relation with other religions, communities, godmen and cultures, opting Basic Reality only or preferring to pay high regard to Unmanifest by avoiding Manifest, have no clash with other faiths and their followers. They permit growth of others religions in a full fledged manner: एकं सद्विप्रा बहुधा वदन्ति (Good scholars speak about that in many different ways). They remain unaware of or do not care for social, political and economic consequences of increase in the number of other competing religions and their followers. However, third level godmen and religions like to establish control over units of Manifest—number of followers, coverage of reformers, family, state, law, economy, polity, trade, resources and influence. These are further used to increase their political, economic and diplomatic power, and also for breaking of other established communities, nations, religions and polities. This they do in the name of supremacy of their religion or for spread of the final Words of God upon earth. Factors behind their expansion can be peaceful, manipulative or coercive conversion of downtrodden classes, alienated communities and oppressed castes of other religions. They end up in colonialism, world wars, establishment of empires. People of fourth and fifth levels do not have to face such problems. They happen to compete and fight against the forces of opposition on secular grounds. Of late, these forces are appearing in form of LPG (liberalization, privatization and globalization), and are expanding at a fast speed. They have to face fierce opposition from them. They try to make use of them for the happiness of common man.

Instruments, Methods and Techniques

Nature of religion or teachings of godmen determine the instruments, methods and techniques to deal with their own followers as well as others belonging to different religions. Messengers, seers, sages, priests, gurus and the like devoted only to Basic Reality or Unmanifest, opt for the ways of meditation, simple life, persuasion, prayers and preaching with the ultimate goal of self-realization. Second and to some extent third level religions grant superior place to the Unmanifest and indulge in, along with meditation, prayers and preaching, several other forms of worshipping idols of deities. The second level faiths also resort to creation of multitude of gods and goddesses (out of actual lives of their great men and heroes), idol worship as profession and faith, celebration of festivals, *bhajans*, *keertans*, dances, music, building of temples, mosques, churches and gurudwaras. Credulous masses blindly obey them. Their priesthood creates huge organizations, institutions, religious literature, makes films and episodes, and uses all forms of communication and media. The secular part of the third level people often manages these matters through discussion, persuasion, creating favourable public opinion and passing of appropriate laws. They also try to prepare themselves for a winning fight against religious fundamentalists, fanatics, extremists, terrorists, crusaders and the like. They succeed after enjoining a tough and united fight. They raise various forms of organizations, well-equipped armies, manufacture superior weapons and develop latest technologies. Ultimately, they join together to resolve their conflicts through peaceful and democratic means. Lack of guidance from the fifth level persons keeps them on brink of war. Fifth level persons adopt all democratic means and resort to force only as a last alternative. Preparation remain in practice to face crises.

Limitations, Consequences and Challenges

Lastly, the believers in Basic Reality, till they remain true to their ethos and understanding, are other-worldly people interested only in meditation and God-realization. They remain happy with what they have. Like Buddha, Mahavira and seers of Upanishads they have no other concern. They consider all human beings as equal members of one family and make use only of persuasion, preaching, meditation and personal living and try to bring all men together. All human beings are considered equal, irrespective of caste, creed, social status, colour, language, ethnicity, nationality and culture. Such religions gain wider acceptance, influence and following. However, all of them in thousands and millions, in terms of their tenets, happen to neglect this world—social life, family, security and sovereignty of the nation-state, agriculture, industry, trade, commerce and the like. They offer no opposition to aliens, intruders, aggressors and strangers and so on. Very soon, evil elements take over and they fall victims to aggression, conversion, slavery and corruption in their religion. Successors and followers of these religions coming after the original godmen, often come down from level one and two to level three. Most of them indulge in egoistic expressions, pleasures and power, and like to stay at materialistic and acquisitive levels. In practice, they do not remain so otherworldly. Later on, one can see them founding empire, evolving big communities, promoting nation-states and mobilizing standing armies, all in the name of God and religion.

Level three religions are very powerful and orthodox both at ecclesiastical and temporal levels. In both these areas, power, wealth and influence abound with them. On the one hand, these religions establish complete control over the conscience, faith and morals of millions of people, and, on the other hand, rule over their secular concerns through the ruler. Even personnel of governance, democracy, administration, law and order, education etc. accept supremacy of that religion. They manage to invest billions of dollars in the conversion of depressed, exploited and poverty-stricken masses of different communities and nation-states, thus to work for the expansion of that religion as power. This they do in the name of God, service, love and human cause. In order to maintain their superiority over others, such duel religions also take lead in all secular areas—science, technology, medicine, trade and commerce, industry and agriculture. In several areas they hold monopolies, patent rights, advance military technology and armament. Their power stands unchallengeable in the fields of warfare, arms and nuclear weapons. Their power is constrained only by the power of other similar religion-state operating in two-pronged ways. During the latter 20th century, most of religion-states have transformed into nation-states. In order to face conflicts and crises, states having identical ethos join together in many types of regional and global organizations.

The fourth level people keep themselves away from first, second and third level clusters and their full and partial religions. The fourth level societies claim to be secular and temporal. They stand for welfare of the people, democratic participation, rule of law, governance based on consent and compromise, and care of the weaker sections of society. But mostly being multi-cultural, plural and democratic societies, they permit freedom of conscience, creed and worship to individuals at all levels. They happen also to grant special rights and privileges to all groups and minorities irrespective of the consideration whether they believe in democracy, nationalism and co-existence of other communities or not. As such, they are forced to grant freedom of religion to their citizens even at the cost of law and order or supremacy of state. Consequently, they look unable to keep all religious matters confined to the conscience of the individual citizens, and disallow apparently pseudo-religious matter from interfering in public life. They fall prey to the forces of fundamentalism, extremism, communalism and the like. These forces operate in the name of religions. In fact, states with such religions can survive and flourish only when they firmly operate at the Manifest level. Their acts have to be open, public, empirical and understandable. When polities grant more room to their members for pursuing goals of religion, they try to overpower the state. Later on, such polities turn unable to operate in a secular manner, and let their people to plunge into communalism, casteism, exploitation, etc.

The fifth level people are non-existent. They belong to Manifest-Unmanifest category. Under this dispensation, all public spheres belong to Manifest. Everyone is left free to act and operate at that level. It depends on the individual himself whether he does it as if he is a part of Basic Reality or not. There is no clash between Unmanifest and Manifest. At this level, godmen or their successors stand at Basic Reality. Even when they find difference between Manifest and Unmanifest, they permit full and free play to them. For them God realization does not mean doing away with the worldly activities or socio-economic and political life. They tend to face the problems squarely and directly: personally in a detached manner.

Clash, Conflict and Cooperation among Clusters of Different Levels

This is point 10 of Table 1. But, at the ground level, there is constant clash among the forms of these levels. They all do not exist peacefully. Even when there is dominance of one level, others constantly try to come up, and take over.

For understanding the scope of religions, the format of a cluster can be shown extending up to ten points: (1) Ultimate Reality: Impact and consequences, location of life—this world/next world; (2) Message or Religion to man, Dharma, religion, incarnation, idol worship; (3) social set-up, hierarchy, varna/caste, individual, caste, supremacy of Brahmins, women, position of lower castes and others; (4) role of knowledge, science, technology, tradition, education; (5) organization of state and government; (6) material conditions, livelihood, agriculture, trade, and commerce; (7) inter-state relations; (8) status of masses, awareness, participation, nationism; (9) relations with other religions, races and communities; and (10) instruments, methods and techniques.

Overall discussion or evaluation can be made separately as point (11) Failures, Limitations and Impact.

All these points, steps or stages are to be discussed after presenting the background for the rise of a cluster or its religion.

It would be observed that level one of Basic Reality covers all the ten points. Level two of the Unmanifest concerns only points 1 and 2. Level three, which is related to both Unmanifest and Manifest, covers points 1, 2, 3-7 and 9. Level four which is concerned mainly with Manifest involves points 3 to 9. So is the case with level five, which is similar to level four also covers points 3 to 9, but if its actors consider themselves part of Basic Reality, they join points 1 to 10 at par with level one.

The Vedicas followers of the Vedas were at level one. Upanishads, Buddha, Mahavira, Adi Shankaracharya etc. belonged to level two. The Vedicas, after their deterioration, transformed into Hindu Dharma with evils of plurality of religions, idol worship of gods and goddesses, other-worldliness, reincarnation, casteism, exploitation of lower castes, degradation of women and the like. All that led them to their domination and enslavement at the hands of Islam and Christianity. The latter religions belonged to level three. Rise of forces of nationalism, democracy, rule of law and industrialization stands at level four. Level five exists mostly as a concept and an ideal.

It is obvious that religions operating at level two have, in view of their challenging background, flourished in terms of number of followers, influence, message of peace, co-existence of religions, freedom of worship, etc. They all are creations of spirituality, renunciation, asceticism, no-actionism (निवृत्ति मार्ग) and way to salvation. They have little concern with rights of individual, social structure, form of state and government, economy and other temporal matters. They often believe in many paths to realization of God or Reality. As such, they have no objection to rise of multiplicity of religion, sects or philosophies. Their overall impact is peace, tolerance, spirituality, non-violence and other-worldliness. When level two prevails intensely over the minds of masses, evils like ritualism, superstition, idolatry, social hierarchy, grace etc. become part of religion. They have little to resist aggression, forced conversion, vandalism, occupation of the country, and exploitation and enslavement of the people. However, top brass of these religions after some decades come down to level three or four. Level three religions or clusters are very powerful. Often, they claim to have emerged on the basis of direct utterance of God to them, or through some Prophet or Son of God to them. This makes them fanatic or extremist believers permitting no change by them in the Message of God. These religions claim action on all points and operate them under the directions of top priesthood. They divide formally or informally all human concerns as religious (Unmanifest) and temporal (Manifest). Under the guidance and control of their religious mentors, the secular life is left apparently free for the common men. But they are given directions about it in detail. In the name of God, Prophet, Father, Pope or Guru they spread their hold through holy wars, conversion, colonization, imperialism and the like. They face difficulties only when new non-religious forces like nationalism, democracy, rationalism, individualism, science and technology stand against them. Level four, being free from all kinds of pressures of religious orthodoxy, tyranny and superstition, devotes itself fully to the cause of newer forces. However, they may permit individuals and groups to nurse faith at the level of conscience. At times, when this concession overpowers the state activities, there is outbreak of communalism, extremism, fundamentalism and terrorism. State may appear powerless before them and split asunder. As stated above, sometimes, level two also transform into level three. It so happens when the top brass of that religion happens to control minds and hearts of millions of people, and enjoys power, sensual pleasure, wealth and power. Both of them, viz., the original level three and corrupted level two clusters, prove much more dangerous to the existence and survival of the rest of the levels. Its mentors claim to speak and obey the utterances of God, the followers appear willing to make sacrifices to any extent. At that time, there appears no difference between the two levels—two and three. Only level four is found fully equipped to deal with them. It is almost free from evils of tyrant priesthood, superstition, multiplicity of faith, elaborate forms of worship, idolatry and the like. It concentrates its energy at the level of Manifest or Secular, and fights with the latest socio-political, industrial, technological and economic weapons against the forces of levels two and three. However, level five is much more advanced as it treats the existence as Basic Reality and operates as Almighty Himself.

In fact, during the 19th and 20th centuries, the whole effort of the Hindu socio-religious reformers and leaders was to transform the Hindu Dharma into an ideology of Hinduism to serve the cause of national awakening and emancipation of the country. These reformers mostly thought that they themselves were like the Vedicas at level one but they were really living at level two. Even at that level, they worked with a God of their own liking, partial, pleasant and imbecile. With that God or religion, they wanted to meet the challenges fiercely posed by religions operating at level three. Dayananda tried his level best to take the Hindu Dharma to the stage of Vedicas, i.e., from level two to level one. He made some awakening in the Hindus, but failed in his ultimate mission. Vivekananda, who stood at level two, appeared to join level three, but could not get rid of the basics of Hindu Dharma. Both were confined to the disability of 'sanyas' and lacked appropriate instruments, methods and tools to realize their goals. Tilak assiduously and vociferously tried to rush from level two to level three by creating men like Lord Krishna and Shivaji, i.e., of level five, but could not succeed very much. He too could not redeem Hindu Dharma fully. His stand on Hindu Dharma could not attract depressed classes, Muslims and Christians. Gandhi directly operated with the basics of Hindu Dharma, and wished to stay at level two. He could not understand that his basics were to the disliking of the depressed classes as well as Muslims in general. Only the Hindus of the prevailing Hindu Dharma stood behind him firmly despite creation of Pakistan and shattering of his dream of Hindu-Muslim unity. A cause of his failure was his avowed goal of achieving self-realization even while taking part in the freedom movement.

In fact, the prevailing form of Hindu Dharma had become the permanent, widely known identity of the Hindus. It had evolved a form, practice and structure, which served the interests of all upper caste Hindus. They never liked to part with it. The present form of Hindu Dharma permits the upper strata of the Hindu society to dominate, control and exploit millions of lower castes Hindus, including women in the name of God and religion. The Hindus themselves do not want to lose this 'identity'. It allows them to do anything they like easily in the name of Shastras, gods, form of worship, rites and rituals, transmigration, grace of God and the like. Any attempt to reform or renovate in a serious manner is likely to result in disciplining the people of upper castes which they never like. Any reform in the Hindu Dharma might put their status, life, ego, pleasures, and livelihood at stake. They somehow want to retain the status quo. In fact, they can lead a carefree life till the Hindu happen to remain in majority in the country. The Hindus hardly care for the coming future when the Hindus would be reduced to one of the other minorities. Most of them are unwilling to anticipate the evil consequences of such an unfortunate situation. Among the Hindus themselves number of such Hindus is fastly growing. They have learnt to lead descent lives at the expense of the Hindus and the Hindu Dharma. Credulous Hindus still regard them as their leaders, mentors and well-wishers. They hardly care for protecting the larger interests of the nation, community and religion. This sight of plight is upheld even by the Hindu scholars, stalwarts and leaders. All other non-Hindu leaders of different walks of life also like to recognize the Hindu Dharma only on the basis of this 'identity'. It serves their purpose, ego and future goals. The present form of Hindu Dharma has been supplying millions of downtrodden, exploited and low caste people to convert and to serve their socio-political and economic interests. It provides soft under belly for hitting them on permanent basis. At this level they have been dismembering and diminishing the Hindus. Utter neglect of the Hindu Dharma by the Hindus themselves at religious, philosophical, rational and secular levels is a matter of perennial attraction to the makers and mentors of Islam, Christianity and a number of other big and small religions.

This perspective enables us to know how the Hindus have been trying to defend and protect their metaphysics, philosophy, culture, polity, and community during various stages of history.

As such, first, we shall discuss level one of the Vedicas and the level two of the Hindu Dharma. From level two we shall go to levels three and four, i.e., encirclement of Hinduism by non-Hindu forces and efforts made by the social, religious and political leaders to awaken masses on the basis of their renovation of Hinduism. An attempt would finally be made to find out a way in form of Hindatva or Indianism or Bharatatva. This Hindatva would enable the different communities of India to unite and be able to face creatively the challenges of democracy and globalization in the present 21st century.[1]

Note

1. A.P.J. Abdul Kalam, *India 2020, A Vision for the New Millennium*, Penguin Group Books, 1998, 2002.

2

Tenets of the Vedic Age

The Vedic Age or Vedicatva or Vedic Dharma belongs to the era after the Aryans settled in India (Bharatvarsha), south of the Himalayas and the north of the Vindhyas. They had passed through constant wars, ideological conflicts, changes in social organization, and political experiments. A long process of change, struggle, migration and settlement had ensued. They had to rationalize, idealize and justify what had gained so far. They had to consolidate what they had achieved, and make for further advancement in all directions. The Aryans were conscious of their superiority in intellectual, moral and political fields, and were linked ethnically with the compatriots of Iran, Persia and Egypt. They continued to refine and develop their social, military and governmental organizations. Large kingdoms came into existence. It was a society that grew later unequal. Labour of some was used by others to maintain the expanding system. There were men of knowledge, warriors, merchants, peasants, and menials. Up to that time it was open, as anyone could join its functional sectors or change it if one liked.

The paramount distinction of the Vedic culture was its spiritual attitude towards life and the world. That spirituality was the core of the Vedic way of life does not mean that they had neglected or looked down upon healthy progress in the worldly pursuits. Their history bears witness to the fact that their religion, science, archaeology, sculpture, architecture, astronomy, mathematics, arts, commerce, trade, economy, etc., were all at the top of the world and that had made fundamental contributions to the growth and enrichment of human civilization and culture. Distribution for welfare and social service, rather than self-obsession and possession, of resources was a great basic value of Vedicatva culture. *Yajna*, the eternal symbol of altruism, dedication, sacrifice and noble deeds, was essential part of this culture.[1]

In the past, there was only one dharma or religion. "It is an established fact that five thousand years ago there was no other religion except the Vedic, for Vedic principles are all consistent with science. Apathy towards the Vedas was the cause of the war of Mahabharata. This apathy led to world-wide ignorance, and the intellect of the people became muddled and different, set up different religious faiths according to their own ideas" (Dayananda).

The terms 'Hindu' and 'Hinduism' are of fairly recent origin as the ancient Indians had no name for their own religion. These names were invented by Persians to refer to the people living east of the river Sindhu. These inhabitants had no name for their religion. One of the reasons for this, was that whereas for "other people, religion is only a part of life; there are things religious, and things lay and secular. To the Hindu, his whole life was religion". For a Hindu, his relation to God and his relation to man, his spiritual life and his temporal life, form an integral whole. His religious theories and practices could not be given a separate and distinct name. According to Chandrashekharendra Saraswati of the Kanchi Kamakoti Peetha, it was the only religion in the world ministering to the spiritual needs of the mankind as a whole. There was no second religion from which it was required to be distinguished. Hence, there was no need for a name for it. It was and continues to be nameless. The Vedas do not owe their origin to any historical personage or prophet. Buddhism, Christianity and Islam are founded religions. Their dates are definite, since their authors are known. No such date or founder can be cited as marking the beginning of Hinduism.[2]

According to the basic philosophy of the Vedic Age or Vedic Dharma, there is abounding Basic Reality having unlimited facets broadly divided for human purpose as Manifest and Unmanifest. Man is related to both these forms. One can go from Manifest to Unmanifest and from Unmanifest to Manifest. But he usually lives in between the Manifest and the Unmanifest or Beyond. Rules of society have to be in consonance with the cosmic order. They are collectively called as dharma. Each society has to have specialization and division of labour in innumerable ways. There must be (a) men of knowledge, (b) men devoted the defence and protection of society, (c) men engaged in agriculture, production and trade, and (d) a large number of people rendering general services and labour. Simultaneously, each man passes through (i) the stage of studentship, (ii) the stage of married life and earning livelihood, (iii) the stage of retirement and if one believes or requires, and (iv) the stage of self-realization. Government or ruling, voluntary or contrived, is necessary. But it must be established only by the persons committed to people's welfare.

The Vedicatva, as an ideology, mission, style of living or religion, can be succinctly summarized in the following manner:

Ultimate Reality and Implications

The Vedas see Life, Reality, Energy or Existence as a whole—a cosmos containing both natural and super-natural. Cosmos is a process, always a change or flux. Consciousness or life is neither separate from the world nor a by-product of matter. Both are blended together. There are three levels of Existence or Reality—first, there is a Beyond, a Supreme Brahma (ब्रह्म). It cannot be fully comprehended or realized. It can only be experienced. Second, there is differentiated reality, which is an extension or manifestation of the Supreme Brahma. Third, there is an effort to connect the cosmos with the Beyond or Brahma. Man can do that.

A part of Nirguna Brahma or causeless cause of the universe at its own, became Manifest through endless cosmic cycles of individuations and differentiations. But the Unmanifest is noetic or mysterious, and cannot be known. It can be experienced through breath-regulation (pranayam), prayer (japa), meditation (dhyana or samadhi) etc. The Manifest is peneumatic or the differentiated creation, and can be known. It follows certain rules (rita). As such, there is some order in the cosmic process. It can be known and communicated with others with the help of reason and experience. Man participates in this process in many ways—pravriti (regulation of desires) and *nivriti* (total eradication of desires). Pravriti connects man to Reality, which is Beyond, through various forms of virtue—and tapa (penance), dhyana (meditation) and japa (prayer). Both men of pravriti and nivriti participate in the cosmic process.

Dominance of Dharma

In the context of society, dharma operates as 'rita' (cosmic rules). It is connected with and derives from the grand architectonic design of the cosmic order. Dharma includes all properties, elements, rules, arrangements and directives, which should be followed by all men.

Dharma enjoins that everyone should pursue good which implies participation in the cosmic process. It leads one to move Beyond. In case of conflict between duties, dharma gives preference or priority over the welfare of the larger group: good of society is greater than good of the individual. Man is alone to discriminate between various goods or relationships. One should not simply oblige his kiths and kins. Virtue or dharma alone elevates one's soul to Brahamahood (ब्रह्मत्व). A man should fulfil obligations of his station or duty in equanimity and gradually earn spiritual merit. In this way, he will join the divine order and attain 'moksha' (salvation). By doing so, he can be a veritable God in this world itself. Thus, at levels one and five, there is no conflict between 'dharma' and 'moksha'. Both sustain the cosmic order. Dharma leads to 'moksha'. There is no hurry. One should move ahead to experience the Beyond from whatever the level, stage or form he is standing on. When one performs his action or duty selflessly or with equanimity, he is virtually at par with God or Creator himself. However, a subtle distinction exists. Those who stay at level one must act alike God, Nature or Almighty. They do not have consideration of Unmanifest or Manifest. No such goal as the greatest good of all or social good or consent of majority or moral values compels them. Level five people act as per temporal conditions and considerations but only for the general interest. They never serve personal or vested interests.

Social Set-up and Women

Obviously, all men could never easily realize or live at the Unmanifest or God or Brahma. Therefore, a scheme was ordained to attain the Ultimate or Basic Reality through proper living at the Manifest level. It could serve the individual as well as society's ends.

This scheme was proclaimed as 'varnashrama dharma'. There had to be four classes or 'varnas': 'Brahmins' (the learned ones), 'Kshatriyas (warriors), 'Vaishyas' (producers and traders), and 'Shudras' (menial labour). The Aryan or the Vedic society was consolidated by providing four categories of human element: (i) knowledge, (ii) protection, (iii) production and exchange, and (iv) labour. Earlier, the basis of classification was self-will, functional, experience and inclination. In this classification, the 'Brahmins', being selfless in the pursuit of knowledge and wisdom and concerned with welfare of all, were given the highest regard, respect and authority. They were supposed to be one with 'Brahma' or 'God'. But still they thought of and taught welfare of the society.

The whole of society and its individuals were divided vertically and horizontally. Vertically, there were four 'ashramas' (orders) for everyone. Passing through them one can attain salvation gradually by performing functions as a householder after attainment of knowledge or education in 'gurukuls'. Human beings are not identical in temperament, capacity and learning. Society too needed diversity of functions and services. Therefore, horizontally, it was broadly divided into four 'varnas' or classes of functional specialization. All the varnas and the ashramas made up 'fullness' of society and presented opportunities for the complete growth of individual's life. This process trained them to attain the experience of Manifest and Unmanifest as identical realities.

Among them, all the householders played the pivotal role. None was allowed to violate the customary social laws. All were obliged to maintain the cosmic order through observation of social laws. The stage of household or family (गृहस्थ) in the ashrama scheme was the highest of all. Family was the foundation of the (Hindu) social organization. Husband and wife must keep each other happy. Gods did not dwell where women were not respected. Being physically weak and vulnerable, a woman was to be protected at all stages of her life—parents, husband and sons. She was neither an object of enjoyment nor a labour. Power, status and wealth were essential for the efficient management of a family. But they were not to be pursued in excessive manner and made instrument of domination over others. Excessive accumulation of property was sin. It was to be earned to the extent of fulfilment of needs and performance of one's duties towards others. A householder was to strive to attain others' happiness. This task of householder was regarded as very important. It was more important than that of meditation and prayers.

Supremacy of Brahminhood

As the Brahmins had experience of the Unmanifest and knew the cosmic rules (rita) of the Manifest, only were they in a position to spell out the moral order (dharma or law) for the society, and also the state. They guided the man to realize his goals here and after.

The true Brahmins were better than the members of other varnas. They knew the Manifest directly and in the light of the experience of the Unmanifest (Supreme Brahma), cosmic order and reason. They rendered selfless services to the society and did not indulge in material and other gains. As they were one with the Supreme Brahma, they performed their duty with equanimity and without caring for the fruits of their actions. They were in-between, but go Beyond. For others, they laid emphasis on customary morality, but to rise far above. The idea of a Brahmin was that of a man who is capable of pursuing and using knowledge without attachment. The members of other varnas could have attachment, but anyone could be a 'Vedic hero' if acted in a selfless manner or larger interest of the society. Later on, this principle was known as 'nishkama karmayoga' of the Gita. It means, a man performing his duties without attachment is alike a selfless 'Brahmin' or God, the Unmanifest. But he continued to observe customary morality or dharma of the social order.[3]

On the basis of such selfless service and living by begging, the Brahmins were highly respected. Later on, the Brahmins, on the basis of high status, began to exercise power and control over the lower strata of the society, and also distorted the canons of dharma to save their vested interests. They made it impossible for others to change their 'varna' without their authority. They changed 'varnas' into castes, based on birth and heredity.

Role of Knowledge and Education

Along with dharma the Brahmins had been given the highest, central and leading place in the polity which included the king. Only they were supposed to be one with the Manifest and Unmanifest Brahma. In the beginning, they stood away from the material things like property, status, land, etc., and lived on alms or begging from the householders. Because of their lifelong education, experience, devotion of dharma and selfless commitment to maintain the cosmic order, they guided, directed and restrained the individuals, castes and the society. The Brahmins, during their whole lives, were devoted to know the Manifest world through reason, experience and devotion. They were considered as virtual Gods who deserved the highest respect from all. Manu, as first law-giver, wrote: "In the beginning of the world, for the prosperity of communities, the Brahma (creator) created the Brahmin out of his mouth, the kshatriya from his arms, the vaishyas from the mid-region, and the shudras from his feet."[4]

A strict code of conduct was laid down for them engaging them in the pursuit of penance, meditation and yoga. A Brahmin capable of pursuing knowledge without attachment and his imparting it to the society without fear or favour was their highest ideal. He was to be different from the priest (clergy or purohit) who got money, property, things etc. gifted to the temples. Having control over senses, the Brahmin was a man of pure mind and pure action. He never hurt others. He learnt even from a Shudra. One who deviates from his code of conduct, had to suffer thousands of hells, received severe punishment, and was not considered as a 'Brahmin'.[5]

Organization, Strong Government and Unified Command

The Vedicas were convinced that the existence of a central authority in India was a necessary condition for the survival and continuation of the dharma or civilization. It could be realized only through a Vijageeshu Rajarshee Samrat—a victory-loving king himself leading an ascetic life as a Vedic hero, or a man-of-detached action.[6] Early tenets were: Goals of Dharma could be realized only through the state, "where there is Dharma, there is victory" (यत्र धर्मो ततो जयः); "For obtaining results of Dharma and Artha, let us salute the state" (अथधर्मार्थफलाय राज्याय नमः); "Root of Dharma is Artha" (धर्मस्य मूलमर्थम्); and "Root of Artha is the state" (अर्थस्य मूलं राज्यम्).

The Vedas stood for knowledge or science. As science, they establish the four varnas and four orders (ashramas) in their respective duties or activities. No society could operate without them. The Smritis recapitulated or repealed these duties. The code of royal duties (Rajdharma) was responsible to maintain the varnasharma dharma.

The king was a means or an instrument to keep them in force. The source or base of the Law of Social Order (society) was Shastra or the Sacred Canon Law. It was a means of promoting individual's security and happiness as well as the stability of social order. Sanctions behind this law were: (a) the law of karma; and (b) the arm of political authority.[7]

The need of making of a strong and expanding polity for India was strongly felt. It was considered necessary that (i) supremacy of state was a must for unity and integrity of India, Aryavarta or Bharatvarsha; (ii) there should be a strong central governance for India as a whole; (iii) it should be protected by a strong army; (iv) the ruler must be 'Vijageeshu' as well as ascetic; and (v) only Vedic or Arthashastra—politics could endure.[8]

The Vedic hero had the tradition of doing one's karma or performing one's obligations to society with equanimity without consideration to personal profit or loss, victory or defeat, fame or blame.[9] One was to lead his life on those lines even after attaining samadhi, salvation or moksha, except at the fourth or last stage of life.

Inter-state Relations

The Vedic ruler was the ideal king, vis-à-vis other states, as 'Vijageeshu' (one who aspires to be victorious). He believes in the expansion of his state and stays as the centre of the rajya-mandal (राज्य–मंडल). He believed in expansion and domination through the process of 'federalization'. A Kahatriya's duty is to achieve victory and not to turn his back in the battle.

Inter-state relations included (a) theory of rajya-mandal; (b) policies of sama (conciliation), dama (bribery), bheda (dissension) and danda (force); (c) six-fold policy; and (d) diplomatic relations. In the beginning, there were hundreds of smaller states constantly at war with each other. In order to realize the goal of a universal state for the Aryavarta (India) or a bigger state, he elaborated the already existing concept of 'rajya-mandal'[10] to universal empire (सार्वभौम वैदिक साम्राज्य)।

Status of Masses and Participation

It was a popular society. Everybody actively participated either in war or in sabhas and samitis.

Material Conditions

As the Vedic society had given full freedom to the people working at the level of Manifest and state of human life, there was tremendous development in all walks of life. India was considered to be the most prosperous and advanced country on earth. There was great development in the fields of agriculture, trade, commerce, village and state industries. Great works were done in the fields of medicine, mathematics, astrology, literature, music, painting, architecture etc. The country was full of natural resources, affluence and pleasures. Exports from India reached every nook and corner of the then known world.[11]

Limitations, Consequences and Challenges

The Vedic society suffered from many weaknesses and shortcomings. The whole social organization was made hereditary which did not allow persons belonging to a particular caste to change it. The Brahmin supremacy was considered fully justified till (a) they were true or real Brahmins, and (b) kept away from power, status, wealth etc. But there was no system of testing, examining and selecting true Brahmins. As such, the whole class was enthroned on hereditary basis. Such people were sure to rewrite the Manu's Code and the Shastras in their favour.[12] None was to be turned out from a varna who had lost traits, experience, inclination or education necessary for the membership of that particular varna. All jobs, functions and professions could not find place in the four-fold classification of society. There was no mention of machinery to implement the ashrama system. The king was ordained to maintain the 'varnashrama' system but his job perhaps ended after the Brahmin supremacy was established in all walks of life. The state, later on, even lost its jurisdiction to intervene in social sphere.

The Brahmins did not provide for change of varnas and ensure propriety through their regular education, training and professional experience. The Brahmanical supremacy or operation of the traditional moral order turned ineffective. The social order got fractured and crumbled from within. It may be stated that perhaps at lower level the two varnas (Vaishyas and Shudras) had merit, aptitude and jobs as prescribed for them, but at the upper level, barring a few persons, there were neither Brahmins nor Kshatriyas in the real sense of the term. The society began to be deprived of required knowledge as well as protection and justice. In a way, it was a society without its leading and protective elements.

The householder, during 'grihastha ashrama', was given a very high and respectable place. But, the woman's position was not clear. She had no 'upnayana' or education or independence. She had to remain always under the control of males—father, husband or elderly children. Thus, half of the society was cut off from active social and moral life. There was degradation of women and the system led to their institutional exploitation, inequality and injustice.

The individual was completely hand-cuffed in the four folds of the varnashrama system. At ashrama level, only the Brahmin male was a full person. The majority of the population, the Shudras and women, were less than human beings. The rest of the upper layers of varnas had been turned, by placing them on the basis of birth and heredity, into castes. Even without merit, temperament and experience, they were permitted to remain members of that particular caste. No arrangement or scheme had been suggested to test their merit or capability for the membership of that caste.

The king has been given a very high place in the society, almost divine and unparallel one. But it was not clear how ordinary people were to be pleased and kept satisfied. Their plan of the consolidation of the Aryan society under the typical Brahmanical supremacy during the period of turmoil worked for sometime, but proved suicidal and self-defeating in the long run. The society tumbled down and was trampled over when it came into conflict with communities having vertical and horizontal equality and freedom to live in a different manner. Such society of Manu proved rotten, dwarfed and half-grown before them. Its women were cut off and crippled; Shudras, the largest segment suffered from exploitation, illiteracy, poverty, and alienation; and the Brahmins had lost their vigour and original 'Brahmanism'. As the latter continued to ride on the neck of the submissive people, there was no hope of redemption or return to the early age of freedom and equality enjoyed by the Vedicas. Obviously, this society was not a dharma order, rather it was operating against all the tenets of their dharma.

Many new religions, besides Jainism and Buddhism, had already come up. Caste system worsened. During the Guptas the Vedicas mostly converted themselves into Hindu religion, with caste system more worsening. It lost its absorbing and assimilating capacity.

Aftermath

Newly emerging philosophies, turned into religions like Jainism, Buddhism, Vedanta and others—successfully challenged the Dharmashastra world-view, and broke the four-fold social order into pieces. The exploited lower castes accepted them as a way to their social emancipation. Millions of people joined the quietude, renunciation and ascetism and began to live like sanyasis (saints) after leaving their families—wife, children and parents. Worldly life, including politics and state obligations, were cause of bondage to them. They did not require any varna or caste status. They were new types of 'Brahmins' (Shramanas, Bhikkhus or hermits) who were now no more concerned with the services of the Kshatriyas, Vaishyas or Shudras. This world was a prison or cage to them. In terms of conventional ashramas, they joined directly the last and fourth order—sanyas or life of meditation and renunciation. They were groups of individuals, each pursuing the good of one's own self. This individual had no concern with society except getting food and protection from it.

The conventional Vedic or Hindu view had no reply to these ideological challenges. The social disharmony, conflict and alienation prevailing in the Hindu society appeared beyond cure. There was no reply from Kautilya and the like that this world was unreal, ephemeral, encaging and despicable. On the one hand, a large number of people continued joining the new religious communities of Jain, Buddha and Vedanta variety, whereas on the other hand, the Hindu society itself began to come under their spell. The latter forgot the Dharmashastra teachings that one can attain moksha (salvation) by performing their varna (caste) obligations. The four-fold social order was necessary for the society as a whole or the goal of moksha was not distant from the other three goals—dharma (virtue), artha (wealth) and kama (pleasure). For the new communities of ascetics, all these were a source of bondage to them.

All was justified in the name of divinity, God and Shastras. Millions of low-caste persons, in search of equality and redemption, were joining the teachings of Mahavira and Buddha. They gave up their worldly life under the impact of new teachings and adopted quietude, renunciation or sanyas. They felt no obligation to family, society or state. Millions of followers of Jainism, Buddhism and

Vedanta were now either Shramanas, Bhikkhus or sanyasis. Thus, they broke up the whole scheme of the dharma order: achievement of salvation by leading their lives first as a householder, and responding to obligations imposed by dharma towards parents, teachers, gods, society and the state. In a way rise of these religious sects and communities was a response to the exploitative social order of the Vedic or Aryan society. The Vedic society now onwards began to move towards other-worldly directions, ascetism, non-violence and neglect of this world. The new religions did not remain confine to spiritual or psychic world, but were fastly influencing the social, political and military matters. Even within the Vedic and post-Vedic (Hindu) society, there was rise of many other sects (Vaishnavas, Shaivas, Shaktas, Tantrikas etc.), which ultimately proved subversive to the prevailing structure of the dharma-society. The new communities hardly had the care that a society to survive must have elements of knowledge, of protection, of production, and of service, and its members before entering into the lives of renunciation, meditation or quietude should actively pass through stages of education and earning livelihood and family.

There were many provisions and traditions amounting to some kind of constitutional constraints of state's (kingly) power. But they were not effective. Neither the pressure of public opinion nor the compulsive consultation of the Council of Ministers was decisive. Some stray examples of their being effective did not make their advice obligatory or binding. All powers vested with the king who in the later centuries became tyrant and oppressive and supportive to birth and heredity based caste system.

Notes

1. It was called as Akhand Joyoti – 'The Light Divine'.
2. Ashok Vohra, Delhi University, *Hindustan Times*, May 9, 2003.
3. The real cause of deterioration of the Vedicas lay in the deformed four-fold varnashrama order. Later on, it was no more a varna system, but a hierarchical caste system based on birth and heredity, which could no more be the guarantee of merit desired in a particular varna (now caste). Dynamism generated by spirit and enthusiasm of man was no more

visible. The four-stage ashramas was not available to the lower varnas, particularly the educational part, and the Vanaprastha and the Sanyas.

4. ब्राह्मणोऽस्य मुखमासीद् बाहू राजन्यः कृतः।
   ऊरू तदस्य यद्वैश्यः पद्भ्या शूद्रोऽ अजायत।। — यजुर्वेद, अध्याय 31 मंत्र 11
5. But nothing is known what treatment was given to such degraded or denounced Brahmins.
6. Besides Chandragupta, Kautilya himself had set an example like a 'rishi' (seer) who had experienced the unknown God or Brahma, but did not confine himself to the cares of ever-lasting communion with the Unmanifest, but came to earth to rescue the people from the clutches of anti-dharma kings and other subversive elements.
7. Kautilya was concerned with the enforcement of social order through the arm of state.
8. With this view, Kautilya (along with Chandragupta) uprooted the oppressive Nanda dynasty and united the warring states under one strong centre, and brought about the Golden Age in all walks of life.
9. See, the oath that the king took at the time of his investiture ceremony:
   प्रतिज्ञां चावरोहस्व मनसा कर्मणा गिरा।
   पालयिष्याम्यहं भौमं ब्रह्म इत्येव चासकृत्।।
   यश्चात्रधर्म इत्युक्तो दण्डनीतिव्यपाश्रयः।
   तमशंकः करिष्यामि स्ववशो न कदाचन।।—महाभारत
10. The proposed 'rajya-mandal' is a group of states around the king's own. The king, desiring victory and expansion, was called 'Vijageeshu'. He (विजगीषु) operates in the centre. Around his state are enemy, middle, and apathetic states. Enemy can be natural (cousin), artificial (evil causing), and neighbour. A neighbouring state, unless otherwise, is always an enemy state.
11. For fn. 7 and fn. 8, see, K. P. Jayaswal, *Hindu Polity*, Calcutta, 1924; Beni Prasad, *The State in Ancient India*, Allahabad, 1928; U.N. Ghoshal, *History of Public Life in Ancient India*, Vol. 1, Calcutta, 1944; and, A.S. Altekar, *State and Government in Ancient India*, Banaras: Motilal Banarsidas, 1955.
12. There was no provision for a learned shudra to change his 'varna'. The shudra had no reach to education or 'upnayana'. He had to remain an exploited hateful labour. It was nothing but rationalization of injustice, exploitation, immorality and inequality.

3

The Hindu Dharma

Ved Vyas of the Mahabharata had long confessed, "With my both hands raised up, I am crying that the Dharma is bestower of both Artha (wealth), and Kama (pleasure), why not that Dharma is being followed."[1] He had uttered at the end of the Mahabharata war, "When politics becomes lifeless, the Triple Vedas sink, all the dharmas (the bases of civilization) (howsoever) developed, completely decay. When traditional state ethics are departed from, all the bases of the divisions of individual life are shattered. In politics are realized all the forms of renunciation, in politics are united all the sacraments, in politics are combined all knowledge, in politics are centred all the worlds."[2]

Still these great seers and scholars continued to commit themselves to the same dharma and politics which had already been losing ground. In fact, they somehow stood for the status quo, and failed to come out with fresh ideas and goals. Challenges from within and outside had been appearing one after another, but they continued to eulogize their early set-up. Both Dharmashastra and Neetishastra traditions failed to recover that lost ground of the Vedicas. The Hindus are unaware of the phenomenon that the form of Hindu Dharma which they respect, love and admire so much is the very source of their decay, downfall and defeats. Under the cover of praise from others, it simply invites insults, humiliation and loss in size, power and influence.

Background

There was rise of several organizations of monks, ascetics, seers and scholars. They all disproved the basics of the conventional Vedic Dharma, and put their own belonged alternative. Often, they, vis-à-vis Aryan monarchical states, to republics where there was greater freedom of thought, individualism and respect for heterodox thinking. Both Jains and Buddhists were highly critical of the Brahmanical system: birth-based caste hierarchy, oppression of the low castes, animal sacrifices, allurement of heaven, performance of ritualism etc. Mahavira and Buddha both came from the Kshatriya families and preached the value of moral life in terms of karma theory.[3]

Buddha preached non-violence. He discovered the reality of constant change in human life as well as nature or material world. Permanence was not a quality or characteristic of the cosmic process, but merely a mental construct. Buddhists denied the existence of soul, God, transmigration and intra-cosmic gods. There was no such spiritual substance. Personal identity was merely a result of the process of psychic life. Only force, result or consequences of action was there. Dharma is a set of principles or rules which bring out order. All metaphysical questions are irrelevant. Simple life and observation of middle path is enough to attain nirvana (salvation). Its four noble truths are: (1) the world is full of suffering, (2) suffering is caused by human desires, (3) there is a way to get rid of suffering, and (4) renunciation of desires is path to salvation.

For salvation (nirvana), eight principles have to be observed: (1) right views, (2) right resolve, (3) true speech, (4) right conduct, (5) proper livelihood, (6) proper effort, (7) proper recollection, and (8) samadhi (meditation). Human life is governed by causal principles. There is no room for divine intervention or grace. Accordingly, attachment to the world is irrational. Attachment in any form should be given up. The virtuous way is withdrawal from the world. The heredity base of caste—superiority or inferiority—is irrelevant. Buddhism, thus, had great appeal, particularly after having converted many kings, scholars and upper caste men, to the lower caste people, who converted *en masse* in thousands and millions.

Thus, both Mahavira and Buddha put up their own original alternatives, challenging all the fundamentals of the Vedic Dharma. In place of their hierarchical unequal and exploitative society, they advanced the ideal of a society of equals. There was no distinction of any kind. All were free to realize emancipation: kaivalya or nirvana.

Thus, both Jainism and Buddhism had utter contempt for the normal activities of life (see Louis Dumont, *Religion, Politics and History* and *Homo Hierarchicus*). They rejected the traditional Purusharthas (virtue, wealth, pleasure and salvation), land, property, sex, power, etc., and found them as obstacles to progress of soul. Higher satisfaction lies in forgoing them. Who conquers his 'self' is superior to a king who conquers millions of warriors. Thus, Mahavira's preaching was purely life-negative—withdrawing from all contacts with society and nature (see G.C. Pande, *Foundations of Indian Culture*). Jainism, thus, had no place for politics. It was non-political. Early Buddhist thought also despised politics as a necessary evil. Property, family, origin of state etc. all indicated fall of man and led to conflict, chaos and anarchy. A king was required to rule according to Dhamma, i.e., the eternal law to govern the behaviour of individuals. According to the precepts of Buddha political obligations of both the king and the people have contractual characters. Some republics had already been operating on that principles of contract. Buddhism stood for the cultivation of 'psyche' through the practice of rational moral principles (dharma). Later, it became a universal religion, not confined to India.

Lokayata, with its view of pleasure and materialism, also rejected the mystical and rationalistic basis of the Vedas. It opposed varnashrama order, idolatry, ritualism and other superstitions. It exposed all animal and human sacrifices, heaven and hell, law of karma, transmigration etc. But both Jainism and Buddhism rejected the Lokayata outlook (see U.N. Ghoshal, *A History of Indian Political Ideas* and *A History of Hindu Political Theories*). Upanishads (Vedanta), Buddhism and Jainism all together upheld the life of sanyas (renunciation), which was separate from the worldly life. Obviously, to them, the life of politics was another name for deceit and treachery. Thus, these seers and saints began to leave the world to itself. The other varnas and orders, while remaining within the dharma order, began to be influenced by them, particularly their quietism, ascetism, life-negation and non-violence. The varnas and orders had already transformed into castes.

Kautilya and others failed to see the fact that the birth-based upper varnas of Brahmin and Kshatriya would never permit the lower varnas of the Vaishya and the Shudra, even unlike the slaves (dasas) of those times, to come up on the ladder of the varna system. No change was permitted in the varna system even for livelihood, as suggested by Shukra or by their transformation in their present merits, training and experience. The linking of the varna system to divinity (God) and law of karma dashed all the hopes of lower castes. Neither the Shastras, nor the society or the Brahmins, made any arrangement to see that only men of merit remain in that particular 'varna' and are turned out of it if they fail to satisfy the varna requirements. Even the state kept itself aloof from that deterioration of society. On the contrary, the whole varnashrama system was declared to be divinely ordained, and the king was asked to uphold it as his primary obligation.

Consequently, millions of the outnumbering Shudras were put permanently under the yoke of inequality, exploitation and oppression. The other varnas too were not permitted to change their caste. But, often, the Brahmin was not a 'Brahmin', though he remained in the Brahmin varna, enjoying the highest status while remaining without appropriate merit. So was the Kshatriya not a true 'Kshatriya'. But ironically, the Vaishyas and the Shudras were forcibly holding their merit under anguish and opposition. Dynamism generated by spirit and enthusiasm of man was no more visible. The scheme of four-stage ashramas was not available to the lower varnas, particularly the educational part, and the vanaprastha and the sanyas.

All was justified in the name of divinity, God and Shastras. Millions of low-caste persons, in search of equality and redemption, were joining the teachings of Mahavira and Buddha. They gave up their worldly life under the impact of new teachings and adopted quietude, renunciation or sanyas. They felt no obligation to family, society or state. Millions of followers of Jainism, Buddhism and Vedanta were now either Shramanas, Bhikkhus or sanyasis. Thus, they broke up the whole scheme of the dharma order: achievement of salvation by leading their lives first as a householder, and responding to obligations imposed by dharma towards parents, teachers, gods, society and the state. In a way rise of these religious sect and communities was a response to the exploitative social order of the Vedic or

Aryan society. The Vedic society now onwards began to move towards other-worldly directions, ascetism, non-violence, and neglect of this world. The new religions did not remain confine to spiritual or psychic world, but were fastly influencing the social, political and military matters. Even within the Vedic and post-Vedic (Hindu) society, there was rise of many other sects (Vaishnavas, Shaivas, Shaktas, Tantrikas etc.), which ultimately proved subversive to the prevailing structure of the dharma society. The new communities hardly had the care that a society to survive must have elements of knowledge, of protection, of production, and of service, and its members before entering into the lives of renunciation, meditation or quietude should actively pass through stages of education and earning livelihood and family.

New religions, besides Jainism and Buddhism, had already flourished. Caste system worsened. During the Guptas, the Vedicas mostly converted into Hindu religion, with caste system more worsening. It lost its absorbing and assimilating capacity. Rather, entry of untouchability in caste and sub-caste system alienated many segments of the Shudras and other lower castes and segregated them out of the normal varna (caste) system.

As a result of disorganization and decay of the Hindu society and constant warfare among the rulers, India became an easy prey to foreign invasions. They could not face the sword of Islam—a religion which negated almost each and every tenet of Hinduism. It was One-God, One-Prophet and One-Holybook religion, which carved out a community of equals. It had a message to spread it everywhere, and crush all non-Islamic infidels. Use of sword was the means to spread its message of peace. India's prosperity, disunity among the kings, and disorder in the society were great attractions to Gauris, Gajanis, Slave invaders, Afghan and Mughal invaders. Indian rulers fell before them one by one. People sought shelter of Islam, out of fear or favour, in massive numbers. As Jains and Buddhas dwindled after the undergoing all evils of Hinduism, Islam soon became one of the major religions of India. It had simple religious precepts to follow with a polity governed by an absolute ruler reigning in the name of God (Allah). Barni and Abul Fazal had spelled out Islamic political ideas, but had no impact either on the people or on the rulers. The Quran hardly encourages independent thinking or reasoning. At lower levels, Hindus and Muslims began to mix up through saints and fakirs. The Hindu saints sought the path of devotion of God as an alternative to the Brahmanical ritualism, casteism, and other superstitions. Hinduism—the major religion—had lost all its touch with reality. Hindus and Muslims were now two separate communities—at crossroads, conflicting and alienated—one ruled and other ruling. Owing to their inner weaknesses, contradictions, otherworldliness and hatred for the lower castes, the Hindus could hardly raise up heads against the Mughal rulers. In fact, the Hindus were mere individuals, further divided into several hundreds of caste groups of higher-lower hierarchies. The Muslims were a 'community of equals' as revealed by Prophet Mohammad—the last and final messenger of God to man. His commands were to be obeyed with absolute fidelity. However, in India, the Muslims also adopted casteism, idolatry and other superstitions in many ways. There was constant struggle among them. It was quite congenial to a third party to apply the policy of 'divide and rule' on such warring groups of India and rule over them.

But, the third party from Europe intervened with new ideas, culture and material goals. They were neither individuals like the Hindus (bound only by consideration of self-realization, God or dharma) nor mere community of servants of God like the Muslims. They were people having new ideas, and a nation. After having a fight among themselves, the English company came out victorious. A trading company of England became the ruler of India. Namely the East India Company defeated the native rulers by sama, dama, bheda and danda one by one and had complete control over the country for another 150 years. The Crown took over this control from the East India Company in 1858. But this Crown itself was a democratic government, responsible to the representatives of the people sitting as parliament. It was a democracy at home, but outside it was an empire spreading over several countries including India. As such, India was to be extracted, exploited and ruled with an iron hand. Still, a democracy cannot rule over another country for long. There were a good number of British intellectuals who wanted to teach India lessons of democracy and allow them fruits of liberty and law.

Often all Hindus cherish and enjoy looseness of Hindu religion (see Diagram 1). They feel free to do whatever they like, and hardly care little for the results. Other proselytizing religions also like that this form of Hindu religions should continue. Under this situation,

Diagram 1
Hindus before Hindutva Movement

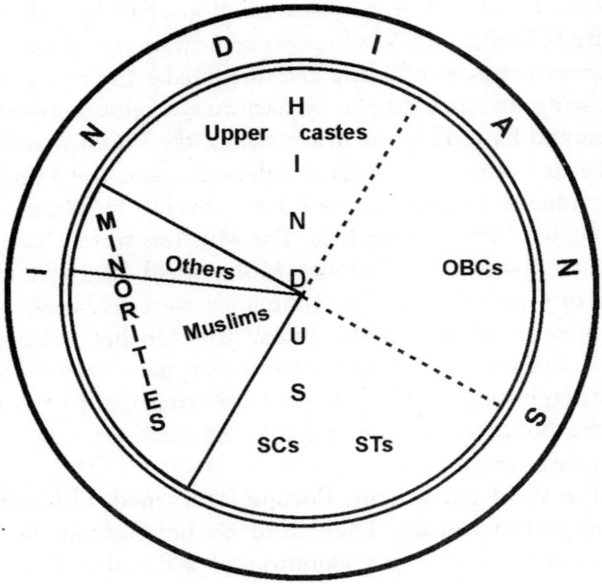

they find opportunity to continue converting millions of the suppressed and oppressed castes of the Hindus.

One after another thinker thought it better to maintain it through the agency of the ruler. Most of them helplessly witnessed the alienation of a major chunk of population. As a whole, social system, which was based on exploitation and hierarchical inequality, was dismantled by the rise of non-Vedic sects like Jainism, Buddhism and Vedantism. The Hindu thinkers hopelessly failed to find any alternative remedy. The orthodox Brahmanism, rather, put more and more restrictions on the lower castes. They were apathetically silent even when Islam trampled over them and ruled the country for over one thousand years. The Hindu mind had no reply to the sword of equality wielded by Islam. Like the latter, Christendom got millions of lower caste Hindus converted to their religion.

Under their influences and own down trends, the ethos of the former Vedicas appeared in form of Hindu Dharma. It carried certain tenets, which have become part and parcel of the widely known and much liked Hindu Dharma.

Tenets of Hindu Dharma

Following are the main tenets of Hindu Dharma:

1. The Brahmanical priesthood has given many metaphysical, moral and religious justifications to the Hindu Dharma. It has been formulated and sustained on the basis of immortality of soul, transmigration and law of karma. On the basis of law of karma, the varna system was translated into a caste hierarchy wherein the majority of the lower strata were subjected to inequality, exploitation and oppression. The metaphysics of Hindu religion became the citadel of caste system which made millions of the lower castes virtual serfs, slaves and sub-humans. This was practised despite their claims to Advaita, Spiritual Absolutism or Abstract Realism.
2. Hinduism learnt nothing useful and reasonable from the equalitarian teachings of Buddha and Mahavira. They were taught and propagated much long before Islam appeared. The Hindu upper castes took them as challenge to its vested interests, supremacy and existence. As the focus of these two religions was nirvana and self-realization (kaivalya), they were mostly neutral to the caste order prevailing in the Hindu society. Spiritual Absolutism of the Upanishads also taught withdrawal from the worldly obligations and showed the path of knowledge and renunciation to the Hindus. Rise of the Buddha and Mahavira orders further boosted the other-worldly quest of the Hindus, treating the society, polity and economy as cause of bondage, sin, and obstacles on path of realization of salvation (moksha). Their other-worldly attitude consolidated and strengthened the caste system to newer heights.
3. In their supernatural world-view, the older heroes, Ram, Krishna and others were transformed into reincarnation of God, coming down to earth as Great Human God.[4] They believed that only some such avatar could save the Hindus from the clutches of evil, oppression and fatalism.[5] Several hundred new gods and goddesses had been imagined and were installed as idols in thousands of temples and holy places. These were ritually

worshipped day and night. The devotees themselves did not do anything except reciting bhajans and reading holy books. It was expression of faith in gods and goddesses. Their prayers were sure to be granted and wishes worldly or heavenly were thought to be fulfilled. This setting became a permanent source of income and livelihood: alms, donations, feasts and celebrations from millions of followers of Hindu religion. All that helped in sustaining the supremacy obnoxious rituals spread by priesthood.[6]

4. The four-fold caste hierarchy too fructified into several hundred upper, lower and parallel castes. Spiritual virtues like non-violence, truth, non-possession, asceticism, piety etc. under the powerful impact of Advaita, Buddhism and Jainism, so much dominated the lives of the people that the whole lot of the fighting caste group got apathetic or became alienated towards in the pursuit of warfare. Millions of the exploited and downtrodden people were interested in the defeat and downfall of the ruling classes and wished welcome to equality-oriented invaders. The overall impact of widespread other-worldliness rendered the Hindu society weak and meek. Their social structure split up into several hundred castes and sub-castes. It also paved way for the recurring successes of the invaders. The latter were accustomed to live in rough weather and lead a very hard life in deserts and mountains, thus, could defeat the Hindu/Indian armies enjoying all comforts. Teachings of peace, non-violence, nirvana etc. had already destroyed their fighting and sacrificing spirit.

5. The Hindu society turned into birth and heredity based caste system. Each caste cut off itself into separate and hierarchical endogamous communities. Consequently, every member of the Hindu society being constrained within was confined to his own caste. He, under the caste system, was dwarfed into one-fourth of the total human personality. Only one-fourth aspect of his personality was recognized and counted on the basis of his birth in that particular caste. For the rest of the three parts he was to depend on the directions of the Shastras and the Brahmin priesthood supremacy. Ultimately, every particular caste became a world in itself and lost support and cooperation from other castes.

6. The lower castes, which had been suffering under the social political and economic regime of upper castes, kept waiting for some occasion of emancipation at the hand of some hero, god or some military leader. They warmly supported and accepted any new dispensation which appeared to redeem them. In many cases, even the torch-bearers of the new dispensation colluded together with the old oppressive classes, and continued to exploit and neglect the lower strata. Historically, there were two such great occasions: one, when the Buddha and Mahavira, to some extent, smashed the whole philosophy or ideology of the Hindus which happened to rationalize and justify this exploitation and oppression; and second, when forces of Islam overpowered these Hindu forces of exploitation, and established their rule in India. However, exploitation and oppression of the lower strata people continued despite the conversion in millions and millions of the Hindus to Islam and, later to Christianity. Before the advent of the British, all this had happened through deposition and imposition of 'monarchs' or 'kings', and the ruling classes connected with them. The ruling classes, including all the big and small kings, were interested in maintaining the societal status quo. The condition of women was equally worse in that prevailing set-up.[7] The Brahmanical mind could not respond creatively to the Buddhist challenge either at the philosophical level or at the societal level. Shankar's response to Buddhism at philosophical level was too late. Buddhism and Jainism both did not attack the unequal social structure seriously. The Brahmanism after turning out Buddhism from the country was satisfied on the latter's connivance at the hierarchical structure of the Hindu social organization.
7. In the name of dharma, and to attain nirvana or kaivalya, an ascetic order (abdication of worldly obligations towards society) had already been justified long ago by Jainism, Buddhism and several others. Great apostle of Advaita (monism) Shankar was instrumental in the disappearance of Buddhism from the country. But he replaced it by his 'mayavada'. It was more subversive in the sense that the whole world was considered to be non-existent or unreal. Hundred of sects emerged during the last one thousand years, which attracted people towards them for direct absorption into blissful God—through either spiritual knowledge (meditation and samadhi) or loveful devotion to

God, respectively known as gyan-yoga and bhakti-yoga. The path of detached action or nishkama karmayoga was left and abandoned, as it was also based on the concept of 'swadharma' or conventional caste order.[8] The underlying principle behind this universal adoption of ascetism and other-worldliness was the exaggerated form of non-violence (ahimsa), which detracted most of the people from fighting against the wicked elements and other evils, including foreign invasions. Their eyes in most cases were fixed on finding glimpse of God only. The path of life-negation was the way to God.

8. Under the impact of Jainism, Buddhism, Upanishads, and Mayavada of Shankara's Advaitism, the culture of the Vedicas or Aryas transformed as Hindu Dharma. The people of India reflected it in form of an attitude of renunciation towards their worldly obligations which were to them Avidya or obstacles in the way of their cherished goal of salvation. Several centuries had passed away in this way. During the Middle Ages, they strived for their salvation by giving up all worldly connections.

   Subject matter or content of the Hindu religion mostly belonged to the world of Unknown, Beyond or Abstract. Any man could say anything about the Beyond. What one told about it could hardly be proved or denied. As a Hindu believed that he comes from the Unknown, before his birth to this world, and goes into it after his death, he easily yields to any Beyond-knower person, or reposes faith in the statements of the person claiming to know that Beyond or Unknown. Such Beyond-knowing persons in due course of time became founders of a new or a particular sect of religion.

9. As most of the concepts of religion and metaphysics are unknown, ambiguous and uncertain, anything could be claimed or spoken about it. No two founders of religions or sects or visualizers of that Unknown Reality agreed with each other. Sometimes they contradicted each other's statements about that Abstract Unknown. It was quite easy, for supposedly good or welfare of man, to find, declare or discover a new pattern of living human life or to form a society by following norms, rules or injunctions declared by that Godman. Almost every great founder of a particular religion had successfully formed a society or a community or a sect in this manner. Such new sect or society was gradually formed by gathering of hundreds or

thousands of his followers. In the beginning, it had to face some opposition, persecution or struggle from the already existing vested interests. The latter too after a few years or decades organized themselves in like manner. All of them gradually grew into powerful sects, community, polity, economy and set of morality. Those who did not act on the norms and rules declared by the founders of new sects were soon declared as heretics and rebels, and were punished, excommunicated, exiled or done away with. The Hindu Dharma connived at all such acts.[9] It had nothing logical or substantial to oppose them. Rather, the Hindus feel proud of this trend, now knowing that every new sect cuts the very roots of the Hindu Dharma, and goes against its survival and existence at moral, political, economic and social levels.

10. Last important tenet of the Hindu Dharma was that it would not change. It maintains that it is God-given, Supreme (Sanatana), Eternal and Universal.[10] It is the most ancient religion of the world, therefore, cannot be overlooked, overcome or overruled by any other faith of later origin. It has made them the Guru or teacher of the whole world. All other religions have to learn a lot from it. They hardly find any difference between the tenets of the Vedicas and the Hindu Dharma as maintained by them.

Thus, its spiritual concerns have kept it confined to the Unmanifest level. A religion merged with the Unmanifest hardly cares for the things at the Manifest level. As such, it was natural that the Hindu Dharma lagged behind in all worldly matters. It desired no change in the status quo. Lastly, in matters of religions, it stood at par with other religions and meekly surrendered before socio-political and economic forces coming from the West.

Imbecility of the Hindu Dharma

Hindu Dharma, thus, stood a poor match to the two dominating religions. Islam had the direct word of God or Allah in form of holy Koran, with no intermediary, no priesthood, and no caste system or hierarchy. Every one was ordained to hold the sword of Islam for its defense. The sword of Islam was also to convert the heretics and punish the non-believers. Moreover, it propounded a uniform familial, social and economic set-up which Hinduism on its path to realization of other-worldly goals never thought of. In several respects, Islam produced a rock-like well-organized society of equals.[11]

The Indian society and polity shipwrecked before the recurring onslaughts of Islam and other hordes of alien races. Islam ruled over the country in parts or/and as a whole for over one thousand years affecting conversions of about one-fourth of the population. Birth and heredity-based upper castes, viz., Brahmins and Kshatriyas, had largely lost their merit, and had nothing to guide the masses. The people had lost all hopes during the medieval period. A part of Hindu masses, after their surrender to the Islamic rule, resorted to 'bhakti' (devotion) marg (path) of Ramananda, Kabir, Nanak, Tulsi, Tukaram, Meera Bai and many others as the only way to redemption. In fact, the 'bhakti' marg has now become the mainstream of the Hindu Dharma.

Soon after the arrival of the Christian missionaries, in the wake of victories of the East India Company or the British Raj after 1858, the vast majority of the downtrodden and frustrated lower castes began to adopt Christian religion for getting better treatment, food and shelter. Impressed by their educational work, which was mostly for the propagation of Christianity, Rammohan Roy warmly welcomed and praised them, without anticipating the consequences for the political and religious future of the country. None of the earlier political thinkers could ever imagine the impact of religion as a political force, as they had always been looking to it only as a way to God. Few could realize the political implications of plurality of faiths and religious conversions. Nobody had the depth and will to spell out the original form and emphasize totality of Sanatana Dharma (ancient religion). Hardly anyone except Dayananda had the courage to expose the deviations, distortions and falsehood added to the original religion which had appeared in forms of various religions, faiths and sects. Owing to the very nature of the then Hindu Dharma, they all continued and flourished, and stood as rivals to it. There was no other way before the Hindus except to accept them at par with the Hindu Dharma, now a non-ruling religion of decadent people.[12]

Future Ahead

The European nation-communities, which had been lagging far behind the Indian people, came out of their dark period. They passed through the Renaissance, Reformation and Enlightenment. Reason gave them science and industrial revolution, and made them powerful nations upon earth. The last and final war of the Indians against the East India Company in 1857-58 made it clear that forces of science, industrial revolution and modernization would win. India's feudalism and the fractured polity would have to give way to new forces.

The great thinkers of the West had broken all restrictions, bondages and religious moorings of man there. Inculcating the new religion of nationalism and science, the western man had become powerful enough to trample over the decadent past of the Indians. A few thousand of Europeans crushed them to ground. They were supported by the element of Indian population which had been crying for help owing to the oppression of the Hindu high castes and the ruthless Muslim rulers. As outsiders they treated all alike. Their neglect of animosities, caste system, hierarchy and backwardness prevailing among the Indians endeared them to the native inhabitants.

Notes

1. उर्ध्वबाहुर्विरौम्येष न च कश्चिद् श्रृणोति मे।
   धर्मार्थश्च कामश्च सधर्मः किं न सेव्यते।।—महाभारत
2. मज्जेत्त्रयी दण्डनीतौ हतायां सर्वधर्माः प्रक्षयेयुर्विवृद्धाः
   सर्वेधर्माश्चाश्रमाणां हताः स्युः क्षात्रे राजधर्मे पुराणे।।
   सर्वे त्यागा राजधर्मेषु युक्ता सर्वा दीक्षा राजधर्मेषु युक्ता।
   सर्वा विद्या राजधर्मेषु चोक्ता सर्वे लोका राजधर्मे प्रविष्टा।।—महाभारत
3. According to Mahavira transcending the cycle of birth and death and rebirth one can attain liberation by his own efforts. The present life is the result of our past karma. Karma (action) particles bind the soul. Jainism emphasized the importance of Karma so much that God or Gods became more or less irrelevant. Human souls themselves have the potential for perfection.
4. Rama was born in the Treta Yuga in Ayodhya, where he spent his childhood. When King Rama moved his capital to Saketa, Ayodhya went into decline. The Rama cult originates from the fifth and sixth centuries AD. According to Hans Bakker, the myth of Vishnu's incarnation as Rama became popular in the Gupta Age. But, the cult in which Rama was worshipped as the supreme form and main manifestation of Vishnu did not rise until the eleventh and twelfth centuries. It began to emerge in the latest period of independent Hindu rule in North India and before

Muslim power was firmly established The spread of devotion to Rama within Hinduism was a gradual process which evolved over a period of several centuries. The widening process was concurrent with the spread over North India of an emotional type of devotion. One important factor of the religious life during those centuries (13th-16th) was the rise of the cult of the name: the practice of repeating the name of God (Rama), conceived of as a sadhana, a way to release. And in the 15th-16th centuries Rama had become the most common word to denote 'God'.

5. यदा यदा हि धर्मस्य ग्लानिर्भवति भारत।
   अभ्युत्थानंऽधर्मस्य तदात्मानं सृजाम्यहं।।–गीता

   None else, but only God Himself can, redeem Dharma, rescue them from demons, and re-establish desirable Social Order.
6. Often all Hindu social reformers and leaders added in the name of reforms, more prejudices, superstitions, irrational beliefs, immoral factors, multiplicity of gods and goddesses, rites and rituals to the faceless Hindu Dharma. There were traditions of Idolatry, Sacrifices and Avatar, which had no sanction in the Vedas or the Upanishads. So was the tradition of human, animal sacrifices and the Suttee. In the latter a widow forcibly against her wish was put on burning fire and made Suttee. There was no religious sanction in the Hindu Shastras. Often, in suttee, a widow was burnt to get rid of the responsibility of her maintenance.
7. After Raja Rammohan Roy, Gandhi was the most important social reformers who worked hard for the upliftment and welfare of the women. He did not regard women as inferior to men on any conceivable ground.
8. Nishkam Karmayoga (performing detached action) is very controversial concept of the Hindu Dharma. It is suicidal, confusing and non-performable. The concept implies that actions can be performed without keeping the result in mind. One should go on performing without taking care of the outcome. Actions performed in this manner, even if they are violent, cruel coercive, do not bind the soul. With this mind, one should go on performing his traditionally given or allotted (caste) functions. On this Dayananda clearly tells that there can be no function without its result. One has to bear accountability for that act. Another overlooked side of the Nishkam Karmayoga is that rational or justifiable act can be performed without keeping its end in mind. Only the acts of a mad or ignorant person are done without consideration to effect, outcome or result. Who is going to allow functions to be done in this manner? Masses cannot depend on a person following Nishkam Karmayoga if he does not do them for the express good of the people. However, a man of high spiritual attainments can perform all types of actions when he acts in tune with or alike God. At that time, he is one

with the Ultimate or Basic Reality. Vivekananda, Tilak etc. were in search of such persons, but they could not succeed. In fact, they were not clear about the concept of Nishkam Karmayoga. The concept should have been fully enlarged saying that actions not performed to serve one's narrow interests, and done to serve the larger interests, fall under the category of Nishkam Karmayoga. But they are done with 'desire' (kamana), 'wish' or 'will'. That desire, wish or will is imbued to serve the common end.

9. Often the mindset of a follower was closed either by heavenly threat, no-contact injunctions, moral exhortation, physical punishment through the ruler, or excommunication or ostracism by society.
10. See the status, role and impact of the Hindu Dharma at level two of the Table 1 in Chapter 1: Levels of Understanding Basic Reality and their Impact on Religion, Culture and Polity.
11. Islam which had ruled over India for about 700 years had already posed a challenge to the Indian thinking. Its sweep and sway was unabated. Its basic tenets remained unresponded to by Hinduism which had failed to absorb it any more. These tenets were: (i) One and One Godhead, the Koran as his last final and direct message, Mohammad only a Prophet or Messenger, total denial of any priesthood or intermediary between God and man, congregational prayer by Muslim on equal footing, common observation by the Muslims of pilgrimage, fasting, *zakat* (beneficence), prayer (samaj) and purity of creed. It ordained egalitarian culture and economy, autonomy of women, share in property and inheritance, and work-culture. Every Muslim had been equipped with duty to defend and protect the rule of Islam by sword or otherwise. It was a solid, organized and armed society, and its members had no right to have second thoughts on it and revise it at will. The Islamic principle of equality was unchallengeable and supreme. There was great need to revise and prepare Hinduism to meet these long-standing challenges of Islam. The Muslim community having faith in the Koran had nothing to fear from Hinduism except its absorbing tendency. But, the latter could not do it for the last 700 years. The only next way was to put the Hindu house in order. The Muslims leadership so far had held its sway over the Hindus through the absolutist rule of their kings, emperors, and sultans. But their defence-mechanism disappeared with the rise of British rule in India. The British rulers proposed democracy which practically was the rule by majority. In order to escape from the rule of Hindu majority, they later opted for separation and communal autonomy.
12. It has been considered as blot on the face of the Hindu community.

II

Hinduism and Hindutva

4

Formulation, Performance and Failure of Hinduism

This chapter discusses attempts made by Hindu seers and leaders to reformulate Hindu Dharma as an ideology and examines its role and efficacy in solving the problems of Hinduism and the people at large.

The Hindus, in the beginning, owing to the very nature of Hindu Dharma, did not care, as it believed in freedom to seek God in many ways. Implications of their rise were not kept in mind. Now, with the growth of forces of nationalism and democracy, the increasing number of followers of alien religions, and unity and organization in them, meant a lot to the very existence and survival of the Hindus. In fact, there were four big challenges before the Hindus: one, suicidal nature of the Hindu Dharma; second, rise of proselytizing and ruling big religions like Islam and Christianity; third, lack of nationalism and democracy and, four, getting rid of the British rule in India. From among the big religious and social reformers of the Hindus, only four attempted to rise to the occasion. They were Maharshi Dayananda Saraswati, Swami Vivekananda, Lokmanya Balgangadhar Tilak and Aurobindo Ghosh. The last one after working as a revolutionary went into exile and gave up all temporal concerns. In fact, he became a big yogi of level two. Mahatma Gandhi too worked a lot for the Hindu Dharma but his object was not to serve solely the cause of the Hindus. However, all the five great men made use of the tenets of the Hindu Dharma to fight against the prevailing socio-religious evils as well as to win freedom for the Indian people. These leaders had no pre-plan to formulate Hinduism as such. They discovered and propounded ideas, schemes and goals which they thought would engender Hinduism used in the sense of humanity.

They took up the task of presenting the basics of the Hindu Dharma in newer forms. Their goal, besides their own self-realization, was to make it an effective instrument for the socio-religious, political and economic emancipation for the people of India. The Hindu Dharma so far had been a silent sufferer as well as a spectator to these evils. These great men studied the Hindu Dharma and its prevailing problems and evils of the Hindu society deeply and seriously, and worked it out in some loose form of "Ideology of Hinduism". Here an attempt has been made to evaluate the performance, achievements and failures of their ideologies to defend Hinduism. The whole analysis has been divided into two parts: Formulation, Performance and Achievements of Hinduism, and Failure, Limitations and Impact on the Hindus and Other Communities at Large.

Formulation, Performance and Achievements of Hinduism

These have been critically examined around ten points given in Table 1 (see Ch. 1). For convenience, these points have further been grouped into four categories A, B, C and D.

Group A involves two points, point 1 is forms of Ultimate Reality and its implications and point 2 is message to man, ultimate goal, religion and idol worship, which added philosophical, metaphysical and religious sharpness to Hinduism.

Renovating Hinduism, Dayananda stood for the Vedas. He had proclaimed that the Vedas (Samhitas) contained the Vedic wisdom, words of God himself, embodying all spiritual metaphysical knowledge and secrets of science. The Vedas belong to all men. He spoke of three eternal substances or realities of God, Prakriti and Jiva (individual souls). Knowledge about them comes from God himself through rishis (seers). The Creator, God, arranges the Prakriti and manages the souls according to law of karma or Purushartha (पुरुषार्थ). He wanted man gradually to attain complete freedom and responsibility within his natural elements, society and others.

The causes of foreign domination in India are mutual discord, diversity of faiths and absence of the Vedic knowledge. Only practising of the Vedic ideals can help them and get rid of their present plight. Progress cannot be made without having common faith, common interests and common feelings.

In place of multiplicity of gods, casteism and confusing plurality of holy books, Dayananda, like the Islam, the Christianity and the Sikhism, gave one single source of dharma—the Vedas. It was revealed by God through learned rishis (seers). Dayananda gave clear, definite and rational interpretation of the Vedas in form of Traitavada (three eternal realities). His Traitvada counteracted the false and mischievous propaganda, conversion campaigns and evils prevailing in the field of religions.[1]

Vivekananda maintained that each country has a theme which is basic and primary: everything else is secondary. India's theme is religion. Social reform and everything else are secondary. He made pure passive and negative Advaita into 'Practical Vedanta'. But he considered the world to be real, but not eternal (like Dayananda). The cosmic purpose can be realized in this very life. One can have vision of God through social service. The individual will have to make efforts. He should have faith within himself. His 'Karmayoga' was a democratic. It could be trodden by everyone—from the humblest to the highest. It involved two elements: (a) renunciation of ego, and (b) service to fellowmen.[2]

He considered the Vedas as 'apaurusheya' (not man-made), coming down from the time immemorial but did not consider them infallible. Hinduism signified to him a body of moral and spiritual injunctions and primordial super-temporal laws for the uplift of humanity. It is the mother of religions. This can be proved and traced out. He introduced once more the practice of proselytism in Hinduism.

Vivekananda was a representative of entire Hinduism from the Vedas to Vaishnavism. He objected to the word 'Hindu'. It was only a geographical name coined by the aliens. He wanted the Hindus to call themselves as the Vedicas or followers of the Vedas. He was champion of Hinduism in all its aspects and phases of its evolution. He did not select one scripture and leave out the rest.

To him, the primal Spiritual Existent or Absolute is the Supreme Real. But this world is also the creation of the Supreme Being. The cosmic Maya or Prakriti (Nature) is behind this creation. Maya operates under the superintendence of the Supreme Being. The spiritual view of creation attributes to man certain amount of freedom and spontaneity. Man has implicit freedom of will. He can try to attain knowledge, and get freedom from bondage. Freedom is a fruition and fullness of the spirit.

In the 'Practical Vedanta' of Vivekananda Brahma is all-pervading and immanent. Accordingly, there is no hard and fast demarcation between religious and secular worlds. In the same manner, it treats society and humanity and also nation and society in identical manner. Ends and means are synonymous. It mixes freedom with equality, and also nationalism with internationalism. It anticipates that there will be neither Hindus nor Europeans, but the ideal humanity conquering both material and spiritual natures. Science and religion stand for each other. In his neo-Vedanta, the Brahma includes the world. Therefore, worldly activity is also sacred. Any selfless activity is not only social, but also spiritual. That way he drew out recluses from their caves, and made them servers of the society.

For Tilak, Brahma or Absolute is all-pervading and all concerning immanent Reality. It permits to include all men and women, irrespective of particular caste, community, faith or culture. Tilak believed in the Advaita or Absolute or Brahma of the Vedanta. Souls are parts of the Absolute, but remain as Jiva owing to the cover of Avidya. The world is only an apparent phenomenal manifestation of the Supreme Being. The Supreme Real or Absolute is total freedom or liberation or Spiritual Creativity.

He was a Sanatani Hindu and had pride in this religion. He had a very comprehensive conception of Hinduism or Hindu religion.[3] For him, the Sanatan Dharma is the Hindu Dharma. During the Vedic times India was a self-contained country and "was united as a great nation".

Lord Krishna, in the *Gita*, teaches the metaphysics of non-dualism, e.g., the foundational and ultimate reality—Sachchidananda. It gives the essence of the Vedic religion preaching that salvation cannot be attained without knowledge of the identity between the cosmic self and the psychic self. Its philosophy of Nishkama Karmayoga establishes a synthesis between knowledge (ज्ञान), devotion(भक्ति) and action (कर्म).[4]

Hindu religion also prompted Gandhi to believe, think and behave according to its tenets. But adoption of truth and non-violence also became a must to launch freedom movement during the British Raj. It was the only path available to the 'religious' people, particularly the Hindus of India. Gandhi also took Hinduism as "the essence of all the great religions of mankind". Religion for him was both a means of personal purification as well as social bond. A true religious attitude meant enthusiastic fulfilment of one's duties (swadharma).

All religions are equal as they are founded on the same moral laws which bind men all over the world. Gandhi time and again had declared that he was essentially a religious man in quest of 'moksha' or salvation. Following the teachings of the Gita, he wanted to live a life of detachment which would lead to attainment of moksha. He engaged himself in the disinterested pursuit of obligations and duties which involved a cosmic and spiritual awareness. The goal of his life was self-realization or to know God through selfless service of man. He also believed in the truth of the saying that not a blade of grass moves but by His Will.[5]

Truth is the end and non-violence is the means. Non-violence is non-injury in thought, word and deed. Gandhi believed in hundred per cent purity of means, i.e., non-violence as creed. He firmly rejected the dichotomy between the end and the means. It was enough to know the means. Means and ends were convertible terms for him. For Gandhi as a saint and mahatma means are everything. As the means so the end. Our progress towards the goal would be in exact proportion to the purity of means. Following the doctrine of dispassionate action preached by the Bhagwadgita, he felt that we have control over the means but not over the end or result.

Gandhi spiritualized politics. According to him, all politics is based on religion. He made morality higher than politics and diplomacy. Moral ends can be realized by moral means only. His religion was humanistic, universal and practical. It resided in the service of man, particularly the poor, the weak and the exploited.

On action side, Dayanand believed in the ethics of concrete behaviour. He freed man from the tyranny of Shastras. Man's actions are judged on the basis of morality alone. He accepted Manu's authority only if it was in agreement with reason. He separated untruth from truth on the basis of reason, and asked everyone to do so.

The Maharshi condemned the Nivriti Marg—the way of renunciation. Even a Sanyasi was not exempted from the requirements of positive moral action. Life should be full of actions—pravriti or purushartha. The Vedas order to do good works.

The Swami rejected all religions and philosophies which suggest short-cuts to moksha, such as pilgrimages, japa, penances, sacrifices of humans or animals, idol worship, fasts, ritualism, mysticism, self-torture, penances, and mere reading of holy books. Any belief in some guru, book, doctrine, or grace cannot give moksha. Dayananda ruthlessly eliminated all other roads or short-cuts to salvation devised by various religions over several centuries. Salvation was to be earned by action of karma alone. Even selfless or detached action has its own results. God never intervenes in the operation of the result of karma. Gyan (knowledge) and bhakti (devotion) do not obliterate the necessity of action or karma (actions). Thus, the Maharshi made the man life-assertive, free, moral and virile.

As God is immanent and abstract spirit, it is sinful to worship him in form of a statue, idol or image.

Swami Vivekananda also saw his God as Absolute Substance or Brahma or Perfection permeating the entire universe, including all human souls or jivas.[6] He wanted to bring about unity of religions, in particular, by making the Vedanta as 'Mother Religion'. Like Vivekananda, Tilak had a very broad conception of Hinduism. It was Sanatan Dharma as old as the history of human race itself. "Religion is an element in nationality", according to Tilak. Dharma means to hold together, connecting the soul with God and man with man. Hinduism as such provides for a moral as well as social life.

Gandhi proclaimed that "those who say religion has nothing to do with politics do not know what religion means". He made it clear that "I could not be leading a religious life unless I identified myself with the whole of mankind and that I could not do unless I took part in politics."

Thus, all teach religion and religious teachings to the Hindus.

Group B includes point 3 social set-up, hierarchy, supremacy of Brahmins and the Individual and point 4 role of knowledge, science, technology, tradition and education. Both show what society and their philosophies had conceived for the Hindus.

From the Vedas Dayananda found that all are equal. At the time of birth, everyone is Shudra or nothing. After undergoing sacred rites (16 sanskaras, 5 yamas and 10 niyamas), and having some attainments, one becomes second-born (dwija) or higher in status as human being. His interpretation of the Vedic religion brought about a sense of unity, brotherhood and spirit of self and social reforms. He rejected Manu's Varnasharma Dharma and replaced it by the system of four 'classes' based on each man's abilities and behaviour. He separated the religious authority from the Shastras, and made the Varnashrama System totally secular.[7]

He uplifted women and family life. The Swami regarded the institution of marriage very important to maintain the basic structure of society—stable inter-personal services, proper care of the young and the old, private property, upholding moral values and so on. He stood for monogamy and rejection of polygamy or polyandry.[8]

Vivekananda, upholding the Gita, said that a man should do his allotted duties according to the four-fold varnas. His soul is reflection of the Absolute covered under Avidya. He can get rid of this Avidya by performing disinterested actions.

According to Vivekananda, only the individual has inherent divinity, and not the society. Vivekananda was liberal in the sense that he granted growth, initiative freedom, activity, strength and resistance to him. All these properties are interrelated. Man is divine, therefore, has right to freedom and equality. All individuals are parts of the Absolute, therefore equal: "Everybody is Brahma".

Individuals are real and spiritual. If they are elevated, the rest of the institutions would automatically be bettered and improved. Institutions, society and others are formed by individuals. They are for the individuals, and the individual is not for them. Therefore, improvement or reform of the social institutions is slow and gradual. Avidya covers man's inner nature, and causes all sufferings. Knowledge and perfection are closer to each other.

To Swami Vivekananda society and social institutions were secondary.[9] Society degenerates owing to role of vested interests, which are related to upper classes and ruling aristocracy. Our high caste ancestors trampled over the common masses of our country making them helpless. They forgot that they are human beings.[10]

Vivekananda felt that the history of the world was manifestation of the four principles which concretize in the four-fold varnas—the Brahmin, the Kshatriya, the Vaishya and the Shudra.[11] He believed in the Hindu theory of evolutionary cycles or movement in wave form. These four waves or stages belong respectively to the Brahmins, the Kshatriyas, the Vaisyas, and the Shudras.

Vivekananda found that India's political slavery rooted in the suppression of masses. The masses had lost or forgotten even their sense of humanity. Such India could never be a match of the foreign invader: "a million or so of Sadhus and a hundred million or so of Brahmins suck the blood out of these poor people". The social tyrants and aristocratic despots of this country exploited the 200 millions of masses. The four demons trampling over them are: (i) priestcraft, (ii) poverty, (iii) tyranny, and (iv) ignorance.

According to Tilak, God or Ishwara is the express or Manifest form of that Abstract Absolute Real. He accepted the notion of a personal God. God is the personalized form of the Supreme Absolute (Avyakta). He was quite closer to the tenets of the Hindu Dharma. For people of less developed consciousness, Tilak accepted the importance of religious symbols. These symbols and their religious efficacy are recognized by the Upanishads and other seers. Everyone through the worship or devotion to God or His Symbols can reach and realize the Ultimate Beyond. That way he had no objection to idolatry. Tilak believed in the incarnation of God. He accepted that Shri Krishna was an incarnation of God. He also accepted the necessity of devotion (bhakti) in the religious life. He was not opposed to religious ceremonies. He did accept that the specific religious ceremonies could and did change. But so long as they were not formally changed, he wanted that they should be observed.[12]

Renunciation of family life is not necessary for a Karmayogi. Tilak authoritatively taught that it is not necessary to renounce the world to obtain spiritual freedom and emancipation of the country. One should voluntarily continue to perform his duties in a disinterested manner, even if he has obtained God-realization. One can have spiritual identification with the Absolute while doing one's duties in a detached manner.[13]

But he was against the ascription of a divine origin to caste system. He considered its divinity "wrong, baseless and incorrect".[14]

But Gandhi's position on caste was better than both Vivekananda and Tilak. Efforts and strategy of Gandhi saved the

Hindu society from further split. He accepted varnashrama and anted to defend the larger interests of Hindu society. It was a good social system and purified of all its evils. He saw rationality behind it and had an evolutionary approach to reform it.[15]

But he was all-out for the abolition of untouchability. Gandhi made herculean efforts, and succeeded to a great extent. He knew that untouchability would destroy the Hindu society itself. He was for equal rights for both upper and lower castes. He put more emphasis on temple entry by the Harijans (untouchables). Such steps were destined to bring about a feeling of self-respect in the untouchables and the upper castes. Hindus would also be changing their attitude towards them. He insisted on marriage-relations, adoption, and inter-dining between the upper and lower caste people.[16]

After Raja Rammohan Roy, Gandhi was the most important social reformer who worked hard for the upliftment and welfare of the women. He did not regard women as inferior to men on any conceivable ground. It was unjust and insulting to consider them inferior. If truth, non-violence, tolerance and morality are kept in view, women can be considered better than men.

The Maharshi put great emphasis on education both in theory and practice. The Shudras have full rights to study the Vedas. "Just as the Lord has created five elements, the sun and the moon for all mankind, in the same way, he has made the Vedas to shine for all." But his inhibition to allow 'upnayana' to the Shudra sons was not justified.

In the same way, the girls had the right to study the Vedas and the Shastras, learn skills required to help their husbands, about medicine, home science, bookkeeping and the like. They have to compete and take part in both public and domestic life. A successful married life involves education of both the husband and the wife. Dayananda had the ideals of the learned women mentioned in the Vedas.

According to Tilak, enlightenment of the people comes through education. Some of the features of his educational contribution were that (a) education should be cheap and ideal-oriented; (b) it should be nationalistic; (c) there should be a synthesis between the east and the west; (d) English is also necessary to generate sentiments of political radicalism, democracy, rule of law and progressivism; (e) knowledge of the Vedas, Upanishads and other scriptures was necessary to generate scholarship and a sense of integrity and devotion to duty; (f) religious education; and (g) industrial education must be encouraged. The teachers engaged in these institutions were to be men of self-abnegation, devotion to the cause of motherland, and service to the society. He considered religious education necessary to inculcate a sense of duty. No religion teaches quarrel, at least Hinduism is free from this evil: "If there be any religion in the world which advocates toleration of other religious beliefs and instructs one to stick to one's own religion, it is the religion of the Hindus alone. Hinduism to the Hindus, Islamism to the Musalmans will be taught in these schools. And it will also be taught there to forgive and forget the differences of other religions."

Group C looks after sustenance of Hindu society through organization, well-being and participation. It pays attention to point 5 organization of state and government, point 6 material conditions, livelihood, science and technology, point 7 inter-state relations, and point 8 status of masses, participation and nationalism concentrate on the form of state, government, inter-state relations. All of them merely present their ideas and propositions, which could not become reality during their lifetime. None of them had occasion to organize and run the Indian State. India was merely a colony of the British who ruled it from England. There were about 600 big and small native states which were in the hands of the native rulers but the latter were also under the control and superintendence of the British bureaucrats. All of them devoted themselves towards the cause of freedom of India. For this, they ignited the message of Swaraj, nationalism and democracy.

The Maharshi presented the renovated Vedic religion (Dharma) as the basis of the national unity. It was further supported by the adoption of Hindi language (Arya Bhasha). All other non-Vedic and anti-Vedic religions, faiths or sects were deviations, additions and accretions of that real Vedic Dharma. He taught the Indians to give up their differences, and adopt it. The Vedic religion was superior, rational, scientific and real to all the prevailing religions and faiths, and was essence of all religions. His nationalism was based on spiritual values or dharma. It was not based on separation of religion and politics (secularism), hatred, violence or materialism. His dharma embraced all humanity. Anyone could accept the Vedic religion.

Both Swarajya and Swadeshi reflected his intense spirit of patriotism as well as nationalism. Dayananda was the first among the Indian thinkers to advocate the use of swadeshi (country-made) goods. He emerged as the staunch supporter of the swadeshi. He fully realized the implications of the use of foreign goods by the Indians. He stood in favour of strengthening the country's economy. Wherever he went, he encouraged and preached the use of India-made articles.

Tilak's greatest contribution is found in his conviction that only political action by the masses can compel the alien rulers in loosening their grip over the country. He placed before himself the goal of activating the masses. Swarajya or Swaraj was the pivot of the whole thinking and actions of Tilak. It was based on the concept of 'Dharmarajya'. Swarajya means divinity. Before 1916, it meant complete freedom without any place to the British Queen. In 1916 and onwards, it carried the meaning of 'limited self-rule', on the pattern of other British dominions. His Swarajya really meant government responsible to the people. The people were the ultimate source of power. Such self-rule was the life behind all of his activities. It was not only of the Hindus, but had to belong to all sections of the people.

For Tilak, nationalism was Swaraj. It was not just a right, but a dharma. He gave a moral and spiritual meaning to Swaraj by relating it to people's political right as home rule: "Swaraj (self-rule) is our birth-right". He regarded only popular self-government as moral government. It was a philosophic and historic necessity. It was pre-requisite of real social, political, economic, cultural and spiritual progress. Therefore, he reminded the people to know their heritage of self-rule. India could be reawakened only on the basis of her past glories, and attain future greatness.

Gandhi also based his ideas on his concepts of religion, truth and non-violence. He also had intense faith in moral and spiritual freedom. Swaraj was part of truth and God. Political freedom or Swaraj could be obtained only by intense suffering. It was never a gift. It was dharma of the Indians. Gandhi was a philosophical anarchist and stood against state. He at the most permitted decentralization or Gram Swaraja or village governance. He was ready to reject the opinion of the majority, and compel all to accept one man's opinion.

Minorities were advised by him to both accept and reject majority decisions.

Dayananda and Vivekananda were not very clear on the material and economic conditions of the country. They did not stand for economic equality. They were not ready to tolerate extreme poverty or luxury. Rather, the rich men might create trouble for the ruler. According to Dayananda, enhancement of prosperity of the country was the primary duty of every ruler. Its importance was next to national independence.[17]

Tilak dwelt on the problems of famine, poverty, land revenue and analyzed the economic factors of the Indian plight. According to his political philosophy, the duty of the government was not only to provide peace, but also to secure prosperity, industrial growth and relief during calamities. If the government did not perform this duty, it was to be forced to do that duty. This was not sedition. At the Calcutta Congress of 1906, he supported the Swadeshi resolution and laid the economic foundations of Indian national movement. To recover from this plight, he suggested the use of the weapons of Swadeshi and boycott.[18] Tilak made use of these weapons through journalism. He put stress on (i) development of national industries; (ii) protection to Indian industries; (iii) technical education; (iv) permanent settlement; (v) peasant indebtedness; (vi) increase of irrigation; (vii) industrialization, and the like.

Gandhi saw economics also from the viewpoint of religion and morality. He did not imagine any economics bereft of morality. Economics should also be based on social justice and equality. He stood for spiritualization of economy also.

His economic ideas were based on (a) opposition to industrialization; (b) support to cottage and rural industries; (c) trusteeship and personal property; (d) non-possessions; and (e) class co-operation. Gandhi supported equality of wages for the lawyer, the doctor, the teacher and the scavenger. This wage equality was a panacea for all socio-economic evils. Man's propensity towards the acquisition of wealth is the central evil. He advocated a wise regulation of riches and absolute social justice. The rich men should recognize the presence of God in all creatures and should take initiative towards non-possession or trusteeship. All should be treated equally. Socialism was not to be realized by capture of political power through an organized party. Only truthful, non-violent and pure-hearted socialists could affect a genuine transformation. He put emphasis on purification of the individual and spiritual socialism for the community.

Brushing aside the prevailing controversy whether political reforms or social reforms should come first, Gandhi boldly declared that not only social reforms should be taken up first, but the economic reforms too have to be given priority. He picked up the spirit of Swaraj and Swadeshi prevailing in 1905-08. To him, the country should not wait till the end of the British Raj and pray to them for amelioration of the economic conditions of the masses. He, on the one hand, used the weapon of boycott (bahishkar) at economic and political levels, and on the other hand, established vast network of khadi and Swadeshi vocations under constructive programme. His 'Charkha' (spinning wheel) was seen as symbol of Swaraj. He was so much worried about the plight of the depressed classes, that after the episode of Poona Pact, he gave up Congress and devoted the rest of his life for the upliftment of the Harijans. It was he who made the entry of Dr. B.R. Ambedkar, the devoted leader of the depressed classes, into the Constituent Assembly possible. Rather, he was given the pivotal role in the framing of the Indian Constitution.

As India was a colony of the vast British imperialism, nothing could have been done by these socio-religious and political reformers. But they had expressed their ideas on inter-state relations and world peace.

On relations among states and awakening of the masses, the Maharshi proposed the ultimate goal of the whole humanity as the establishment of a 'Chakravarti Rajya' (Universal Aryan Empire). This appeared to be the ultimate culmination of his moto, "make the whole world Arya" (civilized). The term 'Arya' means civilized and cultured. Dayananda prayed for the establishment of the Chakravarti Rajya of the brave to God.[19]

It is important to observe that the Maharshi talks of the supremacy of the Aryas. He did not have any particular race, people or country in mind. The Vedic Dharma, as prescribed by him, aimed at making ordinary men into the righteous ones or Aryas.[20]

For Maharshi the culmination of his Vedic teachings was the ideal of a world-state (Sarvabhauma Chakravarti Rajya) or a universal empire.[21] To realize this goal, it was necessary that India becomes a strong state, a nation-state, having one religion (Dharma) and one Arya Bhasha (Hindi).[22] He reminded everyone to remember that the

Vedic Dharma is a not separate sect or a faith or a religion like many others, but the fountain-head of all religions. It gives a way of life that is necessary and would be acceptable to all.

Vivekanand wanted the youth of India more to be football players than mere readers of the Gita. Strength is greater than religion. Nothing is greater than strength. Religion should first give bread to a living man. He was convinced that God was not to be sought from outside this world.

Vivekananda was a monk, a religious preacher and an ascetic, but had tremendous love for the masses. In them he saw his God or Daridranarayana: "I am an Indian, every Indian is my brother, the ignorant Indian, the poor and destitute Indian, the Brahmin Indian, the Pariah Indian, is my brother."

For uniting the peoples of India, he wanted, besides a 'common mother religion' also a 'common language'. That 'mother language' should also be rooted in all the languages of India. Sanskrit could be such 'mother language'. Its superiority and suitability can make it an all-India language.

All of them were leader of the masses. Dayananda started the Arya Samaj, Vivekananda founded the Ram Krishna Mission and Tilak organized the Home Rule Movement and started celebrating Ganapati and Shivaji festivals on mass scale.

Tilak's political thought was a fusion of some of the dominant conception of the Indian thought and the nationalistic and democratic ideas of the West.

Tilak believed in the metaphysics of Advaita (non-dualism) or the all-pervading Supreme Reality or Brahma. As all men are aspects or parts of that Absolute Spirit, they have the same autonomous spiritual potentiality. This spiritual potentiality can grow or fructify only in the presence of freedom. Freedom is the very life of the individual which the Vedanta declares to be identical with God. Without freedom no moral or spiritual life is possible. Freedom was the soul of the Home Rule Movement. Imperialism or the rule of an alien race kills the soul of a nation. Therefore, the British Raj must be fought against. Tilak's nationalism is conceptually a synthesis of the Vedantic ideal of the Absolute Spirit as Supreme Freedom and the Western ideas.

On refusal by Prime Minister Lloyd George to Tilak to attend the Peace Conference as a Congress delegate, he sent a memorandum to Clemenceau, President of the Peace Conference on March 21, 1919. He sent its copy to President Wilson also. Tilak made forceful appeal to get two pronouncements: (i) India would be accorded all the rights of representation in the League of Nations at par with other British self-governing colonies; and (ii) the Indians are fit for carrying on their government and the principle of self-determination should be applied to India so that the Indians could establish a democratic form of government. But nothing could be done till August 15, 1947.

Tilak was far-sighted to suggest the importance of a national language and a common script for all the languages of India. He was the first great political leader to propose Hindi in Devanagari script as the national language of India. Tilak's love for the country was only a step towards cosmopolitanism. He pleaded for reconciliation between the ideal of nationalism and the Vedantic ideal of human unity. The Vedantic ideal was higher and the national ideal was lower. But they were not opposed to each other.

Gandhi made the freedom movement moral and legitimate. Earlier, the movement was dependent on the presence of a great Karmayogi like Tilak—a God-realized person performing Karmas in a detached manner for the good of the people. When he passed away, there was none to succeed him.[23] Gandhi enshrined the conscience of every satyagrahi in place of rarely available Karmayogi's, thus revolutionized the concept of Tilak by implementing it in the heart of every freedom fighter. To Gandhi, everyone's own conscience was a safer and better guide for him.

He transformed, by employing the tenets of truth and non-violence, the apolitical Indian masses into a mighty organized force which did compel the British Raj to quit earlier. During his own lifetime, he converted the freedom movement, hitherto confined to middle and lower middle sections of society, into a huge mass movement. He formulated a religio-moral strategy of political action which put up a tough fight against the alien rule, and forced them to handover the governance to Indians.

Gandhi believed in the concept of 'nationalism' but its basis was the nation as a whole. It was dependent on the feeling of identity with all. His patriotism was not exclusive. It was a part of his creed of Ahimsa. When it is applied along with truth and non-violence, it turned into internationalism.[24]

For him, growth of nationalism was necessary to get over problems of casteism, groupism, etc. Once nationalism is kindled, the nation can make sacrifices to any extent. India may die so that humanity may live. Individual has to live for the family, the family has to live for the village, the village for the district, the district for the province, the province for the nation, and the nation for the world. He wanted freedom for India, so that the whole world may be benefited. The whole world is our family (वसुधैव कुटम्बकम्).

Thus, all the ideals preached by them were already acclaimed by Hinduism. Organization of these on mass scale was the only newer contribution to it.

Group D consists of point 9 relations with other religious communities and point 10 instruments, methods and techniques of political agitation which throw light on ideas of these leaders how they proposed to deal with non-Hindu communities, and made use of various means and methods to realize harmony and cooperation with them.

India, being a multi-religious and multi-cultural country during the 19th and 20th centuries, it is also important to know what Hinduism did to maintain relations with other non-Hindu communities and contribute towards growth of nationalism and freedom.

Dayananda, in order to bring all communities together, taught the Vedas. He severely criticized a number of anti-Veda doctrines and practices of Islam and Christianity. He also criticized some of the tenets of the orthodox Hindu Dharma and opposed their idolatry, casteism, slavery etc. He worked more among the Hindus for their religious and social reforms because they were at the lowest and suffered the most. He asked for no privileged position or concessions for the Hindus. But being a majority community, he considered it more necessary to work for their reform so that a strong and united Aryavarta might emerge to make the whole world Arya (civilized) (कृण्वन्तो विश्वमार्यम).

But Vivekananda's Vedanta as a philosophy and a religion, included every faith of the world. He taught universality of presence of God in all religions—Hinduism, Islam, Christianity and other faiths. As all were identical in their essence, apparently may differ in forms, presentation or details. He accepted the validity of all faiths, and also the authority of their founders.[25] He allowed all mythology, ritualism and fetishism attached with religions to continue.

Vivekananda accepted the right of religions to have independent existence. He knew the consequences of this multiplicity of various sects and faiths. Each religion claimed the exclusive right to live.[26] But he regarded the Vedanta as a rational explanation of the universe. It had all the potentiality to become a world religion. It had all useful social implications. It taught faith in oneself, oneness of all living beings, and the divinity of man. It taught the way of disinterested action. It could also reconcile all religions and sects. In this way, it could serve the purpose of social and political reconstruction.

He thought that only religion could be the basis of India's national unity. By synthesizing Vedanta and the Sufi version of Islam, a single united synthetic religion could be created. It would be a sort of 'mother religion'. But it would preserve all the essential characteristics of prevailing religions of India. With the 'mother religion' uniting them, all these religious sects could function freely, and such act, he thought, would lay the solid foundation of India's unity. However, it would be spiritual unity, and not social unity.

Like them Tilak was also not anti-Muslim.[27]

According to Tilak, a person, thus, working for the interests of India, was not alien, even if he was Anglo-Indian. His Congress Democratic Party stood for religious toleration, and supported the claims of the Mohammedans on the Khilafat.

Similarly, one of the very important ideals of Gandhi was to unite various communities—Hindus, Muslims, Sikhs, Christians, Parsis etc.—and bring about harmonious relations among them. Throughout his whole life he worked assiduously for its realization. More important of them, were the relations of cordiality between Hindus and Muslims. He never accepted that religion could be the basis of nationality. He repudiated two-nation theory propounded by the Muslim League. When partition became a reality, he staked his life to stop Hindu-Muslim riots.[28]

Dayananda's instruments of action were: the Vedas, Dharma, Arya Samaj, religious disputation (शास्त्रार्थ), Purification Movement, Swaraj, Swadeshi and nationalism. From the Vedas, the Maharshi authoritatively proved that untouchability, casteism etc. have no place in the Vedic religion. All are equal—men and women. Varnas follow one's aptitude, job and merit. Heredity and birth have no place in the varnashrama system.[29]

Organization and movement of the Arya Samaj (Society of the Righteous People) was his herculean effort to rejuvenate the scattered people into an Aryan society. It was the first big step towards "make the whole world Aryan (righteous)". The Maharshi gave concrete shape to his ideas and hinted towards the ways to realize them through the Samaj. It was in no way an orthodox or conservative or fundamentalist organization. Rather, the Samaj adopted a modern outlook without leaving the ancient heritage and the goal of going 'Back to the Vedas'. It had a firm faith in reaping the fruits of science.

Dayananda's Arya Samaj had a mass appeal with less ambitious objectives. It had its basic roots in the past, through the call of 'Back to the Vedas', and the return to the 'varna system' in its original form.[30] It also appeared as a challenge to the conversion campaigns of the Islamic and the Christian missionaries. It had launched *shuddhi* or purification (or reconversion) movement for this purpose. But its real goal was to unite the Indian people under one dharma.

Dayananda considered the varna to be the creation of the state. The state can promote a Shudra on merit to a Vaishya, or a Kshatriya or a Brahmin. The state can degrade a Brahmin on his degeneration to Shudraship.[31]

Maharshi Dayananda Saraswati maintained that the Vedic Dharma was the only right religion of man—Godly, and divine and perfect in all respects. Its adoption and practice were the only panacea of all the prevailing evils. Therefore, all should go back to the Vedas. His shuddhi or purification movement was designed to bring all people together on that right path of the Vedas which he found so perfectly justified. It was a purification, not a conversion movement, in form of return to one's own home land. He considered freedom of religion as the inalienable right of everyone.[32]

He did not consider the Muslims or Christians as foreigners or descendants of foreign conquerors. They were Indian nationals who were originally Aryans (or Hindus), but converted to Islam later on. The Arya Samaj looked at the 'shuddhi' as a potent instrument for affecting religious, social and political unity of India. All could come under the banner of the Vedic Dharma.

Vivekananda's methods were propaganda and preaching of Practical Vedanta to the masses within the country and to the West.

Tilak wanted active resistance, no-tax campaign, boycott etc. His policy was to take what he would get and then carry on struggle for the remainder. However, his colleagues in Bengal were more advanced. "We desire to make it (India) autonomous, absolutely free of the British control" (Bipin Chandra Pal). At times Pal and Ghosh spoke in terms of absolute independence. But Tilak never spoke, at least publicly, in terms of elimination of British political connection.

In the beginning he adopted Swadeshi as a primarily economic counterpart of the programme of economic boycott. Preference to India-made goods could give impetus to the Indian industrial development. However, its scope was further widened. Swadeshi could also mean gradual disappearance of visible foreign things, and in due course of time, disappearance of foreign ideas and institutions too. It led towards the spirit of independence. It grew into a movement of national regeneration: to recognize the land of the Aryas as Mother Earth could also be part of Swadeshi movement.

National education was also a logical culmination of boycott and Swadeshi movement. It resulted in the establishment of schools for imparting education with national background. Western education was not to be ignored, but could supplement to knowledge on Indian culture and civilization. Religious education was to be the essential part of the curriculum. New spirit of self-respect and self-reliance in the Indian students could not be expected from the government-run schools.

His other instruments were: Dharma and suffering in jails, use of press and celebration of festivals.[33] Tilak had made immense suffering for the country. It was suffering, at the hands of the British bureaucracy, which had created a fear psychosis in the minds of the laymen like celebrating Ganesh Utsava and Shivaji Festival, and publishing newspapers like *Vande Mataram*, *Rastramata* etc.

At the hands of Gandhi suffering was not to be avoided or feared from. Rather it had to be welcomed, accepted and enjoyed as a part of Satyagraha. People had to court imprisonment and go to jails which were now called as Krishna temples. Fear of British prisons gradually disappeared from the minds of the people. As the Satyagrahis were to be totally non-violent—in thought, word and deed, their imprisonment or ill-treatment made the British Raj immoral, unjust and inhuman. He was sure that this self-suffering could cause conversion of hearts of his adversaries as God or Truth was common to both.

He was for total Ahimsa as a state of mind. As he believed in an all-pervading, kind, blissful, Almighty God, who has created this world, there is no room for any ill-will, hatred, or injury to anybody. Ahimsa was, thus, not merely a detached sympathy towards an enemy, but also the denial of the very existence of an enemy. Complete Ahimsa was a state of soul and mind.

Gandhi used various forms or techniques of Ahimsa or Satyagraha: (1) non-cooperation; (2) civil disobedience; (3) hartal; (4) picketing; (5) strike; (6) fasting; (7) voluntary migration; (8) spinning Charkha; (9) Sitting in meditation etc. He made use of them at national scale, and awakened the masses, and prepared them for winning Indian independence through peaceful means.

Thus, efforts of all these leaders led to awakening of masses as a vital political force.

Failure, Limitations and Impact on the Hindus and Other Communities

However, it is clear that these Hindu leaders tried to formulate an ideology of Hinduism in their own way, but it lacked uniformity and acceptability from all major non-Hindu communities.

Ideology of Hinduism succeeded only in theoretical renovation of the Hindu Dharma. To some extent it awakened the Hindu masses towards political freedom. This ideology of Hinduism could not seek full cooperation both from the majority of the Muslims and the depressed classes of the Hindus. India could obtain freedom only after the Hindu majority was forced to accept partition to the Muslims and constitutional concessions to the depressed classes.

The failure of Dayananda, Vivekananda, Tilak and Gandhi appears in their inability to prove 'religion' as the sole centre of power, politics, culture and pattern of living. They forgot that their own 'religion' was no more a universal 'religion', at par with the Vedicas.

Most of the religio-social reformers tend to forget that every religion after sometimes gets organized, often as a community, society and polity. It becomes a power or a force in temporal terms. It evolves its own patterns of holy books, philosophy, polity, culture, morality, economy marriage system, education and legal code. Its founders command it to enlist or entrap the whole humanity under its order. Even when an original religion, after some time, happens to take a different form or grows into some new forms, it would be hardly ready to go back to its earlier form. Its set up is usually composed of some vested interests, power-holders, large properties, holy places and buildings, scriptures, rituals, gurus (teachers), and millions of followers. As a Maharshi, Dayananda talked only about the spiritual goals of blissful life and moksha, in which most of the other various religions, including Hinduism, were hardly interested. Some others like Vivekananda thought it better to absorb themselves into God directly, and perhaps forthwith, without undergoing the long process performing hard social obligations by observing strict discipline at personal level. Tilak vainly told the people to practise 'detached action' (निष्काम कर्मयोग) and act like Lord Krishna of the *Gita*. Gandhi continued to conduct experiments with truth and non-violence of his own self-realization, but could not attain it. Likewise, most of men of other religions did not think it even worthwhile to adopt renovated ideology of Hinduism. In fact, even Hindu Dharma remained where it was. The ideologues of Hinduism could not understand the nature of their own limitations. As such, it had to experience many difficulties and failures.

Dayananda, Vivekananda and others did not take trouble to find out whether other religions would permit them to consider their own religion as next to Hinduism. They failed to appreciate that every other religion is not only an original way to God, but also a power or force supported by its millions of followers. Why and how would a religion like to give up that status and obedience to it by millions. Vivekananda, like Dayananda and several others, did not intend to found a new religion or replace other religions. But, unfortunately, both the Ram Krishna Mission and the Arya Samaj, even Roy's Brahmo Samaj, had attained the status of religious sect, claiming somewhat different identity from the traditional Hinduism. Every religion carries its own culture, civilization, races, forms of government, patterns of friendship and hostility, modes of economy, particular art, language and literature, and the like. Followers of other religion were ready to listen to Vivekananda till these aforesaid things were not disturbed or challenged. His concern was mainly with man's inner nature, divinity, purity, consciousness or perfection. So his Karmayogi was totally different from Arjuna, devoted only to renunciation and service to man, and not permitted even to make some opposition to the wicked as had been taught by Dayananda in *Satyarthaprakasha*.

Maharshi Dayananda did not explain even to the Hindus why he began with the Traitavada, not with the Unmanifest, Unknown, Abstract Absolute Spirit, Ultimate Reality or Pure Brahma. He was apparently imprisoned by his own perfectionist commitment. This made him look like a fundamentalist and an orthodox to a certain extent.

Criticism of Other Religions and Sects

All this points out how much did it prove futile to criticize various religions, faiths and sects in the *Satyarthaprakasha*. Hardly anyone was ready to change or reform itself. Rather, after Dayananda, several new forms, of religions and sects have come up and gathered hundreds of thousands of followers. They did not look at Dayananda from his own impartial and meaningful angle. He was treated by them as a man of hatred, fundamentalism, secession and monopolist of religion. Under these circumstances, how could his claim be accepted that the Vedas are perfect or they contain the seeds of all knowledge. To such people, Dayananda stood against the law of evolution.

He hardly could explain why, if the first, original, real, and ancient Vedic Dharma was so good, it sank so deep. If it was so perfect in itself, how it was so much defaced beyond identification. He made herculean efforts to recover the identity of the Vedic religion, and was also successful to a great extent. But his own attempts to remodel, reform or renovate the Hindu society were partly accepted, therefore, partly successful.

Overdose of Spirituality and Partial God

In fact, the Vedanta and its faith in spirituality provided limited scope to bring about wilful, planned or contrived change in socio-political structures. In the hands of a sanyasi, its scope gets still circumscribed. Things belonging to the world of Maya cannot get priority over spiritual matters. If, according to Vivekananda, God pervaded everywhere, there was hardly any room for turning out the foreign rulers, eliminating the upper caste exploitation, and destroying the wicked ones. For a Vedantin, realization of the Absolute was more important than doing away with poverty, backwardness, illiteracy or unemployment. Hardly a sanyasi, even if he was Vivekananda, would find himself in a position to provide for the safety and protection of Vedanta or Hinduism from the excesses of other religions and religious organizations. He lacked resources, training, temperament, and manpower to do so. All this has had so far been treated anti-religion by saints and swamis. Vivekananda taught the religious people of India to have more spirituality, believe in unity of all religions, render service without attachment, and live a life of renunciation.

He put again Hinduism on a world map. But he could do little for the Hindus as a community: besieged from without and vivisected from within. His universal Vedantism did not permit him to do much.

His Mayavada actually means that social evils and oppressions are in fact unreal, and a Vedanti should be moderate and remain tolerant towards them. So could be the case with foreign rule, exploitation, racial discrimination etc. At times, he felt that India's social order was but "the reflex of the Infinite Universal Motherhood". This reflects his intense social conservatism, even obscurantism. In his more furious and inspired moments, he talked of a radical elimination of the caste system. On other occasions, he recommended the adoption of the theory of social organic growth. He appeared to be content with teaching of evolutionary growth towards perfection. He was not in favour of any violent reforms and wanted to revive society on the old grounds of universal salvation and equality as laid down by his old masters such as Sankaracharya, Ramanuja and Chaitanya. Like Dayananda, he, even at the end of the nineteenth century, could not understand that even the retaining the use of four terms—Brahmin, Kshatriya, Vaishya and Shudra—were to perpetuate the painful historical memories of social exploitation and suppression

In order to pursue political goals for India, Tilak too made several compromises at metaphysical and philosophical levels.

Gandhi felt that all religions were equal and contained common principles of morality. However, none of these claims could be tested empirically. It is observable that every religion regards itself superior to others. It refuses to regard other religions equal to it. By maintaining his religion and dharma as special and over and above sectarian religions, Gandhi gave the impression to have innovated a new religion. This stand of Gandhi was not acceptable to the orthodox followers of Islam, Buddhism, Christianity etc.

His God was only a part of Total God. As God was ultimate value of Gandhi, it was not subject to any empirical investigation. He is Sachchidananda, perfect, all-powerful, source of morality etc. and resided in form of a divine spark in every human being. Man being a part of His divinity was essentially good. Thus, Gandhi was selective in his appreciation of the attributes of God. He envisioned God more as Creator, Regulator, Benevolent, Blissful, Truth, Sat, Righteousness etc. He avoided His other known aspects, such as, death, destruction, dissolution, violence, power and others. Gandhi's God was preferably a Sanatani Hindu Vaishnava God, preferably liked by majority of the Hindus and were known as tenets of Hindu Dharma. It involved principles of law of karma (action), transmigration of soul, salvation (moksha), re-incarnation (avatar), and personal God, heaven and hell. He claimed to have communion with Him through intuition, 'inner voice', conscience, and prayers. He put faith, love or heart over reason and intellect. The goal of his life was realization of such God through selfless service of man. God or Truth was the supreme end or ultimate value for Gandhi. Nobody could question him about such God and the ways to realize Him through the conduct of freedom movement and tell consequences of his faith to them on these lines.[34]

Both religion and politics, it is observable, were two separate and autonomous categories of life. For leading a religious life, it was not necessary to indulge in politics. Their purpose, nature, form and operation are different. Only to some extent, they might influence each other. Therefore, politics, quite opposite to Gandhi, was not a dispassionate activity or subordinate to religion. For Gandhi, politics or his engagement in the freedom movement of India was a means to the realization of his ultimate goal: self-realization. Few people could agree to this understanding of politics.

Conservativism: Upholding of Caste System

Dayananda considered the classification of the varnas (castes) a political function. He handed over this task to a state board consisting of scholars and saints, for classifying the persons as Brahmin, Kshatriya, Vaishya and Shudra on the basis of their aptitude, merit and action. This was his solution of a centuries-old problem of the wretched caste system. Unfortunately, it came after several centuries when the cancer grew beyond cure. It could not have been done without the help of the state (government). The state was in the hands of the British rulers. Why should the latter take interest in doing so? Who was eager to have oneself classified? What benefit was going to accrue to the society or the polity from that classification? Which family could be ready to have a child transplant to it, and handing over its child to some another on the basis of identity of a particular varna aptitude? How can hundreds of new jobs and varying personalities be classified into the merit based varnas? Even the declared aptitude could go on changing after the classification of varnas was once made. He made no provision for further change after the classification process was closed. In the varna system, Dayananda still appeared to be conservative when he did not permit upnayana to the Shudra children.[35]

For Vivekananda, caste, society, government, state etc. belonged to the finite world of Maya. He put them outside the arena of spiritualism, giving a treatment suitable to the things of nature or to laws of growth. He mistakenly equated 'caste formation' and 'grouping', and maintained that caste was a natural order, not only in India, but throughout the world history. He added further that abolition of caste system would mean uniformity leading to fixity and bondage. His remedy, "therefore, is not its elimination, but mere rationalization of the caste system".

Another remedy which came from Swami Vivekananda was the establishment of the Shudra-raj. This had to come about as a result of the cycle of caste rules operating in the world history. It began with the rule of the Brahmin (knowledge), the Kshatriya (force), the Vaishya (merchantilism), and would end in the Shudra-raj (downtrodden) in order of succession, one replacing another. It means it had to happen by will of God. The spread of the Shudra rule world over would also end up in degeneration of society. The goal of man was to attain Brahminhood, so the cycle of progress would move to its beginning—the rule of the Brahmin. This is the teleology coming from Hero-Prophet of Advaita?

All-out efforts of B.G. Tilak were to have political freedom first, discouraged social reforms towards the eradication of the social evils, abolition of untouchability and equal treatment to the lower castes, upliftment of women and some others. He, thus, happened to neglect half of the Hindu population and bring it amidst the mainstream of the national movement. Even on the varna order, he had no ideas for radical reforms, and wanted them to maintain the status quo, at least till the realization of Swaraj.[36] Tilak and others, such as Lala Lajpat Roy, Bipin Chand Pal, Aurobindo Ghosh etc., had little to respond to the question that how without minorities, women and depressed classes was it possible to put an All-India Front against the mighty British Raj?

Gandhi did not desire to introduce revolutionary changes in the outdated Hindu social structure, though devoted his rest of the life after 1934 to the cause of Harijan uplift.[37]

Limited Knowledge of Democracy, State and Other Political Institutions

Most of the Hindu leaders had perfectionist view of the Vedas. It kept Dayananda away from understanding the West and its sources of strength. His knowledge about the nature of modern state was limited. He did not make any distinction between state, government and society.

Not knowing English and the West, he did not fully understand the forces and working of democracy. Simple election of the ruler by the people or the assembly was not democracy.

Vivekananda mixed society, state and nation. He granted superior place to society which is a divine institution—a full organic whole. It was neither political nor economic, but operated according to scriptural injunctions. His concept of society was based on Vedanta. He wanted an ideal society where the highest truth can be held and practised by all. But he wanted to synthesize the Indian idea of spiritual integrity and the western ideal of progress, but under the supremacy of religion. This religion is to be operated by the individuals striving for to attain goodness and perfection. Society stands next or secondary to the individual. Vivekananda frees the society from the ambit of religion. To him, social institutions, customs and mores have nothing to do with religion. Like caste, untouchability, segregation of women, child marriages etc. are mistakenly connected with religion.

Nationalism of these social reformers was pro-Hindu. Dayananda had galvanized all the factors and forces of nationalism in India—Swarajya, Swadeshi, one language, one religion, Aryavarta, supremacy of the people and the like. Still he was not fully aware of the forces of all India nationalism. But he forgot that it was difficult for the Hindus to give up birth, heredity and exploitation-based caste and sub-caste system which they have ossified through thousand of years.[38] His perfect Vedism or Final Authority of the Vedas could not be applied to all religions. Though he made distinction between an 'Arya' and a 'Hindu', his teachings mostly appealed to the Hindu community only. It was only a part of the Hindu community that liked them most. However, his own mission—the Arya Samaj—turned, later on, into an another sect of the Hindus. During the Freedom Movement most of its big leaders joined the Indian National Congress, and made the Arya Samaj subservient to it. Unfortunately, Dayananda had no successor who would have carried on his task to the desired accomplishment. None of his followers could own his vision in full. Even the cow protection and the 'shuddhi' campaigns ended as damp squibs.

Surely, Vivekananda's appeal was not confined to a narrow section of the Hindus, but all the Hindus belonging to the Vedas to Vaishnava sects. Still it was confined to the Hindus only. His 'Practical Vedanta' did not apply even to the Jains, Buddhists and other atheist religions. The Semitic religions did not pay any attention to it. As he did not mean replacement of any religion by Vedanta, and regarded all religions as valid and good, his appeal ultimately remained confined to the Hindus only.

In the field of inter-state relations, the ideal of Dayananda was superb in proposing to have Universal World Empire of the Aryans, or, Sarvabhauma Chakravarti Rajya through the organization of one strong India united under the Vedic Dharma and the merit-based varna and ashrama order. It had to be a federation-like and democratic. However, it appears to be a mere wishful thinking. Some of basic tenets of his Vedic religion are not acceptable even to religions, faiths and sects prevailing in India, e.g., law of karma, transmigration, varna and ashrama order, Traitavada, impermanent salvation etc. Hardly any other state or religion or community would accept a world-state, dominated and ruled by the Aryans, following the Vedic Dharma. Even various castes, sects, faiths, communities and groups within Hinduism are not ready to accept that ideal. An event established in the dead past may not be repeated again.

In 1894, Vivekanand wrote, "I am not a politician or a political agitator. I care only for spirit". In fact, as a sanyasi, he could not have taken part in political or legal controversies. He was more interested in moral and spiritual regeneration of India. He had no other mechanism or organization to solve other temporal or secular problems of the Hindus.

In fact, no such occasion arose before any one of the socio-religious and political reformers of India, including Mahatma Gandhi.

Tilak openly identified the movement of nationalism with Hinduism. He felt that common factor in Indian society was the feeling of Hindutva (devotion to Hinduism). He overlooked the presence of Muslims and Christians because everywhere the majority in the society consisted of the Hindus. Tilak's stress on Hinduism as an essential and major part of the national movement proved to be a dangerous trend. Identification of national awakening with the revival of Hinduism isolated Muslim masses from the mainstream of national movement.

In view of the degrading conditions of the untouchables, Dr. B.R. Ambedkar observed that Indian society was not a nation: "I am of the opinion that in believing that we are a nation, we are cherishing a great delusion." A people divided into several thousands of castes cannot be a nation. There are two nations here—a ruling nation, and a subject nation; touchables and untouchables.

In the field of making India a viable nation, Mahatma Gandhi was more explicit. National integration, he thought, could be strengthened by (i) removal of caste system, (ii) stopping priesthood to be hereditary, (iii) bringing economic equality, (iv) reorganization of states on the basis of one state and one language, (v) Hindi to be the official language of all the states and until it is so developed, English to continue to be the official language, (vi) central capitals to be at Delhi and Hyderabad, (vii) protection of minorities, and (viii) special provision for the Scheduled Castes and separate electorate for them.[39] But Gandhi's most sincere and ardent efforts to win confidence of the Muslims and the depressed classes did not bear fruit. He was universally accepted as a saintly person but was never able to win the allegiance of caste leaders of the Hindu communities, particularly, the depressed classes. The Muslims largely remained unreconciled. To them, he was an 'outsider' and a Hindu leader. Only the majority of the Hindus stood behind him.

Inherent Inability of Hindu Leaders

In fact, these Hindu leaders suffered from many inherent inabilities. Vivekananda's commitment to religion or spirituality kept a large number of Hindus away from politics on three grounds: (a) politics was a degrading, anti-religion, and anti-spiritual activity—a kind of indulgence in Maya or Avidya; and (b) recluses or sanyasis are not permitted to take part in political (worldly) matters; and (c) religion and morality do not operate under the compulsion of temporal pressure or law. But, owing to the religious nature of the Indian people, these men of religion and their activities gained popularity and acceptance. Another Vedantin, Tilak was a metaphysical defender of altruistic violence, but could never practise. For his own, he followed the legal methods of political organization, propaganda and agitation. He felt that the country was not ready for revolutionary activity. In 1906, he asked the countrymen to avoid violent revolutionary activities. The people were to desist from such activities not on moral grounds but on grounds of expediency. He stated that violence and political murder give opportunity to the bureaucracy to crush the national movement.[40]

It is unfortunate that much against his established image as a great leader of the masses, Tilak in his *Gita-Rahasya* appeared to be solely concerned with taking the services from the liberated souls for the good of the mankind. He himself had realized that such persons of perfect spirituality appear few and far between. Obviously, Tilak's Karmayoga remained limited to a few persons. It was difficult to perform egoless actions in politics. Most of his followers were not having God-realization. Few of them perhaps were having the goal of God-identification or practice of performing their 'swadharma' (varna-allotted) functions in a dispassionate manner. His instructions could also not be applied to non-Hindus like the Christians, Jains or Buddhists. His appeal was mostly to the Hindus. Nationalism taught by him was mostly a Hindu nationalism. He neglected the need of evolving a suitable form of nationalism for the Muslims, and other minor communities. He talked of Dharma-rajya after attainment of self-rule, which was not acceptable to these communities.[41]

Impact of Gandhi Subversive to the Hindus

Many scholars think that leadership of Gandhi compensated the deficiencies of all earlier Hindu leaders. But overall impact of Gandhian leadership was harmful to the Hindu interests.[42]

In practice, his teachings were mostly addressed to the Hindus who likened him to a great avatar, godman, mahatma and saint. Others who were alike the Hindu followers also accorded similar respect to him. Most of them could not visualize that Gandhian apolitical ethics struck at the root of their own total philosophy, social fabric and political interests as a large Hindu community. Non-violence, despite big promises, happened to make them weaker and ultimately compelled them to submit to India's partition. The blind tradition of hero-worship carried on this trend still further. Failures were advocated as successes.

In the end, it can be safely concluded that the ideology of Hinduism so fervently pursued by Hindu leaders was anarchic, contradictory and ill-conceived. It utterly failed to protect the Hindu interests. The country was partitioned with bloodshed despite opposition of the Hindu. Religion was the basis of partition. The Hindus were violently turned out of Pakistani provinces, but more than half of the total population of Muslims remained in India. Dream of Hindu-Muslim unity cherished by Mahatma Gandhi and the Indian National Congress was badly shattered. The 'invincible' non-violence of Gandhi could neither stop nor Pakistan realize Hindu-Muslim unity. The ideology of Hinduism could not make any dent on the form, contents and practice of Hindu Dharma.

All this led to the rise of new ideology of Hindutva.

Notes

1. The Maharshi wanted to take Hindu dharma back to the status of tile Vedicas. He made it fit weapon to stand against monotheism of Islam.
2. Vivekananda stood at level two, but attempted to mix secularism of level three. His Practical Vedanta was an attempt to live Basic Reality.
3. Here, the word 'religion' has been used for *dharma*. The word '*dharma*' is derived from the root '*dhri*' which means to maintain or to hold or to bear.
4. Tilak, metaphysically, believed to live at level two. But his public posture was to stand for the Hindu Dharma. He wanted leaders to work at the level five who should act as men of Basic Reality making no distinction between Manifest and Unmanifest.
5. M.K. Gandhi was a man of Hindu Dharma. But he wished to have self-realization through working for awakening of the masses, Hindu-Muslim unity and India's independence. He actually operated at level two, therefore, failed to fact the forces of level three.
6. When a man like Ramkrishna claims to know God through a particular path, has God-realization for ever. Logically, he cannot test the validity of other paths, even by following them one by one. He is already a man of God.
7. While doing so, despite his being a great sanyasi and Maharshi, he had to face fierce opposition from orthodox elements which hurled abuses, slander and physical threats against him. The purush-sukta was made by them the basis of birth-based caste system. But he cut the very root of caste system by his reinterpretation of the purush-sukta that it meant "in society the Brahmin, man of knowledge was similar to the mouth; the Kshatriya, the warrior, to the arms; the Vaishya the merchant to the belly; and Shudra, the servant to the feet". He cut the very roots of caste system based on birth and heredity.
8. But he supported Niyoga. It was a contract, made in public knowledge, between a widow and a widower to procreate child and be broken off after the birth of two children. It was a temporary legal union initiated by a widow.
9. See, how Unmanifest of level two was misleading Vivekananda? He stood for caste and advanced arguments to retain it. But he wanted society to cultivate a liberal and assimilative outlook.
10. Praising the ancient varna system, he stated that it was a stepping stone to civilization, making one rise higher and higher in proportion to one's learning and culture.

11. Like Herbert Spencer, Vivekananda had an evolutionary vision of society. His thoughts were inspired by the Hindu sources, alike August Comte's stages of social evolution—theological military, critical-metaphysical, and industrial-scientific.
12. Tilak claimed to be operating at level two. But, he actually supported all evils of Hindu Dharma, such as, idol worship, reincarnation, caste system etc. It was a matter of baffling contradiction that he wanted men of detached action to work for freedom of India. His ideal was to work at level five.
13. According to the Gita, even after one has identity consciousness with the Absolute, duties relevant to varna order need not be given up, and should be performed in a spirit of disinterestedness (asanga) and Godward surrender (Ishwar samarpana).
14. Tilak discussed Bhakti or devotion as a part of spiritual metaphysics. It also led to the realization of tile Absolute Real. However, devotion is only a means of knowledge, not the final objective (Nishtha). According to the Gita, there are only two Nishthas—Gyanyoga and Karmayoga.
15. His programme of social unity and reforms centred around (a) re-orientation of the varna-system, (b) abolition of untouchability; (c) communal unity, (d) upliftment of women, and (e) basic education.
16. He purposefully called them as 'Harijans' (people of God), that they serve the society more than anyone else despite their being looked down upon.
17. The Swami developed all arguments against cow killing, particularly in his book entitled *Gokarunanidhi*, e.g., a cow can feed one lakh people, but its meat only 80. Actions that cause injury to others are sinful. Animal slaughter leads greater dependence on agriculture. He stood for the protection of the whole animal world. Their protection ensures better forests, better rainfall, and pollution-free atmosphere. But he took up the cause of cows first, as the ancient Aryans provided special care to it.
18. Sardar Ram Singh of the Kuka community had made use of boycott in 1870. In Maharashtra, Vasudeva Balwant Fadke, the political guru of Tilak, had spread the message of Swadeshi and organized peasants rebellion against the British Raj in 1870.
19. The Chakravarti government is to look after the welfare of its constituent units. The governors of a thousand villages would report to the governors of ten thousand villages. The governors of ten thousand villages would report to the Rajasabha of a hundred thousand villages. All such state assemblies would report to the Supreme Maharaja Sabha or the Chakravarti Supreme Assembly which has to rule over the whole world.

It was to be a kind of world federation. Its central power would be in the hands of an assembly composed of the representatives of different sovereign states. It would be ruled over in accordance with the prescriptions of the Vedas.

20. An Arya is one who practises true dharma.
21. ....the whole drift of Dayananda's teaching is far less to reform Hinduism than to enlighten it into active resistance to the alien influences which threatened, in his opinion, to denationalize it" (Valentine Chirol). He was a true prophet of nationalism, rather militant nationalism.
22. The Maharaja of Jodhpur on his advice ordered use of the khadi cloth produced in Marwar. The term 'khadi' had wider significance for him. It involved use of one Indian language—Arya bhasa (Hindi) also.
23. Tilak had returned back from Extremist to Moderate posture in adopting the goal of Home Rule—a limited colonial status for India within the British Empire. He did so out of fear from the clutches of law and from being treated as a criminal indulging in sedition. Even a small instalment of concession in form of the Government of India Act, 1919 had made Tilak and others to postpone the freedom struggle.
24. It can be observed that Unmanifest of level two enabled them to go beyond nationalism.
25. His master (Ramkrishna) had validated it one after another by realising God by observation of the disciplines of several religions: God is one but wise men speak on Him in various ways (एक सद्विप्रा बहुधा वदन्ति).
26. He accepted horrors, fiercer hatred, bitter enmity, and blood shed caused by religions, but counterpoises benefits brought by them to humanity in form of building of charitable institutions, hospitals for men and animals, or spreading brotherhood.
27. Zacharias (Renascent India) consider him as the spokesman of an anti-Moslem retaliations. Powell Price (*A History of India*) talks of the rise of Muslim League because of the possibility of self-government raised the spirit of separation which "the intolerance of Tilak had emphasized". Chirol reported that due to Tilak's extreme orthodoxy the Muslim members of the Poona Sarvajanika Sabha left that body. Similarly, Palme Dutt (*India Today*) blames that his revival of Hinduism cut off the Muslim masses from the national movement.

    But all these charges are partial and incorrect. M.A. Jinnah, Dr. M.A. Ansari and Hasan Iman had praised the nationalistic sentiments and spirit of compromise of Tilak. His wise counsel and moderation brought out the Lucknow Pact, 1916. Both Shaukat Ali and Hasrat Mohani respected Tilak as their political guru.

28. All were convinced that without a unified front of all religions, castes, communities; and a common national language, they cannot wrest freedom from the British hand. To realize this goal, they advanced plans and strategies to take non-Hindu minorities, particularly, Muslims with them. But their grounding of Hindu Dharma could not allow them to endear Muslims to them wholeheartedly.
29. It was a political matter to be performed by the state.
30. Unfortunately, this remedy was proposed 2000 years late.
31. When disqualified from his work, a Brahmin at once becomes de jure or automatically Shudra. Similarly, a Shudra who attains that merit, becomes *de jure* or automatically a Brahmin. But neither of them becomes so *de facto* at his own will or the will of others, as long as the state does not recognize them in like manner. Dayananda gave a moral basis to his newly proposed social order by declaring that, "If someone commits adharma (impious acts), his sacred thread (yagyopavita) should be snatched away". Thus, in his theory of the perfect (Arya) society, the division of society into birth-based castes would be replaced by the original varna system based on merit and action.
32. As such, every Christian or Muslim, or anyone else, should have the right to adopt the Vedic Dharma or religion which was in fact their own as that of any Hindu or Arya. One could rejoin it, if one had attraction towards it and wanted to accept it out of his own choice.
33. However, Tilak was convinced that nationalism can be built up only on the foundations of past values, culture and civilization or in one word 'dharma'. He maintained that nationalism was a spiritual and psychological conception. As India did not have one common language, common religion and common culture, he thought it proper to reinforce the spiritual and psychological elements of nationalism. He stated that India cannot move forward as the nation of the Hindus only. He rather added economic elements to the formation of Indian nationalism. He advocated boycott, swadeshi and criticism of the 'drain' of Indian prosperity to England.
34. In order to justify non-violence as means and end, Gandhi presented only one-sided picture of God. This partial advocacy of God caused immense harm to the Hindus.
35. "In practice, it will be immensely difficult to prevent the four varnas from degenerating into four castes. Hence although I agree with Dayananda in his theory of ashramas, I strongly differ from him in his theory of varnas." –V.P. Varma
36. His area of action was mostly Maharashtra only. In 1920, he thought of contesting elections of the Bombay Legislative Assembly only. He was also not an all-India leader. Despite his vocal support to many other socio-

economic programmes, he had little time to devote to other socio-economic activities, e.g., rural reconstruction, development of rural and cottage industries, prohibition, elevation of the depressed classes and women reforms. He was unaware of the consequences of industrialization, Western democracy and aggressive nationalism.

37. Even after losing several crores of Hindus by conversion to Islam, Christianity and other religions, these Hindu leaders continued to stand in support of caste system and exploitation of the lower caste people. It divided the country into pieces, weakened the Hindus by raising anemic and threatening minorities, trampled over their culture, and enslaved them for several countries.
38. In fact, their faith in the supremacy of Unmanifest at level two did not permit them to think beyond their own past or team modernity, democracy, nationalism and dignity of individual form the West. Even Gandhi was lost in the world of his truth and non-violence. He could not go beyond trusteeship and Gram Swaraj.
39. More than any other social reformer herculean efforts were made by Dr. Ambedkar to reform the Hindu society. Following footsteps of Kabir and Phule, he while remaining as a Hindu, fought against the evils of Hinduism—untouchability, exploitation, oppression and inhuman treatment. He exposed the history, philosophy and mythology of Hinduism, including its Shastras. He fully exposed the caste system and its evils in the book *Annihilation of Caste* and also put forward proposals to reform it. He put pressure on the Hindus in form of various satyagrahas. Very soon, he came to the conclusion that the Hindus would not reform themselves. Therefore, he made efforts to get the 'untouchables' declared as a 'minority' and have separate electorates. Only attainment of political power, according to him, would compel the Hindus to bring about change in their attitude. After the Poona Pact, the requisite change was visible to a certain extent. He declared in 1935 to renounce Hinduism and created a flutter in the caste-Hindu circles. With the help of the British rulers, before their exit, he tried his best to get a minority status and separatist political settlement but could not succeed. However, when he found that Hinduism remains unable to change itself and accord equality to the Harijans, he chose Buddhism as his religion just before two months of his death. According to him Buddhism was the only true religion preaching liberty, equality, and fraternity. In a way it was an acceptance of his failure to reform Hindu society.
40. He had learnt all about the failure of the violent struggle of 1857-58, of rebellion of 1876-80 by Vasudeva Balwant Fadke against the British rule. But he did not deny from any possible armed rebellion in distant future.

41. Tilak had had to give up his earlier goal of 'Swarajya' (complete independence) in 1914, and adopt the revised goal of limited self-rule or Home Rule. This he did to escape from the clutches of law of sedition or otherwise had to undergo further suffering. After adopting the policy of 'responsive co-operation', almost all his weapons Swadeshi, boycott, passive resistance and others had become out of use. Hardly there was any scope for his leadership in future. Swaraj was dharma. This dharma was Hindutva or Hindu Dharma. Aurobindo went to the extent of equating nationalism with Hinduism or Sanatan Dharma. None was able to present a united front before the alien rulers.
42. For this topic, see, infra, Chapter 17, "Reconsideration of Gandhi".

5

Ideology of Hindutva

An 'ideology' usually is said to be a system of political, legal, ethical, religious and philosophical views and ideas.[1] R.M. MacIver observes it as "any scheme of thinking characteristic of a group or class". Robert A. Dahl defines it as "a set of more or less persistent, integrated doctrines that purport to explain and justify leadership in the system". Lyman Tower sees it as "a value or belief system that is accepted as fact or truth by some groups". In it, Eugene J. Meehan includes (a) a pattern of belief relating to some particular aspects of social, political or economic life, (b) a programme of action, and (c) element of irrationalism or absolute faith". It is clear that an ideology is not philosophy, theory or approach. Often ideologues, even scholars, knowingly or unknowingly, present their 'ideology' as 'Bible', 'Koran' or 'Gita', philosophy and theory. The ideology of Hindutva also joins this category.

Now let us analyze the (i) background, (ii) tenets and forms, and (iii) achievements of the ideology of Hindutva.

Background

As has been discussed earlier, Hindu Dharma has long been bearing a particular type of suicidal and castrated nature of its own. All ruling classes, upper strata of the Hindus and non-Hindu religions have had been liking the Hindu Dharma to carry on that nature. That form of

Diagram 1
Major Religions of the World

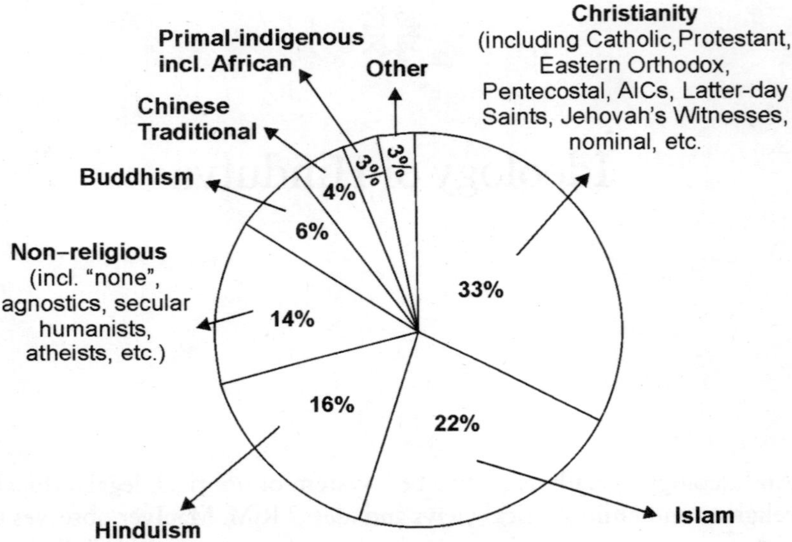

Hindu Dharma had always been helping their attempts to succeed in the past, and had and has been cherishing praise from them. In the past, the Hindus did not and could not care because of the prevailing monarchical or authoritarian governing systems (see Diagram 1). At that time they considered these matters related to the freedom of religion to have own path to God. The increase in the number of followers of non-Hindus did not matter much. This neglect or wanton apathy has largely been responsible for their present plight, dishonour and insults.

During the era of Islamic invasions, what Will Durant called the bloodiest period in the history of mankind, many Hindus gallantly resisted, knowing full well that defeat would mean a choice of economic discrimination via the 'jaziya' tax on non-Muslims, forced conversion, or death. It is no wonder that countless Hindus over the length and breadth of Bharatvarsha, from present-day Afghanistan to present-day Bangladesh, thought it better to die gloriously or face cold-blooded slaughter. Hindus never forgot the repeated destruction of the Somnath Temple, the massacre of Buddhists at Nalanda, or the pogroms by Muslim invaders and the Islamic rule of the Mughals.

In modern times, Hindutva gained momentum when the Muslims made the greatest abuse of Hindu tolerance: the demand for a separate state and the partition of India, a nation that had had a common history and culture for countless millennia. Thus, the Muslims voted for a separate state and the Hindus were forced to sub-divide their own land. They obtained with the consent of the majority a separate state of Pakistan, and also retained their status and position in the remaining part of India that is Bharat. The number of Muslims living in India is greater than that of Pakistan. With the influx of immigrants from Bangladesh, the number is fastly increasing.

After partition, in Pakistan, Muslim superiority was quickly asserted there and the non-Muslim minorities were forced to flee due to the immense discrimination in the political and religious spheres, bloodshed and conversion. The Hindus could not respond to such an onslaught. Hindu majority in India continued the Hindu ideals by remaining tolerant, secular and accommodating the minorities at par with them.

India even gave the Muslim minority many more gifts, such as separate personal laws, special status to the only Muslim majority state—Kashmir, and other rights that are even unheard of, even in the United States of America. Islamic law was given precedence over the national law in instances that came under Muslim personal law. The Constitution was changed when the courts, in the Shah Bano case, ruled that a secular nation must have one law, not separate religious laws. Islamic religious and educational institutions were accorded a policy of non-interference. The list may go on.

More painful for the Hindus was the forced negation of Hindu history and factors that gave pride to Hindus. Hindu customs and traditions were mocked as remnants of a non-modern society, things that would have to go if India was to modernize like the West. The self-proclaimed guardians of India, the politicians of the Congress Party, who called themselves secularists, forgot that it was the Hindu psyche that believed in secularism and enshrined it in the Constitution. They continued to mock at their religion, gods, culture and traditions.

When Hindus realized that pseudo-secularism had reduced them to the role of an innocent bystander in the game of politics, they demanded a true secularism where every religious group would be treated as the same and a government that would not take Hindu sentiments for granted. Hindutva awakened the Hindus to the new world order where nations represented the aspirations of people united in history, culture, philosophy, and heroes.

Hindutva is not a religion; it is a political movement which began in the early twenties of the 20th century and had picked up momentum in its last two decades.

The real moving spirit behind this vast national activity is the ideology of Hindutva based ultimately on the tenets of Hindu philosophy. It has been their firm faith that Hindutva is the only solution for all the ills. A deep inner awareness tells us that Hindu philosophy is based on laws which are not just Hindu laws but universal laws applicable to all. This philosophy is called Hindu philosophy only because these laws were discovered by ancient Hindu sages. In reality, this philosophy is a universal philosophy.

According to the principles of Hindu philosophy, man is composed of four elements: body, mind, intelligence and soul. Hindu philosophy seeks to bring about a balance of all these elements. It asserts that every individual is a part of the universe and represents the cosmos in miniature in himself. An individual cannot be separated from his family, society, country, mankind and even the whole of creation itself.

This Hindutva philosophy (after Dayananda Saraswati) was seriously taken up by the founder of the Rashtriya Swayamsevak Sangh (RSS), Dr Keshav Baliram Hedgewar. Only he could observe that the Hindu society, which had earlier produced this wonderful philosophy of oneness, was deeply divided within itself in many ways and had forgotten its identity. In order to bring this society back to life, this philosophy was to be re-awakened in the minds of Hindus. He emphasized two things. First, we must put into practice our philosophy which was the best in the world. Without practice, it is meaningless. Secondly, it must be remembered that nobody accepts any philosophy because it is best. One has to back up this philosophy with a powerful force of the society and its disciplined organization. The RSS founded by him is engaged in this dual task for the last 80 years.

In order to create this awareness, he set about the task of creating an organization of selfless workers dedicated solely to extending this philosophy to all spheres of national life.[2]

In a broader sense, contribution to Hinduism/Hindutva has been made by many great men and organizations: Maharshi Dayananda, Veer Savarkar, Swami Vivekananda, Rabindranath Tagore, Gandhiji, Rashatriya Swayamsevak Sangh and others. Recently, Swami Chinmayananda, Maharishi Mahesh Yogi, International Society for Krishna Consciousness, Muni Susheel Kumar etc. can also be counted among contributors of devotional Hinduism. Vishwa Hindu Parishad and Bharatiya Janata Party form religious and political wings of Hindutva respectively.

After attainment of independence, the Hindus began to feel that freedom was yet to come. Freedom from imperialism to all people meant that they would have control of their own destinies. The Hindus would have their own heroes, their own stories, and their own culture. They would also have opportunity to condemn the holocaust that Muslims rulers heaped on them. They would be able to do away with the racial discrimination and the economic imperialism practised by Britain. Freedom for Hindus had to mean that their heroes such as Ram, Krishna, Shivaji, the Cholas, Shankaracharya, and Tulsidas would be respected. They would be able to offer the Ramayana and the Mahabharata to humanity as examples of the brilliance of ancient Hindu thinking. They expected that their Bhagavad Gita, the Vedas, the temples, the gods and goddesses, the art, the music, and the like would be respected.

This freedom should have meant that all Indians, regardless of religion, language, caste, sex, or colour, would openly show respect for their greatest hero—Ram—throughout Hindustan.[3]

All these sentiments, expectations and ideals make up the contents of Hindutva. It must be noted that Hindutva is a nationalist, and not a religious or theocratic, concept.[4]

Tenets and Forms

As a term 'Hindutva' is derived from the two terms 'Hindu' and 'ttva', which literally mean Hindu principles, Hinduness, Hinduism or essence of being a Hindu. These Hindu principles have come down from the Vedas and related holy books of knowledge and enlightenment and action.[5]

According to Savarkar, the term 'Hindutva' does not mean only the religion Hinduism; it covers the complete Hindu civilization and history. Hinduism is only a fraction of the civilization called Hindutva. That is why, he used the term 'Hindu' to refer to the collectivity of the people of India—Hindus, Muslims, Christians, Sikhs, Parsees, etc. In the rising nationalist movement at the end of last century there are some examples proving that this kind of 'loose' vocabulary was accepted among different religious groups. For example, the Muslim nationalist leader Sir Syed Ahmad Khan (1817-1898) used the term 'Hindu' to mean "the inhabitants of Hindustan".[6]

The most important thing is that 'real' Hindus accept natural and thus right attitudes towards their land. Savarkar emphasizes that "a Hindu means a person who regards this land of Bharatvarsha, from Indus to the seas as his Fatherland as well as his Holyland, that is the cradle land of his religion". Like Savarkar, the RSS leader M.S. Golwalkar has stressed the importance of defining the natural borders of Hindustan. In his most famous book *We or our nationhood defined* (1939) Golwalkar means by India or Hindustan the "lands from sea to sea". In fact, the map on the cover of his book gives the outline of his geographic limitations of India, which stretches from Afghanistan to Burma and also includes Sri Lanka.[7]

Until the 19th century, the word 'Hindu' had no specific religious meaning and simply referred to the people who lived east of the Indus river, whatever their beliefs. (The Indian Supreme Court itself has held that "no precise meaning can be ascribed to the terms 'Hindu' and 'Hinduism' "). It was only when the census introduced by the British colonial authorities in 1871 included 'Hindu' as a religious designation that many Indians began to think of themselves and their country as Hindu.

The Sangh Parivar's central organization Rashtriya Swayamsevak Sangh (RSS) was founded by Keshav Hedgewar in 1925. Hedgewar was influenced by V.D. Savarkar, who believed that Hindus were the descendants of the ancient Aryans and properly formed a nation with a unified geography, race and culture. Savarkar's 1923 book *Hindutva—Who is a Hindu*? declared that those who did not consider India as both fatherland and holy land were not true Indians—and that the love of Indian Christians and Muslims for

Diagram 2
Encirclement of Hindutva

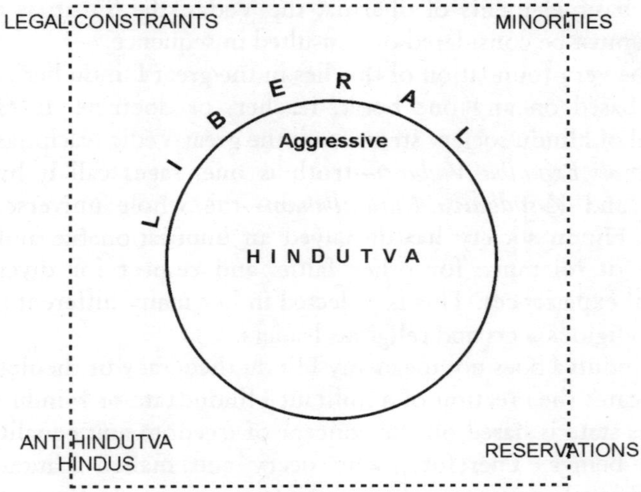

India was 'divided' because each group had its own holy land in the Middle East.

After the failure of non-responding Hindu Dharma[8] and half-attempting Hinduism[9], Hindutva stood up to meet the challenge (see Diagram 2).

Hindutva is the proactive ideology of the hurt Hindus to defend and protect the Hindus, by propagating and through organizing to defend the Hindus, their vital interests, culture, ethos, status and honour. It is a Hindu right to stand, exist and claim superiority of talents and attainments. The Hindus claim to live in their own home. It likes to welcome all those who agree to live as brothers and sisters. But, on the basis of its sad past experience, it likes to keep a watchful eye on strangers, aliens and intruders.

Tenets

Pivot of Hindu Dharma, Hinduism or Hindutva is dharma. The Vedas (as knowledge) are regarded as the main source (root) of dharma. Others are the traditions (Smritis) and practice of those who know the Vedas. Dharma is declared by the Vedas and Smriti. In case of absence of such declaration, the practice of the Shishta (moral behaviour of the ideal men) is the authority for finding out the basis of dharma. Manu and Yagyavalkya also agree to it. In case of conflict on the basic elements of dharma, the Vedas, the Smriti is and the Shishta must be considered or consulted in sequence.

The very foundation of this lies in the great Hindu heritage that is not based on any one book, teacher, or doctrine. In fact, the pedestal of Hindu society stems from the great Vedic teachings: *Ekam Sat Viprah Bahudha Vadanti*—truth is one, sages call it by many names, and *Vasudhaiva Kutumbakam*—the whole universe is one family. Hindu society has displayed an unquestionable and proud history of tolerance for other faiths and respect for diversity of spiritual experiences. This is reflected in her many different philosophies, religious sects and religious leaders.

Hindutva does not mean any Hindu theocracy or theology. But, it advocates the creation of a militant Hindu state or Hindu rashtra. But this state is based on the concept of freedom and equality of all human beings. Therefore, who decry and malign Hindutva are utterly biased, ignorant and wicked.[10] In this sense, the fanatics among the Muslims and Christians in India are treated to be as 'invaders'.[11]

The global Hindutva in the 21st century is ushered by the RSS in all walks of life.

Hindutva is in line with Indian ethos and culture. It asserts that the Hindu nation has existed for 8,000 to 10,000 years and Hindustan has been in possession of Hindus for at least that length of time. Therefore, for proper running of democracy in India, the majority community, the Hindus, should have a dominant role.

Only the Hindus, in the entire world, are liberal enough to treat other cultures and communities in a proper and just manner. No other non-Hindu country in the entire history has permitted the minority religions and communities to co-exist in peace and harmony.

Unlike Semitic religions—Christianity, Islam, etc.—Hindutva is a purely non-dogmatic religion. To counter coercion, dogmatism and intolerance of Islam and Christianity(especially as propounded by their clergy), there are attempts to 'semitise' even the Hindu religion around one deity (Ram), some holy books (Geeta, Vedas, Smritis) and a few specified Vedic scholars.

To discourage conversion by Christian and Muslim organizations, Hindutva is now educating the adivasis (Tribal, indigenous people) and other non-Hindu communities into the Hindu mould, providing a welcome faith for them.

To rejuvenate Hindu culture, which is tolerant and flexible, Hindutva has been taking up a number of programmes like the ban on cow slaughter, Sanskrit as a compulsory language, abolition of the second status language (in some states) with alien script (Urdu), uniform civil code etc. But it is not dogmatic about the cultural, aesthetic, economic and social norms, to the extent of imposing its specific values on the whole of society.

Hindutva is a set of values and a way of life. It is the majority of the Hindus who have permitted the present Constitution of India to come into force. Hindutva does not intend to impose Hindu Dharma on all Indian citizens. Hindutva is not specific religion.[12] Manohar Joshi for his election speech in which he claimed that if elected he will make Maharashtra as the first 'Hindu Rajya' of the nation, the judgement also said that Hindutva is not just a religion, but it is a way of life.

Surely, it is more concerned with the upper varna elements, particularly, the protective element, to defend and re-establish Hinduism as the supreme religion, culture and community of India. It was 'indestructible and eternal'.[13]

Forms

Presently, there are two forms or modes of the ideology of Hindutva: aggressive and reformative or liberal. In its *aggressive* form, it exposes the evil designs of other religions, related communities and organizations, which happen to attack Hindu interests, openly or secretly or in collusion with other similar elements. Such attempts have been made and are being made by the organized elements of non-Hindu religions and communities, particularly Muslims and Christianity. When such attempts are reduced to minimum, they eagerly adopt a reformative, conciliatory or liberal attitude: forget, forgive and live together.

In brief, the phenomenon of aggressive Hindutva carries the attributes of

(i) claim of Hindus as owners of India, as their motherland;
(ii) over confidence and fighting spirit;
(iii) absolute faith in the supremacy of Hindu Dharma;

(iv) Hindu Dharma is the only path to success, here and after;
(v) dislike of the alien religions, cultures and communities;
(vi) justification of varnashrama system, plurality of sects, goals, cultures and philosophies; and
(vii) preponderance of the Hindus over polity, economy and lifestyle in India.

Liberal or *reformative* Hindutva differs from it. It (1) regards India as motherland and commits oneself to defend and protect the honour, territorial integrity, independence and sovereignty of the country; (2) inculcates feelings of brotherhood among all Indians, irrespective of their different castes, colours, religions, languages, regions and cultures; (3) pays respect to all diverse religions, languages and cultures and great persons related to them with condition to oppose people trying to destroy this diversity; (4) enjoys one's rights and duties in a way to realize all-round development of the nation to distribute the gains equitably among all; (5) endeavours 'especially' to help the poorest, the most deprived, illiterate and backward of the society for bringing them at par with others; (6) upholds the democratic system wherein more and more persons would share power in the decision-making processes; and (7) works for peace, progress and cooperation among the peoples of different nations and ensure sovereignty, dignity and freedom of India as a powerful member of the United Nations.

These two forms of Hindutva are not identical. They have been differing, conflicting and clashing with other.

Aggressive Hindutva

Dissatisfaction with the outcome of Hindu Dharma has been the main cause of renovating it as Hinduism. But performance and failure of Hinduism also in the long run disappointed the Hindus. Most of them found that it is no more possible to tolerate. They felt that the Hindu leaders, supposed to be the well-wishers and caretakers, have, despite their claim to ameliorate the socio-political conditions of the Hindus, caused greater harm. They were fed up with the non-violence and Muslim appeasement by Mahatma Gandhi, which appeared in form of partition of India, bloodshed, arson, migration of population on unprecedented scale, and increased Muslim arrogance. Muslim appeasement and anti-Hinduism was further taken over by the

Congress under the leadership of Prime Minister Jawaharlal Nehru and the communists and carried on for another two decades. They launched a Constitution which largely stood against the Hindus. The Hindu leaders felt that it is no more possible to tolerate Muslim appeasement and large-scale conversion of the Hindus by the Christian missionaries. They ultimately found that the number, size and power of the Hindus decreased considerably. They were feeling alienated in their 'own' country. In their eyes Hinduism was imprisoned and disabled. All minorities—Muslims, Christians and others, and a large portion of anti-Hindutva forces had usually been praising the Hindu Dharma which has caused the Hindus to come down to that level. All these anti-Hindu forces had upheld this Hindu Dharma as the real 'Hindu Dharma' and liked it to continue as such. They had been opposing every type of big and small change or reform in it. All such attempts were maligned as 'communalism'.

Reacting to the anti-Hindutva forces, the 'Kshatriya' or virile elements among the Hindus, particularly from the Hindutva Parivar, the RSS, Vishwa Hindu Parishad and others, rose to the occasion. To realize their goal they rightly chose 'Ram' as their hero (God)[14] to crush and trample the Ravanic or demonic elements. Thus, they adopted the ideology of aggressive Hindutva. This ideology though rooted in Hindu Dharma and Hinduism is Hindutva. It stood up to protect, defend and serve the Hindu interests, and is not Hindu Dharma or Hinduism. It was not satisfied even with the RSS.[15] It opposed the role of Mahatma Gandhi and his policies.[16]

They were under apprehension that some anti-Hindutva minorities are organizing to replace the present rule by majority communities. Now, it is becoming difficult, rather uncomfortable and unacceptable, even to stand for and support Hinduism. It is surprising, they felt, that only minorities as permanent groups belonging to some religion, language and culture find place in the Constitution of India.[17] It does not recognize any majority community related to religion, language, caste or culture. There are provisions in the Constitution in connection with 'minorities' which tend to move even the majority community towards division and split. During the last 58 years, this tendency of disintegration of the majority community is clearly visible. Total neglect of the position and strength of the Hinduism or Hindu community is one of the most deplorable weaknesses of the Constitution of India.

All of these deprivations have appeared in form of demolition of the Babri (mosque) structure on December 6, 1992, Ekatmata yatra in 1995 and the Gujarat election of December 12, 2002.[18]

Jai Lalita also expressed similar views. Presenting the Tamil Nadu Prohibition of Forcible Conversion of Religion Conversion Ordinance, 2002 in the State Assembly, she said: "I do not want a strong country to be handed over to a political trader, whose rapacious Italian relatives and friends have made country a happy hunting ground for their operations." She repeatedly referred to Sonia Gandhi by her maiden name Antonio Maino. She alleged that Gandhi was involved in "antique smuggling case" and Bofors deal.[19] Togadia and Bal Thackery went long in that direction.

Unfortunately, the aggressive Hindutva does not know its socio-political limits, and force lying behind the Constitution of India. The VHP's resolve to ride the Hindutva juggernaut across the country with the aim of forcing the Muslims and others to 'acknowledge' India as 'Hindu Rashtra' within two years, was clearly anti-law. It said that "our commitment is not to NDA but only to Hindutva and there is no compromise on this". It could not side with those who were not for Hindutva. It challenged that "it is essential for the BJP and Congress to review their political ideologies and change their organizational set-up or else they will be rendered inconsequential by the emerging political forces".[20]

All this led the BJP in utter confusion. In its two-day conclave (23-24 December 2002) all top leaders were swearing by 'Hindutva', but insisted that "Hindutva and extremism cannot go together". Praising the Supreme Court's idea of Hindutva as a noble and elevating concept, Naidu reiterated that "Hindutva and intolerance cannot go together". He announced time and again that in one hand he would carry the BJP flag and the NDA agenda in the other. He forgot that only Hindutva enabled him to hold the BJP flag, and lead the NDA in the present manner. In the absence of Hindutva, both would be snatched away. It simply showed the way its leaders were living in a world of make-believe. The VHP did not stop and continued its acts of aggressive Hindutva.[21]

Liberal Hindutva

But, the BJP did not yield space to VHP. When Vajpayee denounced the VHP talk of Hindu Rashtra in two years, Advani asserted that the Gujarat polls would have been won even without Godhra killings. The BJP read out the Supreme Court's verdict on Hindutva to Parivar hawks. It did not let the VHP to come near it. The BJP saw no utility for the Modi or Praveen Togadia brand of politics outside Gujarat. It did not prefer the term 'Hindutva' to be used all the time. It talked of 'cultural nationalism', which was defined in varying ways, depending on the political situation. In fact, the Supreme Court's observation in a judgment that Hindutva is a "way of life" and does not necessarily refer to a religious faith had come handy for the BJP.

All this was liberal Hindutva, the ideology of then-in-power, represented by Prime Minister Atal Behari Vajpayee, Deputy Prime Minister and Home Minister L.K. Advani and other colleagues. They could not favour Hindutva of VHP. They stood in favour of prevailing form of Hindu Dharma or Hinduism and asked the people to see it as Hindutva and Indianism or 'Bharatiyatva'.[22] The then BJP President Venkaiah Naidu, in his address to the party's national executive, skirted the Ayodhya issue for the coming Lok Sabha polls in 2004. Its General Secretary Pramod Mahajan said the NDA had dropped the idea of parliamentary legislation as a solution to the Ram Temple. Naidu remained silent on the issue to avoid any confusion among the NDA allies. He claimed, "Hindutva is not an electoral issue to be negotiated in political battlefields. Cultural nationalism is our lifeline and Hindutva is the soul of India." The BJP carried on non-Hindutva programmes in a sincere manner. They were, as usual, opposed by the non-Hindu forces of the country and outside.[23]

But their ideological somersault was clear. The liberal advocates of Hindutva did not take the parent organizations of RSS and the VHP into confidence. Owing to sudden change at the surface, the Hindus at large did not support them, and the BJP lost 14th Lok Sabha election.

Thus, there arose clash between aggressive and liberal forms of Hindutva. The RSS leaders advised the two BJP stalwarts Vajpayee and Advani to place their point of view before the assembly of top RSS leaders at Hardwar conclave. A strong section of RSS maintained that the BJP continued to be a coterie-driven outfit and had deviated from the basic ideology of the Parivar. The VHP leader Ashok Singhal, who had been critical of both Vajpayee and Advani, had advised them to retire from active politics. In fact, the RSS-BJP relationship is at a crossroad and everyone knows that it is the BJP which needs the Sangh for its survival.[24]

In fact, liberal Hindutva cannot gain ascendancy without doing proper spadework or simply on the basis of state power transform into Indianism or Bharatiyatva. It had to convince the RSS (Rashtriya Swayamsevak Sangh) and Vishwa Hindu Parishad and get clearance for this changeover. Liberal Hindutva is actually Hindu Dharma or at the most Hinduism. It is pseudo-Hindutva. On this count, the RSS had asked the top leaders of the BJP to give way to the younger generation of the Parivar.

However, it is surprising that the RSS, even while supporting the VHP, is taking up the line of liberal Hindutva. RSS sets out to woo minority community—the Akhil Bhartiya Sah Sampark Pramukh of the RSS, the ideologue, Indresh Kumar wanted the BJP and VHP to stop making Ramjanmabhoomi issue a question of their existence, thus hurting the sentiments of crores of people "just for Babar". Kumar said, "Once an enemy is always an enemy" is not the formula for those who work for nationalism and humanity. The National Muslim Front (NMF) came out of Eid-Milan function at Chanakyapuri in New Delhi about two years back which was attended by Sangh chief K.S. Sudarshan.[25] This NMF also organized the function at Jaipur in February 2005.

Opponents of Hindutva

It is a fact that the Hindus are the majority community. They shoulder all responsibilities of taking care of the country as a whole. They bear the burden of defending, developing and operating democracy in India. In addition to these, the majority community is also accountable to the minority communities for their protection, safety and welfare. They have given, despite its being against them, the present Constitution which is successful in operation. Still, there are individuals, scholars, leaders and reformers who happen to stand against the Hindus, Hindu Dharma, Hinduism and Hindutva.

They know well that democracy is a game of number. Somehow their ancient forefathers gave this number and today luckily they are having their own government but are perhaps unaware that their neglect in this direction would lead to creation of hostile states, communities and nationalities.

From the very beginning since independence, every political party—from Congress to BJP—is enjoying power at the cost of the majority of credulous, ignorant and helpless Hindus. Even political parties in opposition are playing this role on this assumption that they are safe till the majority of the Hindus in India last.

The innocent Hindus for having an undivided India relied upon Gandhi for his tall claim in the might of non-violence and were found betrayed. Standing on this very ground, Nehru stepped in-between Jammu & Kashmir and gifted Tibet and parts of territory of India to the Chinese. Indira Gandhi surrendered hard earned victory to incorrigible Pakistan. Perhaps, the majority tolerated their misgivings consoling themselves over the fact that their leaders were Hindu by birth and that they would not have knowingly harmed Hinduism and the Hindu interests. But, the Hindus have suffered at their hands. They have a Constitution and laws made thereunder which do not permit even to speak out their losses and inner feelings.

However, the BJP leaders with their pro-Hindu past in family, RSS and the Jan Sangh, did the same considering them to be the fittest one to harm the Hindu-majority state. They took initiative to go to Pakistan by the Lahore bus without paying any attention to Kargil. Hundreds of jawans were killed because of this neglect. The ruling elite was bold enough in offering concessions one after another unlearning their past history. The Congress (UPA) is busy in implementing her past policy of appeasing the Muslims.[26]

If we consider Hindus and others as majority (about 80 per cent), and Muslims and others as minority (about 20 per cent), the latter and some others from the majority do not want the people of majority to organize, unite and maintain their cultural traits and existence. But, the minorities want to organize and strictly stick to maintain their separate identity, often refuse the same right to the majorities.[27]

For critics like Ashis Nandy Hinduism and Hindutva are two different yet closer phenomena. They now stand face to face. So far, they have confronted each other. But, in near future, confrontation will have to sharpen some day. It will be a struggle unto death.[28] The ideology of Hindutva is an attack on Hinduism. To those who live in Hinduism, Hindutva is one of the pathologies. For such scholars, Hinduism is a toothless religion of the poor, old, helpless, and god-fearing people of India.

Such people fail to understand that the Hindutva movement presents itself for establishing a strong nation, based on the tenets of Hindu Dharma. At the social and political levels, this movement presently derives its strength from upper castes, but also co-opts some lower castes within its fold. Apparently, they see it as an ideology and programme which suppresses the legitimate and much overdue social, economic and political aspirations of the deprived, disadvantaged and depressed sections of society, who are on the lower rungs of the social hierarchy. These people regard Hindutva as return of the rule of exploitative and repressive Brahminhood.

Organization

Hindutva moves on the pivot of RSS and similar organizations. The aim of RSS is to unite all Hindus.[29] This work has been going on continuously since the last 80 years. It has mushroomed into many other institutions like the Bharatiya Janata Party (BJP), Bharatiya Mazdoor Sangh (BMS), Vishwa Hindu Parishad (VHP), Akhil Bharatiya Vidyarthi Parishad (ABVP), Kisaan Sangh and mass organizations in nearly every sphere of activity. In the field of co-operative movement, it has established 'Sahakar Bharati', in industry, it has 'Udyog Bharati' and in the field of arts 'Samskaar Bharati'.

All of its organizations and their sub-organizations or branches are popularly known as 'Sangh Parivar'. But, in its broader form, it is Hindutva Parivar. It consists of the Rashtriya Swayamsevak Sangh (RSS—the mother organization after which the label 'Sangh Parivar' is coined), the Bharatiya Janata Party (BJP—Hindutva's constitutional front that fights elections etc.), the Vishwa Hindu Parishad (VHP), the Shiv Sena (the fascist front), the VHP of America (Hindutva's overseas arm) and the Hindu Students Council (VHP of America's student wing). Other organizations of the Sangh Parivar are Akhil Bharatiya Adhivakta Parishad, Akhil Bharatiya Sahitya Parishad, Akhil Bharatiya Vidyarthi Parishad, Bharatiya Majdoor Sangh, Bharat Vikas Parishad, Bharatiya Itihas Sankalan Yogna, Bharatiya Kisan Sangh, Bharatiya Shikshan Mandal, Deen Dayal Sodha

Sansthan, Hindu Jagran Manch, Pragya Pravah, Rshatra Sevika Samiti, Sanskrit Bharati, Swadeshi Jagran Manch, Sewa Bharati, Samajik Samrasta Manch, Vigyan Bharati, Vishwa Hindu Prishad, Vidya Bharati, and the Vanvasi Kalyan Ashram, etc. Major organs of the Sangh Parivar can be described in the following manner:

1. **The Rashtriya Swayamsevak Sangh (RSS)**: The RSS, founded in 1925 by Keshav Baliram Hedgewar, is the ideological fountainhead of the modern Hindutva movement. Organized around the concept of Shakha[30], a local cell formation, where young men gather for physical and ideological training, under the tutelage of a brother or dada. The RSS ideology has always been espousing the national cause. Madhav Sadashiv Golwalkar, who was appointed head of the RSS shortly before his death had clarified the idea of the nation in his treatise, *We, or Our Nationhood Defined.*[31] However, only those who are imbued with the spirit of Hindutva can follow it comprehensively.

2. **Bharatiya Janata Party (BJP)**: This is Hindutva's parliamentary front which constantly makes efforts adopting positive type of secular orientation through parliamentary actions—elections and pushing for legislations of various kinds. Their ideology is visible in limited and constitutional ways within mainstream political discourse. The BJP came into existence after the collapse of the Janata Party which came to power after Mrs. Gandhi's fall in 1979. The erstwhile Hindu parliamentary party—the Jan Sangh—had merged itself into the Janata Party in the wake of Emergency. The top party leadership with few exceptions came from RSS cadre. The party often participates in joint meetings with RSS leadership. The election campaigns of the party are often significantly shaped and helped by RSS cadres of the local region. In short, in more than one ways, the relation between BJP and other Hindutva organizations is quite visible.

3. **Vishwa Hindu Parishad (VHP)**: The VHP was founded on August 29, 1964 in Bombay with the clear aim of being the activist wing. It undertakes aggressive actions in civil society as a whole. The VHP's goals are clear. It is to organize the Hindu world to save itself from the evil eyes of Christianity, Islam and Communism.

The VHP has also spread out as an extra-parliamentary force throughout India and outside. Its primary functions in India are to mobilize forces for agitational and violent purposes. It took part in the Cow Protection Movement throughout the 60s and the 70s. The entire Babri Masjid movement was orchestrated by the VHP. It steadfastly refuses to enter into negotiation, rejecting the right of the judicial system in adjudicating on this issue. It mobilizes often violent events with the clear intent of polarizing society and creating political movements within public discourse of Hindutva—the Rath Yatras of the 80s and the final demolition of the Babri Masjid in 1992 conducted in association with its youth wing—the Bajrang Dal. The strategy of the Hindutva combine as a whole is palpably apparent. BJP leaders participate in VHP sponsored events, but when the results of such events come out—such as violence and killings—the BJP conveniently distances itself temporarily from the VHP.[31]

Apparently, the leaders of the RSS had successfully taken over Hindu India. It appeared as if most of the Hindus, in the wake of Babri structure demolition, were behind it. The BJP—the RSS's political wing—had dominated the coalition government (NDA—National Democratic Alliance) in New Delhi (1998-2004). Both Atal Bihari Vajpayee, India's Prime Minister, and his Deputy and heir apparent, L.K. Advani belonged to the RSS. After the defeat of NDA in the Lok Sabha elections, the UPA (United Progressive Alliance) under the leadership of Prime Minister Manmohan Singh (actually Mrs. Sonia Gandhi) has taken over. Hindutva has been badly hit. A large number of Hindus, the Scheduled Castes, the Scheduled Tribes and some Other Backward Classes, have either backed out of it, or stand passive and frustrated onlookers.

Achievements

The initial concern of aggressive Hindutva movement (RSS and Hindu Mahasabha) was to counter the politics of Muslim League and to influence the Congress towards a pro-Hindu direction.[32] RSS was mainly focusing on shakhas, training volunteers for Hindutva movement and Hindu Mahasabha was taking part in electoral politics. After independence, the number of cadres of RSS kept on increasing and the Hindu Mahasabha gradually went into oblivion. It lacked organization and leadership both. By insisting on extremism, coercion and violence, it became anti-law and anti-state. At that time, the people who were fully confident to get independence for the whole of India had rallied behind the Indian National Congress and

Gandhian leadership. The RSS was not an active force during the freedom movement. It stood for Hindu Rashtra without anti-Hindu Muslims and Christians. It simply enjoyed an unrealizable dream for the Hindus. On the failure of Gandhian non-violence to win freedom for undivided India and victory of Muslim League demand of Pakistan, the Hindus were taken aback and felt deceived and frustrated. One of the Hindu leaders from Maharashtra and ex-pracharak of RSS, Naturam Godse, murdered Mahatma Gandhi in 1948. The RSS was banned for some time. The Enquiry Commission and the courts did not find anything against RSS. Ultimately, the ban was lifted. As gesture of showing nationalism, the RSS volunteers began infiltrating the army, bureaucracy, media and educational institution. In course of time multiple RSS-controlled organizations were started countrywide.

The RSS became very visible with its anti-communist tirades during the Indo-China war and projected its 'nationalist' and 'patriotic' fervour. Its political wing—the Jan Sangh—undertook the campaign to 'Indianize Muslims' and turn out the China-supporting communists.

The RSS joined the JP movement to oppose the imposition of Emergency by Indira Gandhi on June 26, 1975. Its political wing—Jan Sangh—joined the Janata Party. When it came to power, Jan Sangh got vital ministries. It further infiltrated the bureaucracy. It left the Janata Party on the issue of double membership (Janata Party and RSS). As it did not want to leave the RSS, Janata Party broke and Jan Sangh re-emerged as Bharatiya Janata Party (BJP) on the plank of 'Gandhian socialism'.[33] The opportunist politics of Indira-Rajiv Gandhi[34] led to Sikh pogroms in Delhi, the Shah Bano fiasco and opening up of the locks of Babri Masjid. The BJP started the campaign of Hindutva. V.P. Singh's implementation of Mandal Commission recommendations incited a backlash of upper castes. To cover up the loss of Hindus to the left out Janata Party, the Sangh Parivar cleverly organized pro-Hindutva movement of Rath Yatra and used various religious symbols. The Rath Yatra aimed at building a temple of Lord Ram at Ramjanmabhoomi in Ayodhya. This movement awakened the Hindu masses for the first time at the national scale. The Hindus solidly stood behind this movement. The Kar Seva of December 6 resulted into destruction of the Babri (mosque) structure and signalled the victory of Hindutva.

The day of December 6, 1992 completely shattered the old and weak roots of Hindu society, and with it, their old political and intellectual structure. The destruction by the Kar Sevaks of the dilapidated symbol of foreign dominance was the last straw in a heightening of tensions by the government, and the concomitant anger of more and more Hindus to rebuffs of their reasonable demands.[35] During the Mughal periods, over 30,000 Hindu temples were destroyed and mosques were built on them to vindicate the Islamic victory over the Hindus. All was said to be done in the name of Islam. The ruthless last-ditch effort of the powers-that-be was the banning and suppression of the Hindutva leaders. The effort of the rulers reminds one of the strategy of all ill-fated rulers.

The masses retaliated in the Lok Sabha election, and the Congress government was replaced by non-Congress government at the Centre as well as in several states.

The Hindus now felt at last free. They controlled their own destiny. There was no power that could control them except their own tolerant ethos. Real India in turn was finally free. Having ignored its history, it suffered from its repressed conscience. The destruction of the structure at Ayodhya was the release of the history that Indians had not fully come to terms with. Thousands of years of anger and shame, so diligently bottled up by the anti-Hindutva interests, was released when the first piece of the so-called Babri Masjid was torn down.[36]

Virile Hindu Dharma and righteousness[37] had won. Truth prevailed only when the Hindus, realizing that truth could not be won through political or legal means, took the law into their own hands. Hindus have been divided politically and the laws have not acknowledged the quiet Hindu yearning for Hindu unity. The Hindus so far had been granted a back seat to economic development and Muslim appeasement. The Congress so far had been claiming to make India a 'nation'. That game was now fully exposed. The Hindus were taken for a ride.

On constructive side, the Hindutva forces have been trying to gain confidence of and reclaim the lower castes and tribal communities. The leadership of the RSS has taken up many projects and programmes of social amelioration. It now considers the tribals as

Vanavasis (forest dwellers) on par with Gramvasis (villagers) and Nagarvasis (city dwellers) Hindus. As a result of this fraternal approach, today, there are over 4,000 service projects run in tribal areas by the Parivar volunteers. They plan to eradicate untouchability by spreading: first, social awareness, second, religious awareness of the basically non-Hindu nature of untouchability, and third, practical activities which bring people of all castes together.

If the Sangh, along with its emergence, would have explained the basics of its own preferable religion, it would have solved the problem of inequality, exploitation and repression of the depressed classes and among the various castes and sub-castes of the Hindus by putting them at par with each other. As a progressive organization of the Hindutva it would have done away with the conversion movement of Dr. B.R. Ambedkar from Hinduism to Buddhism. The basics of Hindutva would have pointed out the lack of total or full life of man in Buddhism and in other ascetic and life-negating religions yet having the possibility of the same goals of self-realization in Hindu Dharma. Still it is in the hands of the Sangh leaders to educate all the people on the need of specialization and division of labour for the speedy progress and advancement of every society. No society can survive and remain vibrant without contribution from some of its people to knowledge, defence and protection of its culture and community, production, exchange, trade and commerce, and skilled and non-skilled jobs common to all. While going upwards, in governance, industry, business and social set-up, one has to be recruited or admitted on the basis of his attainments of merit in schools and colleges, earn livelihood and lead a social life in family and community, rest in retirement after performing his role, and live peacefully in view of his physical, mental and biological disability. In a democracy, everyone is free to do any job and live a pattern of life by choice and attain success passing through certain 'ashram'-like stages at vertical levels.

With this understanding of classification of the people on the basis of functional specialization and specific stages of human life for individuals (varnashrama), they would be appreciating the totality of Hindu social system. It could have been easier to expose the segmental approach of minority religions and communities. There would have been no lower, depressed, downtrodden or untouchable classes in the Hindus, thereupon, no place of attraction for their joining other religions by abrogating Hindu religion. But, the Sangh remained stuck to old form of Hindu Dharma and to ignorance on the basics of total reality.

The Hindus do not realize that Parivar's attempts are small and limited ones. Amelioration of the conditions of lower and tribal castes is not a part of the programme of Hindu awakening. These programmes lack professional orientation. Despite the fact of the Hindu social workers or volunteers being connected with the grass-roots and their living in India, they are unable to compete with the alien agencies. The Hindutva forces can see the magnitude of their challenge to it. Islam and Christianity—the two largest organized religions—are, for the last several centuries, engaged in their mission of converting millions of tribals and the depressed class people of India. They do so as part of their religious service to God for obtaining heaven. Billions of dollars are being sent continuously from the Gulf and the Christian countries to the organized cadres of various religious or denominational organizations.[38] Their trained and devoted personnel spend that money on converting the native people. Besides personal contact, and living among them, they extend education and social traps attached with sectarian religions, give medical aid and money to the poor, render help in earning livelihood and job, and political support to gain power and sympathy for the donor countries. Often, the ultimate object of these conversions, besides serving the cause of religion, is to earn allegiance for the alien donor countries. Therefore, even if some small efforts are made by the native religions and organizations to discourage or stop them, constant hue and cry is made by the interested parties working for the alien goals. The efforts made by the Parivar or similar agencies, therefore, are too small before them. As a part of their imperial expansion, even these native efforts are not tolerated by these outside forces. Often, the Government of India and its leaders, out of ignorance or in collusion with them to get grants and aids, stand by them. The RSS is working against heavy odds.

Notes

1. It was first used in the 17th century by Destutt de Tracy of France as 'ideologie' (French) or 'ideology' (English) which meant 'science of ideas'. Since then it carries many meanings.
2. The Hindutva philosophy countered the principle of class struggle effectively by the principle of 'Vasudhaiva Kutumbakam' (the world is one family). The slogan "Workers of the World Unite" was replaced by "Workers Unite the World", and the concept of class conflict by the concept of class co-operation. As a result of this approach, the Bharatiya Mazdoor Sangh (BMS) today ranks as the largest apex trade organization.
3. Klaus Klostermaier's *A Survey of Hinduism*, Munshiram Manoharlal Publishers Pvt Ltd (Delhi, First Indian Edition, 1990). The book was first published in 1989 by the State University of New York Press, Albany, New York, United States.
4. Some of the main Hindu beliefs and practices of Hindutva are:
    1. At the heart of Hinduism is the monotheistic principle of Brahmin, that all reality is a unity; the entire universe is one Reality. This Reality is simultaneously visualized as a triad of three-pronged power, namely,
    (a) Brahma, the Creator, who is continuing to create new realities;
    (b) Vishnu, the Preserver, who preserves these new creations;
    (c) Shiva, the Destroyer, is at times compassionate, erotic and destructive.
    2. That society requires four elements: (i) knowledge, (ii) protection, (iii) production and exchange, and (iv) service or non-specialized labour. While doing or attaining preferably any one element, one can attain peace and bliss in this very life and after.
    3. For this the individual has to pass through four stages of (a) getting education, (b) leading a life of householder, (c) retirement, and (d) renunciation or recluse.
    4. Sacrificial fire (yagya) prayers or worship are done to remind these obligations.
5. Simultaneously, many hundreds of Hindu Gods and Goddesses are worshipped as various aspects of that unity. Depending upon one's view, Hinduism can also be looked upon as a monotheistic, trinitarian or polytheistic religion.
6. Gyanendra Pandey (ed.), *Hindus and Others: The Question of Identity in India Today*, New Delhi: Viking, pp. 238-272.
7. Yechury, Sitaram, *What is this Hindu Rashtra? On Golwalkar's fascistic ideology and the Saffron Brigade's practice*, 1993, Madras: A Frontline Publication, p.6.

8. See, back, Chapter 3, 'The Hindu Dharma'.
9. See, back, Chapter 4, 'Formulation, Performance and Failure of Hinduism'.
10. Madhav Sadashiv Golwalkar, supreme leader of the RSS until 1973, expressed the tenets of Hindutva, the Hindu extremist ideology, in his manifesto "*We, or Our Nationhood Defined*". In it he said that Hindus could "profit" from the example of the Nazis, who had manifested "race pride at its highest" by purging Germany of the Jews. He also had declared 'Hindu Rashtra' as the goal of RSS.
11. Vamadev Shastri (David Frawley), an authority on Vedas, Director of the American Institute of Vedic Studies and an author of many famous books, during his sojourn in Mumbai, had delivered a lecture on 25th December 1996 on "Global Vision of Hinduism in 21st Century".
12. The Supreme Court had delivered its judgment on December 11, 1995. Going by the judicial precedents, Justice J S Verma's Bench has rightly observed: "These Constitution Bench decisions, after a detailed discussion, indicate that no precise meaning can be ascribed to the terms 'Hindu', 'Hindutva' and 'Hinduism'; and no meaning in the abstract can confine it to the narrow limits of religion alone, excluding the content of Indian culture and heritage. Also, Jagmohan, Hinduism and Hindutva: What Supreme Court says? *Hindustan Times*, January 8, 1996.
13. According to Girilal Jain (1994: 45), there are three notable points in Swami Vivekananda's *Religion of Patriotism*: firstly his identification of Mother India with the supreme God, secondly his attempt to reintroduce the Kshatriya element in the Hindu psyche, and thirdly his conviction that India was destined to be a teacher of the human race in the spiritual reality. On his return to India from the meeting of the Parliament of Religions held in Chicago in 1893, he declared that the indebtedness of the universe to India knew no bounds. While civilizations had come and gone, the civilization of India was 'indestructible and eternal'. And the message of this civilization had to be spread throughout the world.
14. The *Rama cult* originates from the 5th and 6th centuries AD. After the 16th century, the story of Rama became so popular that it wove its way inexctricably into the fabric of rural culture and religion. Rama came to be worshipped as the ideal man, hero king, and an avatar of Vishnu. Rama is often heavily armed, ready for war, and alone. Now, he is not fighting against Ravana but against Muslims. This was the newly carved path of the aggressive Hindutva.
15. In the nationalist movement the RSS remained rather nonpolitical until India's independence in 1947. For example, V. D. Savarkar, who was

elected president of the Hindu Mahasabha, frequently denounced the RSS for its 'purely cultural'. Andersen, Walter K., and Shridhar D. Damle, *The Brotherhood in Saffron: The Rashtriya Swayamsevak Sangh and Hindu Revivalism*, New Delhi: Vistaar Publications, 1987, p. 36.

16. Praveen Togadia now slams the Mahatma. He thundered, "The Congress adheres to the philosophy of Gandhi and Nehru. Their ghosts have rendered us impotent as a people. This battle is not between political parties, it's between ideologies." He described the Congress as a "Muslim party" and "an enemy of the Hindus". *Hindustan Times*, December 8, 2002.
17. See the J&K Permanent Residents (Disqualification) Bill, 2004. It seeks to deny free education, voting and property rights to women marrying persons who are not the permanent residents of J&K State and also disqualifies such women for government jobs.
18. The violence in this state earlier in 2002 set the tone for the Gujarat election of December 12. In February 2002, VHP activists coming back home from Ayodhya—where they had gone to demonstrate in favour of building a Ram temple at the former site of the Babri mosque—were attacked at Godhra railway station in Gujarat. The train compartment they were travelling in was set on fire and 58 of them burnt alive. The assailants were identified as militant members of a local Muslim community. The incident triggered religious clashes across Gujarat. In the two weeks that followed, over a thousand were killed, mostly Muslims. Chief Minister Narendra Modi (BJP) was accused of not doing enough to restore law and order and not cracking down on VHP cadres. At the same time, Modi sensed that the anger against militant Islamism in general and Pakistan-backed terrorism in Jammu & Kashmir in particular had found fertile ground in post-Godhra Gujarat. With the VHP's help, he swept the election.
19. *Times of India*, September 3, 2002.
20. *Hindustan Times*, December 17, 2002.
21. Praveen Togadia of the VHP was arrested under Arms Act and anti-state activities, on outlawed ceremony of the distribution of *Trishuls* in Rajasthan. *Rajasthan Patrika*, May 3, 2003. He is still undergoing criminal trial for his anti-state activities.
22. *Rajasthan Patrika*, December 25, 2002.
23. With BJP support, laws have recently been adopted in Tamil Nadu and Gujarat states that restrict the ability of Hindus to change their religion, and proposals for national restrictions have been made. Pope John Paul II described these developments in June 2003 as 'unjust' and said they prohibited "free exercise of the natural right to religious freedom". Paul

Marshall, Hinduism and Terror, *First Things: A Monthly Journal of Religion and Public Life*, June 1, 2004; His books are *Islam at the Crossroads* (2002); *God and the Constitution: Christianity and American Politics* (2002); See also Amulya Ganguli, Batting for the BJP, *Hindustan Times*, August 22, 2003.

24. *Hindustan Times*, November 11, 2004
25. *Hindustan Times*, October 21, 2004; also, *Rajasthan Patrika*, February 12-13, 2005.
26. The HRD Ministry had issued an order, reserving 50 per cent seats in post-graduate and professional courses for Muslim students. Later, the High Court overruled this order, saying the university did not have a minority status. *Hindustan Times*, January 11, 2006. In striking down the AMU Amendment Act of 1981, that granted the university minority status, the Allahabad High Court (upholding an October 4, 2004 judgment) has played spoilsport for the politicians. Now this power, side-tacking the Court, has been given to control the State Universities. *Rajasthan Patrika*, January 13, 2006.
27. P.R. Ram, *Fascism of the Sangh Parivar*, EKTA (Committee for Communal Amity), 1999.
28. Ashis Nandy, Hinduism Versus Hindutva: The Inevitability of a Confrontation, *Times of India*, February 18, 1991.
29. Article 3 of the RSS Constitution states: "The aims and objects of the Sangh are to weld together the diverse groups within the Hindu Samaj and to revitalize and rejuvenate the same on the basis of its Dharma and Sanskriti, that it may achieve an all-sided development of the Bharatavarsha."
30. In the RSS organization the basic units are called 'shakhas' (branches). The membership of each shakha varies between 50 and 100 male participants. Nowadays, it is estimated that there are around 3,00,000 shakhas all over the country.
31. M.S. Golwalkar, *Bunch of Thoughts*, Bangalore: Jaagarana Prakashana, 1980. The basic purpose of the book was to establish that India was always a Hindu nation and continues to be one. For him, India meant the lands from sea to sea.
32. Vinayak Damodar Savarkar (1883-1966), apart from his utmost sacrifice for complete independence of India and rejuvenation of Hindutva, wrote many important books on Hindutva: *The History of the War of Independence; Hindutva; Hindu Padpadashashi; My Transportation for Life*, etc. Savarkar worked hard to protect minority rights. During the celebration of Hindu festivals, Savarkar visited Muslim and Christian homes to promote goodwill. He encouraged intercaste marriage and

assisted Dr. Ambedkar in the liberation of the untouchables. He appealed for a wider use of Hindi as the mother tongue and suggested reforms to the Devanagiri script to facilitate printing. At the end of his five year confinement in Ratnagiri, Savarkar joined Tilak's Swaraj Party and founded the Hindu Mahasabha as a separate political party. He warned of the Muslim League's designs of partitioning the nation. In 1937, Savarkar was elected President of the Hindu Mahasabha. He toured the nation widely and delivered the simple message that followers of Vedism, Jainism, Buddhism and Sikhism were all Hindus.

33. In fact, the Hindutva ideology had nothing to do with either 'Gandhi' or 'socialism'. It simply reflected bankruptcy of mind on part of the whole of Hindutva Parivar, particularly, the BJP. Like the RSS (Rashtriya Swayamsevak Sangh), the BJP could not muster courage to call itself 'Hindu Janata Party', which only reflected its 'pseudo-Hindutva'. See also, Uma Bharati veteran BJP leader and former Chief Minister of Madhya Pradesh, "in 1980, ideology was bound to take the back seat. To become an alternative to the Congress, the BJP had to have Congress-like values. These two were accepted more as slogans than conviction. Compromise with ideology became the BJP's destiny the day it replaced integral humanism with Gandhian socialism without explaining how the two could be taken as the same". Uma Bharati, *Hindustan Times*, December 12, 2005.
34. Both Indira and her son Rajiv were not, in any sense 'Gandhi'. It was simply a political trick to use immense popularity earned by Mohandas Karamchand Gandhi. On the basis of Gandhian faith and ideology, none of them can be considered as 'Gandhi'. They could very well use the word 'Nehru', but they preferred to use popularity of 'Gandhi'.
35. Grievances of the Hindus are historical and many: Gopal Sharma, *"Karseve se Karseva tak"*, Jaipur: *Rajasthan Patrika*, 1993; see, also, infra, Chapter 12.
36. On this, Shri V.S. Naipaul, in an interview with *The Times of India* (July 18, 1993), had the following to say: "What is happening in India is a new historical awakening....Indian intellectuals, who want to be secure in their liberal beliefs, may not understand what is going on. But every other Indian knows precisely what is happening: deep down he knows that a larger response is emerging even if at times this response appears in his eyes to be threatening...."
37. In 1989, the RSS and BJP, led by L.K. Advani, started a campaign to build a Hindu temple in the north Indian town of Ayodhya over what they believe was the birthplace of the God Rama. There was only one problem. A Muslim mosque, the Babri Masjid, already occupied the site, and had been there since the 16th century. The RSS claimed that the

Mughal emperor, Babur, destroyed an ancient Hindu temple to build the mosque. He may well have done so, since Moghul emperors destroyed thousands of Hindu temples during their conquest of north India, often replacing them with mosques. In December 1992, BJP leaders organized a mob of Hindus that demolished the Babri Masjid, while shouting "Death to Muslims". At least 1,700 people, most of them Muslim, were murdered in the riots that followed. In March 1993, Muslim terrorists retaliated with simultaneous bombings that killed over 300 civilians and destroying hundreds of temples and idols of gods in the wake. The RSS controls the VHP (World Hindu Council), which has sponsored the carving of foundations and columns for a Hindu temple on the site of the Babri Masjid. Regularly, trainloads of Hindu militants descend on Ayodhya to demand that construction should commence. So far, they have been blocked by court order and the security forces of the Centre and the state governments. The Archeological Survey of India (ASI) has just found evidence that a structure resembling an ancient Hindu temple may lie under the ruins of the mosque in Ayodhya. Hindu nationalists say the findings prove that a Hindu temple should be built on the site. Next, they would want Hindu temples to replace structures in Varanasi and Mathura.

38. NGOs in the country attract as such as Rs. 5,000 crore from foreign donors every year but though the government knows the money is coming in, it is clueless about where it goes. This is why, the Centre has decided to come out with a comprehensive legislation to monitor the functioning of NGOs. *Hindustan Times*, May 10, 2005.

6

Limitations and Disabilities of Hindutva Parivar

Hindutva cannot be understood by applying either a Western-parity democratic gauge or a Marxist-socialist pattern. Its potential has much to do with the wounds of Hindus. Throughout the ages, the high-caste Hindus asked the people to live for the causes that were mostly of transcendent importance for which ordinary human values and considerations had to be renounced.

Apparently, it is a movement for building 'Hindu Rashtra' or Hindu nation, which expresses the aspirations not of all the people of this country but only of upper-caste Hindus. It leaves out the vast numbers of backward castes, Dalits, minorities and women. On the authority of religion and Shastras, it assigns subordinate roles to: (a) minorities, who should live by the ideology of the Hindu nation, claiming nothing and deserving no privileges, (b) women; who are to cultivate themselves as 'ideal' mothers, wives or daughters, subordinate to her husband, father or son; (c) workers, who are supposed to treat the employer as the part of their family and to do production for 'national good' dumping their rights in the backyard; and (d) Dalits, who are supposed to forgo 'reservations' so that the 'merits' acquired through education and employment continues, paving the way for upper caste monopoly on jobs and other social privileges coming along with 'merits'. This cannot be called a Hindu Rashtra. It has to be a Hindutva Rashtra. A Hindutva Rashtra must be of all Hindus, preferably the majority of the Hindus.

Few Hindus are ready to listen that the very foundation of Hindu Rashtra is antithetical to present Indian Constitution, which upholds the sovereign, democratic, secular character of the republic; stands for equal opportunities for all, for affirmative action for the disadvantaged and leaves no room for religion to influence state policy, while the goal of Hindutva is an Indian state based around the interests only of Hindu elite.[1]

In the coalition government (NDA), the BJP was the dominating partner. It found that there was little which it could do exclusively for the Hindus. Even its attempt to make change in the Indian Constitution was opposed even by the President of India. Ultimately, it had to yield and only the task of the review of the working of the Indian Constitution could be undertaken.[2]

Latest failure of the cause of aggressive Hindutva is Gujarat and the denial of the US visa to Chief Minister Narendra Modi.[3] Opposition to Hindutva is not confined to the non-Hindus of India. The whole world appears to oppose Hindutva for different reasons.

Thus, *aggressive* could not realize its goals in full. The RSS supplied a vast and indoctrinated organization of the Hindus throughout length and breadth of the country. After launching the Rath Yatra and demolition of the Babri (mosque) structure, the Hindutva forces gained power at the Centre and in several states. However, all Hindus were not behind it. In spite of the absolute majority of the Hindus in the country, the BJP at the Centre was only a dominating partner of the National Democratic Alliance. For this it had to give up its three major Hindutva programmes: construction of Ram Temple at the Ramjanmabhoomi of Ayodhya, Uniform Civil Code, and removal of Article 370 from the Constitution.[4] During its regime it could do little except conducting experimental explosion of nuclear bombs for attaining the status of a nuclear power, launching Right to Education as a Fundamental Right and expansion of Information Technology. Despite humdrum of 'India Shining' and 'development' in the Lok Sabha elections, it was badly defeated.

Liberal Hindutva and the Aftermath

To continue in power, the political wing of the Hindutva distanced itself from the aggressive Hindutva forces. It was found that after overplay of aggressive Hindutva, the percentage of the Hindus supporting the Hindutva movement had considerably gone down from forty to twenty, whereas the percentage of anti-Hindutva Hindu forces had increased from twenty to thirty-five. The anti-Hindutva non-Hindu forces, about 30 percent, organized further in form of different political parties and organizations. The majority of the depressed classes, which were so far neutral, had joined the last two segments of the Indian population. The rest of the population, consisting mostly of Hindus, was floating, apathetic and ignorant (see Diagram 1).

Diagram 1

Hindus after Hindutva Movement

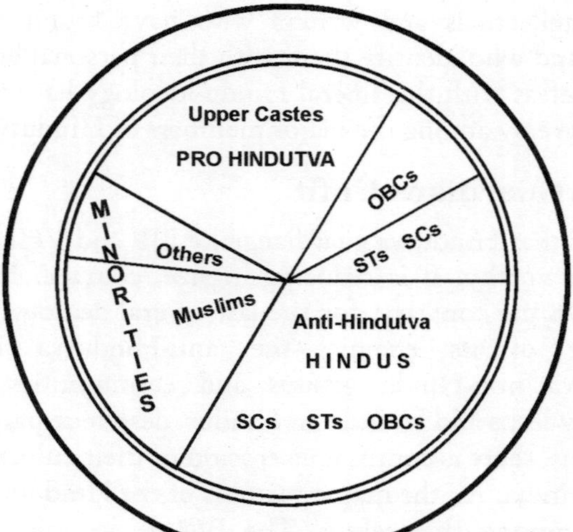

The BJP wanted to woo the Hindu masses by giving the impression that construction of Ram Temple without court judgment was no more a party issue. So was the recourse to launch uniform civil code. Prime Minister Atal Bihari Vajpayee, along with Deputy Prime Minister and Home Minister L.K. Advani, declared time and again that Hindutva is Bharatiyatva (Indianism) and Hinduism stands for 'dharmanirpekshta' (secularism) and 'sarva-dharma-samabhava' (equal respect to all religions). They began to go closer to all types of die-hard Muslims and Christians. All these attempts come under the 'liberal' or 'tolerant' form of Hindutva. But, the Parivar, particularly the RSS and the VHP, did not accept their versions.

Proponents of *liberal* Hindutva felt that Hinduism as a religion has to be less doctrinaire. It has to be less clear-cut than mainstream Christianity, politically less fanatic than Islam, and ethically less abnegating than Buddhism. It would offer something to everybody, whether one is a Hindu or a non-Hindu, it would delight one by its richness and depth.

For them, Hindutva will spread not so much through the gurus, saints and swamis, who attract a certain number of people looking for a new commitment to hate and attach or a quasi-monastic lifestyle or seeking salvation. They believe that it will spread mainly through the work of intellectuals and writers who have found Hindu ideas convincing and who identify them with their personal beliefs

BJP's defeat with this liberal Hindu ideology has triggered off a sharp controversy among the major members of Hindutva Parivar.[5]

Hindutva Guardians Unfit

It is obvious that Hindutva guardians like BJP and VHP are proving unfit and unworthy. It is reducing in size, courage, resources and influence. On the contrary, for the last several decades, the number and power of its enemies—the anti-Hindutva Hindu and anti-Hindutva non-Hindu groups and communities have been increasing by leaps and bounds. In Hindus, despite apparent majority of the Hindus, there is continuous erosion of their culture, status and influence in India. All the major partners of the Hindutva Parivar are quarrelling among themselves. The BJP is secretly and silently gulping its humiliation because it changed its colour of *aggressive* Hindutva to *liberal* Hindutva overnight.[6] The VHP has lost all self-confidence, courage and fighting spirit to the extent that it is demanding to form, in place of present Congress, like BJP, one another Fighting Front of the Hindus.[7] Under the circumstances, the RSS with a sense of guilt is discovering new strategy to deal with revival of Hindutva.[8]

Even, the RSS lacks understanding, courage, perspective and planning. It has yet to become a powerful and unchallengeable instrument of Hindutva in the 21st century. Hindutva is facing the crisis of its existence. The RSS, as the backbone of Hindutva, is shaking. It rightly disapproved of attempts to seek reservations for converts from Scheduled Castes (SCs) and said it was against reservation on the basis of religion. "If the demand of the converts from SCs was conceded, it would render 'great injustice' to SCs, as a larger share of the benefit for which they were rightfully entitled would be grabbed by the converts", it said in a resolution at the conclave.[9] Whenever it attempts to protect the Hindu interests, and organize, its acts are dubbed as 'Fascism'.[10] Few want to allow it to "Hinduize the Hindus".

An analysis of the outcomes of the efforts of these organizations shows that their performance on Hindutva attained so far has proved them unfit and unworthy of the cause. Including the parent organization Rashtriya Swayamsevak Sangh (RSS or the Sangh), all have miserably failed. Main factors of this situation are 'inherent' disabilities of these organizations. These 'inherent' disabilities are independent of their present form, type of personnel, amount of resources, and ignorance of required training, and tools and techniques to accomplish the mission. They are basically ideological.

The Hindutva Parivar mainly consists of three big organizations: RSS (Rashtriya Swayamsevak Sangh), BJP (Bharatiya Janata Party), and VHP (Vishwa Hindu Parishad). In the following pages, we shall study their ambitions and disabilities one by one.

Rashtriya Swayamsevak Sangh (RSS)

RSS is the parent organization of the Hindutva Parivar. It is basically a defensive, introvert and collaborative organization aimed at uniting the Hindus to protect their religion, culture and communities. It has little concern with reform or change in the Hindu Dharma.[11] It accepts whatever is said to be in the Hindu Dharma. It has no opinion on what actually Hindu Dharma is? The Hindus are basically attached with various forms of Hindu Dharma, therefore, it is very essential to know and ascertain the basics or essentials of Hindu Dharma. But the RSS does not bother to know them. As it keeps away from its basics, it remains unable to measure or evaluate the 'Hinduness' of various forms, sects and panths coming under the umbrella term Hindu Dharma. It follows exactly the position held by the Supreme Court of India.[12] For the apex court, Hindu Dharma,

Hinduism and Hindutva are unanimous. For it, they are lifestyle, a tolerant culture or a way of living. As RSS is not concerned with the basic forms of Hindu religion, it stands unable to speak out what particular form of Hindu Dharma should in the prevailing circumstances be? Owing to the same reason, and suffering from this ignorance, it cannot justify which of the prevailing forms of religion is basic Hindu religion. Therefore, it accepts what is spoken to it about Hindu religion. It cannot judge or ascertain the core, real or basic elements of Hindu Dharma in case of conflicting statements made about it. With this perplexing background, it cannot give an outline of the format of Hinduism or Hindutva to canvass, propagate or fight for. Its leaders want to bring about unity by defending and supporting all such conflicting or collaborative positions. It is exactly the level two position.[13] It fact, it cannot prove or uphold that it is a religion of humanity, not an ideology of communalism or fascism. Advocates of Hindutva belonging to RSS speak about two types of Hindutva: aggressive and liberal. It is not clear to which it belongs to. M.S. Golwalkar stuck to the former but his successors appear to move towards the latter. But all remain unable to spell out how social, political, economic and defensive set up has to be based on their fundamentals.

This position of ignorance, aloofness or apathy towards the basics of Hindu Dharma has compelled it to adopt the precept of 'equivalence' and equal respect to all religions (सर्वधर्मसमभाव). When one does not know the contents of one's own religion, he has to accept the givens of all other religions. A votary of Hindutva, before paying respect to all other religions and regarding them equal, has to know not only the outlines of all other religions but basics of his own universal or sanatan religion too. If one does not know the basics of Hindutva, how can he ask others to advocate, speak and fight for it. This was the position of religion appearing at level two in the ancient times. They had nothing to speak against, stop or discard the undesirable teachings on their formulation adopted by the masses at large.

There is no difficulty when religions discover truths at metaphysical level. They are free to differ with one another or accept what has been said or felt earlier. There is no harm even if their experiences conflict with each other. There is no problem when they do so in this abstract, internal, spiritual or mental area. Any new or old religion might be at par with earlier basic Hindu religion when it talks about the path to self-realization or his recourse to the Ultimate Brahma or Consciousness.

But in rest of the matters appearing social, political, economic or temporal, a new religion, if it overlooks human limits, and in the name of God or revelation or intuition goes in a different direction, it puts a challenge to the very existence of society, polity or economy prevailing before its emergence. Only after assessing the impact of such religion, one should declare it to be at par with the religion prevailing earlier. Without doing it in a proper manner, one cannot put any new religion at par with his own religion.

In a different way, Raja Rammohan Roy, Dayananda Saraswati, Vivekananda, Lokmanya Bal Gangadhar Tilak and Mahatma Gandhi tried to convince the non-Hindus of India that the basics of Hindu Dharma were similar to the teachings of their religions, therefore, there could be one religion for all Indians—Hindus and non-Hindus. Rather, they invited the non-Hindus to return to their earlier religion, but few came back. All such attempts in the long run have proved futile, hopeless and retrograde. The RSS in a different manner had declared, on the basis that all those living in India (Hind) are Hindus, therefore, they should be treated as Hindus.[14] On this basis it considers itself 'National' (Rashtriya) and has tried to speak and stand for all.[15] But few are convinced with that logic. The non-Hindus connect the term 'Hindus' only with Hindu religion which they had known for the last several centuries. So far, even all the Hindus of India have not come under its banner. Therefore, the RSS appears to have been compelled to coin a new term 'Hindutva'.[16]

Shortcomings in the concept of Hindutva held by the Sangh are due to several factors.

The RSS, in the beginning, could not take a positive stand on depressed classes and minorities. If it could have really stood and spoken for all the Hindus (residents of India—including depressed classes and minorities), it would have spearheaded the movement for equality and eradication of exploitation and repression for the depressed classes long before what Mahatma Gandhi and Dr. B.R. Ambedkar had done for them. Such was the overdue requirement of their Hindutva. However, at that time, it was not so broader. In fact, it could not distinguish between a Hindu and a Hindudharmi. One would be 'Hindu' in the sense that he was born in the country widely known as 'Hindustan', a land of the Hindus in geographical sense.. He could also be called as 'Hindavi'. One who's 'religion' was Hindu is Hindudharmi (follower of Hindu Dharma). All Hindus are not Hindudharmis. By sticking to the superiority of the Brahmins as a class and of the upper strata of the Hindu society, the RSS cannot win over even the two-third Hindus of the depressed classes to Hindutva.[17] The Sangh, overlooking its basic disabilities is living in a world of dreams to reconvert the minorities to Hindutva.[18] It is obvious, near about two-third population of India is unwilling to accept Hindutva as 'Indianism'.[19] The RSS is unaware of the prevailing image of 'Hindutva' at popular level.[20]

The RSS has also to critically analyze and revise the oft-repeated shakha-stories on role of Prithavi Raj Chauhan, Maharana Pratap, Shivaji, Guru Govind Singh, Laxmi Bai, Subhash Chandra Bose and the like. It should, instead of worshipping them as a whole, discriminate and isolate the role which is not out of date. So is the case with their emotional surrender to Hindu gods and goddesses abounding at the levels of mythology, and in national, regional and local areas and their being worshipped day and night in thousands of temples and religious places whereas Hindus pray to them to do every work for them in lieu of their offer of some sweets, recitation of prayers or sitting in silence for a few minutes. Most of the Hindus have grown habit to throw their own responsibility to do a particular obligation upon their idol gods. So, should the RSS update its methods, tools, techniques to educate the masses in modern and popular ways. In the age of science, technology and IT revolution, giving emotional colour to every big and small event is not enough, particularly when it has to fight for long. It would not be out of context to comment that the Sangh should update its modes of publicity and knowledge in the areas of democratic politics, management, social, medical, military and natural sciences.

The repeated declaration of the former Prime Minister of India Atal Behari Vajpayee was not believed that Hindutva is Bharatiyatva or Indianism. For the Sangh too it is very far-fetched that minorities would convert to the Hindutva even while retaining their own faith intact. The RSS has not been successful even in transforming the various differing Hindu organizations, sects and faiths to Hindutva. Obviously, the non-Hindus cannot be votaries of Hindutva as such.

Taking old Hindu Dharma for granted as Hindutva cannot serve any purpose for bringing about unity and integration among the differing and conflicting religions, cultures, forms of worship and goals of life. Few are able to conceive that old Hindu Dharma is out of tune with the requirements of present polity, economy, social harmony and international LPG.[21] The Sangh, the Hindus and the depressed classes were silent spectators of the making the present Constitution of India. They had accepted it in toto. Now, they cannot disobey or revise it by force. It speaks more for the non-Hindus, particularly anti-Hindus. It is to them a kind of sword and shield. The Hindus now have to live with it. Great men like Dayananda, Vivekananda, Lokmanya Tilak, Mahatma Gandhi etc. tried their best to make Hindu Dharma as vibrant Hinduism, but failed. The RSS too cannot succeed even with the Hindu Dharma covered with the cloak of Hindutva.[22] Adoption of the ideal of 'integral humanism' makes no substantial change.

Still, the Sangh is the only remaining force behind the Hindutva movement. It is because of its choosing Hindu realities and symbols as indicators of Hindutva. It upholds worship of territory of India as Mother, unity of India and culture as Flag of Victory, and taking birth in India. It will keep it free from all types of slavery as enough for one's being a 'nationist'. This is good but not enough. It has to convert its ideology of Hindutva to Hindatva, Bharatiyatva or Indianism. Nobody is going to call oneself as 'Hindu' simply because one happens to live in India or the Hindutva Parivar persuades him to say so. The word 'Hindatva' (हिंदत्व) means Hindus as well as non-Hindus. The non-Hindus include Hindus, Muslims, Christians, and other communities. It should upgrade the meaning of the adjective 'national' from 'nationalism' (राष्ट्रीयता) to 'nationism' (राष्ट्रत्व), and make an appeal to all minorities, classes and communities to give up their own out-of-date and anti-Hindatva elements.

Bharatiya Janata Party (BJP)

The BJP and VHP are the two offshoots of the RSS.

The BJP is a political party.[23] Its members usually are taught and brought up by the Sangh which itself is a non-political, cultural and nationalistic organization. The party is taught in terms of Hindutva or Hinduism or cultural nationalism. It has already been pointed out that the RSS neither knows the basics of Hindu Dharma nor has acquainted itself with the latest developments in Political Science, Economics, Sociology and the like. Owing to the very nature of its being a military-like organization it is almost blank in these areas. Only a few retired people from these disciplines and services have recently joined it.

Whatever little the Sangh knew about Hindu Dharma or Hinduism, it taught it to the BJP. As has been stated earlier, the BJP never fails to harp on Hindutva, as it understands it. Actually, it has done nothing for the erosion of awareness in Hindus about Hindutva. In fact, with its lack of focus about the religion whose cause it claims to be championing, the BJP has ended up giving it a colour that Hinduism has never had in its history. The BJP's approach to Hinduism has only heightened its ignorance about Hinduism.

BJP officially claims to follow the ideology of integrated humanism (एकात्म मानववाद), propounded by Deendayal Upadhyay. But hardly any BJP leader has been able to explain it in some depth. In fact, it is equivalent to level two type religion which has been the root cause of the downfall of the Vedicas, later reduced to Hindu Dharma. The ideological vacuum in BJP is filled by new ideology of sycophancy, i.e., boss is always right. The BJP cadres looked up to Atal Bihari Vajpayee and LK Advani. The RSS, which claims to be the mother organization of BJP, has lost its moral heights to lead Hindutva in right direction. Presently, it is also following the footsteps of the liberal Hindutva adopted by the BJP to win Lok Sabha election. RSS still supplies bulk of manpower for BJP. But, for a BJP leader, utterances of Atal-Advani are more important. BJP loyalists like to live a life of luxury with all the trappings of power. The BJP without guidance and direction from the RSS is a political party without ideology.[24]

The BJP, in order to broaden its base, had adopted the ideology of Hindutva. But it lacks commitment and understanding. As a result of its leadership in the Rath Yatra and participation in the demolition of the Babri (mosque) structure, it committed itself to build a Ram Temple at the Ramjanmabhoomi, Ayodhya (Uttar Pradesh).[25] It got nationwide Hindu support in the 13th Lok Sabha election, but it could not obtain majority. However, it was a dominant partner in the ruling coalition (National Democratic Alliance—NDA, 1998-2004) at the Centre. But it succeeded in seeking utmost cooperation from the coalition partners after publicly giving up its three Hindutva promises made in the election manifesto.

Unfortunately, it could neither fully implement the Hindutva programme nor transform itself into a real 'Bharatiya' (Indian) Janata Party. Most of its members are from the lower and lower-middle class Hindus engaged in service, small business and shopkeeping residing mostly in urban and semi-urban areas. Like the Congress it was controlled by the upper strata of the Hindus and some others. During its rule, it could not bring the depressed classes—STs, SCs, and the OBCs—at par with upper castes. They drifted away from it during the 14th Lok Sabha elections.

So was the case with the Muslims and the Christian minorities. In the wake of the demolition of the Babri (mosque) structure on December 6, 1992, the RSS was banned for the third time, and the four BJP state governments were dismissed and put under the President's rule. It was the leading party of the Ramjanmabhoomi movement. But, after forming the NDA government, it distanced itself. While as the ruling partner of the NDA government, it could not do anything towards the prevention of the Gujarat massacre. It could not even tell that it actually flared up in the wake of burning of 58 kar sevakas alive by some Muslim extremists.[26] The whole burden and blame was borne by the aggressive Hindutva of the Vishwa Hindu Parishad and the present Modi government. On both these occasions, the Hindus were taken aback. Despite its being known as a pro-Hindu party, it did greater harm to Hindutva. This left the Hindus in lurch and utter disappointment. They found the role of the BJP no better than the early ruling Indian National Congress.

In fact, the BJP as a group of Hindutva political workers, coming mostly from the Sangh, knows little about democratic politics.[27] Few of them know about the constraints and directions enshrined in the Constitution of India. They are unaware of the organization, culture and working of the Indian bureaucracy. Under the impact of rapid economic development and IT revolution, they forgot that poverty, unemployment, concentration of wealth etc. have grown immensely. With these developments, the enmity against the Sangh Parivar had also consolidated. BJP, with overconfidence to have an easy walk over, ordered Lok Sabha election four months early. Its claim to have done what the Congress could not do in its 45 years' rule fully exposed its slogans of 'development' and 'India Shining'. In place of nourishing its Hindutva constituency, it kept busy in cajoling Muslims and Christians. The BJP was rejected by the majority of the people. It was praising its unique success, in comparison with earlier coalition governments, in running a coalition government at the Centre for six years. Following the same pattern, the Indian National Congress succeeded in forming a majority coalition government (UPA—United Progressive Alliance). All non-NDA and non-BJP political parties joined together and won the 14th Lok Sabha election and replaced the BJP-led government.

Now, the parent organization, the RSS is taking it to task for giving up the Hindutva agenda and also for the defeat of the BJP. In fact, the whole Hindutva Parivar is unaware of the factors responsible for the defeat of the BJP. The nature of the two organizations—RSS and BJP—is different. The former is a cultural organization deeply rooted in old pattern of Hindu Dharma, and wants to enact Hinduism as an ideology.[28] But it cannot control and direct a political party (organization). But it is not willing to accept it. Ultimately, they will have to separate. The two organizations are different from each other in matters of goals, motivation, incentives, methods of work and environment of their operations. The RSS has not developed appropriate control mechanism except withdrawing support during elections. The BJP has no cadre of its own. Perhaps, presently, it lacks capacity to do so.[29]

The BJP has lost on account of its liberal Hindutva. It has no ideological reply to the tenets of Islamic terrorism or Muslim violence and to the tactics of Christian expansion through conversion. The only available way to it is to give support to the surrender Hindu interests and outright grant of concessions to the minorities with a view to surpass the non-Hindu and anti-Hindutva Hindu organizations.

BJP broke all records of liberalism and tolerance, when its President L.K. Advani made all-out praise for Jinnah and partition.[30] He ultimately had to abdicate, and hand over the charge of BJP to pro-RSS President Rajnath Singh on January 2, 2006.[31]

Vishwa Hindu Parishad (VHP)

The VHP represents the stock of utmost faith of the Hindus towards Hindu Dharma appearing in form of various sects, gods and goddesses, and ways of worship and prayers.

It is represented and organized by upper caste Brahminhood which for the last several centuries has been living on the exploitation of religious feelings and emotions of the Hindus. It is thrust on the Hindu masses as universal, God given, permanent and unchangeable dharma. It continues on the basis of the authority of some specific holy books, designated saints, acharyas, munis and recluses. Hindu Dharma, as they advocate, is based on trinity of gods, reincarnation of Lord Vishnu from time to time, varnashrama transformed into caste and sub-caste system, idol worship, hundreds of religions, sects and paths to self or God realization and so on. Such religions go on multiplying. Every Hindu is supposed to be depending upon 'leela' (game) of God which cannot be disturbed, changed or reformed by human beings. A Hindu is born as such and is not permitted to renounce it.

The VHP represents the conglomeration of pluralities of spirituality in Hindu Dharma. It hardly reflects the basics of Hindu Dharma except its spirituality and plurality. There is no room of any united organization or action or concern towards safety and protection of what each one of them stands for. Their Hindu Dharma still stands in between the 11th and 20th century. Only the office bearers of the VHP feel this vacuum and work out to fill it.

The highest body of the VHP consists of all Hindu saints, acharyas, mahants, gurus, swamis and mathadheeshas of different sects, panths, branches and religions of the Hindus. All are different except that that they put on clothes of saffron colour (prescribed for the sanyasis or recluses) and are sanyasis. But each one of them is conscious of his high position in his religious sect, special types of robes, decoration and symbols, custody of riches, offerings, buildings, jewellery, land, property and wealth. Temples are their perennial source of wealth. Each is connected with millions of devotees, followers and admirers who congregate at pilgrim places. They inherit gaddis, chairs or positions in some prescribed manner. In a sense, every one of them is like a monarch or raja of his religion's regime. They are sovereigns in their respective areas, unwilling to meet with one another and arrive at some definite steps to ameliorate the social, economic and moral conditions of the Hindus living in the 21st century. They tend to leave all these matters to God, Brahma or Almighty. Most of them are status quoists, happy with the continuation of what they have inherited or obtained from their devotees, and want to maintain them at all costs. Throughout centuries, they have transformed the mythological gods and goddesses in form of idol to be worshipped in a particular routine set on daily time-table and calendar. The number of these saints, gurus etc. is increasing. Every one is free to preach or invent a religion of his choice. Though all the saints formally stand out of the varna system, they strictly support the supremacy of the Brahmin priesthood.

This congregation of saints (sant mandal) is hardly concerned with poverty, illiteracy, backwardness, disease and superstitions prevailing in the Hindu masses. They presently think only in terms of building a Ram Temple in Ayodhya, which is likely to result in form of worship of an idol whereat millions of devotees would put offerings— sweets, gold, jewellery, money, donations property etc. Thousands of Brahmins and their henchmen would gain and earn livelihood and live in palatial buildings. None of them thinks in terms of creating personalities of Ram to emancipate the Hindu Dharma in real sense. They are hardly aware of modern concepts of democracy, nationalism, rule of law, accountability, liberty and equality. Progress in the fields of science, technology, management, economics, medicine, social sciences and the like belongs to a different culture.

The VHP is a bridge between the saints and the BJP. However, the power behind the VHP is the blind and traditional faith of the 10 per cent of the Hindus in their traditional Hindu Dharma. This part of the Hindus hardly stands for change. It does not yield even to the calls of the RSS. But it is willing to stand with the BJP during the elections. The whole of the VHP officialdom depends upon their faith and belief in the Hindu Dharma. To keep its constituency safe and reserved, it is away from the problems like casteism, degradation and exploitation of women and depressed classes. Their ideology seems to be the defence and protection of the Hindutva by maintaining status quoism of the Hindu Dharma. Otherwise, it has no other training and tools and techniques of working with the Hindus at large. With increase in the awareness among the Hindus, this support is likely to dwindle in future.

The Hindus during the freedom movement stood behind the leadership of Mahatma Gandhi. They, in line with their own teachings of Hindu Dharma, believed in the invincibility of non-violence of Mahatma Gandhi who had promised the Hindus to win independence of united India against the British Raj and to bring about Hindu-Muslim unity on permanent footing. Both of the goals could not be realized. The Hindus did not lose faith in Gandhi and the Congress even after the partition of India and bloodshed and migration of population on mass scale in the wake of independence of India won and ruled for over forty years. They continued to have faith in the conventional Hindu Dharma. They could not realize that the Constitution of India which was framed for long three years had rejected all of the basics of Hindu Dharma: religion, family, subjection of women to men, status of lower castes, special rights to minorities (Muslims, Christians, Sikhs and others). In fact, they were left without their own land, culture and Hindu Dharma. The Hindus stood unaware that some of the basics of the Hindu Dharma vis-à-vis the Constitution of India had been rendered anti-law and anti-Constitution. The RSS under these circumstances came forward. To keep Hindu Dharma alive the Sangh organized the VHP as its wing of Hindu religion.

The Sangh stood for the Hindus and the Hindustan. It unfortunately did not distinguish between Hindu and Hindudharmi. They were not synonymous. On the basis of concept of 'nationalism' and the nomenclature of 'India' as 'Hindustan', it wanted to call all the inhabitants living in India, of whatever religion, culture, ethnicity etc., as 'Hindus'. Their term 'Hindu' included 'non-Hindus' also. It also did not distinguish between 'Hindu' (a person living in India, on the other side of the Sindhu river) and 'Hindudharmi' (follower of Hindu religion). In their sense, all the people living in India are Hindus. Out of these 105 crore 'Hindus', there are over 80 crore namesake Hindudharmis. The actual number of Hindus following Hindu Dharma, that is, real Hindudharmis, is much less. In this specific sense of the term 'Hindudharmi', the number of religion-believing Hindus is much reduced. Both RSS and VHP forget that the Hindus coming under the category of Hindu Dharma is not more than 35 to 40 percent of the total population of India. It is now no more a 'majority'. Majority, that is, more than 50 per cent of the total population, is considered to be decisive in a democracy. It is this fact which explains the reason why the RSS or the BJP has not been able to involve all the Hindudharmi Hindus and non-Hindudharmi Hindus, and capture majority to form its own government at the Centre and in many states. To call a person born in Hindu Dharma as Hindu or treat him as Hindudharmi does not work. The VHP fails to understand that this part of Hindu majority living on blind faith and some superstitions cannot be powerful enough to deliver goods in democracy. Presently, the whole of the Indian political system, the bureaucracy, the lower judiciary, the rest of the Hindus and the non-Hindu communities appear to stand against VHP. They fail to know that all Hindus are not behind it. The opposition against the RSS for this reason is also increasing.

The VHP is blindly enamoured of Hindu majority. In fact, only one-third of the Hindus are with it. Only a small part of religion-based Hindus is Hindudharmi. It hardly understands that the whole of the Indian Constitution, judiciary and legal set-up, democratic system and its institutions stand against its understanding.

The format and actions of VHP have been giving an impression that it aims at imposing the rule of Brahmin priesthood again on the Hindu masses. Under such self-same allusions, they want more and more temples which, they think, are likely to result in their more and more hold on the Hindu masses. All gods and goddesses of the Hindus are claimed to be in their favour. The lower castes are very much alarmed. Its success in building the Ram Temple wholly depended on the formal and official support of the BJP (in the NDA). The apex court disallowed all such attempts. The BJP started negotiations between the two communities—Hindus and Muslims—but could not succeed. Being in the NDA, the BJP had officially given up its promise to build Ram Temple at Ayodhya. It could not do so until it got absolute majority in the coming Lok Sabha elections. The VHP felt deceived and frustrated, and desired to form a Hindu front for this purpose. In the 14th Lok Sabha elections, the BJP following liberal Hindutva could not get majority and the NDA lost power to the UPA led by the Congress.

Thus, the VHP is feeling disabled from all sides. Only the RSS stands by it, but it is not a religious organization speaking with certainty on the Basics of Hindu Dharma.

Presently, Uma Bharati, Govindacharya and VHP appear closer to each other, therefore, likely, to form a front, group or party to stand by Hindutva.

Notes

1. The RSS supremo K.S. Sudarshan called for the need to rewrite the Indian Constitution which was the revised edition of the Government of India Act, 1935 and several clauses were adopted from the unwritten Constitution of Great Britain. Even Dr. Ambedkar was not satisfied with the present shape of the Constitution. Dr. Ambedkar had said: "I did what I was asked to do." Dr. Ambedkar added that given a chance, he would have been the first person to burn it. There is need for a mass awareness on the issue so that the country can get a Constitution as per its needs and aspiration that fulfill the expectation of the people. *Hindustan Times*, November 6, 2005.
2. Commission on the Review of the Working of the Constitution of India was constituted. It appears that when late President K.R. Narayanan cautioned the government against 'revising' the Constitution, or the parliamentary form of government, it was Advani who prevailed on the Prime Minister to issue the necessary clarification, after a Cabinet meeting, that the proposed review would be within the framework of parliamentary form of government and that the basic features of the Constitution would be out of its purview. Thus, the BJP failed to realise its ultimate goal.
3. In a severe rebuke to Gujarat Chief Minister Narendra Modi, the United States has denied him entry to America. Taking a strong stand against the senior BJP leader and Hindutva icon, the US Consular division denied him a 'diplomatic visa'. BJP General Secretary Pramod Mahajan also has said that the Bharatiya Janata Party's second regret after the Ayodhya issue is the Gujarat riots. He added that the riots are a 'black spot' for any civilized society. *Hindustan Times*, May 9, 2005.
4. In an article Uma Bharati exposed that "the party developed two anomalies after 1996. First was the continuation of the dilution of ideology. The second was to sacrifice issues such as security, swadeshi, probity etc. in order not to displease foreign power while running a coalition government. Article 370, the uniform civil code and Ramjanmabhoomi were put in the backburner." *Hindustan Times*, December 30, 2005.
5. The RSS leaders advised the two BJP stalwarts Vajpayee and Advani to place their point of view before the assembly of top RSS leaders at Hardwar conclave. A strong section of RSS maintains that the BJP continues to be a coterie-driven outfit and has deviated from the basic ideology of the parivar. On the last day of the RSS's national executive on October 22, general secretary Mohanrao Bhagwat said the replacement will be someone who would stick to the five point agenda suggested by

the sangh: primacy of Hindutva, strengthening the organization, training cadres, ethical conduct and consultative mechanism in the party. Also, the BJP leadership would have to be a collective one, not personality driven. Bhagwat said that the Sangh favoured the principle of collective decision making and team-work in the party as these formed the basis of a democratic system. RSS said that its business was to ensure that the BJP was moving in the "right direction" and any deviations by its leadership would be dealt with firmly. "The Sangh is firm on its ideological stand and all swayamsewaks are bound by it." *Hindustan Times*, October 24, 2005.

6. Devi who is the RSS representative at the celebrations read out the Sangh's elementary rule book, "The BJP is not a party of individuals but of ideology. It is an organization of people who accept this ideology. They have the ability to solve no matter what difficulties arise." He reminded the BJP of the pre-eminence of the RSS. "It's an all-India set-up. Even our rivals acknowledge our ability to do what we se to achieve." *Hindustan Times*, December 27, 2005.
7. On expulsion of Uma Bharati from the BJP, she indicating to form a new party thundered that "I am the real BJP". *Rajasthan Partika*, December 30, 2005; Govindacharya, of Swadeshi Jagran Manch had already made a declaration to form a New Party for the Eighty Crore People of India. *Rajasthan Patrika*, December 16, 2005.
8. RSS also sets out to woo minority community—the Akhil Bhartiya Sah Sampark Pramukh of the RSS, the ideologue, Indresh Kumar wanted the BJP and VHP to stop making Ramjanmabhoomi issue a question of their existence, thus hurting the sentiments of crores of people "just for Babar". Kumar said: "Once an enemy is always an enemy is not the formula for those who work for nationalism and humanity". The National Muslim Front (NMF) came out of Eid-Milan function at Chanakyapuri in New Delhi about two years back which was attended by Sangh chief K.S. Sudarshan. This NMF organized the function at Jaipur in February 2005. *Hindustan Times*, October 21, 2004. It simply shows that RSS has lost its ideological clarity.
9. The Mangalore conclave pointed out that "there is already a large section of converts from SCs, who continue to hold on to Hindu names and enjoy reservation benefits. These crypto-Christians, who constitute about 2.1 per cent of our population, are depriving SCs of their opportunities." Reservations were intended to undo the damage caused to a section of Hindu society due to caste discrimination, resulting in their social disability.
10. Basu, T. et al (1993), *Kakhi Shorts, Saffron Flags*, Orient Longman, New Delhi; Andersen W. and S.D. Damle (1987), *The Brotherhood in Saffron:*

The RSS and Hindu Revivalism Vistaar, New Delhi; Gopal S. (1990), "Anatomy of a Confrontation: The Babri Masjid RJB Issue", *Viking*, New Delhi; Pandey, G. (1993) (ed.), "Hindus and Others: The Question of Identity in India Today",Viking, New Delhi; Nandy A. et al (1995) *Creating a Nationality: The RJB Movement and the Fear of the self,* Oxford University Press, New Delhi; and, Thapar, R. (1985), "Syndicated Moksha", *Seminar*, September 1985.

11. Some of its leaders feel proud to say that Hinduism is both a civilization and a congregation of religions; it has neither a beginning nor a founder, nor a central authority, hierarchy, or organization. Hindu scholars are never ashamed of several crores of the Hindus that left to other religions. In place of searching reasons for their predicament, they apparently are satisfied that Hindus at least are surviving.(see back Chapter 5)
12. Arun Shourie had made it clear that what for the Hindutva Parivar fights is not at all Hindu Religion. In the Court's view what we practice and have faith in is not a religion at all. It is so diverse. It does not have one book, it does not have one prophet, nor one over-arching Church as a religion has. "Therefore it is not a religion." Arun Shourie, 'The Hindutva Judgements: The Distance That Remains', *Hindustan Times*, April 24, 1996. According to him the Court expects the Hindus always to be tolerant, broad-minded, and plural. It means they should not do anything against communities and religions even if they plan to kill them?
13. See, back, Introduction.
14. "We Hindus—have been in undisputed and undisturbed possession of this land for over eight or even ten thousand years before the land was invaded by any foreign race and therefore, this land, came to be known as Hindusthan, the land of the Hindus" M.S. Golwalkar. *We or Our Nationhood defined* (Bharat Publications), 1939, p. 6.
15. The word 'National' has been used here over and above the term 'Hindu' to allay any apprehensions about its scope and nature. Punj, op. cit.
16. See, Chapter 5, 'Ideology of Hindutva'.
17. The RSS was founded on Dussera day in 1925 by Dr. Kesav Baliram Hedgewar at Nagpur for "Hindu Revivalism". During the last 80 years there have been only four Sarsanghchalakas namely:

    K.B. Hedgewar 1925-1940 Brahmin

    M.S. Golwalkar 1940-1973 Brahmin

    Bala Saheb Deoras 1973-1994 Brahmin

    Rajju Bhaiya 1994-1999 Kshatriya Conspicuously removed?

    K.S. Sudarshan 1999-Brahmin

The Sarsanghchalak is considered to be the guide for the corporate Hindu Nation.

18. RSS set out to woo minority community. The National Muslim Front (NMF) came out of Eid-Milan function at Chanakyapuri in New Delhi about two years back which was attended by Sangh chief K.S. Sudarshan. This NMF organized the function at Jaipur in February 2005. *Hindustan Times*, October 21, 2004; See, also, *Rajasthan Patrika*, February 1, 2005.
19. *Rajasthan Patrika*, December 25, 2002.
20. Present Image of Hindu Religion or Hindutva has been outlined in Chapter 3.
21. Former Prime Minister Atal Bihari Vajpayee criticized RSS attempt to restrict thought process: "It is a constantly evolving process; there should be room for fresh thoughts." "It is difficult to pinpoint the final principle of any ideology. It is, therefore, not right to adopt an attitude that what we have accepted as the final principle of our ideology is the ultimate truth." "It is essential that our ideology stands the test of being beneficial for human kind as a whole. The thought process will evolve constantly. Exchange of ideas will also take place." *The Hindu*, September 26, 2005; See, also, Chapter 25, "Challenges of Globalisation to Indian Democracy".
22. Actually, the present Hindutva of the RSS is Hindu Dharma or at the most Hinduism as explained in 'The Hindu Dharma' and 'Formulation, Performance and Failure of Hinduism'. Punj quotes Pandit Deen Dayal Upadhyaya the ideologue of the Rasthriya Swayamsevak Sangh (RSS)/Bharatiya Janata Party (BJP) that the ideal of the Indian state has been Dharma Rajya. Tolerance of and respect for all faiths and creeds is an essential feature of the Indian state. Freedom of worship and conscience is guaranteed to all and the state does not discriminate against anyone on grounds of religion, either in the formulation of policy or in its implementation. It is a non-sectarian State and not a Theocracy'. BJP believes in 'Integral Humanism' as its basic philosophy, which visualizes a harmonious relation between individuals, individual and state, state and world, individual and humanity. The most important cementing factor has been the Hindu religion. north or south, east or west, wherever you may travel, you will find the same religious ideas, the same culture and the same tradition. All Hindus look upon India as the Holy Land. Thus the word 'Hindu', with its derivatives 'Hinduism' and 'Hindutva', has a nationalistic rather than religious or sectarian origin in hoary past of civilisation. The Sanatana soul of Hinduism has to survive in the world it needs the body called Hindutva. Balbir K. Punj, *'Hindu Rashtra'*, op.cit.

23. The Jana Sangh party was formed in 1951 to act as a political wing of the RSS. Some leaders felt that 'though the RSS had mass following, it had no political voice'. But the new party was also strongly opposed by some senior RSS leaders. The Bharatiya Janata Party (BJP) replaced Jana Sangh in 1980. By the mid-1970s, when a state of emergency was declared by Prime Minister Indira Gandhi, the RSS was banned a second time among other political parties. During the Emergency years 1975-77, the RSS and the whole Hindutva movement adopted a more liberal interpretation of Hindu nationalism. This also meant that the mutual suspicions of the RSS and its political opponents were reduced significantly. The organization took at least partial credit for the defeat of Prime Minister Gandhi in 1977. The Janata Party then won 298 out of the 542 seats. The share of the Jana Sangh party was 93 seats in the Janata alliance. Gurdas M. Ahuja, *BJP and the Indian Politics. Policies & Programmes of the Bharatiya Janata Party*, 1994 New Delhi: Ram Co. p. 17.
24. After the dissolution of the Janata Party the main concerns of BJP leaders were to strengthen their claims to being the 'real' Janata Party. While staking such a claim before the Election Commission, they adopted the Janata Party's constitution as their own. It is worth mentioning that the Janata Party constitution was taken from the Congress-O constitution, which was a carbon copy of the Congress one. Uma Bharati, *Hindustan Times*, December 30, 2005. As such, the 1984-85 elections recorded an unprecedented defeat for the BJP which won only two Lok Sabha seats. After separating from the V.P. Singh Government, writes Uma Bharati, the hurry to reach power somehow was evident when the 13-day government was formed despite the BJP not having the majority. This hurt the party's team spirit and the image of the leadership. ....Instead of traversing the distance from Ram Temple to Ram Rajya, BJP leaders demonstrated their lust for power by forming opportunistic alliances. In 1998, finally the NDA came to power. During this phase, BJP's work culture changed fast. The top leadership grew more intolerant of dissent. Opportunists, power brokers and the corrupt gained prominence and principled and ideologically committed workers were sidelined. Uma Bharati, *Hindustan Times*, December 30, 2005.
25. Court cases are pending against its leaders for taking part in the illegal demolition movement.
26. It could not muster courage and emphasize that the real cause of the riot was terrorism led by the Muslims extremists and Islamists. To create confusion two Inquiry Commissions have been set up.
27. RSS stalwart Dattopant Thengadi, the founder of the RSS-affiliated Bharatiya Mazdoor Sangh (BMS) and the Swadeshi Jagran Manch, attacked the NDA government, particularly the PM on the issue of

labour reforms and the WTO. He also attacked Disinvestment Minister Arun Shourie, saying he had projected "wrong image" of B.R. Ambedkar in his book, *Worshipping False Gods. Hindustan Times*, April 16, 2003. See the former prime minister Vajpayee's initiative to go to Pakistan, by the Lahore bus without any attention to Kargil. Hundreds of jawans were killed because of this neglect. See, also, PM's allotment of petrol pumps, and LPG and kerosene dealerships which the Supreme Court had to quash from January 2000. *Hindustan Times*, December 21, 2002, and also the army expedition on the Western borders. Writes Noorani, "As a front of a unique body, the RSS, the BJP is a unique political party. With its brand of politics, India's parliamentary democracy has suffered a lot and will continue to suffer more." A.G. Noorani, *Stuck in a lotus position*, *Hindustan Times*, January 10, 06.

28. The RSS constitution Article 4(c) clearly states that the "Sangh is aloof from politics and is devoted to social and cultural fields only."
29. "In 2005, the party is directionless, frustrated and faction-ridden. It appears that the player has lost everything in a bet with no sign of rejuvenation." Uma Bharati, *Hindustan Times*, December 30, 2005.
30. Advani's four cardinal sins—1. Ayodhya demolition was the "saddest day of his life"; 2. "the Partition as an irreversible process" thereby violating the Sangh concept of Akhand Bharat; 3. there was no difference between Indians and Pakistanis; 4. Praise of the Qaide-Azam as a secular person. Pankaj Vohra, Advani's requiem, *Hindustan Times*, December 30, 2005.
31. He is choice of the RSS, though his election his been unanimously endorsed by the National Executive of the BJP on January 20, 2006. With this, the BJP under Rajnath Singh has accepted all the items of its old agenda. *Rajasthan Patrika*, January 21, 2006.

III

Attempts to Renovate

7

Steps in Four Directions

Attempts to renovate Hindutva have to be made in four directions: (i) Toleration, (ii) Secularism, (iii) Conversion, and (iv) Reclaiming Full God and Great Men for Man.

Toleration

Almost everyone teaches the Hindus to have toleration and extend cooperation to the minorities, particularly the Muslims. This is done both inside and outside of India. The Hindus have already been acting on such advice for several centuries in the past, so much so that the numerical strength of the Muslims, who had arrived here as aggressors, which was about one lakh or so, has now risen to 45 crores (15 crores each in the two sovereign Muslim states of Pakistan (1947) and Bangla Desh (1971) and the rest in India).[1] Among others there are about 4 crore Christians and 3 crore Sikhs. Pakistan, since its inception, has been trying to create another sovereign state of Azad Kashmir, grabbing the remaining territory of Jammu & Kashmir by proxy war, i.e., by force, infiltration and creating terror. Perhaps such persons want the Hindus to go on learning and practising 'toleration' till they end themselves or disappear from the scene or give up defending themselves.

Few have courage to teach the same lessons to the minorities.

The Hindus themselves are largely responsible for receiving such sermons. They have been living with a withdrawing, deformed and dwarfed form of Hinduism. It avoids and decries this life and this world, and while living here yearns for the indefinite next-world. The latter is told to be the indicator of superiority and identity of their Hinduism. For this, they, living at level two, have chosen the path of spirituality, non-violence and toleration. The Hindus respect poverty, meekness, humility, compassion, contentment and submission. They are always eager to resort to various ways and means to surrender their self to God and wish to become selfless. Their surrender is, firstly, before their man-made gods and goddesses, and secondly, when their prayers remain unfulfilled, they go to Almighty God.

Pre-Independence Era

When India was prosperous, affluent and well-protected in ancient times, the sages of those times meditated and thought it proper to teach the people to move towards realization of higher self or preparing for the next life. They stood for truth, non-violence, love, compassion, abnegation, toleration, penance etc. to obtain the goals of *moksha* (salvation) or self-realization. These other-worldly teachings continued for several centuries which mostly resulted in the neglect of this world—state, society and life. Spread of Buddhism, Jainism and Advaita further aggravated their other-worldliness. Only in exceptional cases, some of them could display resistance. During that period, aggressors arrived in big hordes from time to time and looted the wealth and honour of the country, and also made converts to Islam in millions. Before the advent of the Mughals, the aggressors in most cases looted the country and returned to their native lands. But, the Mughals, after the Slaves and the Afghans, settled here and ruled over India for about five hundred years. They thrust Islam upon people by force, threat and tricks. Every Muslim was to act as the soldier of Islam. There was no other way available to the subjugated people except showing toleration. After the Mughals, there were the Britishers, though different from the Mughals in matters of religion, who spread Christianity through rendering organized missionary service among the poor, depressed and the aboriginals. Before the might of the British Raj, again, there was no other way except showing toleration. During the whole freedom movement, the people of India under the leadership of Mahatma Gandhi who firmly believed in the tenet of non-violence, were finally nurtured in toleration and non-violence. The final outcome of the centuries-old toleration was the partition of India in form of Pakistan with bloodshed and hostility in the wake.

After Independence

The partition of India created two sovereign states of Islamic Pakistan and Secular India. In India, there is majority of non-Muslims, particularly the Hindus. Therefore, after India's freedom, defending and protecting the country should have been the primary duty of the Hindus. Obviously, this cannot be done only on the basis of teaching toleration to its majority on the ancient lines. In a way, those leaders and scholars who continue to do so, knowingly or unknowingly, support that loot, vandalism, life negation, military aggression and wishing India to keep where it has been. Such preachers of toleration to the Hindus on their part feel no concern for the defence of the country or to have self-respect for it. It simply shows that they feel pleasure in encouraging anti-national interests, attitudes and elements. They have little courage to extend the same lessons of toleration to the enemies of the Hindus and ask them to return their lost honour, population and property to the Hindus. They say it is not possible to undo their past acts. They are also unwilling to prepare themselves and teach them to stop such heinous happenings in future. The best course, according to them, is to follow the policy of peace, non-violence and toleration.

For the first time, the RSS tried to reverse the trend. In place of the Hindus, it advised the Muslims to seek cooperation and goodwill of the Hindu majority. However, the basic urge of the RSS also appears to tread on the beaten track. The RSS is willing to support and help the Muslims if they display goodwill towards the Hindus. It means under the leadership of RSS on finding their goodwill it would be willing to accommodate their demands. They fail to understand that it can be in form of another partition of the Indian territory. The governments in the state of Jammu & Kashmir are already moving in that direction—demand for greater autonomy. The Hindus, for the time being, are unable to envisage the result of their increasing number of demands and appear satisfied with the Muslims on showing goodwill towards them.[2]

Toleration, if it is at all required, must apply to all concerned. One-sided toleration is found counter-productive and harmful. What actually is required is protection of the rights of the individual and welfare of all by all democratic means and arrangements. In place of display of toleration, there is urgent need of effective implementation of law, efficient administration of justice, law and order and responsive and participatory democracy. As the sources of fundamentalism and terrorism mostly relate to some holy books, they cannot be fought against on the basis of the directives given by any other religion. These evils can be encountered only by secularism. Adoption of secularism at state level is fruitful for both majority and minority communities. Use of Constitution-ordained secularism in place of one-sided teaching of suicidal toleration to Hindus is the best way to combat all forms of communalism and maintain peace in state and society.

Toleration should not mean pleasing minorities even at the cost of suffering heavy loss to one's own person, group or community. Basically, it is against rule of law, spirit of justice and prevention of crime. On the one hand, it deprives the Hindus of their legitimate rights, honour and effective participation in democratic governance, and on the other hand, it encourages the minorities to indulge in injustice and crime. Thus, more the Hindus show toleration, more the minorities inflict tyranny and misbehaviour to them.

Secularism

A holistic Hindu mind when he claims to cherish the reality as Brahma and Brahma as reality, he is greater than any other secularist of western variety, and also a greater spiritualist than any one of the Upanishadic adherents. He lives in the total whole. Such Hindu mind feels authorized by his total dharma to deal with the worldly matters at secular or temporal level. While dealing with worldly matters in a secular manner, he is still a hundred per cent Hindu mind. A truly Hindu mind does not confine himself or have preference only with spiritual matters, or with living at 'secular' level. He has both worlds (in fact one) in his hands.[3]

The only way to strengthen the Hindutva ideology and the Hindus is the adoption of secularization at political and governmental levels. The Hindus should assimilate secularism in such a manner that it appears as their identification. Only secularism, with primacy to worldly consideration, can save Hinduism from decay or extinction. This understanding must be learnt by the Hindutva believers at their earliest. This matter may not be confined to the Hindus only. But everyone should work in that direction. More than any one only Hinduism provides wholesome environment—material and spiritual —for the all-round development and welfare of man and mankind. In the long run this perspective would benefit both the majority and minority communities. The Hindutva people for their own safety and progress should now enthrone it by accepting a prominent position to it.

The Constitution, neglecting majority community and its values, has granted priority to the minority community and their interests and created serious imbalance. There are many provisions which if used make the minority community stronger than the majority community. With this trend there is possibility that the majority community would be compelled to accept another partition. Opponents of the Hindutva are encouraging them to do so. Provisions (Articles 28-30) under Right to Freedom of Religion relate to minorities go in many ways against secularism. Fathers of the Indian Constitution have not only granted the status of fundamental rights to the rights of minorities, even the Supreme Court of India in many cases has reinforced and elaborated them. The only way now left for the majority community is to accept and act upon it.

There is great imbalance between the requirements of secularism and the grant of rights and opportunities to the minorities. But, the same rights can be claimed, though the Constitution makes no specific mention, by the majority which may resort to religious extremism to the same extent. That clearly creates a situation of communal tension and riots. The only way to counter this imbalance is to resort to positive secularism in an effective manner.[4] In case secularism is not put to action, rights to religious freedom tend to open the floodgates of extremism, terrorism and fundamentalism. When the sources of fundamentalism or extremism relate to God, some Holy Books or prominent leaders of religion, it cannot be restrained by any other similar pattern of fundamentalism. The two opposing forms of fundamentalism connected with their respective Gods, Holy Books and leaders of religion usually end in communal riots, civil war or partition of the country. If one of them has accepted the path of peace, toleration and non-violence, only that has to yield to the other religious fundamentalism or 'jehadi' fanaticism, and has to face injustice, untruth and humiliation. The only just solution to the problem lies in the adoption of positive, strong and clear form of secularism. Only secularism can objectively separate good from evil in the society and punish the evil doers. However, secularism can be effectively exercised only by the state and its agencies. In the absence of a secular state, religions feel free to cross over the boundaries of law and morality, and put the lives of common men in jeopardy. If the government is concerned with secularism in a half-hearted manner, notwithstanding constitutional provisions, it remains unable to restrain religious fundamentalism which makes claims to work on the authority of God. Therefore, the urgent need is to constitute state and government on secular basis. Secularism accepts only the authority of man and seeks his welfare. When there is religious freedom, pure and simple religions like Jainism and Buddhism continue to tread on their usual path of peace and toleration, but followers of religions like Islam and others may consider it a congenial opportunity to indulge in fundamentalism, aggression and violence. They are able to do so under the cover of the Constitution itself. It is obvious that anti-social, illegal and violent activities caused by the extremist elements of a religion cannot be stopped without resorting to an effective form of secularism exercisable by the state. That can be done only at the level of the government of a country.

Organizing a Secular Government

The Indian Constitution has not construed any special provisions to organize the government on strong and effective secularism both at the central and the state levels.[5] It has not made laws to forestall anti-secular steps usually resorted to by political leaders while seeking power. Occurrences of communal riots time and again confirm lack of understanding of secularism on the part of political leaders of this country. In India, so far, secularism has found place only at the level of state and its Constitution. Secularism has to be operationalized at the level of government. The government can be made directly responsible to administer it. Depending on judiciary for this purpose is not enough. It has also to be seen that the secular provisions are not abused by the non-secular forces.

Sometimes, a few political leaders apprehend that after launching of secularism they might lose power on not getting majority at the hustings. On the contrary, leaders resorting to bigotry, extremism and communalism may win favour of the electorates. All such eventualities must be effectively checkmated beforehand, and not allowed to happen. Law must ban leaders and their political parties contesting elections on the basis of religion, particular faith or sect. The Hindutva leaders also should take a vow immediately to adopt a 'higher' or 'superior' form of secularism. The vow demands that they should rise above all other secular and non-secular political parties and pursue 'super-secularism'. They would adopt super-secularism when operating at the state level. Briefly it means that (i) a minister, MP, MLA or a member of an elected body would have no connection with any religious institution, practice, festival or demonstration; (ii) political leaders not observing this prohibition would be deemed to have been immediately and automatically removed from their office and their charge taken over by their superiors/subordinate office-holders; (iii) public servants after their appointment to an office would lose it in case they are found to instigate a particular caste/sub-caste, language or culture to commit violence against other communities; and (iv) everyone would have to subscribe to an oath of allegiance to the supremacy of the Constitution of India. In the end, the state shall gradually withdraw from having control over and administration or management of all type of religious institutions, except in case of emergency or by the verdict of a court for a limited period, and hand it over to the leaders of the community concerned or to some authority constituted for this purpose.

Conversion

A five-judge division bench of the Supreme Court under Chief Justice A.N. Ray has already decided that Article 25(1) only allows a person to profess and propagate one's own religion but does not permit him to convert some one else's religion. To convert other's religion is not a fundamental right.

Law in some states ensures every member of a religious community that none of them can be asked to convert his religion under any fraud, force or allurement. It disallows a mischief monger, at his own instance or at the direction of outside elements to spread communalism or carry on anti-social activities by demanding conversions. Thus, it protects the followers of all religions from falling prey to racket of conversion. This law defends position and interest of all religions. It should be enacted by all the states and the Centre. But, unfortunately, its enactment has been demanded only by the Hindutva organizations like the BJP, Shiv Sena, VHP, RSS and the like. It serves interests of all religions and religious communities.

However, the ordinance or similar law enacted in other states does constrain the business of individuals, sects or organizations that get crores of dollars in lieu of converting millions of the innocent, illiterate, ignorant and poverty-stricken people of India. The donors send money for this very purpose on the basis of past and prospective performance of the managers of conversion. Till today, these managers must have received billions of dollars as can be calculated on the basis of ever-increasing size of their activities, number of persons converted, needs and skills. Opening of schools, hospitals, orphanages and woman homes, installing of social services, distributing cheap books, leaflets etc. are mostly geared towards the goal of greater number of conversion. Barring a few cases, all conversions are mostly based on helplessness, poverty, illiteracy and need of the affected people. In place of ideas, the managers often use force, fraud and allurements on them. If these conversions are effectively stopped, business, trade, racket or profession of thousands of missionaries would be affected and with the decrease in the number of conversions, they would not get that much of amount, honour and recognition from their donors. In fact, a silent, unknown and innocuous war is being launched by the missionaries and their distant donors against the Indian people for the last several centuries.

But only a legal ban on conversions on grounds of allurement, force and fraud and exploitation is not enough to nip evil in bud.[6] Their causes, processes and impact must also be known to all to stop them altogether. The magnitude of such illegal, anti-constitutional and anti-national conversions would be known only when a survey is conducted at the central and state levels of all conversions done after India attained independence. The proposed step should involve study of causes, means and methods, sources, structures of various organizations engaged in conversions, and their impact on society and polity. When the real perpetrators are finally known, they can be suitably punished under law, their financial sources stopped and properties confiscated.

However, even this investigation conducted at the state or communitarian level would not serve any purpose if the related religious communities do not organize suitable rehabilitation programme for the return of converted. The converted people, at their own, should be free to join their previous religions or community, and also any other if they like. However, they would like to do so only when the problems of poverty, inequality, unemployment and lack of respect to them are properly addressed to by the welcoming religions. None of them would like to return to their earlier religion or community simply because they formerly belonged to it. Particularly, the Hindutva people who are considering this law as most urgent and necessary for their survival should bear in mind that these separated people would hardly like to remain in Hinduism unless:

(i) Hinduism is fully renovated and made attractive, respectable and workable. As the Hindus living at the lower rung of the social hierarchy find Hinduism exploitative, degrading and painful, they desire to get rid of it at the earliest.
(ii) Birth-based caste and sub-caste system is abolished and all persons including women having low social status are treated equally with respect to others.
(iii) All the persons at the lower levels should be provided social and economic security, particularly in old age and unemployment.
(iv) The managers of communities willing to re-admit the converted people must undertake responsibility of marriage of their children when they attain adulthood in social groups desired by them.
(v) People freed from their present religions would hardly like to be burdened with unnecessary and complicated and wasteful rituals, taboos and traditions after rejoining their earlier and new religion.
(vi) The new religion must be able to teach is followers to isolate and punish the corrupt and evil elements, train and equip them to fight against the perpetrators of false, undesirable irrational religions.
(vii) It must be a life-engaging and life-assertive religion, eschewing evils of withdrawal, submission and other-worldliness.

Hindutva leaders hardly realize that their religion does not pass these tests. It does not have what other religions, particularly Christianity, have to offer. It has neither money, nor livelihood or social security to give to the downtrodden people, which they direly need. It does not give what Hindutva can easily give to them, such as (a) respect as human being, (b) liberal and plural approach to socio-economic matters, (c) compassion, (d) message of *karma* as way to worship of God and salvation, and (e) will to fight against irrationalism.

However, it can be reiterated that even after the passing of this ordinance as law meant for the whole of India, there would be little change either (i) in the present form and condition of Hinduism, and its millions of the tribal, downtrodden and dalit people, and also (ii) in the ways, means and operations of missionaries who would go on converting their people into Christianity or some other religions at their own will or under pressure from outside elements or transnational organizations. As usual, they would employ the same means and methods, continue to render social and educational services and behave in a manner that the neglected sections of the Hindus, being poor, helpless and exploited, would hardly refuse their conversions for those gains. They would do so despite hue and cry from the Hindu leaders as well as punitive hand of law.

Reclaiming God and Great Men for Man

Originally, matters of faith were related to spiritual development and realization of God or salvation. But, for the last several centuries, faith has been commercialized in almost all the religions of the world. This commercialization of faith has appeared at three levels: (i) relations between man and God, (ii) about conceptualization of God Himself, and (iii) super-naturalization of great men. Commercialization of faith at these levels has mostly hit and harmed the Hindus. Majority of the Hindus, being backward, poor, illiterate and helpless, have fallen prey to the evil of 'commercialization of faiths'. Followers of religions can be saved only by rectifying and putting the faith back to human use or precisely, by practising 'humanitarianism'.

Commercialization of Faith

Every person to some extent knows something about relationship existing between man and God. In this area, he also seeks guidance from some great man of his liking. But he remains uncertain and lost in-between. His uncertainty is exploited by the vested interests. From the very dawn of human civilization, there has been a class of persons who exploited their assumed or imagined knowledge of the relationship among man and God. They can be considered as religion-related brokers, middlemen or intermediaries pretending to take devotees and aspirants to doors of God. They really lack actual experience of divinity but claim to possess it. Those who have real knowledge or divine experience are a class apart and rarely make any such claim. They are literally free from all worldly desires, e.g., wealth, power or fame. On the contrary, the brokers of religion in due course of time very skilfully turn their knowledge of that esoteric relationship into a lucrative business, profession or expertise. They appear as experts in getting the desires of a man realized through divinity of gods and goddesses by performing *puja*, *havan*, recitation of *mantras* etc. Such trends have appeared in almost all religions of the world. In some religious communities, as in India, such activities have turned into a big evil. As in case of other religions, this evil has eaten into the vitals of the Hindu community. This evil has ruined and emasculated the Hindus considerably. The intermediaries accordingly have been teaching the Hindus that they can approach God or Gods through prayers, *havans*, *yagnas*, recitation of some holy books, repetitions of *mantras*, observing fasts, offering charity etc. and get all their work done or difficulties removed automatically on the basis of power generated by those acts. These acts can be performed either by themselves or through experts like priests or other religious professionals. They claim to have the capacity, knowledge, expertise and art to invoke divinity, grace or power of some gods (ghost or spirit) and make something impossible as possible. For this the client has to make very small effort, contribution or undergo some suffering. These intermediaries are mostly known as *purohits*, *pujaris*, priests, saints, *siddhas*, godmen, *tantrikas*, *gurus*, *bhaktas*, *yagna* experts, *kazis*, *mullas* etc. They have been claiming to practice this profession for the last several centuries.

Unaware of their insult to God they concoct mysterious stories that God incarnates to help his devotees and comes down upon earth in human form. As if God is not permitted by some one to help or rescue from distress directly. They go on elaborating myths, imagery, beliefs, farsighted intelligence or sheer hypnotic experience that God the Almighty has incarnated himself in form of a human being to do some great thing. As if God is unable to help the devotees directly. They claim that God has endowed someone with his divine power or sent his own messenger or representative or someone has caught his glimpse and attained Godhood. It is never made clear that how could they know about this entire affair. Such myths or make-beliefs do not withstand for ever, and are ultimately exposed by another set of religious leaders. However, the common man, despite exposure from intelligent people, continues to believe in what was revealed or taught earlier in any form, and hardly cares to think for changing their former unverified beliefs. Great beneficiaries of such habits of the people are the consecutive successors of the founders of such religions. This is the area where these intermediaries find open arena for their operations, thus, strengthen their hold over masses.

Man-Made God

Only thinking men would realize that it is direct insult of God or the Almighty when one says that he (i) incarnates himself in human form to avert some big evil or (ii) sends his messenger or representative to teach people to be good or (iii) takes *avatar* or (iv) enters the body of a devotee or reformer to enable him to face the devil. When one utters such things, intuitively or on any other ground, he hardly remains a person knowing the power of God. He simply concocts stories or puts his imagination in compelling words, poetry or *bhajans*. God himself is powerful enough to do all those things directly as he has been visibly doing them in case of nature.

In their habit of depending upon God, the Hindus have amputated even God according to their wishes and likings. This enables them to make the practice of their profession simple and easier. Their God is mostly made of attributes like pity, pardon, sympathy, repentance, abnegation, self-satisfaction, toleration etc. The Hindus worship, meditate, pray, praise and dream of God having only these attributes. They are completely unconcerned towards other equally important constituents of God. The God of the Hindus is made of attributes what they prefer or like, and not of what actually are his. Thus, their God is artefact, incomplete, amputated and subjective. They have suppressed or separated his other equally important attributes, such as destruction, death, anger, force, violence and the like. Some of their smaller gods and goddesses also are equipped with arms and weapons, which are merely showpieces or are used after long sufferings and heart-melting prayers of devotees. The Hindu *bhaktas* are supposed to learn only to tolerate, pray and surrender. God, accordingly, does everything, inclusive of incarnating in human form (*avatar*) in the world to protect saints and redeem the desecrated dharma. The *bhaktas* (devotees) are simply to pray, praise and sing songs of his might. The Hindus depend on the grace and kindness of divinity. As they are not encouraged to make efforts and exert in all possible ways they remain unable to fulfil their desires, aspirations and needs. They are asked to follow the path of peace, self-satisfaction and toleration, and are left to depend on fate. Under such dispensation of God the Hindus are asked to act on their long tradition of toleration and contentment.

Deification of Great Men

These intermediaries, taking steps further, have converted most of the great Hindu heroes, from human beings to gods and goddesses, and declared them as incarnation of God himself. Following similar lines, they also assert in having the capacity of using the power of the soul of a great or good man after the latter passes away. In this process of divinization they have put their heroes or great men in form of statues, and started adoring and worshipping them in temples. The moment the heroes are transformed into ritualized gods and goddesses, they stop inspiring the people to perform brave deeds alike them. Worshipping them makes the Hindus merely devotees (*bhaktas*) who repeat pious *mantras* and prayers with great pomp and show. They do so in the hope that these gods and goddesses would be pleased and do their desired work, such as healing diseases, helping to get food and protection, defeating the enemies and so on. After some time, performing duty or doing work in place of worship is considered as a sign of disbelief in these gods. This type of understanding has become almost a habit or second nature of the Hindus.

These great men have been the best examples of human attainment, but are now treated as God's agents to perform desired acts or things. Almost all great heroes of the past are regularly worshipped as gods. This has traded a death blow to Hinduism as a religion of man meant for man. Today, they have millions of gods and goddesses to worship them and look after their pictures and statues and avoid all types of labour.

In order to boost this profession, these middlemen encourage masses and individuals to build more and more mosques, *dargahas*, *mathhas*, *vihars*, *gurudwaras* and temples. In temples they ask devotees to consecrate statues of gods and goddesses, perform big and complicated *yagnas* and many kinds of religious ceremonies. They sometimes defy the rules of the state, society or conventional morality. They remain untouched even when their state or society stands dishonoured, dismembered and subjugated. They are more concerned with their earnings through commercialization of faiths of the people. They teach the people that everything can be done by invoking some spirit or soul. In place of doing hard work, seeking knowledge, and producing wealth, the followers have to remain satisfied with less troublesome acts like devotional attendance in temples, making some contribution towards religious celebration and the like.

All this has made the followers fatalistic, parasitic, dependent and lethargic. The Hindus, particularly in the countryside, appear as God-oriented, inactive and life-negating. They depend on these gods to get their needs and necessities fulfilled and to obtain protection and prosperity. As regards the increasing number of temples, even majority of these religious places are not even properly looked after. In some cases they have turned into haven of vices. Still, the Hindu leaders, knowing the people's bent of mind, encourage them to have more and more temples and various forms of religious places. Constructing religious places is like politico-religious opium administered to the people.

Reclaiming God and Human Heroes

There are only two ways to get rid of this plight: One, by exposing these intermediaries and by dismantling their structures of commercialization of faiths. People should be brought closer to reality by using reason, science and technology. Two, by discovering, recovering and reclaiming Full God with some understanding of his immense powers. His powers do not need the presence of any human instrumentality or of intermediaries. Similarly, all great men transformed as gods and goddesses should be freed from the clutches of intermediaries and taken back as ideal human beings. We have to emancipate them for the coming generations. After humanizing them they would be able to get inspiration from them and follow their heroic deeds. Presently, there is complete stand off between the deified Hindu past and needs of an inspiring present. Conservative devotees of Hindu gods and goddesses may continue worshipping them as gods and goddesses, but for the rejuvenation of the new generation of the Hindus efforts should urgently be made to humanize all important gods and goddesses. During the last several years, big statues are being erected with great pomp and show which later on may be converted into a new kind of temples. This would entail huge expenditure on their protection and maintenance. In case they are broken by some miscreants, it could turn into one of the new causes of communal tension. The proposed conversion of gods into humans would stop such untoward incidents.

Other communities too, if they feel the need to do so, can also make way to reclaim their God, gods and great men, separated from them by their religion-related brokers. There is urgent need of making this world more human than leave it to mysterious divinity distanced from them by the middlemen.

Notes

1. Acharya Dharmendra of VHP said that those who do not comply with family planning programmes must be deprived of citizenship rights. The than leaders did not accept 'transfer of population' plan put by Jinnah. Muslims who were about three crores presently are over fifteen crores. See *Rajasthan Patrika*, September 16, 2004.
2. See, the J&K Permanent Residents (Disqualification) Bill, 2004 passed by the Mufti Government.
3. See, level-one and five in Introduction, Chapter 1.
4. S.L. Verma, *Theory of Positive Secularism*, Jaipur: Rawat Publications, 1986.

   The RSS in its Kanyakumari resolution passed by its national executive urged the Indian government to lodge protest with the Pope for his uncalled for exhortation to Christian missionaries to carry on their campaign of conversions. The resolution condemned it as a direct challenge to the sovereignty of Bharat. It pointed out that it was force, fraud or allurement was at the root of mass conversion, which was rampant in the conversion. *Times of India*, July 7, 2003. The RSS has done very right, but it should work for the reconversion of the converts undergone conversion in this manner. Let me add that only 'force, fraud or allurement' is not the cause behind these conversions. One another very important cause of conversion is the confusion relating to the tenets of Hindu religion as well as maltreatment of the lower class people.

5. The forces of false or pseudo-secularism, since the days of Congress rule in India have been very strong. For example, the subject of a Uniform Civil Code, which would remove special religion-based provisions for Muslims and Christians from the Indian Constitution, is thus one of the main political planks of Hindutva. Followers contend that in a secular democracy it makes little sense to allow Muslims, for example, to marry more than once, but to prosecute Hindus for doing the same. Muslims are also funded for the Hajj, a pilgrimage to Mecca, while Hindutvawadis claim they are accorded no similar privilege for their own pilgrimages. Recently, the ill-conceived move of the Congress government in Andhra Pradesh to grant reservation to Muslims has been struck down by the Supreme Court. But it lays bare the Congress mentality. In a recent Muslim rally, organized by the Jamait-ul-Ulema-e-Hind in Delhi, a demand was raised for reserving posts for Muslims in government jobs, college admissions, legislative assemblies and in parliament. This is on the lines of the demands of the Muslim League in pre-partition India and the result of that cleavage is for everybody to see. Vjay Kumar Malhotra, One over others, *Hindustan Times*, July 20, 2005; Again, there is plan to amend AMU Act. The reservation of seats for Muslim students is likely to continue at AMU despite the Allahabad High Court's order terming the university a non-minority institution on October 4, 2005. The Congress minister of UPA government Mani Shanker Aiyer managed that metaphorically and with a great degree of cleverness when he removed that plaque to Veer Savarkar, one of the original bearers of that flag, at the cellular jail in the Andamans with one dedicated to Gandhi. Once the BJP cried foul, he said he wasn't disrespectful to Savarkar, merely giving Gandhi the respect due to him. *Hindustan Times*, January 23, 2005; The UPA government plans to track all textbooks for convents, Madrasas, RSS (Rashtriya Swayamsevak Sangh) run schools on radar: the Ministry of Human Resource Development decided to set up a Textbook Regulatory Council to regulate education in madrasas and missionary, RSS run and private schools. Once the council starts working it will have the power to act on complaints or take suo moto action to summon any textbook outside the government system for scrutiny. It will also be able to get books withdrawn from school. See *Hindustan Times*, October 20, 2005.
6. Tamil Nadu Prohibition of Forcible Conversion of Religion Ordinance, 2002.

8

Majoritarianism and Opinionization

Since the day India attained freedom, Indian politics has been moving along with the roles of 'majority' and 'minority' communities. If one set of political leaders threatens minorities by exaggerating the dominance of the majority community, the other one instigates the majority community to save itself against the danger of minority community. All this is being done without probing into the existing socio-political demographic reality. Everyone from ruling to opposition sides has fallen prey to this colossus misunderstanding, causing immense loss to the Indian nation. 'Majoritarianism' has become a mystery. Those who blindly bank upon majoritarianism and neglect minorities lose ground, and those who out of frustration leave it and surrender to minorities also do not win. Therefore, reality lying behind majoritarianism must be made clear.

All this has happened due to confusion arising out of the mistaken use of the terms—'majority' and 'minority'. These are opinion words, which indicate greater or less number of people holding opinion on a particular issue or subject. This number may go on changing, turning a 'majority' into 'minority' at one time and a 'minority' into 'majority' at another time. Use of these words may be proper for topics of immediate or short-term interest. But, for better and deeper understanding, these words should be explicated or elongated respectively as 'majority opinion group' and 'minority opinion group'. There is constant change in the size and number of persons holding opinion on some issue. But democracy does not operate on short-term arrangements. Democracies work on constant and viable support from communities formed on the basis of permanent values.

But stable majority or minority opinion on specific topics, issues and world-views may permanently reside in particular communities. Such communities might be permanently formed on the bases of religion, ethnicity, language, culture, region and political goals. Close association or assimilation with them connects a 'majority' or a 'minority' with specific groups and transforms into 'communities'. It is done through the process of opinionization or idea-ization. Constant 'opinionization' or 'idea-ization' consolidates opinion groups into communities. Opinionization spread with inculcation of ideas based on reason, emotion or interest. Its purpose is to bring out identity of views on some common cause for action or decision. It may create temporary or permanent impression in the minds of man. Assimilation of ideas converts a 'majority' or 'minority' opinion into 'majority community' or 'minority community' (*bahusankhyak* samudaya, (बहुसंख्यक समुदाय) or 'minority community' (*alpasankhyak* samudaya (अल्पसंख्यक समुदाय). The use of the terms *'bahusankhyak* (बहुसंख्यक) and *'alpasankhyak'* (अल्पसंख्यक) connote respectively larger and smaller 'communities'. But commonly known words 'majority' and 'minority' simply reflect size or number of people holding 'opinion' with reference to a particular issue.

In view of the need of a majority to support the edifice of Indian democracy, a large number of people try and claim that there is already a majority in India which is constituted out of some permanent values. They think that there is a democracy-supporting majority in India. It is popularly addressed as 'majoritarianism'. This term is often equated with the Hindus who consider them to be the majority. But all do not agree with them. They challenge the very concept of 'majoritarianism'. According to them, such majority community never existed in the past. Had there been any such Hindu community, the invaders who came in very small number could never have succeeded against them and ruled over India for over six to seven hundred years. The same success was achieved by the British rulers after the fall of the Mughal empire.

Challenge of Majoritarianism

For the last five decades most of the communities of India have been struggling for or against the phantom of 'majoritarianism'. On the basis of their past impression, they equate 'majoritarianism' with Hinduism or Hindu community. But, they fail to trace out the factors responsible for making up this community. The Supreme Court of India did not find any one specific factor. However, some people find religion, language and culture among these factors. When 'religion' is kept in view, it would be found that there is no such Hindu community believing in one particular religion or faith. In fact, the Supreme Court tried its hard to find some common religion of the Hindus, and came to the conclusion that Hinduism or Hindutva is not a particular religion. The Hindus are divided into thousands of religions, sects and *panths* etc., which often are contradictory and inconsistent with each other. Followers of Ram, Krishna, Ganesh, Durga, Bhairon etc. in the past have even waged wars against each other. Their faiths, ethos, ways of worship, dresses and dining, facial prints etc. have differed. The Sanatanis, the Arya Samajis, the Buddhists, the Jains, the Brahmos and the like are strangers among themselves on philosophical and religious grounds. From the viewpoint of 'language' as the base, we see the people of India using more than 290 languages and over 2,000 dialects. Languages of north are not only different from the southern languages, but in some cases their users are hostile against each other. Already in the past, the country has suffered from many language riots.

The people of India do not have one specific culture. People are very different from each other. Looking to their differences from the moment of birth to death, in matters of thoughts, dresses, social customs, marriage restraints and the like, they can hardly be put into one particular group. The Hindus were never one community at least for the last two thousand years. This can be witnessed by the presence of hundreds of castes, sub-castes and sub-sub-castes within one caste group. At state level, over one-third of the Hindus are formally categorized as SCs (Scheduled Castes) and STs (Scheduled Tribes). Out of the rest, there are over 70 per cent people divided into several thousand castes, who are now known as OBCs (Other Backward Classes). Under the compulsion of the Supreme Court verdict they are granted only 27 per cent reservation. The former have 15 and 7.5

per cent reservations. These groups and classes are already divided into separate castes and communities. All worship different gods, have separate saints and genealogies and myths. They hardly have any common element to bind them. Some of them even do not like to call themselves as 'Hindu'. Thus, there is no Hindu community as such. Therefore, addressing the Hindus as a majority community is a myth and wishful thinking. Their presence cannot be identified as 'majoritarianism'. On the basis of available facts, majoritarianism is merely a ghost, at the most a contrived story or a myth. It continues on the basis of Hindu-named groups of the Hindu community that existed perhaps some centuries ago. It is sheer politics and untruth to put it as a majority community.

Some vested interests have resurrected that 'ghost' either to make a show of strength or to threaten the minorities for pressing them to join their side. The non-ruling groups and parties encourage the minorities to prepare and fight against their contrived Hindu dominance. Considering them as guardians of minority interests, they go on concocting stories about the exploitation and repression of the minorities by the Hindus. In this manner, they try to alienate them from the mainstream of democratic politics. In fact, among various communities in India, there is not even one single group which can be considered as 'majority' community. Sometimes, standing against the hostile minority communities, the Hindus give impression of being a united community while in practice they have never done so. Many large groups do bear the name of 'Hindu' and are attributed as the Hindus, but are not individually a Hindu 'majority community' on the basis of ground realities. These Hindu-named groups have members from some hundreds to millions but no group can be considered as a majority community. There are five to ten big communities of the Hindus, but none is bigger than the largest minority community or have more than half of the population of India. Normally, the Hindus are a bulk of many minorities.

After ascertaining the actual condition of the Hindu-named groups, it is now necessary to look into the realities of the minority communities in India. It would help us in knowing how these minorities hiding their real face are playing politics under the cover of 'majoritarianism'.

Condition of Minority Communities

Muslims, Christians and Sikhs are the known major minorities of India. Everyone of them is from five to ten fold bigger than any of the biggest Hindu-named minorities or groups. To illustrate, the purest and the top placed sacred Brahmins consider themselves in practice separate and over and above from other Hindu communities, but their number is less than 40 lakh in the whole of India. This number is sub-divided into different languages, regions, faiths, sects, and world-views. In comparison to them, known minorities are about Muslims 14 crore, Christians 5 crore and Sikhs 3 crore.

In comparison to Hindu-named minorities, the known largest minorities of India are ideologically monolith and socially well-organized. These minorities mostly originated from following the teachings of one Messenger, Guru or God Incarnate. They further expanded on the basis of conversion, use of force and propagation. Most of these teachings are known, written, specific and binding. None is permitted to entertain doubt, revise or challenge. Followers of all climes are required to read, meditate, study, preach, propagate and follow them in letter and spirit. None is allowed, particularly in case of Islam, to raise any doubt or argue against it. If someone indulges in that direction, he is entitled to be punished by any other co-follower of his community or the Islamic state. Followers of these exclusive religions are required to keep away from all other religious discourses, preaching and literature. Most of them stand for one particular language which they regard it as the base of their culture and religion. Earlier, in India, they were a few hundred, now they are over several crores. All of these minorities have obtained protection from the Indian Constitution, which has further been upheld by the Supreme Court (2002). The bulk of Hindu minorities, mistaken under the false notion of one Hindu community, have not been provided such protection. The Hindu minorities at this level of consideration stand next to large minorities.

For example, the Muslim minority community is bigger than the size of any other community. All the Hindu minority communities lag far behind the three larger minority communities. Among these three largest minority communities, the Muslim community in India having 14 crore is the largest one. Christians and Sikhs are about 3 and 1 crore respectively. It has been pointed out that Christians are divided into seven or eight prominent sects. Biggest of them are Protestants and Roman Catholics. So are the Sikhs divided into four or five important groups or sub-communities? The Muslims too have two broad groupings—Shias and Sunnis, besides several other smaller ones, their approximate number respectively being 11, 3 and 1 crore. But, their ideological, religious, social and communitarian bind of the structure leaves all other communities far behind. The Muslims have grown from merely one lakh to 45 crore in the entire Indian sub-continent. Despite strong opposition from all other communities, it had been successful in partitioning the British India and obtaining Pakistan within a short period of six years. Even after the dismemberment of Pakistan in 1972 and formation of Bangla Desh, the Muslim minority in India remains as powerful and solid as it was earlier. Indian Muslims, besides Pakistan, have 56 Muslim countries behind their back to support them. Similarly, from the point of view of external religious support, the Christian minority community, compared with other minority communities, also does not lag behind. The whole of the West and the North American countries stand by and continue to help it. In this respect, the Hindu-named minority communities, even if they appear larger than all together, lag far behind the two minority communities—Muslims and Christians.

Opinionization

Democracy requires opinion groups. It necessitates transformation of majority or minority communities into majority or minority opinion groups on specific issues. Democracy demands operations at opinion levels. But communities are made of structures which may obstruct opinion formation. However, community structures are not immutable. Structures of community can be loosened and relaxed by renovation of cultural values, reinterpretation of orthodox segments of religion and philosophy, modernization of norms and practices, and reforms in patterns of social control and relations. It can usually be done in the name of Christ, Buddha and Nanak. Such efforts are further supported by forms of economy, education and institutions. They can be reinforced by forces of science and technology.

Transformation occurs even at the structural level of communities. Structures, big and small, undergo change. Even if a community is structured on some permanent basis, it evolves and cannot remain standstill. The majority community of the Hindus of the long past has split asunder into myriad of namesake Hindu communities—big and small. Other large minorities too, over a period of time, to some extent, have divided into several groups and communities. Structures change as a result of constant pressure of opinionization. When opinionization ossifies, it turns into structure. This phenomenon of transformation of communities specially affects the fate of political parties. The latter tries to remain constantly connected with some majority or big minority community. They also try to keep the structure of that community intact if not augment it. While doing so, sometimes, they lose their grip over the actual demographic reality. Owing to their conservative attitude or ego they continue to consider a previously known majority or minority still as a majority or a minority community. Blinded by their own narrow interests or some misconceived notions, they remain unable to see the changing reality, and fail to understand the problem. They forget that majority or minority communities at their own do not remain as they were earlier. One has to make continuous efforts for a long time to maintain the same structure or towards its enlargement in size, number and influence. Otherwise, their earlier unity might fructify into diversities and unyielding autonomies.

Opinionization of Communities

Opinionization is inculcation of new ideas and values. Transformation of communities is done by using the process of 'opinionization' which can be called also as 'ideation' or 'moralization'. It appears in two forms: (a) ossified, and (b) dynamic. Opinionization consolidates through constant propaganda, indoctrination and education and ossifies in form of community structures. In this process, the expansion of 'opinion' or 'ideas' or 'moral values' is made the basis of structural transformation or change of communities.

But communities do have their dynamic parts. In these areas, they are vague, vacant and uncertain. Dynamic opinionization moves in these areas very speedily and begins to take them under its influence. It may take the community as a whole or a part of it under its dominance. Communities change into opinion groups. A big community may turn into small opinion groups, or a small but whole community may come out in form of a big opinion group. Operationally, the total process may be captioned as 'opinionization' of majority community (structure) into a 'majority opinion group' and of minority community (structure) into a 'minority opinion group': *bahusankhyan* (बहुसंख्यन) of *bahusankhyak* (बहुसंख्यक) community and *alpasankhyan* (अल्पसंख्यन) of *alpasankhyak* (अल्पसंख्यक) community. When opinionization hardens it turns into structure. It is an action process of majority and minority formation.

On structural side of communities, the members of the collectivities continue to stick to their permanent bases like religion, sect, style of worship, language, culture etc. and try to defend and protect them against all odds. Sometimes, such attempts—ideological orthodoxies, tend to make the structure of that community still smaller in size and effect. For example, the Rajput community in the direction of maintaining their purity, superiority and status went on shortening their size, and were left only with a few Sisodia or Hara Rajputs. In this process, the bases of religion, caste, language etc. remain intact, but clinging to them begins to alienate periphery of the community.

In *dynamic* opinionization, there is inculcation of new ideas, norms and values. It may overwhelm, first its own community, and later on, attract other communities. It may so happen only at structural or opinion level. At opinion level, expansion is often temporary limited to issues at stake. Size of opinion groups may increase or decrease on the basis of adoption of new ideas and moral values. Majoritarianism, which means majority communitarianism, moves towards majority opinionism, and minoritarianism or minority communitarianism into minority opinionism. On particular issues, communities begin to act as opinion groups.

There can be two stages, inter and intra, of transformation of majority into majority opinionism and of minority into minority opinionism. In the first stage, people belonging to preconceived narrow notions or confinement to their shrunken size of micro communities, smaller sub-castes or sects in the Hindu context, cross over their earlier boundaries on specific issues, and enlarge their narrow interests or ideas to that of the larger group or community. They can also go back and remain a community. In the second stage, their opinionization enlarges further and crosses over the structural boundaries of their communities, and by adopting new ideas and values spreads over to broader regions, nation and state. A minority community like the Muslims too, on the basis of broader ideas or values, can envelope the whole of the Muslim community passing through region, nation and state. They do not remain merely Sunnis or Shias. This process can be captioned as 'minority opinionization' of a 'minority community'. It can also cover the whole world. The key to this change is the widening of opinionization of communities into larger opinion-entities. They may retain their identity both as 'community' and as 'opinion group'; and also move towards either side. Democratization makes them move towards opinion side.

Opinionization is the weapon of politics. Political leaders like Subhash and Jai Prakash have made effective use of it. But, both of them can be wielded by one man as did Gandhi during freedom movement. They can be used by two separate or closely related agencies: one might be engaged in structural renovation like the RSS, the Arya Samaj etc. and the other can be undertaken by the political parties and the NGOs. The latter remain connected with spreading opinion and ideas for gaining or opposing power. Politics uses the weapon of dynamic opinionization. It can encourage or accelerate the process for a good cause or exploit it to serve vested interests. Though by nature opinionization may appear temporary and ephemeral, yet it can overwhelm the community and ossify in form of its structures. Outdated structures do obstruct the flow of opinionization. But power opinionization can overpower each and every structure of a community.

Opinionization during Freedom Movement

In the Indian context, fate of the political parties has been found attached with ossified and dynamic opinionization of communities. A proper understanding of this process and action on it has determined their success and failure in electoral politics. This phenomenon of transformation of communities specially affected the fate of political parties. The political parties in the past have tried to remain constantly connected with some big or small minority community. They have also endeavoured to keep the structure of that community intact if not augment it. While doing so, sometimes, they have lost sight of its actual demographic reality. Owing to their conservative attitude or own ego, they continued to consider that community as it was seen sometime ago. They forget that majority or minority communities at their own do not remain intact. One has to make continuous efforts for a long time to maintain the same structure or towards its enlargement in size, number and influence.

Long before, freedom movement of India came up, there were majority and minority communities based on some permanent variables. There were several hundred autonomous and separate communities in the country. It was under the leadership of Mahatma Gandhi that an attempt was made to convert mega group of all 'communities' into one 'opinion group'. Initially, Gandhi ventured to include all the communities of India. He wanted to transform all the communities into one solid structure of nation or through opinionization of nationalism. But he could operate only at the opinionization level and could not penetrate the structures of all the communities. He through the Indian National Congress tried his best to opinionize or opinionate all the Indian communities but could succeed largely in case of the Hindus communities only. Opinionization of the Hindu communities by him took about 10 to 20 years. Muslim leaders like M.A. Jinnah did that work for their community within 5 to 7 years. Gandhi's opinionization was challenged by M.A. Jinnah who considered it merely as opinionization of the 'Hindu community'. He asked the British rulers to divide the country into India and Pakistan on the basis of communities.

However, the Congress in the general election of 1937 was benefited to a large extent by the opinionization of the Hindu communities. It also helped the Congress to remain in power for over 25 years of India's independence. After the assassination of Mahatma Gandhi, the Congress could not continue the process of opinionization of all the communities of India. Later, the Congress was so overwhelmed with the success of minority communitarianism witnessed in form of getting Pakistan that in order to stick to power it shook hand with 'minorityism' or 'minority communitarianism'. It continues to bank upon it. It also purposely allows opinionization of the Hindu communities to shrink and push them to Hindu community structures, and to hide its attempts by raising the bogey of 'majoritarianism' or 'bahusankhyakvad' (बहुसंख्यकवाद). The Congress already knows that the Hindus are a namesake mega group or a community of many divided minorities.

Use of Opinionization

After the Congress shook hand with minoritarianism, the Jan Sangh, now Bharatiya Janata Party (BJP) and its allied organizations, took up the task of opinionization of the Hindu named minorities as Hindutva or Hindu communitarianism, and succeeded largely in transforming it into a majority opinion group. This opinionization of the Hindu named minorities or majority opinionism took it closer to power in many states, and at the Centre. However, after the attainment of power, the BJP and its allied organizations went back to majoritarianism of the Hindus as the majority community, popularly known as Hinduism or Hindutva. These organizations are no more engaged in opinionization of differing Hindu communities. They are resorting to majoritarianism without translating it into opinionization of the Hindu communities. Thus, the BJP has lost opportunity of enlarging and making use of the process of opinionization, left long ago by Mahatma Gandhi and L.K. Advani in the recent past.

On opposition side, the Indian National Congress and other prominent political parties, instead of opinionization of minority and majority communities on the Gandhian lines, were crying wolf of really non-existing majoritarianism. In response to the minoritarianism wooed by the Congress and other opposition political parties, the Hindu diehards and fundamentalists were relying on false majoritarianism. The dynamic process of opinionization had apparently been abandoned by all concerned.

Thus, majoritarianism as a fact hardly exists at all. Still some political parties wanting to get political power are resorting to it in vain. None is engaged in opinionization of the Hindu named minorities. In order to realize their vested interests and obtain power, they are simply trying to overawe the minority communities by posing the threat of majoritarianism, and pressurizing the Hindu named communities by posing the danger of minoritarianism. Reality of the communities is very different. In fact, only minorities or small groups exist. Still they go on calling some (Hindu) minorities by grouping them as one majority community. The only demographic reality in India is that of the existence of big and small minorities. At one place, one particular minority may be powerful and more dominating, while at some other place, there can be some another minority community in position of dominance.

Presently, to contest elections, the Congress and all other big and small political parties have been seeking support of comparatively more organized minority communities. They foresee no gain by joining Hindu named but non-existent majority community. It is now being increasingly recognized by them that this imaginary majority community is merely a group of many minority groups which have further divided into SCs, STs and OBCs. The BJP is losing because of its preconceived notion that the Hindus are still one majority community. Other political parties have realized that they will have to face defeat if they depend on the support of the existence of some non-existing majority community and do not depend on the strength of well-knit minority communities inclusive of the Hindu named smaller communities. Suppose there are eight candidates in a particular constituency. They, individually and separately, by banking upon scattered Hindu votes may obtain 20, 15, 10, 5, 8, 7 and absentees 10 per cent votes, but one connected with some large minority community by obtaining 25 per cent votes may be elected in that constituency.

In this way, opinionization appears to be the sole weapon to contest elections successfully. It can take over both 'structural' and vacuum parts of a community. Structures of a community and its vacuum relate respectively to 'ossified' and 'dynamic' processes of opinionization. It is related to both of them. Both can go together to be opinionated. Opinionization can change community structures. It may also fail to bring about change in community structures. Sometimes this change is temporary and the community can resume its earlier form. When opinionization remains ineffective, the political parties have simply to support the structures of the community. There is no way out. But it should not stand for the false structures like majoritarianism.

As a short-term goal of gaining power, one has to make a compromise. Where a community is not impressed by opinionization, he has to support its structures by redefining or reforming them. A leader always has to keep in mind that the process of making or influencing structures gravitates around the past and likes to stick to its old culture, while dynamic opinionization prefers to go along with the present and move towards future. However, opinionization can prevail if it is skillfully managed by effective use of media and press, and by contacting the masses.

The only way available for democratic politics of India to win elections is to transform the communities into opinion groups and win their favour through opinionization.

9

Pseudo versus Viable Hindutva

Pseudo-Hindutva comes from former Prime Minister Atal Bihari Vajpayee and his followers. He made a declaration in 2003 that Hindutva is *dharmanirpekshata* (secularism) as well as *Bharatiyata* (Indianism).

He began with the assertion that acceptance of the diversity of faiths is the central feature of secularism in India, therefore, Hinduism stands for secularism. Secularism as such enjoins upon the state the duty to respect all faiths and to practise no discrimination among citizens on the basis of their beliefs. Therefore, "Hinduism's acceptance of the diversity of faiths is the central feature of secularism in India". He defines Hindutva by its acceptance of diverse faiths and identifies this quality as the central feature of India's secularism.

Further, he wrote that true understanding of Hindutva is forward-looking and reform-minded, taking one to meet the challenges of the modern world or that does not stick one in the grooves of the past. In comparison with the conventional secularism, he appeared to present it as 'super-secularism' but in fact it is merely 'super-spiritualism'.[1] According to him, Hindutva is a noble and elevating way of life, having its own 'viraat darshan'. It emphasizes the inseparable relationship between the individual and society, as well as between man's material and spiritual needs. Like most of saints, devotees, seers and mahatmas, Vajpayee spoke only of God or

Creation with man or his identification of man with the Infinite. But he forgot that God or Creation also involves death, destruction, transmutation and remaking of evil and removal of the unwanted and the undesirable. Presentation of one-sided or much-liked aspect of Creation is unjust and denigration of Hinduism. It is motivated amputation of totality of Hinduism or Hindutva. After explaining Hinduism (presently equated with Hindutva) as an open space available freely for all religions, Vajpayee maintained silence without owning any responsibility to guard openness of that space at least for the Hindus. His concept of Hinduism has no concern for Hindutva.

Forgetting all what had happened with Hinduism in India, he reproduced words of Swami Vivekanand's article, "The Future of India": "It is the same India which has withstood the shocks of centuries, of hundreds of foreign invasions, of hundreds of upheavals of manners and customs. It is the same land which stands firmer than any rock in the world, with its undying vigour, indestructible life. Its life is of the same nature as the soul without beginning and without end, immortal and we are the children of such a country." Vajpayee here appears ready at least mentally to welcome similar foreign invasions and upheavals in manners and customs. Quite obviously, he is willing to admit similar downfalls without an iota of repentance but to save his 'pseudo-Hindutva'. Could India's polities, cultures and civilizations in the past ever stand in 'rock' like manner except in Vajpayee's poems?

Two Forms of Hindutva

The VHP, RSS and others are quite right in opposing Vajpayee's Hinduism as 'Hindutva'. In fact, there are two broad forms or aspects of Hindutva.[2] The first belongs to swamis, maharshis and mahatmas, which had mostly been part of religious mythology, archaeology, literature and history. Alike many others, it is this aspect of Hindutva which has been opted, elaborated and praised by Vajpayee. Another form of Hindutva is that of a crying child who had believed in his mother like spirituality but was wounded, mutilated, insulted, deceived and defeated, yet has been struggling to survive like any other communities. It is this Hindutva which is being claimed, fought and propagated by the VHP leaders like Praveen Togadia. He considers extremist Hindutva as an unfortunate and unacceptable interpretation that runs totally contrary to its true spirit. The RSS and VHP have rightly expressed disagreement with Vajpayee's Goa musings. The RSS helplessly reminded him of his own description (in rhyme) of a real Hindu as one who wages relentless war against evil.

Misconceptions underlying Pseudo-Hindutva

The central proposition lying behind his pseudo-Hindutva is that "India is secular as Hinduism is secular and liberal".[3] He failed to explain how can a state be secular if it has to (i) look after or keep various religious faiths intact; (ii) constrain itself by their beliefs, styles of worship, practices and taboos; and (iii) deal with them on the basis of number of their followers or size of organizations. Secularism simply means that the state has no faith or religion of its own and is not constrained by them in its normal functioning. Only on this basis, its citizens render allegiance to its regime. Cantwell Smith defines a secular state as "a form of state so contrived, as to win and hold and deserve the loyalty and warm allegiance of any citizen, of whatever religion, or of none". Secularism has no concern with 'diversity of faiths' or 'no faith' or 'equivalence to faiths'. Religions in a secular state concern with minds of citizens in their individual capacities but leave them to live as a developing yet well-protected country.

Therefore, it is wrong to assert that India has been 'secular' since the beginning of her known history.[4] It may nominally be called, at different times, as 'a state permitting diversity of religions' or 'a multi-religion state'. We did not accept partition because of our secularism. It is false to write that Pakistan could not have been possible "if the majority of Indians were not secular".[5] Pakistan was the victory of the leadership of a violence-prone religion over the leader of unarmed community made to believe in the invincibility of non-violence and spirituality. Vajpayee wanted to lead India perhaps on the same old lines and wished to claim superiority of India's spirituality over others. Even for political reasons, it was false for him to declare India 'secular' from the very beginning or because several faiths could flourish at that time. The state in ancient times had its own religion. It is also not proper to declare Hindutva or Hinduism as 'secular' simply because it permits diversity of faiths and religions. Conversely, in its innermost corner of his heart the then BJP-led Indian state considered itself related to some form of 'religion'. Had the Indian state been 'secular' it would not have talked of granting equivalence to religions (*sarvadharmasambhava*) or no concern with sects/religions (*panthnirpekshata*). A secular state is not interested 'in allowing a variety of faiths to exist', or 'treating them at par' with each other, but in keeping itself away from them, and performing its acts on temporal basis. The claim to call itself 'panthnirpeksha', cunningly means to avoid sects, but have 'dharma' (bigger religion) with it. Advocates of this trick forget that to treat one's own (Hindu religion) faith as dharma or bigger religion is the root of their hatred or apathy against the Hindus. When the state stands careful for granting respect to diversity, equality and places, styles and practices of religions, administers and manages religious institutions and places of worship, and gives grants on regular basis, it cannot be considered 'secular' in the normal sense of the term. The Indian state itself might not believe in some super-natural entity or God or deity, but it grants autonomy in small or big areas occupied by various religions in the socio-political life of the country. This anti-secular withdrawal by the state prompts the leaders of these religions to call the present Indian state as 'secular'. Communalism spreads when grants, norms of administration, distribution of favour and facilities are given by it to them in an unequal or disproportionate way. The pro-religion persons also promptly declare it 'communal' or 'non-secular' when their demands are not met in their desired manner.

So far 'Hindutva' has been treated in a partial, subjective and conflicting manner.[6] It has not emerged as an effective ideology. Recently, it is being updated as the ideology of Hindutva, and made effective and identical with Indianism. But, the Hindutva leaders are not clear about it and have been contradicting each other over its meaning and contents. Some orthodox Hindu leaders, ideologues and intellectuals are also trying to do it but their work has not been accepted so far. In fact, they stand more for Hinduism or Hindu religion. Their Hindutva does not relate to all the sections of the Indian people. It does not connote a system of governance, it could not be, according to Vajpayee, an issue in the coming elections.

Paradigm of Viable Hindutva

However, it can be studied and understood as an independent 'ideology', i.e., a meaningful statement of thought, approach and action. In the contemporary situation, Hindutva has an independent status. It is a composite whole which is closely concerned with almost all the segments of socio-political, cultural and economic life of the Indian nation. Culture, polity, economy and religion make up its constituent elements. As a set of ideas it is quite different from Hinduism, Hindu community and Hindu religion. Hindutva is in fact an ideology of the whole Indian polity. It is an ideology of vibrant and virile Indianism. Hindutva is totality, covering all aspects of life found in temporality. Temporality and spirituality both operate in their respective fields, and also may go together. But, the former dominates in the societal matter and stands neutral to spirituality. It does not, as it did in the past, support or remain subordinate to spirituality. In worldly matters, it is able to overpower and direct the latter. The present would control future. At this level, the concept embraces all the communities, religions, cultures and lifestyles. In this way, it is both temporal and spiritual. As it is related to the cosmos or living world as a whole, it accepts the responsibility to maintain it on the basis of certain rational principles. It would manage to react sharply if these principles are violated. As it stands close to the faith believing in rebirth or transmigration, it would like to fight fiercely over the events of violation of humanity. From this point it stands for broader and higher form of 'secularism'. However, this secularism is of Indian variety. It provides for welfare and development of the people in a way that they, if they like, can also make for spiritual growth in line with their own experience and understanding. But, it is not a 'super-religion' or 'super-Hinduism'.[7]

Concerns of Hindutva Paradigm

As an 'ideology', it concerns various issues like fundamentalism, secularism, Hinduism, nationalism, culture, lifestyle, casteism and so on. These are discussed in brief so as to determine and trace out specific form of the 'Hindutva paradigm'. After it is formulated, it would be analysed on the basis of its controversial relation with 'extremism' and its probable use in politics.

Non-secular Hindutva has often been failing to deal with religious extremism or communalism. A large number of people now realize that terrorism or *jehadi* fundamentalism or fanaticism comes down or mostly emerges from religions proclaimed by God or

Messenger Himself. It cannot be denied, refuted or opposed by any other religion even if it also likes to draw its authority on similar grounds. In case of conflict, followers of the two Gods or religions would appear fighting against each other. The former, having an assumed monopoly over God, therefore, can feel free to exercise force or violence in the name of religion. War would break out or continue, as it happened in crusades, if there are people having the same type of religion or divine message to fight against each other. Apparently, such *jehadis* or the fanatics can be controlled or stopped only when there are communities of their type preparing to fight against each other. In such controversies, only war-overt or covert decides the outcome that which side correctness of 'their' God lies. Therefore, a peace-loving community, which does not have any such authority directly or through someone from God, simply has to tolerate, keep patience and suffer silently, or get converted to save their lives, honour and property. To avoid such eventuality, the only alternative left to them is to stand firm and resort to 'secularism' unattached with any kind of religion.[8] That secularism can create conditions conducive for peaceful settlement or courageously launch war without using the name of God or religion.

For this, the new Hindutva identifies itself with 'secularism' in full.[9] Owing to several reasons, all may not be willing to accept it. It may also be pointed out that if, in the present context, India really adopts 'secularism' in its true and operational sense, perhaps, it may be opposed by some minorities in a fight to finish manner. If measured on the scale of secularism[10] it would be found that all the minorities, including Buddhism, are much more non-secular than Hinduism taken as a whole. However, only the emerging Hindutva secularism is 'secular' which should not be mixed with the Vajpayee brand of 'plurality of faiths' claimed by him as secularism. His is 'multi-religion secularism'.

Hindutva secularism, being flexible, does respond in proportion to the extent a person, group or community is secular. In a state observing 'rule of law', elements of non-secularism or fanaticism or *jehadi* terrorism are controlled and captured by greater force of valid secularism which obviously deals with it by means of law-enforcing agencies. But before such operation begins, it is useful and important for the state to watch and supervise the available patterns of thinking, behaving and responding of the people who claim to belong to the past hordes of invaders, killers and rulers of various princedoms and native states. It has to be seen whether they have reformed and changed themselves, or have kept on their connections and actions practised in the past. Much depends on the types of their mindsets, learning of particular precepts of their religion and making preparation to act accordingly. Such people can be considered as peaceful citizens if they have improved themselves or have made solemn promises to their fellow-citizens to follow the norms of society and laws of the country.[11] In case all or some of them do not show any such inclination, the society or the state in its behalf will have to put them in the categories of suspects and also make all preparations to defend and protect the peaceful communities.

Hindutva considers Hinduism close to it. Hinduism as a plural religion is acceptable to all. As Hinduism of the Hindutva now claims to come out fully reformed, renovated and modernized, it can to a large extent be equated with Indianism.

Hindutva should not be identified as 'cultural nationalism'. This term does not carry the meaning and content of Hindutva in full. It mistakenly confines the reality of Hindutva merely either to 'culture' or 'nationalism' or both. Nationalism should not be narrowly attached with particular culture.[12] Hindutva is not what 'nationalism' conventionally stands for. It concerns 'nationism' which is territorial and material. In fact, there is no need to equate 'nationalism' with Hindutva. The concept of 'cultural nationalism' is inadequate as it does not reflect the full form of polity. Hindutva means common allegiance of all citizens, and paying respect to all of their great men and women. Only in this sense it can be an engine of communal harmony.

At societal level, foundation of Hindutva lies with the persons and families of hitherto neglected communities, such as SCs, STs and OBCs, women and other very small economically backward minorities which have depended on labour for centuries. It has to give special regard and consideration to them, by way of reservation, special training and education programmes, loans, subsidies, allotment of houses and lands and the like. The lowest among them must be its first priority. This level needs more and more cultural cohesion. Consolidation of Hindutva to them should (i) show the way of leading the modern life of Hindutva; (ii) enlist people of different communities, forms of worship, regions and cultures, particularly the Muslims and the Christians, into the fold of its ideology; and (iii) open the teaching and training wings of politics, administration, management and warfare to tide over crisis situations. It also means to denounce and reject casteism completely in all its forms. To make recurrence of casteism impossible no one should be treated as superior to others. No profession, trade or calling should be considered as the monopoly of a particular person, group or community.

Economically, Hindutva also involves vigorous 'swadeshikaran' (domestication) of labour and talents to have India's domination world over in the fields of security, trade, industry, science, technology and material progress. Small, rural and local crafts must be granted protection constitutionally to reduce poverty and unemployment. Excessive domination of the Indian economy by the MNCs (multi-national corporations) owing to LPG (liberation, privatization and globalization) should be opposed at non-state level by the Gandhian means of boycott, non-cooperation and asceticism.

Thus, the Hindutva paradigm presented above finds Vajpayee's Goa musings as hollow and helpless. Let us be very clear that it was 'extremism', 'rigidity', 'commitment', and 'fighting spirit' which was required to defend and protect the Hindutva. They had to force all to acknowledge that India is a Hindutva Rashtra. Praveen Togadia, the only leader after Shivaji, Guru Govind Singh and Tilak, declared rightly that there should be no compromise on this and one should not side with those who were not for Hindutva. For this, the leaders of VHP and RSS had to renovate, explain and propagate it, and arrange for education and training of the youth and also of the conservative Hindu masses. They had to do a lot to equate Hindutva with Rashtra (or India).

The liberal Hindus including Vajpayee failed to convince the people whether Hindutva could be saved without showing and exercising 'extremism' (which simply means will to survive and try to set the things right) throughout history.[13] Was the 'Rathyatra' not an exercise of extremism? Is defending one's own people who had been kept downtrodden, neglected, exploited and insulted in their land of birth an exercise of 'extremism'? Their extremism never meant threatening, torturing or killing members of other communities. It is simply an attempt to put the Hindus at par with the minorities. Diversities of all types are to be respected in our country, but who is going to prevent, punish and eliminate the elements which commit themselves to destroy them and are taught to impose their own dogmas on others? When governments fail to stop extremism launched by a particular community, in the exercise of self-defence, it is the right of the aggrieved community to protect it by all available legal means. They fail to understand that Hindutva without 'extremism' (proactivism) is no more viable, workable and attractive even as a party ideology. Without proactive extremism the BJP like the Congress would be identified with minorityism.

In place of developing the concept on the basis of some pre-conceived emotional attachments, now, Hindatva has to be built on territorial or geographical foundations. It should aim at bringing out some kind of culture-oriented demographical equilibrium. Ideologically, India or 'Bharat' should now onwards mean the territory of India, which includes all its natural resources, maintenance of healthy ecology and pollution-free environment. People have to adopt 'nationism'. Indian nationism should work for occupying decisive partnership in the making the achievements of 21st century. Hindatva should transform the prevailing form of Indian nationalism as Indian 'nationism' by giving more importance to its land and people, and less to religion, culture and language.[14]

However, Vajpayee must be praised for his great step of boldly equating Hindutva as 'secularism' (*dharmanirpekshta*) and 'Indianism' (*Bharatiyata*). The pro-minority parties after Vajpayee's explanation of Hindutva (Hinduism) were now left with nothing to say. They could only talk on socio-political and economic matters. Vajpayee had placed the saffron flag on the top of the Mount Everest of Indian politics. But he could not pay any attention towards the need to have some organization and an armed protection for guarding the unfurling of that flag. It was left to be lost in the Himalayan glaciers. However, Vajpayee had had taken the foresighted lead in taking the concept of Hindutva closer to the modern and indisputable concept of 'secularism' and Indianism. In that had made great contribution towards the making the ideology of Hindatva.

Notes

1. Had it ever been 'super-secularism', India would never have fallen prey to social-religious evils, disintegration of society, ignorance and surrender to foreign forces and religions. Secularism, pure, temporal, humane and simple would never have permitted these evils. But he fails to understand that acceptance the existence of diverse faiths is not secularism.
2. For knowing distinction between these two, see, Chapter 20, "The Path of Hindatva".
3. The Congress chief Sonia Gandhi, while addressing a function at Ramakrishna Mission on January 12, 1999, had spoken these words. See *Hindustan Times*, January 1, 2003.
4. Prime Minister Atal Bihari Vajpayee's musings, 'Secularism can't be pitted against Hindutva', *Hindustan Times*, January 1, 2003.
5. Ibid.
6. Words standing closer to the term 'Hindutva' are: Hind, Hindu, Hindi, Hinduism, Hindu community, Hindavi, Hindustani, Hum, Hamara etc. Conceptually, it is a composite whole or an entity made of several elements. It connotes all that is contained of or related to specified land, economy, power, cultures, population and communities, religions, languages, goals, norms and values, demands and aspirations, some special features and characteristics, socio-political set-up, ethnicity, family patterns, fads, taboos and the like.
7. The Samata Party welcomed Vajpayee's statement linking secularism with Hindutva, but cautioned that secularism, and not Hindutva should be used in future references. "We agree that Hindutva is a way of life. But in its place the word, which has been used in our Constitution, should be used."
8. Looking to our misunderstanding on the nature of secularism required for a strong India, it can be anticipated that it would take another 100 years to make India really secular.
9. For details, see, Chapter 5 "Ideology of Hindatva".
10. Verma, S.L., "Muslims in Rajasthan: A Political Study", in Seminar on "Economic and Political Conditions of Muslims in Rajputana/ Rajasthan" January 11-12, 2003.
11. For this, see, Chapters 21, 22, and 23.
12. One should be careful while using the concept of 'composite culture'. The demand for having a 'composite culture' often means that the non-Hindus remain where they are, and are free to continue their thinking and behaving, whereas the Hindus and other non-Muslims

should transform themselves to the satisfaction of the non-Hindus and seek accommodation with them with cost.

13. Those who oppose 'extremism' or 'aggressiveness' of the Hindutva wanted there should be no reaction to the burning of the karsevaks alive, and wait for the culprits for years together without any consequence. They also want that there should be no cry over the forced migration of the Kashmiri pandits numbering over three lakh. They are being so badly and inhumanly treated in India itself. Why one does not talk to take back the PoK from Pakistan.? They also want that there should be no mention or talk of destruction of temples, forced conversions of the Hindu masses and torture of men and women in millions. What these minorities, raising hue and cry over the rise of Hindutva, are doing for them? It means the Hindus must not only suffer insult and humiliation, but also work and die for the safety and protection of the minorities without expecting any mutuality and reciprocity from them.
14. See, infra, Chapter 20, "The Path of Hindatva".

10

Mutual Responsibilities

There are many kinds of minorities—religious, ethnic, cultural, issue or opinion based etc. Most important among them are religious or faith-based minorities. Other minorities except ethnic can transform or change at temporal levels. They relate mostly to worldly matters. But religious minorities are connected with both worldly and other-worldly matters. They are more stable, effective and deep-rooted. Big and small communities grow and organize around religions. Worldly matters to them are subordinate to other-worldly goals. However, even within one religion, minorities can situate inside or outside.

The Hindu Dharma has been under attack from many inside and outside minorities. They mostly have arisen or appeared owing to its deep-rooted weaknesses and disabilities.[1] Basically it suffers at four levels: (a) lack of cohesion and unity about Basic Reality; (b) over-emphasis on abstract forms of life, such as, soul, super-soul or Brahma or Absolute, salvation, transmigration and the like; (c) exploitation of lower castes by upper castes; and (d) challenges of non-Hindu religions and communities. As Hindu Dharma, from the very beginning, suffers from lack of cohesion and unity about Basic Reality, it could not specify the basic elements of that Reality. In the absence of the knowledge of those basic elements, it conveniently moved in different directions of unlimited abstractness. Behind these varying abstractions, the Brahminhood, in collaboration with other upper castes, declared a large number of people as lower castes whom they jointly exploited, repressed and segregated as 'untouchables'. The number of these lower caste people went on increasing as more and more persons were deprived of education, livelihood, equal treatment, property and the like.

Contribution of Minority Religions

New religions appeared with force and conviction. Buddhism taught 'spiritual equality', and disproved all Hindu bases of social inequality. It created millions of Buddhists out of orthodox Hindus. So were the Jains. But there was no change in the form and nature of Hindu Dharma. Inequality, on the basis of 'karmas' (acts) done in past life and their results in the present life, was considered to be the essential element of Hindu Dharma. Thereafter occurred invasion of Islam which brought the message of absolute equality among men both in religious and temporal matters. Equality of Buddhism was mental and spiritual; therefore, it was of little consequence to the depressed and downtrodden classes. Equality of Islam was real as it was declared divine and had the support of arms and army. Millions of suppressed and outcaste Hindus vis-à-vis upper caste Hindus and Brahmins welcomed it. Still, the Hindus did not give up the inhuman practice of caste inequality. They considered it as the sole feature of their religion. In consequence, millions of Hindus, in search of equality and simple faith, under force and persuasion, were converted to Islam. In India, now, it was a powerful counter-community of non-Hindus. It ruled over the Hindus for over one thousand years. However, after sometime, even among the Muslims, caste system or inequality of the Hindus percolated. With the advent of the British Raj, came the message of 'love' through Christian missionaries, trained and organized for proselytizing the downtrodden castes, outcastes and tribals of India which formed about two-thirds of the Hindus. Again, millions of poor, repressed and exploited people changed, under coercion or persuasion, their religion to get better food, medical aid, love and equal respect, provision of livelihood and protection of the arm of the state. The Hindus, despite strong protest movements, organized by Mahatma Gandhi and Dr. B.R. Ambedkar, could not extend love, respect and human status to the exploited castes and tribals. The Hindus have still not learnt and adopted, despite conversion of several crores of their followers to Islam and Christianity, the desirable attributes of equality and love to their lower caste followers. This makes the existence and survival of the minorities in India essential and desirable. Hindu Dharma, because of its megalomaniac attitude and inability to absorb their contribution into its fold, makes its presence essential. The Hindus are unwilling to learn these attributes because of the selfish interest of the Brahmin priesthood. If the attributes of spiritual equality, socio-political similarity, and love and respect for all human beings, irrespective of class and caste differences, are accepted, the Brahmins feel that their status, power, influence, affluence and control over the Hindu society would be jeopardized. As the Brahmin priesthood would never permit those qualities to be engrained by the Hindu society, presence of minorities becomes necessary.

Inclusion of these attributes in human beings makes them whole, total, equal and respectable. As the very central element of Hinduism is Brahma, God, Ultimate or spirituality, its presence in every human being puts them at par with each other, implying respect, love, equality and grant of free status to each other. This is rather fulfilment of Hinduism as religion. Inculcation of these attributes subserves the Hindu set-up. Therefore, either the Hindu Dharma should generate these attributes or elements from within and apply them to the society at large or accept its inadequacies in an open and broadminded manner. Till it does not do so, it has to permit co-existence of minorities.

Their presence, till the Hindu Dharma does not develop those qualities in their society, contributes to the very purpose and goal of Hindu Dharma. In fact, minorities arose or invaded the country of Hindu Dharma, because it lacked these very essential attributes of man. Whenever there is lack of or decrease of any one of these attributes, religious teachings from outside get into such deficient religions, communities or societies. The Hindu Dharma could not deprive two-thirds of its population of such essential attributes, and still claim to be supreme and the best religion of the world.

Plight Hindu 'Majority'

Hindutva organizations like the RSS (Rashtriya Swayamsevak Sangh) operate on an unfounded premise that the Hindus form a majority community and they want to remain a consolidated majority in India. The Hindus of past centuries had also been thinking in those terms. They also opined that the lower caste Hindus, despite their exploitation and repression by the upper castes, would always like to remain a part of the Hindu community. Their Hindu religion would compel them to stand by the majority of the Hindus. The Hindus also entertained a false notion that the Hindu culture is the best among all. No other culture, religion or community would dare harm their position. Only the Hindu civilization, when others have died or disappeared, remains in tact. In terms of their own self-praise, they so much exaggerate that they do not see (i) the loss of several crores of Hindu followers; and (ii) the rise of three competing and winning religions—Christianity, Buddhism and Islam—which have snatched the first and the highest position from the Hindu Dharma.[2] The Hindus happen to be so myopic that they, despite their decrease in terms of number, size, power, position and influence, still regard themselves as the greatest of all other religions. It tends to forget that whenever there was rise of any minority religion—Islam, Buddhism and Christianity, the Hindu Dharma lost several millions of its followers within no time. These converts, in every possible way, refused to identify themselves with the Hindu religion. Religious leaders like Dayananda, Vivekananda and Gandhi prayed, tried and advanced serious arguments for their return to Hindu fold, and recently Hindutva leaders also appealed the minorities for home-coming but all in vain.[3]

All this did happen, besides loss of power and authority in political terms, due to their failure to present the basic oneness or inherent unity in the tenets of Hindu Dharma. They stood scattered, divided, conflicting and plural before the onslaughts of the religions of oneness. This phenomenon, which obviously is the fatal weakness of their decay, defeat and downfall, is proudly praised by the Hindus, including the Sangh, as the sign of their greatness, superiority and ideal form.[4]

Lessons to Segmental Minorities

On the part of minorities, while their contribution to the Hindu Dharma should be praised with an open mind, they must be seen as partial, incomplete and segmental religions. None of them is total. For example, non-violence of Buddhism and Jainism is very important, but for them it is all-in-all. Depending on pure and minutest possible non-violence, no state, society, legal or production system can sustain. Buddhists and Jains stand only for non-violence so much so that they reject need of army to fight, engage in agriculture, fisheries etc., use pesticide, awarding punishing to hardcore criminals and anti-social elements. As they do, acts of those who are engaged in the maintenance of these institutions cannot be considered as 'violence' or sin. The law and order agencies or security forces commit such 'sin' to keep the larger number of people safe and sin-free.[5] It is quite easy to attract lower caste Hindus and convert them by saying that the 'varna' system of the Hindus leads towards hateful caste system, structural societal hierarchy, exploitation, repression etc., and deprives millions of people from their essential human equality. The poor Hindus, instead of producing a rational justification of the varna system, went on defending this deterioration in the worst form of caste and sub-caste system on the basis of divinity and divine sanction.[6] None of the Hindu scholars, saints and seers could claim that the varna system as functionally specialized classes of a society, whether that society is Hindu or non-Hindu, is universal. Shastras or divinity is not needed to prove its essential utility. Rather, no society can survive or make progress without it. Those who do not have any functional specialization also remain within the varna system when they serve the society in any unspecified way. The varna system is overall classification of the people on the basis of functional specialization. It is not necessary that there should be only four 'varnas'. They could be raised to any number. It remains even without calling it 'varna system'.

Therefore, let the minorities or anti-Hindutva Hindus forget that varna system is formally related to the Hindus and their Shastras. It has nothing to do with religion.[7] Each society, for its maintenance, peace and progress, requires people of four specific elements: one, knowledge, two, courage, sacrifice and fighting, three, production, trade and commerce, and, four, general services or labour. An element is an empirical concept representing a category of related knowledge, activities and attributes. It is a societal requisite or essential. Of course, a society would like to have 'equilibrium' of these elements. But, at some specific time, it may like to overweigh one or two particular elements. During war time, more emphasis may be given to the second element.[8] Success in the prevalence of market economy of the 21st century demands expertise in element three. However, no society can sustain or survive in the total absence of or absolute decrease in any one of the four elements. For the requirements of the 21st century in the prevalence of LPG (Liberalization, Privatization and Globalization) era, the number of the categories of elements can be increased including provision of 'mix' of two or more elements.[9] As very few persons can be 'all in one', the caretakers of society have an eye over the lack of some elements. They make special efforts to increase the quantum of that element(s), and bring out required 'balance' among them. More the 'balance' among these elements in the functional formation of a society more would it be viable and strong enough to face different kinds of crises. A society lacking balance among these structural elements or requisites would not be able to face crises, and would gradually recede, decay and disappear. Minorities, thus, help in bring out a 'required balance', and also disturb the existing balance leading to its further deterioration and death.[10]

Similar is the problem of 'ashramas' (आश्रम), stages of preparation, conduct and progress in individual's life, in the Hindu system. If the ultimate objective of an individual to have self-realization or salvation or identification of an individual soul with the Ultimate Reality or Bliss or Peace is accepted by all religions or communities, there would be four upward or vertical stages of human life. But, a particular individual or a religion may reject or accept this goal also in a different manner. A man, of whatever faith, ethnicity, culture, region or language, to realize his worldly and other-worldly goals, has to pass through stages of (i) education and learning, (ii) lead family life containing children, wife and elders with earning livelihood, making property and desiring status with honour, (iii) retire from the second stage of active life while contributing his experience and knowledge to the new generation, and (iv) renounce all connections and activities to live in peace here and after. In fact, these stages are only suggestive.

One can skip over any one two of them. After attaining knowledge, one can directly go to the stage four of renouncement. Or, someone may skip over the stage of family life, and devote oneself to the service of the poor, the sick and the disabled ones.

It is useful to add here that these 'varna' elements and 'ashrama' stages (overall classification of the people on the basis of functional specialization and stages of preparation, conduct and progress in individual's life) can be formally prescribed by some authority or informally followed up by the members of a community. Formally, they can be imposed on any one of the bases: holy books, law, morality, public opinion, democratic means or traditions. Their inclusion can also be subject to the principle of 'demand and supply'. Still no formal provisions are really needed as their observance is natural and unavoidable. They are a 'must' for each and every society. It may learn by undering trial and error, but, in the long run, it may become part of its culture and societal set-up. However, those who do not like the 'varnashrama' (element and stage) scheme, considering it essentially a part of the Hindu Dharma and maintaining its adoption as conversion to Hinduism, can keep them away from it. But those societies or their members would do so only at the expense of upkeep, maintenance or survival of their society. If a society discards, as the Hindus did, a particular element of a varna system, it would be lame, lopsided and disabled. A wholesome society would require that an individual passes through all the 'ashrama' stages. But it would like to put more emphasis on the first and the second. These are creative and production-oriented stages, and no society can sustain without them. Knowledge is the primary stage through which every individual should stay at. Householders or families make up community, nation, state, profession and the like. It is said to be the cradle of civilization and culture. The old ones have to 'retire' and pave way for the younger generation which remains in search of fresh life, ideas and attainments. A society composed only of hermits, saints, priests and recluses would be of no use for the worldly people. A community only of fighters and soldiers means an invitation to war, bloodshed, destruction and massacre.[11] Dominance of the third element would result in cut throat competition, materialism, physical pleasures, accumulation of wealth, and machine like human living, colonialism and fight for control over markets.[12] Religions often prefer the fourth stage. They move around either on meditation, freedom from bondage of 'karma' (कैवल्य), surrender to God, attainment of heaven, non-violence as absolute value, love as God and the like. This approach makes them lopsided, segmental and limited. Their societies ideologically operating at level two[13] are not self-sufficing, though their followers are taught to consider it 'complete' or 'perfect' in all respects. Most of the religions have failed to understand that all the goals of meditation, freedom from bondage of 'karma' (कैवल्य), surrender to God, attainment of heaven, non-violence as absolute value, love as God and others necessitate an environment which should make man materially free from hunger, disease, poverty, danger to life and cruelty, and, thus, provide peace, protection and order, and encourage love and fraternity among human beings. A religion demanding absolute faith, blind obedience and elimination of other faiths cannot form a total society. Belief in one's own faith cannot demand non-existence of differing faiths. If it proposes to do that, it would mean that it is not a religion, and is engaging in expansion of power, accumulation of property, exploitation of lower classes and rejection of morality. Such religions manoeuvre towards coercive conversion of others to non-religion. They are political war-mongers putting on some attractive cloak of religion. Only a bigger power can frustrate their evil designs.

Such attempts should be frustrated and opposed to the largest possible extent. All such measures adopted by particular politico-religions are really anti-religious and should not be tolerated. Even apathy or neutral attitude towards them is suicidal and harmful to humanity at large. However, opposition to such religions is possible only when they have clear and open understanding of their basics of religion, maintain a societal set up composed of an appropriate 'balance of elements', and observe normally all the stages of human life.

When a minority community at its own acts on the tenets and stages of 'varnashrama' and restores a workable balance of elements, it would not find itself very different from a wholesome Hindu society.

However, there are some trends visible in some of the sections of the Muslims which show that are coming close to the Hindus.[14]

Societies operating on Functional Specialization and Stages

A dispassionate observation of some of the progressive societies would convince us that they are made of all these four elements and have been maintaining a requisite balance among them. They are devoted to education, defence, production and service. Members of these societies often pass through schools, colleges and institutes for knowledge which mostly is responsive to the job market. After or along with attaining success at that level, they form a family. When they grow older, they retire, get some kind of pension and enjoy social security. During the last period of life, they pursue peace as they are intelligent enough to know their physical, biological and psychological limits. Other-worldly or spiritual goals are optional for them.

After the downfall of the Vedicas, the Hindu Dharma lost its 'balance' of societal elements and was overrun by the forces of minority religions. It was overwhelmed by one or two elements and actually operated at level two.[15] Some minorities are also treading on the same path. Keeping the plight of the Hindus in mind, each one of them carried the flag or dominance of that particular element which the Hindu Dharma lacked at that particular historical time. Each minority succeeded over the vast but dissipated Hindu majority. The Hindu Dharma succumbed to it in that particular area. As such, the Hindu Dharma can be advised to maintain its equilibrium of societal elements, and observe the 'varnashrama' stages needed for the individuals of a wholesome society. So should a minority do it at its own. If a minority fails to maintain that societal balance of elements, and sticks to one or two particular elements, they would grow weak, and have to face the opposition from another wholesome society or some minority religion. Until a minority becomes fulsome, it would fail and face difficulties in the area of its elemental vacuum. That vacuum may occur in the fields of knowledge, defence, production or service. It would not succeed until it recovers its lost ground. Minorities would lose even if its priesthood falsely consoles its followers about the factual conditions of its elemental structure of the society or deceives them in the name of God or claims of inherent supremacy of their religion over others.

On the basis of the experiences of the Hindus and downfall of their Hindu Dharma owing to the transformation of the 'varnas' (classification people on the basis of functional specialization) into callous caste system, societal hierarchy, inequality, exploitation and repression of the depressed classes under the cover of divinity, social status or birth based on past 'karmas', and the like, it can be said that a minority would also have to face similar fate if it follows the path of the outworn Hindu Dharma. It has to be emphasized that the proposed societal balance of elements is free from religion. A society belonging to whatever religion may or may not adopt it. Modern institutions of democracy, rule of law, independence of judiciary, adult franchise, elections etc. can set up the 'varnashrama' scheme, without naming it as such, but keeping it totally free from all religious constraints and limitations. One may or may not accept it. A community, after accepting it may subsequently forsake it. Everyone is free to put it into action or stop its operation. Even when a man of religion acts on the principle of 'detached action' (निष्काम कर्म), it is not necessary for him to follow the hereditary or traditionally ordained jobs. The principle of detached action does not lead to the strengthening of the orthodox or status quo society. The only thing in the performance of 'detached action' (निष्काम कर्म) is that they should not be done to serve narrow personal, caste or vested interests. Their end must be good of all without expecting any personal gain from them. Performing of acts pertaining to societal elements is wholly dependent on personal understanding and attitude of a man. One may look towards or take decision on the basis of discussion, democratic consent, job requirement, tradition, pecuniary consideration or commitment to a mission. His decision would belong to him alone. However, every individual is influenced by his surrounding, environment and prevailing societal order. Therefore, the caretakers of a society must make suitable changes in the conditionality and environment wherein decisions may be taken independently to serve the best interests of all. This may amount to doing duties in the name of God or surrendering their results to Him. Of course, such decision, apart from the real good of the individual, would also give priority to the greatest good of all. In the greatest good of all, he as an individual is automatically included.

Notes

1. See, Chapter 3, 'The Hindu Dharma'.
2. It is estimated that there is somewhere between 800 million and 1 billion Hindus living in the world today. Approximately, 79 per cent (750 million) of India's population is Hindu. Nepal has an even greater concentration of Hindus in comparison to other faiths. Eighty-nine per cent, or 17 million people follow Hinduism in Nepal. Hindus account for 11 per cent (12.6 million) of the population in Bangladesh, 2.5 per cent (4 million) in Indonesia, 15 per cent (2.8 million) in Sri Lanka, 1.5 percent in (2.12 million) in Pakistan and 6 per cent (1.4) in Malaysia. In the United States, Hindus only account for 0.2 per cent (0.9 million) of the population.

   An analysis showed that in 1881 there were 79.32 per cent Hindu and 21 per cent Muslims in India. In 1991, Hindus were 68.03 and Muslims 30 per cent. In 1881, Christians were 0.6 per cent who in 1991 grew 2.1 percent. At this rate, by 2060, Hindus would be reduced to a minority. *Rajasthan Patrika*, December 13, 2003. In Great Britain, the Muslim minority is demanding partition. *Rajasthan Patrika*, October 18, 2004.
3. *Rajasthan Patrika*, February 12-13, 2005.
4. Such people proudly say that it is a mind-boggling phenomenon: For 500 to 600 years we survived the invasion of Islam as no other society did. The whole of Arabia, which had a much evolved civilization, was run over in a matter of just 20 years. Persia collapsed within 50 years. Buddhist Afghans put up a brave resistance for 300 years but, in the end, they also collapsed. In all of these countries, today, there remains nothing pre-Islamic worth the name save for some broken down architectural monuments from their pre-Islamic past. How did our society survive the Islamic onslaught? We have survived not only physically, but intellectually too. We have preserved our culture. The kind of music that was heard 1,500 years ago is heard even today. S. Gurumurthy, *Semitic Monotheism: The Root of Intolerance*; and, also, what makes them proudly distinctive is that many formidable invaders have been assimilated into its stream like a satchel of salt. Compare Hindus with mighty civilizations in Middle-East like Sumerian, Babylonian, Phoenician, Egyptian, Carthagians, Canaanites, Abyssinians which have been Arabized and Islamized in 7th century by a victorious expedition originating in Hijjaj and Greeks, and diminished Assyrians follow their ancient language but have undergone change of religion. Balbir K. Punj, *Hindu Rashtra*, op. cit. He also quotes Allama Iqbal from his Tarana-e-Hind in 1904 "Roma ho Yunan ho sab mit gaye jahan se, magar baki hai ab tak nishan hamara/kuch baat hai ki hasti mit-ti nahin hai hamari/sadiyon raha hai

dushman daur-re jahan hamara/sare jahan se accha hindoositan hamara". Also, R.C. Mazumdar, H.C. Raychaudhuri and Kalikinkar Datta, *An Advanced History of India* (Macmillan, 1978), pp. 135-6.

5. Force, coercion or violence used as a matter of duty or obligation to preserve and protect society or justice, and for serving personal or narrow interests or for evil, is not considered 'sin' by Hinduism. Such acts are part of wider concept of 'non-violence' (अ–हिंसा)––वैदिकी हिंसा हिंसा न भवति।
6. ब्राह्मणोऽस्य मुखमासीद् बाहू राजन्यः कृतः।
ऊरू तदस्य यद्वैष्यः पद्भ्या षूद्रोऽ अजायत।।
(यजुर्वेद अध्याय 31 मंत्र 11)
7. Dayananda cut the very root of caste system by his reinterpretation of the purush-sukta, (ibid), that it meant "in society the Brahmin, man of knowledge was similar to the mouth; the Kshatriya, the warrior, to the arms; the Vaishya the merchant to the belly; and Shudra, the servant to the foot". He considered the varna to be a political institution, made by the rulers for the common good society. S.L. Verma, *Representative Indian Political Thinkers*, Jaipur: Jain Prakashan Mandir, 1999, p. 177.
8. The Hindutva movement was organized on ideological and proactive attempts to practice the second category elements of the varna system to uphold Hinduism. Vivekananda preferred to call it 'Kshatriya' spirit.
9. It can be 'sarvavarni' society.
10. In fact, the Hindutva movement was an attempt by some organized elements of the Hindus to restore this 'balance' of elements.
11. Aggressive Hindutva put all emphasis on the second element. It had to face many legal and constitutional problems as it was involved in violence. Communal riots flared up in its wake.
12. Present dominance of LPG (Liberalization, Privatization and Globalization) is demanding predominance of this approach everywhere.
13. See, Chapter 1, Introduction.
14. G. Parthasarthy, "Time to Move on, and Ahead", *Hindustan Times*, October 5, 2003; and, *Rajasthan Patrika*, December 13, 2003.
15. See back, Chapter 3, "The Hindu Dharma".

11

Reconsideration over Gandhi

Most of the great men and world leaders, after sometime, are transformed into objects of admiration, ideological eulogy, ritual, and worship disabling the successive generations from giving a serious consideration to their ideas and actions. For Mahatma Gandhi, Einstein made the statement that generations to come "will scarcely believe that such a man, as this, ever in flesh and blood, walked upon this earth."[1] The only way to save him from being converted into a mere "hero" is to examine his ideas and actions and give them some critical consideration. Scholars of political science and other allied disciplines have already expressed the feeling that Gandhi has been completely lost to the world of religion and ethics and very little effort has been made to redeem and claim him back.[2]

Gandhi has been equated with the Buddha and Christ and with Socrates and Bhakti saints of medieval India.[3] Few great men, in their own lives, achieved such worldwide attention. He has been likened to several gods and heroes of the world.[4]

Gandhi was the first great religious leader who made use of religion to get freedom for a subdued nation. He happened to be the greatest apostle of peace when he organized mass movements several times on the basis of truth and non-violence alone and led them to the goal of independence. Gandhi did this during his own lifetime and for his countrymen but proclaimed the power of those values and ideals for all times to come. He put them before the whole of mankind.

Goals and Values of Gandhi

From the very beginning, Gandhi grew as a man of religion or Dharma, which is different from sectarian religions. All the ultimate values of the Gandhian philosophy and thought emanate from religion. His religion is made of God, truth and non-violence. He believed in God or an omnipresent fundamental spiritual reality or an all-embracing 'Living Light' called Brahma, Rama, Truth, etc. True religion puts emphasis on the moral values of man as spirit. All religions are equal as they are founded on the same moral laws which bind men all over the world. Gandhi believed in the moral governance of the universe. Religion to him was not merely a means for personal purification but also a creative force of human history.

Gandhi had an absolute faith in God which he identified with *sat*, existence, or all living beings. God or Truth was the end or supreme value to Gandhi. Truth (*sat*) is the substance of all morality, while 'Satya' is the essence of Dharma and implies that nothing exists in reality except Truth.

Politics is part of religion. In the Gandhian scheme there is no politics devoid of religion. Politics bereft of religion is a death-trap which kills the soul. It has to subserve religion.[5] He was interested in destroying the dichotomy between religious values and political norms, and ethical principles and political expediency. As early as 1915, he declared his aim to spiritualize political life and political institutions.

Background of Popular Acceptance of Gandhi

It is now desirable to analyze the contextual factors and forces which made up the Gandhian leadership.[6]

(i) It is almost commonplace to say that only India could have accepted non-violence to such an extent. It can be largely attributed to the religious nature of the people of India since time immemorial. All major religions of the country, Hinduism, Jainism and Buddhism, including Christianity and Islam, uphold non-violence or Ahimsa (non-violence) as one of the foremost values or goals of life. Apart from his family upbringing, it was natural for Gandhi to tread on the path of religion and make use of its objects, idioms and ends.

(ii) The people of India religiously pay highest regard to their godmen, religious leaders, priests, saints, gurus and preachers. The masses deeply appreciate their way of renouncing worldly comforts, undergoing all kinds of sufferings for them, praying for the upliftment of their souls, and living a life of an ascetic. As a matter of age-old practices, the greater they undergo suffering, the greater they get respect from the people. Gandhi compounded all these elements in his ideas, lifestyle and leadership, and based them all on the ideal of non-violence.

(iii) After 1858, India was unarmed and without martial leaders for about 100 years. The people, having no sense of being a united nation, were divided into so many castes, sub-castes, cultures, languages, races, historical animosities, and had been living under torpor of other-worldliness. The country was seething under an exploitative economy where most of the people were engaged in stereotype agriculture and were cut off from the rest of the world. There was little impact of industrialization modern science, and technology on their living and thinking. Such disorganized people could hardly think of waging war against the British Crown.

(iv) However, some spadework was done by the leaders of the Indian renaissance like Raja Rammohan Roy, Dayanand Saraswati, Swami Vivekananda, and several others. Slowly, people began to react against the exploitative and humiliating British Raj, and began to put forward the demand of reform and self-government for the nation-in-making. The failure of both the moderates and the extremists, even with their eventual unity in the Congress and their understanding with the Muslim League during World War I, could not bring about the desired results. By the year 1920, the whole country was without an all-India leadership.

(v) The British rule, in comparison with other colonizing European nations elsewhere, was less autocratic and less ruthless. Efficacy of non-violence required the presence of some civilized and liberal government which respected, to a certain extent, human values and dignity of man. The British understanding of law and justice also enabled non-violence to flourish. Courts, big and small, in order to punish a culprit, were primarily concerned to ascertain the nature of intention or motives underlying acts of causing harm, insult, injury, or assault. In the absence of commensurate intention, the result, outcome, effect, or consequence of an act was not very important, and the person, even if found guilty, could be acquitted.

Moreover, Gandhi himself was found to be the most potent force. His techniques proved to be so successful that there was hardly any other alternative left with the people. He was a great leader who could mobilize all sections of the people at the national level. With his entry into Indian politics, all his contemporary leaders were relegated into the background. Gandhi was foremost in putting his life at stake for the cause of India's freedom. People were so much overwhelmed by his words and deeds that they developed a kind of faith in what he said about the power of non-violence which itself came down to them from ancient times. As the majority of the Indian people, particularly the Hindus, had already a legacy of spiritualism the adoption of non-violence as a fighting technique appeared quite congenial to them.

For Gandhi, non-violence was all in all, universally applicable, both in its negative and positive forms. In its negative aspect, it was non-injury to any living being by body or mind.[7] It does not cover suffering caused to the wrong-doer by natural acts, not proceeding from ill-will, of the non-violent person. Ahimsa requires deliberate self-suffering, not a deliberate injuring of the supposed wrong-doer. The positive aspect of Ahimsa means the largest love or charity. For him, violence was, as it involved evil intention and behaviour, to cause harm to others. But, for Gandhi inflicting pain on one's ownself or undergoing voluntary self-suffering for others was non-violence as it caused no injury to others. He was sure that this self-suffering could cause conversion of hearts of his adversaries as God or Truth was common to both. This led him to adopt 'non-violence of the brave' which was at the top of other two forms of non-violence.

Power of Non-violence of the Brave

Gandhi stood for the enlightened non-violence or non-violence of the brave, the highest or purest level of non-violence. He regarded this form of non-violence as the best, the most pious, and the most powerful upon earth, and aspired to attain it as a *sthithapragya*, a *mahatma*, or a saint. He also calls it soul or spiritual force which is invincible and never-failing He stresses the potency of soul force in the individual and society. It has the unique capacity of winning adherents, building up morale, and invoking sacrifice, arousing public opinion, and weakening the adversary.

Gandhi was so much anamoured of the might of non-violence that he suggested a plan to meet the menace of foreign armed aggression during the Second World War, to Churchill, the then Prime Minister of England.

His plan of Ahimsa implied not merely a certain attitude of detached sympathy towards an enemy, but also the denial of the very existence of an enemy. On such an occasion, even if some votary of Ahimsa dies, still, by dying he realizes his goal of *moksha* or self-realization. Such a *satyagrahi* is never defeated. Ahimsa is adopted not by painful necessity but by inner conviction based on moral considerations.

From the Gandhian viewpoint, in inflicting suffering on the satyagrahi, the opponent helps in his own defeat. The satyagrahi thrives on repression and no amount of violent coercion can crush him. Ahimsa is most efficacious in the face of the greatest himsa. There is no such thing as defeat or failure in non-violence because in satyagraha, to suffer is to win. The satyagraha struggle may seem to be a slow, long-drawn process, but it is the wisest, for it is the surest. It touches not the body but it touches and strengthens the moral fibre of those against whom it is exerted. It is a method of conversion and is based on its ability of reaching the intellect and the heart. For him, non-violence involves power only as influence or persuasion, pressure or moral force, but not in its violent and compulsive forms.

Gandhi preached and practiced non-violence of the brave as his supreme religion, *swadharma* or creed. It stood on the firm foundation of God or Truth. It was soul force. It was invincible and never-failing and had the unique capacity of winning adherents, building up morale and invoking sacrifice, arousing public opinion, and weakening the adversary.[8] Superiority over physical strength is the core of such non-violence. Such non-violence under the leadership of a person like Gandhi or some true satyagrahi could change the heart of even armed foreign aggressors or pilots intending to drop atom bomb on peaceful population. Gandhi alone was enough if he had the power of non-violence as such. But he felt that perfect non-violence was impossible as long as man in human body was living. Such perfection was unattainable. He could not try his personal creed of non-violence as stated in his *Hind Swaraj* anywhere. His statements about the power of non-violence of the brave proved to be merely a wish, possibility, or imagination. Gandhi's own experience with people like B.R. Ambedkar, M.A. Jinnah and Subhash Chandra Bose does not corroborate the existence of such power of non-violence.[9]

As a true satyagrahi, Gandhi, throughout his long life, underwent immense suffering. He was sure that this self-suffering would cause conversion of hearts of his adversaries. God or Truth was common to both. He maintained that inflicting pain to one's ownself or undergoing voluntary self-suffering for others was, as it caused no injury, non-violence. Barring a few cases, Gandhi was not very successful in causing conversion of hearts of his enemies. It has also been critically observed that even if the winning over an adversary has happened on the basis of his self-suffering, it does not amount to have gained victory of his total truth. The adversary might enter into compromise on account of many other factors: shortage of time, vested interests, fear of condemnation and the rise of counterforces.[10]

He continued to strive for the status of a *sthitapragya, karmayogi,* or a *mahatma*. But, he could never attain it. As such, he did not get the opportunity to exercise the power of non-violence as a creed on a mass scale. He could actually apply non-violence only at policy and expediency levels. He happened to conduct only 'experiments' with Truth, and could not attain any finality. However, despite Gandhi's rebuttals,[11] the masses, owing to their religious background, kept believing that the Mahatma had mastered non-violence of the brave and would be able to attain all his goals for them. The people were so eager to find their image of the Mahatma real that they overlooked the role of many national and international events, and liked to conclude that the realization of India's freedom was the result of the power of non-violence. Gandhi, following the rules meant for a satyagrahi strictly and meticulously and by asking others to do so, looked like attaining the height of a *yogi* and a *rishi*. But, according to his own confessions, he did not reach that stage. The tragic assassination of the Mahatma and the propaganda made by the post-Independence leadership, the ruling Congress party, and the press cemented the popular impression. His non-violence appeared to have an irresistible force. But, the response and reaction of his adversaries, the British Raj, Muslim League, and other political parties was different.

However, Gandhi, without giving up the theoretical level of non-violence of the brave, continued to operate at the level of non-violence as a policy or expediency. Perhaps, all the major successes of Gandhi may be attributed to this form of non-violence.

Non-violence as a Policy and Expediency

Finding the Indians, particularly the Congress, weak and helpless, having very limited capacity to undergo self-suffering and moral conviction, Gandhi proposed non-violence as a policy or expediency. According to Gandhi, if it was pursued honestly and scrupulously, it was capable of achieving results to a certain extent. However, observation of the outcome of the two freedom struggles of the 1920s and the 1930s does not support the statement of Gandhi that it was less effective than non-violence of the brave. Being conducive to the background and wherewithals of the country, the policy of non-violence was wholeheartedly accepted by her people. Somewhat liberal and civilized nature of the British Raj also helped its encouragement. However, it is difficult to ascertain whether there was some change of heart in the British rulers. It is on record that the objectives of both non-cooperation and civil disobedience movements could not be achieved. Even if there was some effect or change of heart, it is doubtful if it was due to the impact of the policy of non-violence or physical pressure of the non-cooperators in 1920 or due to the fear of anarchy and chaos owing to the spread of civil disobedience movement. Nobody can be sure whether the Quit India Movement changed its policy of non-violence to something else and still claimed to remain under the purview of Gandhian non-violence.[12] Under the then prevailing circumstances, the question arises which was more powerful—non-violence of the brave (as a creed) or non-violence as a policy and expediency? For an analytical understanding, if both of them are taken together, it can be stated that effectiveness of non-violence requires a leader like Gandhi who wholeheartedly subscribes to and advocates the efficacy of non-violence (as a product of faith in religion, God and Truth) and has a large number of followers.

Non-violence as a Cover for a Coward

This was the third level of Gandhian non-violence. But Gandhi discarded cowardice displayed under the cover of non-violence. He liked to prefer violence to it. But he stood only for exceptional cases of violence. It appears, for certain unknown reasons, even after witnessing several failures of non-violence of both types, Gandhi did not make any provision in favour of use of 'force'. To him, the latter was violence committed with evil intentions. As a great leader of truth and non-violence, and confronting the British Raj, he never liked to be a votary of violence. He preferred death and self-suffering more than to resort to violence even when attacked by foreign aggressors and advised many other European nations to do the same. But he made concessions to violence in certain cases. Most important among them relates to his approval of the use of the Indian troops in 1947 to repel the Pakistani aggression in Kashmir. He was asked to justify his advice to Churchill and Hitler to adopt non-violence and yet permit the use of 'force' by India. He replied by saying that a believer in non-violence could himself not resort to violence in defence of anything, and he would also put no impediments to those whose lives are not governed by non-violence.

When we look at the actual operations of the movements of 1920, 1930 and 1942, it is difficult to ascertain whether it was based on non-violence of the brave or cowardice covered with non-violence. The Quit India Movement of 1942 was not operated under the leadership of Mahatma Gandhi, but its denouement shows what happens to a mass movement which, even if it is guided by him to run on policy of non-violence? Perhaps, the latter quite easily transforms into the non-violence of the cowards, rather both cowardice and violence.

Reconsideration

Gandhi has to be reconsidered at many levels:

1. Confusion was created when Gandhi, time and again, till the end of his life, continued to say that he had not as yet realized the Truth, God and non-violence, and still was groping in the dark: "If I was a perfect man I owe I should not feel the miseries of life which I always do. ....Mine is a struggling, striving, erring, imperfect soul." He continued to make experiments with Truth,

and had no finality. He was rarely clear on his position in matter of ultimate values. The whole edifice of Gandhi was primarily based upon credulous faith of the Indian masses. Its actual force was based on the number and power of the non-cooperators. The majority of the masses had developed absolute faith in him. It made them one with their leader who, in their minds had visualized those values and steadfastly fought for them. He came out of popular expectations, in thought, word and deed. He always was ready to stake his life for upholding those values, and make all necessary sacrifices which no other leader could do. People were so much overwhelmed by his words and deeds that they developed a kind of faith in what he said about the power of non-violence.

2. The ultimate values of Gandhi from religion to non-violence come out of subjective experience, tradition, belief or intuition. By maintaining his religion and Dharma as special and over and above sectarian religions, Gandhi gave the impression to have innovated a new religion. This stand of Gandhi was not acceptable to the orthodox followers of Islam, Buddhism, Christianity etc. "Raghupati Raghav Raja Ram" did not indicate broader view of his religion. It was not historically correct that religion has always been a creative force. Rather, in many cases, it has been a disruptive force causing wars, communalism and other evils. It was one of the factors of India's partition despite Gandhi's best efforts made in this direction. Principles of morality, as claimed by him, are also not uniform.
3. Both religion and politics, it is observable, are two separate and autonomous categories of life. For leading a religious life, it is not necessary to indulge in politics. Their purpose, nature, form and operation are different, and to some extent, may influence each other. Therefore, politics, quite opposite to Gandhi, was not a dispassionate activity or subordinate to religion. For Gandhi, politics or his engagement in the freedom movement of India was a means to the realization of his ultimate goal: self-realization. Few people agree to this understanding of politics.
4. Like any other man of religion, Gandhi is selective in choosing some of the specific attributes of God. His is a part—God. As God is ultimate value of Gandhi, it is not subject to any

empirical investigation. He is Sachchidananda, perfect, all-powerful, source of morality etc. and resides in form of a divine spark in every human being. Man being a part of His divinity is essentially good. Thus, Gandhi is selective in his appreciation of the attributes of God. He visualizes God more as Creator, Regulator, Benevolent, Blissful, Truth, *Sat*, Righteousness etc. He avoids his other known aspects, such as, Death, Destruction, Dissolution, Violence, Power and others. Gandhi's God is preferably a Sanatani Hindu Vaishnav God, involving principles of law of *karma* (action), transmigration of soul, salvation (*moksha*), re-incarnation (*avatar*), and Personal God, Heaven and Hell. He claimed to have communion with Him through intuition, 'inner voice', conscience, and prayers. He put faith, love or heart over reason and intellect. The goal of his life was realization of such God through selfless service of man. God or Truth was the Supreme End or Ultimate Value of Gandhi. Nobody could have questioned him about such God and the ways to realize Him.

5. As Gandhi's Truth or God is immanent, ubiquitous and all-permeating, everything else turns a part of it. Both ends and means being aspects of Truth are identical. To pursue means is to realize ends. God or Truth was the End or Supreme Value. But he regarded this end as unattainable, so he moved towards the relative truth. The latter permitted experimentation, trial and error, and slow progress based on personal experience. Ahimsa as relative truth was the means. Ahimsa was the means to realize Truth—absolute or relative. When this concept is adhered to, both end and means, Truth and Ahimsa, would appear relative. They are part Truth and part Ahimsa, now attainable to man. In other words, one particular end or goal can be realized by varying means. A particular means may also lead to differing goals. Means automatically does not take up to the end. Result is attained in proportion to action; means to end. But Gandhi does not agree. He regards them both ends and means as part of Truth. In this he converts his means into ends, but not vice versa.

Thus, Gandhi exaggerates and makes Ahimsa (means) all-in-all. Having adopted it he does not like to think about the Truth (end). Reverting back from his position, he declares both end and means as inseparable and parts of Truth; sides of the same coin. Thus, he goes against his own concept of relative truth. In suggesting means as end, he turns back to his goal of 'unattainable' Truth. If it is so, how can means, as claimed by him, lead to end.

But it may be, perhaps, a legal requisite which required to tell the British rulers, courts and authorities that Gandhi, the leader of the movements of 1920, 1930 and 1942, had nothing in mind but non-violence based on Truth. Each crime under British law necessitates to prove wilfullness or ill intention. In its absence, no act of Gandhi and other satyagrahis could be termed or considered or adjudicated as 'crime'.

6. The use and choice of the term violence by Gandhi is value-laden. Non-violence, to him, was non-injury to any living being by body or mind. Then, violence should be considered only as injury. It means violence could also cause injury or harm without ill-will. But, for Gandhi, it was causing harm with evil intention. Thus, like non-violence, it did not remain a neutral term. Gandhi made it an ethico-religious concept—every act of injury was considered to have been committed with evil-intention, and was 'violence'. It means no act of injury, causing harm to an enemy or adversary could be done without evil-intention. All such acts were automatically treated as 'violence' (*himsa*), hence ethically wrong and deprecable. Thus, Gandhi treats all acts of force, coercion, compulsion etc. as violence. Even state-acts to punish criminals would appear 'violence.'
7. Men of soul-force or spiritual power are always found few and far between. Even if they are found in some hundreds, they remain mostly confined to their spiritual pursuits. They could hardly be considered as dangerous to any government, group or society. They rarely have any power in material or physical sense. If the adversary had no change of heart and the creed of non-violence had failed, there was no other way left to him except putting the life at stake by fasting unto death or facing death face-to-face. Apparently, his success would surely lay in ending life for the sake of Truth and attain the ultimate goal of self-realization. Gandhi, after the sacrifice of his life, perhaps could have no problems. But how others, followers and the

people, who have not adopted the goal of self-realization, would be provided safety and protection?

He hardly thought of the situation when both non-violence of the brave as well as non-violence of policy or expediency fail to deliver goods, and the society is left unprotected. Some such thing had happened at the time of partition. What would happen in the event of clash among four or five Gandhi like leaders fighting for their respective communities having millions of followers? Evidence is not available that a few non-violent persons are ever able to turn out the aggressors after they are permitted to enter and settle down in a country. Non-violent measures undertaken later often fail to stop their misdeeds.

Similarly, anti-social elements finding non-violence as ineffective or dormant can perpetrate much more violence to society than that of a limited use of force by some trained armed persons would do some harm but defend the larger segments of society in a disciplined and legally permissible manner. What would happen if there is no civilized or liberal government available to permit the use and spread of non-violence? How would a society or community like to leave their fate in the hands of a leader whom for their defense and protection is not an end but a means to him for the realization of God? Here Gandhi appears to have been treating the whole nation as his means to realize his own personal end. Even Ahimsa was to him an end in itself.

8. Impression of non-violence a total reality and whole truth does immense harm to the cause of knowledge on the one hand, and weaken the fabric of state and society on the other. Excessive praise of non-violence as an invincible force or culmination of truth and justice would result into neglect of factors and forces making the state as viable. It would demoralize the forces strengthening the state and loosen the defence preparedness of governments. It would also embolden the elements which care little for the much praised power of non-violence.

Democracy operating on the principle of fundamental rights of the individual, periodic free elections, free press, independent judiciary, political parties, egalitarian society, welfare state and responsible government has hardly any place for the dictates of 'inner voice' and anarchic devices like fasting, non-cooperation or civil disobedience. A person, group, community or a party, having attained any height of spirituality, cannot be permitted to claim to be the only repository of Truth. The state should, instead of stopping at the gates of soul-force or non-violence of the brave, directly deal with the actual physical power of the agitating sections of masses and the use of probable potential power of the people by their leaders. Democratic politics is an inter-play of probable potential powers, direct physical power wielded by groups and parties, and counter-power of the opposing groups. Morality, religion and soul-force appear only as initiating formative power which ultimately operates on the basis of direct physical power or probable potential power. A state would neglect probable potential power of the masses at its own peril.

9. Promise and provision of non-violence in pure form for the society as a whole is futile as well as suicidal. Even a great man like Gandhi could not adopt it successfully and always found himself in an experimental stage. Neither his non-cooperation and civil-disobedience movements nor the venture of Hindu-Muslim unity could witness its complete realization. In fact, a social structure built on pure non-violence is likely to suffer erosion and break up at the hands of vested interests and inside and outside oppressors. Ordaining non-violence to one segment of society and allowing the rest to exercise their own choice amounts to put the former at the mercy of violence-prone communities.

   It happens to be more deplorable when that segment of society has already been suffering owing to her misconceived notion of Ahimsa for several centuries. The Indian history is witness to the fact that such unarmed, non-violent and peaceful communities are rarely able to stand against the onslaughts of even small bands of aggressors. Once an organized group of aggressors set foot on soil, it remains difficult to drive out them or persuade these people to adopt the pious faith of truth and non-violence. They rule over and control the rest of the credulous masses for long.

10. Attributing all superiority to non-violence often disheartens and demoralizes the persons in uniform using force and arms for the protection of society, such as, Kshatriyas classes, armed forces and the police. The ideal of non-violence which neglects all other

forms of power also discourages even the training of its armed forces and from developing and equipping them with the latest weapons. It tends to treat even its failure as success which has a deadening effect on the minds of common men. Men of non-violence like Gandhi are often devoted more to self-realization or their identity with God. They do not care much even if others do not follow them and go on indulging in their own religion. These godmen have little time for the reorganization of society and state on realistic basis. By the time, a good number of people begin to develop absolute faith in them, they happen to disappear from the scene leaving the society in vacuum, rather in worse condition. Sometimes their non-violence becomes a cover for their negligence, cowardice, imbecility and servility.

11. Often 'intention' is considered to be the core element of non-violence. But, a pious wish or faith in peace is not enough. Society is largely concerned not with mere intentions or motives, but with short and long term results, outcomes and consequences of non-violence. The partial truth of Gandhian non-violence so far has resulted in an imbalance among societal forces. Its overall impact has made even some of the smaller segments or minorities of society more powerful and dominant than bigger ones. The former have refused to adopt non-violence at latter's cost. In order to maintain balance and harmony, both state and society should concentrate on actual physical force and probable potential power of the people and act sagaciously. Votary of absolute non-violence, in public life, often claims to regard himself greater than God. The latter perhaps has not worked out the world in non-violence alone. But he claims to do so.
12. On Dalits, Gandhi gave the functional interpretation of the division of society and endeavoured to rationalize the 'varna order'. But his attempt was superfluous as the division of labour was long replaced by the ascription of status on the basis of birth, and the castes became hierarchically arranged closed occupational groups. He did not desire to introduce revolutionary changes in the outdated Hindu social structure, though devoted his rest of the life after 1934 to the cause of Harijan uplift. He worked for creating an 'integrated society' but could not find

'chemical' which would dissolve the separatist clots in the blood veins of the Indian society.

His most sincere and ardent efforts to win confidence of the Muslims and the depressed classes did not bear fruit. He was universally accepted as a saintly person but was never able to win the allegiance of caste leaders of the Hindu communities, particularly, the depressed classes. The Muslims largely remained unreconciled. To them, he was an 'outsider' and a Hindu leader.

13. His ideal state or 'Ram Rajya' existed only in heaven. No state can exist without some organization of police or army. Moral means during crisis cannot replace them. Gandhi was there at the time of communal riots in the wake of partition which he could not stop. Use of moral means in maintaining proper management-labour relations is not always helpful. Non-cooperation, civil disobedience, fasting, picketing, ostracizing etc. do not change the essential nature of exploitative capitalism. Control on economic power by these means is not feasible. Rather they give opportunity to the capitalists to become more powerful. In a way, his thinking of class cooperation, rejection of class struggle, repudiation of violence, advocacy of trusteeship etc. proved more supporting to the capitalists. Sometimes, he was considered to be friendly with the bourgeoisie. His trusteeship principle kept all the property (factories, workshops, wealth etc.) in the possession of the capitalists. There was no objective standard to judge that a particular capitalist has turned into a trustee of the property already possessed by him and would make use of it for the welfare of the society. His own suggestion contradicted himself that in case a capitalist does not adopt the trusteeship principle, his property can be nationalized and put under the joint management of the state and the labour.

14. Gandhi's ideas are not clear about democracy, representation, public opinion, civic rights, nature of state etc. He was ready to reject the opinion of the majority, and compel all to accept one man's opinion. Minorities were advised by him both to accept and reject majority decisions. His grounds of eligibility of a candidate for contesting elections are not practicable. In his sub-ideal state, police and army remain but without ever using force in the performance of their duties.

He had decried the western democracies in the *Hind Swaraj*, but ironically he had to work throughout his life for the realization of similar western type of democratic system in India.

15. Gandhi revered as mahatma and apostle of peace and non-violence has been completely lost to the fields of religion and ethics and very little efforts have been made to redeem him from the clutches of religion and morality. Such efforts have of late gained momentum with the limitless increase of the power of violence to the extent of elimination of humanity from the entire earth. Some peace-loving scholars, associations and leaders are having been finding equally viable remedy in the Gandhian non-violence. In the matter of mass awakening and resultant achievement of Swaraj, all praise has been showered on the spiritual and moral elements of non-violence relegating its material and potential aspects to ignorance and oblivion.[13] This has resulted in immense loss to the cause of knowledge of state and society at large. Blind faith and dependence on the power of non-violence may result in (a) lack of making adequate usual preparations to fight violence by violence, and (b) greater loss to man and society by resorting to non-violence. Its power should be evaluated in proper manner.

    Gandhi was unable to see and spell out the political forces lying behind non-violence. It was because of his incessant desire to realise his ultimate goal of self-realization or *moksha*. In this sense, the total thrust of his ideas and action was apolitical, or non-political, even anti-political. He could not appreciate that politics is a worldly activity and it stands to make life better here and now through human efforts. Therefore, Gandhi is more useful for those who want to live closely to religion, morality or spirituality and resort to non-violence at all costs.

    It also means there is no place for non-believers. Followers of Gandhi have to adopt his brand of faith either by reforming has own conventional religious perceptions or abandon some of them for good. In practice, his teachings were mostly addressed to the Hindus who likened him to a great *avatar*, godman, mahatma and saint. Others who were alike the Hindu followers also accorded similar respect to him. Most of them could not visualize that Gandhian apolitical ethics struck at the root of their own total philosophy, social fabric and political interests as a large Hindu community. Non-violence, despite big promises, happened to make them weaker and ultimately compelled them to submit to India's partition. The blind tradition of hero-worship carries on this trend still further. Failures are advocated as successes.

16. A good number of people regard the Gandhian thought relevant for the present as well as future. It claims to be relevant for all times and stands for all-round development. Dr. Nelson Mandela observes, "Gandhi holds the key to human progress." Some Gandhian enthusiasts are unable to conceive of the modern world without Gandhi and his thought. They say, Gandhi is more relevant today than ever before. We have to choose between "Atom" and "Ahimsa," "non-violence" and "non-existence," and between "Sarvodaya" and "Sarvanasha" (total annihilation)" (N. Narayanasamy in *Gandhi Marg*, 1996). These eulogies do not look into realities of life, society and state.[14]

Notes

1. Albert Einstein, "On Peace and Gandhi," in Norman Cousins, ed., *Profiles of Gandhi* (Delhi: Indian Book Company, 1969), p. 100.
2. V.R. Mehta, *Ideology, Modernization, and Politics in India* (New Delhi: Manohar Publishers, 1983), p. 135; and Loius Fischer, *The Life of Mahatma Gandhi* (London: Harper and Row, 1983), p. 93.
3. S.L. Verma, *On Grounds of Gandhian Polity* (Jaipur: RBSA Publishers, 1990), pp. 1-14.
4. Raghavan N. Iyer, *The Moral and Political Thought of Mahatma Gandhi* (Delhi: Oxford University Press, 1973), p. 5. Gandhi has been likened not only to Lord Krishna, Rama, St. Francis, St. John, Weslet, but also to Cromwell, Jefferson, Cobbett, Mazzini, Lincoln, Lenin, and Sun Yat-sen, and yet again to Rousseau, Thoreau, Marx, and Tolstoy.
5. V.R. Mehta, *Foundations of Indian Political Thought* (Delhi: Manohar, 1992), p. 213.
6. S.L. Verma, *On Grounds of Gandhian Polity* (Jaipur: RBSA publishes, 1990) pp. 1-14.
7. See Bhikhu Parekh, *Colonialism, Tradition, and Reform: An Analysis of Gandhi's Political Discourse* (New Delhi: Sage Publications, 1989), and his *Gandhi's Political Philosophy: A Critical Examination* (London:

Macmillan, 1989). See also Sudhir Chandra, "Difficulty of Understanding Gandhi," *Economic and Political Weekly*, Vol. 29, No. 50, December 10, 1994, pp. 3143-46.

8. Gandhi considered Unity of India and Hindu-Muslim unity as the two final truths, but he failed to protect them. He stated in *Harijan*, April 6, 1940 that he would never be a willing party to the vivisection of India. On Hindu-Muslim unity he wrote, "I do not believe that Muslims, when it came to a matter of actual decision, will ever want vivisection. Their good sense will prevent them." The two-nation theory is an untruth. Hindus and Muslims of India are not two nations. Those whom God has made one, man will never be able to divide. Still he agreed to the Rajagopalachari formula. He also agreed to the partition plan. The Simla Conference pushed Gandhi to the background leaving the party to be led by Nehru, Patel and Azad. Negotiations failed now not on political issue between India and Britain, but on the communal issue dividing different Indian groups. Failing on these two issues, he began to make politically impractical suggestions like that Jinnah should be the prime minister. Padma, op. cit., pp. 214-17. In 1940, he had described Pakistan as an untruth and had refused to accept the two-nation theory. But in 1944, he changed his views. He was prepared to go to any length to accommodate Jinnah for the sake of Hindu-Muslim unity. He was even ready to concede Pakistan provided the Muslim population was in favour of it. Oftentimes he assured his Congress colleagues that so long as he was alive, he would never agree to the partition of India and that he would not allow the Congress to accept it. But he continued to support the Rajaji formula and the Desai-Liaqat Pact. Ibid., pp. 208-18. He even did not want independence at the price of partition. Ibid., p. 224.
9. The net result of Gandhian non-violence was not necessarily love and affection from the adversary—Churchill, Linlithgow, even Wavell besides Jinnah other. See, Padma Ramkrishnan, *Gandhi and Indian Independence*, (New Delhi: Blaze Publishers & Distributors Pvt. Ltd., 1994). In the context of Hindu dominated majority of Indians, pure non-violence got him the prestige of a 'Mahatma' to the maximum by 1930, thereafter, Gandhi wanted to convert the whole Congress with his creed of non-violence. When he could not he left the Congress by October 1934, but the aura of being a Mahatma, because of his creed, continued. He carried the mass-following. Most votes for Congress candidates were a vote for Gandhi. Padma, op. cit., pp. 20-71.
10. "Jesus, Gandhi's exemplar, could not cast a spell over Judas, the Roman Pilate or any of the orthodox Jewish Priests." Quoted from Bhikhu Parekh's book, *Colonialism, Tradition, and Reform: An Analysis of Gandhi's Political Discourse*, pp. 180-81. On election of Subhash Bose as

President of the Indian National Congress by 1580 to 1375, Gandhi uttered, "Pattabhi defeat is my defeat". Bose had to tender his resignation. Padma, op. cit., pp. 93-98. Later on in 1942, Gandhi in a way acknowledged the rightness behind Bose's approach. The 1942 struggle brought Gandhi and Bose ideologically nearer to each other. The movement was a triumph of Netaji's policy. Ibid., p. 100.

11. Ashutosh Lahiry, *Gandhi in Indian Politics* (Calcutta: Firma KLM Pvt. Ltd., 1976), p. 47. See also Nirmal Kumar Bose, *My Days with Gandhi* (Calcutta: Nishana, 1953), passim.
12. Gandhi never thought in terms of a mass struggle on the dimensions of the Quit India Movement. This struggle was a forced upon the country by the arrest of Gandhi and the leaders without allowing them to parley with the Viceroy. The arrest of Gandhi and other prominent leaders suddenly plunged the country into a mad frenzy of revolt which the government hit back with all its might. However, it strengthened the Congress as political force and as the symbol of Indian nationalism. Padma, op. cit., pp. 142-44.
13. S.L. Verma, *On Grounds of Gandhian Polity*, (Jaipur: RBSA Publishers, 1990), p. 3; Geoffry Ashe, *Gandhi: A Study in Revolution*, (Bombay: Asia Publishing House, 1968), p. 144; Purshottam Mehra, 'Politician as Saint', *The Hindustan Weekly*, October 20, 1974.
14. Raghvan Iyer, op.cit., p. 13; Michael Edwards, *The Myth of Mahatma*, (New Delhi: UBS Publishers, 1986), pp. 179, 191, 203, 215, 224 and 250; and also see, Bhikhu Parekh, *Colonialism, Tradition and Reform: An Analysis of Gandhi's Political Discourse* (New Delhi: Sage Publications, 1989), and, *Gandhi's Political Philosophy: A Critical Examination*, (London: Macmillan, 1989), p. 248.

IV

Internal Threats to Hindutva

12

Communalism, Fundamentalism and Terrorism

The three problems of communalism, fundamentalism and terrorism are closely interrelated. All the three spring up from self-justified explanation and understanding of 'religion'. For such people, religion is a worldly activity conducted in the name of God. Few have for various reasons tried to throw light on the root causes of communalism and fundamentalism in India. Without understanding them properly, communal harmony, cannot be ensured.

Communalism

Few people in India know about the real roots of *communalism* in India. Even if some of them know, they, under the prevailing circumstances, act as if they do not know anything about it. Some others even when they know it in full lack courage and capacity to spell it out. A lot of people, as the circumstances permit, feel free to offer comments on communal events in India and also suggest remedies for them. They avoid in tracing out its deep roots. The problem of communalism cannot be properly addressed to simply by talking of secularism, law and order, religion or human brotherhood. It cannot be mitigated only by singing *vandemataram*, national anthem, and some emotion-pervading songs. The tricks of crying unity songs or asking people to forget the past or re-write history books as often desired by the ruling governments also do not solve the problem. To attract serious attention, some of the causes of the problems relating to communal harmony or Hindu-Muslim unity or Hindu-Christian brotherhood in India are mentioned here:

1. The Hindus are unable to forget the atrocities of the fanatic Muslims, visible almost at all important places and written in the pages of history of India, done in the past on the Hindus, Hindu institutions and Hinduism as a religion and on its different sects. Every government in India, in the interest of its survival, insists on forgetting the communal events occurred in the past. They often engage historians for rewriting history so as to disprove wars fought for religion.
2. There has been increase of the number of the Muslims from one lakh or so to presently 45 crores in the Indian sub-continent, about 30 crores in the two sovereign Muslim states of Pakistan and Bangladesh, and the rest in India. This increase has taken in the past mostly by exercise of force, violence, threat and falsehood. As there is rule of majority in democracy, more toleration on the part of the Hindus would result in the end of their existence. If this trend of displaying toleration continues, the proportion of the Muslims is likely to increase and result in the decrease of the proportion of the Hindus, ultimately resulting in the end of their survival as a majority community. This is likely to happen in near future. As a result of the acceptance of "family planning measures" by the Hindus, and their rejection by the minorities, particularly the Muslims, the Hindu proportion of the population is likely to shrink very fast. The Hindus as a minority will nowhere be allowed to survive in Muslim countries.[2]
3. God-ordained hostility of the Muslims against the non-believers (non-Muslims) and idolaters and their absolute Prophet-directed faith that their religion is the last and final message from the God, therefore, has to be accepted by the rest of the mankind. There is no room for democracy in Islamic dispensation: freedom of thought, expression and discussion, doubt or test of finality and spirit of compromise. On account of suffering violence, oppression and excesses perpetrated by Muslim invaders and rulers in the past, when doubt, criticism or

correction is entertained in the teachings of the Holy Quran or Islam, such persons are subjected to death by the believers using all possible means and methods.

4. In Islam, there is total isolation, separation and alienation of the Muslims (in line with the teachings of Islam) from other religions. Nothing can be permitted to learn from them. It has been ordained that, Islam being all-perfect, the believers have nothing to learn from any other religion.
5. Faith in the unity of Muslim community (Umma) of believers, which rejects all modern entities like state, nation, rule of law and citizenship. The believers are not bound to obey any other law coming even from the international community organizations sch as the United Nations.
6. Islam by itself is an absolutist, obligatory, temporally expanding and soldierly religion, which carries uncompromising and dominant attitude towards other religions and cultures. Rest of the Indian religions are pluralistic, rational, ascetic, other-worldly and primarily committed to seek spiritual self, hence are non-violent and tolerant in their way of life. They can hardly withstand the force and pressure of Islam. Unless there is radical transformation within Islam, other Indian religions find it difficult to put it at par with them.
7. In India, on ground of religion, caste, language or culture, there is no majority community, i.e., numbers having more than half of the total population. Only minorities, big or small, exist. Among these minorities, Muslims form the largest, most organized and divinely-ordained community. The Muslims, as a community, is already supported and strengthened by more than fifty Muslim countries whereas the Hindus (as it has happened with the Pandits of Jammu & Kashmir) lack safety, protection honour even in the country of their birth.

Thus, hardly anyone can try to solve the above mentioned grievances and difficulties of the Hindus. In place of solving them amicably and justifiably, the matter goes to the 'extremist' or 'fundamentalist' elements entrenched in both the communities. Almost all the political leaders happen to speak, for political reasons, on these lines.[3] If they do not do so, the members of their communities are likely to oppose them. This may affect their vested interests and political careers. They talk with two voices. However, in order to build up their public image, they tend to speak in general and ambiguous terms. This makes up the sole cause of the communal conflagrations from time to time. The need of the hour is to spell out the precise meaning of these terms.

Fundamentalism

Fundamentalism or extremism emerges out of above situation. It briefly means

1. to hate, do disrespect and sharply criticize other religions, its heroes and followers and their teachings and practices in the name of one's religion or God;
2. to conspire to kill prominent saints and teachers of other religions;
3. to destroy, forcibly possess or ruin property, institutions and women belonging to the members of other religious communities;
4. to organize, collect and equip co-religionists with sharp weapons, arms, bombs, swords, bows etc. to kill, create terror and threaten others;
5. to engage in the name of one's own religion in subversion, insurgency or rebellion at the instance of alien powers, organization or states;
6. to indoctrinate children and co-religionists through educational institutions, press, books, leaflets, media, speeches at religious congregations, hustings etc. and recruit them for violence;
7. to earn, donate or collect funds and arrange payment for the people engaged in such activities;
8. to indulge in activities which create and cause loss of unity, harmony, cooperation among the people of a country and encourage them towards separatism, vivisection and dismemberment as an immediate or distant goal; and
9. to organize festivals or demonstrations causing law and order problem and to threaten others at political, social, financial and religious levels.

Negatively, one is not fundamentalist or extremist if he believes in religious tenets, observes rituals or worships God in form he likes, or spreads teachings at his individual conscience level and without hurting others. When they give shape in form of action, organization, community, identity and influence, they do not reflect religion, but material interests, power and politics. But, it is important to throw light on what those tenets are. These tenets are to be evaluated on the basis of their utility toward common peace, law and order, and co-existence. Following of such tenets becomes 'fundamentalism'. It is harmful and destructive leading to communalism, even terrorism. A fanatic follower of religion acts on them doggedly in the prescribed fashion, and does not care for the results. Some people go on supporting such acts in the name of religion.[4] He is not fundamentalist when he voluntarily helps the police, intelligence services and other public agencies so as to isolate the elements of fundamentalism, before and after the occurrence of riots or communal disturbance in any form.

Terrorism

Terrorism is much more fierce, destructive and cruel than both extremism and fundamentalism. It is 'jihad' when committed in the name of God, Guru, Prophet, Holy Books or their advocates. According to the draft prepared by the Law Commission of India, a person commits a terrorist act:

- By using explosives, firearms, weapons and chemicals, which cause injury, death, destruction of property and defence equipment and disruption of essentials.
- By being a member of a banned outfit under the Unlawful Activities (Prevention) Act, 1967, and by abetting such outfits.
- By conspiring, advocating, or inciting terrorist acts.
- By harbouring a terrorist.
- By holding any property derived from terrorist crimes.
- By threatening witnesses in terrorist crimes.
- By concealing information which may be of material assistance in prevention of a terrorist act.
- By carrying weapons of explosives in a notified areas in contravention of the Arms Rules, 1962.
- By contravening any provision of the Arms Act, 1959; the Explosives Act, 1884; the Explosive Substances Act, 1908; the Inflammable Substances Act, 1952.

If the terrorist act results in death, it is punishable with death or imprisonment for life and liable for fine. Any other crime is punishable with a minimum imprisonment of three to five years. This could be extended to life term and is also liable for fine. Proceeds of terrorism, properties and assets acquired by terrorist acts are liable to be forfeited.

Often those who commit the acts of terrorism are not individuals or scattered persons. They are well-organized, equipped, trained, and financed by governments and non-governmental organizations. This makes, every kind of big and small terrorism, a kind of war on non-conventional lines.

Terrorism as War

Fight against terrorism must be treated not only as 'proxy war' but a war, which could be longer, multifaceted, more fierce and complicated. It is not 'merely terrorism' as such. It is intermixed with religious fundamentalism. There are two ways to fight terrorism. Firstly, it has to be met by force, if possible, before its occurrence, otherwise after it. The second way provides long-term solution. It requires separation of religion from religious fundamentalism and its variants. In place of religion one may also have absolute faith in some ideology. Separating religion from religious fundamentalism or fanaticism is still much more difficult. This separation has to be defined, supervised, enacted and properly implemented. Conducting war against terrorism and apprehending the terrorists, both before and after they commit the crime of terrorism, cannot be possible under the ordinary common laws of an individual country.[5] The process of law is slow, dilatory, costly and ineffective. By the time the case is decided the terrorist would have committed several fresh terrorist acts. After a few years of judicial trial, one terrorist might be sentenced to death. But before that happens, he would have killed hundreds of innocent men, women and children. Ordinary law entails so many loopholes, which are fully exploited by the terrorist links. The West has learnt this lesson quite recently but India has not followed it so far. India happens to treat 'terrorism' as mere hard 'communalism', and fails to deal with it effectively and promptly. Only the *US*, from 9/11 onwards, has shown the way to deal with it.

Prevention and containing terrorism involves suffering all sorts of pain and injury, including death, on the part of innocent people. It is the necessary price, which has to be paid by the people and their government for lack of vigilance in keeping a watch over all overt and covert activities of the terrorists and terrorists in-making. Both war against terrorism and implementation of ordinary laws and human rights as means to prevent it cannot go together. Containment of terrorism demands full or partial sacrifice of rights, conveniences and privileges in varying degrees.

The Supreme Court of India has said that fanatics had distorted religion, thus spreading the messages of terror. In a philosophical tone, the apex court said no religion propagated terrorism or hatred as love for all was the basic foundation of almost all the religions. It made these observations while upholding the life sentence awarded to all the accused in the Kolkata serial bomb blast case in the aftermath of the demolition of the Babri mosque in December 1992. "The cover of self-protection, when pierced, unravels a sinister design to unleash terror," a Bench comprising Chief Justice B. N. Kirpal, Justice K. G. Balkrishnan and Justice Arijit Paswayat said. In its attempt to find a definition of the term 'terrorism', the court found itself in the proverbial "Gordian definitional knot" and said, "lack of agreement on the definition of terrorism has been a major obstacle to meaningful international counter-measures. Cynics have often commented that one state's 'terrorists' are another state's 'freedom fighters'."

The Bench further said: "Terrorism has not been defined under TADA nor is it possible to give a precise definition of terrorism or lay down what constitutes terrorism."[6]

So, who is a fundamentalist? The fundamentalist has his own version or history, his own definition of culture, his own interpretation of religion and his own brand of nationalism. Behind all the impassioned sloganeering and pretensions of defending culture, religion and nation, the real agenda is to legitimatize an unjust and an exploitative system.

It is not that every fundamentalist sees his worldview (theocracy) as a political instrument. On the contrary the large majority of those who subscribe to such views are sincerely committed to them. But these are merely pawns and minions who have been brainwashed. And, among them, those from the economically weaker sections are often used as a canon fodder. But for those who are pulling the invisible strings, fundamentalism remains but a political strategy.[7]

Notes

1. The present UPA (Congress-led) government from 2005 onwards is seriously engaged in re-writing history and other NCERT books revised last during NDA government.
2. *Rajasthan Patrika*, December 13, 2003: In India, minorities coming from outside like the Jews and the Parsis are negligible. 90 per cent Muslims and 99.9 per cent Christians living in India belong to India. However, in 1881, there were 79.32 per cent Hindus and 21 per cent Muslims in India. In 1991 they respectively became 68.03 and 30 per cent. Christians in 1881 were 0.6, increased to 2.1 per cent in 1991; see also, fn. 1, Chapter 7; Seeds of communalism may be witnessed in the Constitution of India in the sense that its Article 30 authorises minorities to have educational institutions without any control of the state whereas it does not authorize the 'majority communities', to do so. Such attempt was rejected by the Supreme Court when the Ramkrishna Mission tried to avail of those rights after its declaration to be a minority under Article 30. But ruling governments often make use of this provision to appease minorities.
3. For example, the bone of contention is not Ayodhya but a particular plot. Not even a particular plot but an area of a mere 80×40 square feet 'sanctum sanctorium' of the proposed Ram Temple. If it could be located a mere 30 feet away the dispute could be resolved. However, the other alternative is much more easy and just. But, the "once a mosque, always a mosque" claim of maulvis and mullahs is nothing but a lie. They cannot deny that in many Muslim countries, mosques have often been shifted even to broaden highways. So, the insistence that a mosque must be rebuilt at the exact spot is anything but religious.
4. Asghar Ali Engineer has his own view. To hide his own fundamentalism, he writes, "Fundamentalism should not be confused with fundamentals of religion. Those who believed that every word of the Bible is literally divine word were called fundamentalist. (Ali uses this logic). To follow Islam or Hinduism should not be described as 'fundamentalism'. Even to follow orthodox traditions of religion should not be dubbed as 'fundamentalism' though one may not agree with orthodox practices." *Secular Perspective: Fundamentalism and Terrorism*, Vol. VI, No. 1, January 1-15, 2003.
5. See, Chapter 19, "War against outer and Inner Form of Terrorism".
6. *Times of India*, September 7, 2002.
7. Javed Akhtar, "Beyond real Estate-Ayodhya: The choice isn't between a temple and mosque. It's between democracy and totalitarianism", *Hindustan Times*, July 15, 2003.

13

Jihad as Terrorism

Fanatic followers of Islam, by their acts and understanding, have made it a religion preaching terrorism. It may not be a whole truth. But a large number of people have found that whenever anyone raised any kind of doubt, suggested, reformed or changed or examined veracity of some of the tenets, teachings and events inscribed in the Holy Books of Islam, he is put under the threat of 'fatwa' or death sentence.[1] As soon as one questions its formulations or teachings, every Muslim considers himself authorized by God to punish him. Man is a rational animal by nature, but the Islamists promptly forbid use of reason. Most of the Islamic rulers, Muslim communities and clergy stand by and support all such acts of violence, which are usually considered as terrorism.

Internally, the whole of Islam may not be teaching or preaching terrorism. But there must be some statements in the Holy Books which authorize them to indulge in terrorism.[2] It might be done just to obey the divine directives or punish the non-believers or propagate it by deeds of violence. Thousands of terrorists claim to act on these divinely-ordained statements. Millions of Islamists apparently do not appear to agree with them. But, only few come forward openly to denounce, boycott or oppose them. Because they do not organize to stop these fanatics from blaming terrorism on the Holy Books, it is taken for granted that they believe in the religious base of their violent acts. It appears that the terrorists are doers and others are merely passive onlookers. The terrorists do not see these passive onlookers as believers of Islam.

Thus, its followers feel authorized to go to the way of terrorism. It is divine path to them. They see the whole world as anti-or non-Muslim.[3] Therefore, in the name of Islam, they can commit any kind of violence. They are ready to make any sacrifice. No power on earth can stop them. Weapons, diplomacy, technology and politics are unable to restrain terrorists. Islamic rulers, dictators and political leaders make full use of their commitment to Islam. No other religion or ideology has been able to come up to face this encounter. Terrorism is treated as an unfailing weapon of religion. Religions that thrive on teachings of peace, toleration, other-worldly bliss and non-violence simply have to surrender to them. It has disabled the nation-state, superiority of democratic systems and well-equipped standing armies.

A large number of scholars, intellectuals and leaders already knew the power of Islam, but only a few realize that presently it is the perennial source of terrorism in the modern world. But for the sake of their own survival, fear of widespread communal disturbances, dependence on goodwill of the Muslims for protecting their vested interests and maintenance of fragile polities, they do not speak out the reality. The killing sword of Islamic terrorism continuously hangs over their head. Muslims and non-Muslims all suffer from this threat. So far, there is no remedy available to man to escape from this type of divine scourge. Predicament of man is that he cannot even express his agony. Any attempt to analyze or discuss the mystery, or casting doubt, making criticism or suggesting correction, reform or remedy in the tenets of Islam is likely to result in severe punishment, humiliation, destruction and death of the person or persons engaged in such activities. Islam authorizes every believer to stop and punish such acts.

In all other religions, it is possible to discuss and evaluate their contents by saying that God exists or does not exist.[4] It is possible to opine that He is different from what is said about Him. As He is Almighty, it is suggested that there is no need to send any messenger, or specially produced son, to incarnate Himself or make direct appearance to convince human beings about His existence or give directions how to lead good life. It can be discussed whether His utterances are misleading, doubtful or irrational, or are wrong. They can even be subjected to correction. Other religions permit man to think and find if their teachings are outdated, impractical, irrational or unacceptable. Even the acts, utterances or lifestyle of the preacher, messenger or godman can be evaluated in a different manner. Some of his teachings can be given up without any serious difficulty. Surely, the priests, guardians and leaders of these religions make all attempts to keep their teachings intact, try to ostracize non-followers from the community and threaten divine punishment in the next world. However, this punishment is said to be awarded by divine agencies—gods, goddesses and devil. Humans are not authorized to punish non-believers, idolaters, renegades or sceptics for violation of divine injunctions. Non-Islamic religions do not imprison the human minds by disallowing their doubts, discussion, analysis and suggestions of reform. They command no threat to their lives.

Islam stands on quite different footing from them. It does not permit anyone of these outlets. A follower of Islam has to have full faith in many tenets of his religion. Some of the obligatory tenets are given below:

1. God has very kindly made revelation, given commands and directions to their community at the appointed time and place.
2. It is believed that these commands and directives were given to the Prophet or Messenger who declared them to be obeyed by all persons, irrespective of time and place.
3. The Message written in form of the Holy Quran after its revelation to the Prophet is the last and final one. It can never be amended, revised or changed by any human being.
4. God or His Messenger in that revelation has authorized the believers to bring all others to that faith, by all means.
5. One can attain Bliss, Grace, Heaven or Divine Favour only when a follower himself acts on or compels others to accept and follow these teachings. He is assured of all pleasures here and hereafter.
6. Those who do not obey are liable to be punished by the followers of Islam or the Islamic courts or the rulers of the Islamic state.
7. Islam demands complete faith, total surrender and strict adherence to it in letter and spirit.

8. Islam claims to envelope all the followers of the world as its community, and does not permit any other institution like state, nation, constitution or creed to stand before or run parallel to it. It demands undivided loyalty to it.
9. The rest of the social, legal, political and ritual set-up is also ordained to be the part of the Holy Quran. It has to be accepted by all, irrespective of differences of race, caste, colour, social status, language and culture except slaves, non-believers, women and animals.
10. Islam literally means peace, but it permits the use of force or violence. In this respect, Prophet Mohammad has asked the followers learn from his life and actions.

Thus, most of the tenets make up and generate, if one accepts them, the basic spirit of terrorism in varying degrees—Islamism, communalism, extremism, fundamentalism, fanaticism and terrorism. Islam being the best and the last revelation has to be adopted by mankind. A believer is authorized to pursue all peaceful and violent means and bring out rule of Allah or the Holy Quran. Critics of the Holy Book have no right to exist. All other laws and institutions are subordinate to the Islamic injunctions.

Maulana Saud Alam Qasmi says that the Islamic believer can kill a person in retaliation of murder and/or if he spreads mischief in the land (verse 32). In other words, a Muslim is duty-bound to oppose 'oppression' and not to oppose any other person if he incites violence with 'justification'. He is permitted to kill a person for a murder and for spreading 'mischief' in the land. Obviously, the meanings of words like 'oppose', 'oppression', 'violence', 'justification', 'mischief', 'murder' etc. can be stretched to the extent of joining terrorism. Every righteous person has been given the duty to 'oppose' injustice and oppression to anyone everywhere.

Islam appeared in a non-state and non-nation society. It was a favourable situation in the hands of the Prophet and his successors for the spread of the message of Islam. There were communities, religious groups and hordes of nomads in Arab. Prophet Mohammed successfully converted almost all to accept Islam.[5] The Holy Quran was made the sole guide. There were no entities like state, nation and citizenship, which could bind a believer or follower of Islam. Thus, Islam appeared global by nature. Being the last message of God, the Holy Quran stood over and above everything. It is the religion of the whole Ummah (the community of the believers) who are inhabiting the world over. Every Muslim is equipped with the divine right to use force in self-defence and fight against oppression anywhere in the world. Operationally, every believer has the right to be a practitioner of violence. However, in case of adverse circumstances, he is directed to remain silent or submissive till opportune moment arrives.

It means a Muslim can live and follow his tenets only when he lives in a community without having a state or nation. However, if he is compelled to live in a state, or a nation or a community different from a Shariat or Quran ruled entity, he stands at war with it. He can be at peace only in a society of Islam. In a Muslim state too, which is not run according to the tenets of Islam, he finds himself at war with it. From this point of view, a state, where there are persons belonging to Islam or Islam-like religion, unless it is run in accordance with the injunctions issued by that religion, they are bound to consider themselves at war with the prevailing dispensation.

Iqbal A. Ansari reiterates that the Koran (Quran) validates use of force for self-defence when people are subjected to extreme persecution to the extent that they cannot practise freely their religion and have been forced to flee their homes. It can be exercised against the 'kafirs' who drive Muslims out of their homes and who are bent on annihilating Islam. Force is legitimized for liberating a people who have been oppressed and tyrannized beyond endurance: "In cases of lawful use of force, it is ordained by the Shariat that force will be used when all other methods of redress of wrong have been exhausted."

Whether one is Muslim or a non-Muslim, he has to accept the Holy Book as the last and final word of God. None is allowed to discuss it. One cannot raise any objection to statements made in it. If someone dares to do it, he can be killed on spot. Every Muslim considers it as his prime duty to kill the person raising doubt or objection in those holy statements. Such killers regard themselves as 'soldiers of religion' and 'loving sons of God'. He is destined to go to heaven directly. Overwhelmed with such feelings a believer can unhesitatingly engage himself in the job of killings or terrorism.

A Muslim has to appear diehard, and there is no way out. The moment it appears that he lacks some faith in the Holy Book or tries to interpret it in a different or subjective manner, he would be declared renegade, non-Muslim, 'kafir' and the like. The punishment for committing such heinous crime or appearing to do that can go to any extent. Being the last message of God, the Holy Quran stands over and above everything. There can be no change in it. It has to be obeyed by the whole of Ummah (the community of the believers) spreading world over in billions. It is the final law over and above every other law. Islam is global by nature. Supporters of entities like state, nation and citizenship, foolishly complain that the Islamic extremists in the name of 'jihad' are attempting to mould the whole world into their ideology. They forget that they are doing what they are directed to do it. Every Muslim is equipped with the divine right to use force in self-defence and fight against oppression anywhere in the world. All this prompts the believers to operate as extremists, insurgents and rebels. There is no way to advise them to live like good citizens. All depend on their own conscience and understanding. Only the follower has to decide on restraining his obedience to certain parts of the Holy Quran. The believers are judges unto themselves and have divine sanction to use force. It depends on their individual understanding, training and education that to what extent they fight for the cause of religion. All from simple believers to hardened fanatics, fundamentalists, extremists and terrorists can legitimately claim to commit acts of violence in the name of religion almost everywhere.[6]

Thus, terrorism committed in the name of Islam is 'jihad' (a religious act) for such Muslims.

Geopolitical Terrorism

There is one another source of terrorism—of both religion-related and secular. The two can be represented respectively by Al Qaida and LTTE. Presently, the world community is worried about religion related, fundamentalist or Jihadi terrorism. It appears beyond any remedy, cure or compromise. This form of terrorism comes out of excessive communalism and extremism or fundamentalism. It appears when the adversary or enemy is state, and because of its power, violence perpetrated by communalism and extremism fails to achieve the desired result. Their desired goal is achievement of a sovereign Muslim state, or at least autonomy in all internal affairs. Finding itself unable to win the battle, it resorts to religion-related terrorism. Jihadi terrorism is the offshoot of extremism emerging via communalism. It is directly related to the increasing density of Muslim population in a part of a country or state. This intensification of Muslim population can be natural, contrived or planned. It remains natural till the native or local population of the area is unaware or does not pay any attention to it or is hardly able to think about its long-term interests. It can be contrived or planned. Such intensification of Muslim population is being created in some of the districts of the north-eastern states of India. It can also happen as the result of large-scale conversion of the people belonging to other religions. It so happened about two centuries ago in parts of Jammu & Kashmir. Such examples can be multiplied from several parts of India and some other countries. Much depends on the spirit of a particular religion. The formula of this religion-related terrorism is—Muslim majority—communalism of violence—extremism—acts of terrorism. Its goal is attainment of autonomy or a separate sovereign state for a Muslim area. Briefly, it is exercise of murder and violence for power in the name of God. Its basic urge comes from some specific religion.

Everywhere, terrorism is breaking out in this manner. Chechnya is a province or part of Russian Federation. It happens to be a Muslim majority area. There communalism is flagrating into terrorism via extremism. Islamic terrorists there are committing terrorist acts of the worst type. So is the case of Philippines a country of Christian majority. It has also an area of Muslim majority, which has been treading on the same path—from communalism to terrorism via extremism.

Next comes Great Britain. During the freedom movement, Britain following the policy of divide and rule used to encourage the Muslim majorities in different parts of India for demanding autonomy. It resulted into partition of India into two hostile states: India and Pakistan. It had patronized the same policy—Muslim majorities in some provinces, special rights for the Muslims, encouraging their demands for autonomy, spread of communal violence, acceptance of self-determination, grant of partition and status of a sovereign state to the Muslim majority areas. Now, the Muslims of Britain also want to have the same. The Al Mukajiran organization of Great Britain, after dissolving its separate existence, has given a call to all British Muslims there to speak with one voice for making a demand to have a sovereign Muslim state out of Great Britain. According to its leader Sheikh Umar Vakri Mohammad, the British Muslims should declare to have a war between Islam (Muslims) versus

Satan (Great Britain). Finding exercise of communalism and extremism difficult and inadequate, they have resorted to the path of religion-related violence. To realize their goal, they are treading on the same path. They have gone far ahead of communalism and have opted for terrorism. Thus, densification of Muslim areas as the result of mass immigration and constant misuse of environment of civic freedom has shown them the much known route of terrorism.

Britain was never serious on fundamentalism growing there. Abu Qatada, a radical Islamic cleric, known as the godfather of world terrorism, was granted asylum. For years he drew a monthly £ 1,000 benefit from the British government. He was named as the person directly involved in inspiring the September 11, 2001 attacks in the US.[7] For years, the British and other western governments have followed the enigmatic and inexplicable policy of giving shelter to foreigners whose political or religious followers carried out a campaign—quite often violent and secessionist—in their countries of origin, e.g., Jagjit Singh Chouhan, A.Z. Phizo, and several others. Al Qaida mainly comprised Arabs but the London attacks were carried out (on July 7 and 27, 2005) by British born persons of Pakistani origin and connections.[8] British Prime Minister Tony Blair believes that the terrorist bombers who struck London in July were motivated by the same kind of hatred and fanaticism as terrorists in Kashmir and Afghanistan. He said, "The roots of this go very, very deep. And the roots are found in the teaching of hatred at a very, very, early age". The bombers had Pakistani origins and had attended Pakistani madrassas. It was necessary to tackle "the culture and ideology of extremism that breeds it".[9] Mohammad Zia ul Haq has observed that foreign Muslim religious leaders, who have been residing in Great Britain for the last several decades, are misusing mosques for inciting Muslims against that country. They would have either been sentenced to death or put behind bars, had they been living in some other state.[10]

Great Britain is conscious now. It has taken many steps, besides standing by with the US in the war against terrorism. All new British citizens are required to take pledge of loyalty. The 1,12,000 people, who became British citizens each year, will have to pledge loyalty to their new country as part of their citizenship ceremonies. The citizenship oath and pledge follows as: "I, (name). (swear by Almighty God)/(do solemnly and sincerely affirm) that, on becoming a British citizen, I will be faithful and bear true allegiance to Her Majesty

Queen Elizabeth II, her heirs and successors according to law. I will give my loyalty to the United Kingdom and respect its rights and freedoms. I will uphold its democratic values. I will observe its laws faithfully and fulfil my duties and obligations as a British citizen."[11] But, in view of living there, UK is also timid and lax. An estimated 85 per cent of the 2,000 imams in the UK are foreign born and have mostly come from Pakistan and West Asia. It was suspected that many radical imams had entered the country and were misleading young Muslims there. Still, Tony Blair liked to scrap the Britishness test for them. This is the second climb down by his government in a week. The proposal to seal mosques suspected of having extremist links was dropped a few days earlier.[12] However, his understanding on terrorism is better than that of the American, as he rightly said: "The roots of extremism go very, very deep. And, the roots are found in the teaching of hatred at a very, very early age. They will see any issue to justify what they do. But actually the fundamental point about their ideology is a hatred for anyone different from them."[13] But, so far, the UK has not done anything in this direction whereas the US makes fierce attacks on terrorism directly and promptly.

The outcome of this demographic phenomenon, i.e., densification of Muslim population is the cause of growth of separatism and demand of autonomy in the beginning and of formation of a sovereign state after a few decades by the organized elements of Muslim community.

The partition of India took place simply on the basis of this trend. It was imposed as a result of the claims of autonomy to the areas where Muslims happened to be in majority. As formation of an independent state on the basis of religion (Islam) was rejected by the Indian National Congress in the beginning, the demand of partition was converted from religion to nationality by the Muslim League. It was advocated as right to self-determination. This conversion took place from religion to nationalism through the exercise of violence, often practised by forces of communalism, communalism invites extremism. Behind the partition of India, apparently, there appears the facade of two-nation theory, but in fact, it was the result of the creation of Muslim majorities happened to emerge in different parts of the British provinces. These majorities were organized by the Muslim League under the banner of Islam. It can also be seen as geopolitical or territorial terrorism. Pakistan was realized just through the exercise of communal violence. No need was felt to resort to extremism or terrorism.

Under the Indian Independence Act, 1947 the native states were permitted to join India or Pakistan or stand free in agreement with the two newly born states: India and Pakistan. It was for the native state to decide. The state of Jammu & Kashmir was one of them. Pakistan made an illegal claim, that being a Muslim majority there, the state of Jammu & Kashmir has to join Pakistan. To the misfortune of Pakistan the Muslim majority of Jammu & Kashmir was not willing to join Pakistan. In spite of making of all-out efforts, the Muslims of Jammu & Kashmir somehow did not come under the sway of communalism or got involved with extremism. After the failure of Pakistan in the mobilization of communal forces and in launching it from its territory, it, violating international law illegally and forcibly, occupied parts of Jammu & Kashmir. After losing four wars, Pakistan found terrorism as the only way to grab Indian parts of Jammu & Kashmir, particularly the Kashmir valley, where the Muslims form an absolute majority. During the cold war, Pakistan had already exercised the weapon of 'Jehad' for helping the USA in uprooting the occupation of USSR in Afghanistan. Pakistan had succeeded in organizing the fanatic Talibans to take over Afghanistan. America gave immense military and financial aid to Pakistan for this adventure. After the 9/11 attack, America again sought the help of Pakistan for crushing the Al Qaida and the Talibans and took over Afghanistan. With this experience, Pakistan has made a vow to apply the same formula and launched the weapon of Jihad in India. Since then, it has regularly been dispatching the terrorists in form of extremists and infiltrators expecting help and rebellion from the Muslim majority of Jammu & Kashmir. But its strategy of creating an independent Muslim state by partition on the basis of intensification of Muslim majority, and by conversion of their rights into demands of autonomy through spread of communalism, inciting the communal forces to practices large-scale violence or extremism against the ruling government or the majority community has so far has not succeeded. therefore, Pakistan has been resorting to acts of terrorism, calling the terrorists as 'freedom fighter'.

Geopolitical terrorism, ultimately, is also based on religious fundamentalism. Some ways to deal with it can be: (i) inculcation of liberal education, (ii) settlement of strong non-Muslim communities there in large number, (iii) provisions of preventive detention and award of prompt and severe punishment to persons committing crimes in the name of religion, and (iv) special governance.

Notes

1. See, back, Chapter 12, "Communalism, Fundamentalism and Terrorism".
2. Mani Shankar Aiyar is an atheist. Arun Shourie a Hindu who rejects the existence of a compassionate God and subscribes to the Buddha's belief in all pervading *dukh* (sorrow). Quoting the book *Confessions of a secular Fundamentalist* (Penguin) Khushwant Singh writes about Shourie's reply to Airyar's questions that "Adhering to Islam in purity would make it impossible to live in a multi-cultural, multi-religious society and still abide by the tenets of Islam". Aiyar again asked, "If you are faithful to the edicts of Islam as enshrined in the Koran and the Shariat, would you have difficulty in being a good Indian". Shourie answered in the affirmative and went on to define a good Muslim: "If 'good Muslim' means brotherhood of man and so on, then there is no difficulty. But if it means as 1,000 verses in the Koran say, "Spread Islam, have nothing to do with these kafirs, kill them, they are untrustworthy, they are unclean", then?" The Hadith is full of this. There are rewards for killing the kafir. If this is a good Muslim, then a multi-religious society in India would become impossible.' "More secular than thou", Khushwant Singh, *Hindustan Times*, February 26, 2005.
3. Osama bin Laden in his recently released tapes again has threatened US that he has not attacked America after 9/11, 2001 only because of lack of adequate preparation. The US should get away from the Muslim areas at the earliest. *Rajasthan Patrika*, January 20, 2006.
4. See, Chapter 14, "Questions and Culture of Liberal Muslims".
5. The whole of Arabia, which had a very evolved civilization, was run over in a matter of just 20 years. Persia collapsed within 50 years. Buddhist Afghans put up a brave resistance for 300 years but, in the end, they also collapsed. In all of these countries today there remains nothing pre-Islamic worth the name save for some broken down architectural monuments from their pre-Islamic past.
6. British Prime Minister Tony Blair believes that the terrorist bombers who struck London in July were motivated by the same kind of hatred and fanaticism as terrorists in Kashmir and Afghanistan. Blair said, "The roots of this go very, very deep. And the roots are found in the teaching of

hatred at a very, very, early age". The bombers had Pakistani origins and had attended Pakistani madrasses. It was necessary to tackle "the culture and ideology of extremism that breeds it". *Hindustan Times*, September 8, 2005; See, poetic expression of from the diary of an Afghan terrorist:

We saw Russia disintegrate
Now we will see India fall apart
In the flames of Jehad
We will see America ablaz

7. He is a Palestinian whose real name is Omar Mahamood Abu Omar. *Hindustan Times*, May 22, 2003.
8. About 80 British Muslims, most of the originally from Pakistan, had joined the Iraqi resistance. Another 3,000 British Muslims had attended Islamic training camps in Pakistan, Afghanistan and Central Asia and then returned home, Vikram Sood, 'The aliens have landed', *Hindustan Times*, July 28, 2005.
9. *Hindustan Times*, September 8, 2005.
10. Mohammad Zia ul Haq, 'Attempt to save Islam from Extremists', *Rajasthan Patrika*, November 4, 2005.
11. *Hindustan Times*, July 28, 2003.
12. *Hindustan Times*, December 21, 2005.
13. *Hindustan Times*, September 8, 2005. In comparison with this view, the American understanding is simple and does not go deeper: US ambassador to India Robert D. Blackwell said, "Those who murder innocents for political motives and who seek to bring down the very pillars of our democracy in New York, in Washington, at the Assembly in Srinagar, at the Parliament in New Delhi, and presently every day in J&K, are terrorists. These murderers are not misunderstood idealists. They are not disadvantaged dissidents. They are not religious perfectionists. And they are not freedom fighters." *Hindustan Times*, July 18, 2003. With this understanding USA cannot be expected to go deeper towards elimination of religion related Terrorism. As it does not have areas occupied exclusively by Muslim majorities, it overlooks this internal form of territorial Terrorism. The US connives at Al Qaida people who have access to crude nuclear bombs. George Tenet, former CIA Director, finds Pakistan's father of Pakistani Nuclear bomb A.Q. Khan is at least as dangerous as Osama bin Laden. In the light of the CIA warning of Al Quida's readiness to use "dirty bomb" against the US, the latter must investigate the full extent of Pakistan's role in nuclear proliferation. A.Q. Khan had been running a private company for the dissemination of nuclear weapons' know how blueprints, technology and equipment, as he did with Libya and Iran. P.N. Khera, "Weapons of Choice", *Hindustan Times*,

November 30, 2004. For more, see, fn. 34, Chapter 19. Besides this, see also, for an American road to jehad: The US News and World Report reveals that in the 1990s between 1000 and 2000 US citizens left the country to take up to jihad. Since 1989, some 400 recruits have left the US and Canada to be trained in Pakistan and Afghanistan alone. *Times of India*, June 15, 2002.

14

Questions and Culture of Liberal Muslims

There are many questions and problems arising in Muslim minds. A Muslim cannot dare to express them to anyone. He is socialized, trained and forced to avoid them. Nobody can rescue him from this predicament. But his rational mind constantly fights against himself. These are concerns, especially, of a liberal Muslim.

Few Muslims are able to think that their orthodox adherence of the Holy Quran and other religious books in the present form and their wishful efforts in keeping them intact are proving self-defeating.[1] Rather, the majority of the Muslims by their doing, believing and behaving in the present form are narrowing down the goals underlying the revelation. Some questions and the outcomes emerging from their non-response are being posed here:

About Man's Status

- Does religion exist for man or man for religion?
- Should one regard 'man' and his 'reason' as the final source of authority to judge things for himself or not?
- How can the utterances of God or Prophet appearing in the past be right for the man of today?

- Why should one accept by order, threat or early education thrust in childhood all that what has been said and written in the Quran and other holy books? Without voluntary acceptance, how can it be called morality or religion?
- Should not one accept teaching of the holy books only when he himself feels and is convinced to believe after having his or her experience?

About God

- If Almighty God is powerful as he himself is supposed to have uttered in the holy books that he can do everything for man and his cosmos could there be the need to make revelation at his own will or at man's request through some human agency?
- Was God himself not capable enough to give his message to all human beings at the same time? What is the need to do it, particularly, when several messengers had already done it? Is he not intelligent and free enough to see that everyman does, even after having any message, what he feels, needs and wills something to do at his own specified place and time?
- Why should the God/Prophet bind himself with the declaration that now onwards none else would not come to speak, reveal or declare directions in this manner?
- By doing so does not the Quranic God appear doing something 'personal' or showing his hidden ego in giving direction that all men are under obligation to acknowledge his existence and obey him in the manner he has ordained without using their reason?

About Messenger

- Why should a man, community or group of people of today accept a particular revelation (the Quran) that had happened in the past at a particular time and place and among the members of some particular community and made in a particular language as useful, last and final one?
- How would it be verified that it was revealed by God only or through someone called as Prophet or Messenger?
- What is the status of those Muslims who realize God without adhering to the Shariat injunctions, and claim to have reached that stage and realized him? Why should they be not accepted as

Prophet if they begin to preach and announce the revelation of God to man? Who will, how and why one should deny them from doing so? On what basis one can oppose them, in case such objector has or has not realized him?

- How any godman, messenger or representative of God or 'Avatar' can, appearing as a man like him could be treated as the final arbiter of good or evil acts for the rest of the mankind?

About the Use of Force and Violence

- Should every Muslim individually and the Islamic groups and rulers generally be equipped with the divine right to use force in 'self-defence' and fight against oppression anywhere in the world? The historical-institutional Islam had used this divine injunction to wage wars and convert peoples and communities. It is quite obvious that the Koran does not stand for absolute pacifism.
- Is use of force for self-defence still valid when a few Muslims here and there are subjected to extreme persecution or they find them unable to practise freely their religion or are forced to flee their homes? Can the use of force in this nuclear age be legitimized for liberating a people who have been oppressed and tyrannized beyond endurance? Will not the liberator die along with the oppressor in a nuclear war? Does such act not grant legitimacy or authorize him to kill the self-same liberator beforehand?
- Is it still valid neglecting plurality of religions to authorize a believer to bring all human beings to join that faith by all means so that he may attain bliss, grace, heaven or divine favour? If he acts on or compels others to follow these teachings he is assured of all pleasures here and hereafter. Those who do not obey are liable to be punished by the followers of Islam or the Islamic courts or the rulers of the Islamic state. Does it not amount to elimination of other religions and communities?

About Islam as Power of Final Religion

- Is it proper, justifiable and permissible for the Muslims to make Islam as the only power of the world?
- What would happen if some other religion also directs its followers to be like Islam?

About the War with Non-Islamic State

- Can Islam and modern state go together?
- Can a modern state be organized and operated on the tenets of Islam and vice versa?
- Should Muslims be permitted to consider themselves to be at war when living in non-Islamic states till it is ruled over by Islam? Would it not make them suspects or criminals everywhere?

About Democracy, Rule of Law and the UN

- As Islam requires absolute faith in religion and does not allow supremacy of state, law and other non-Islamic regional and global arrangements, is it possible for it to work within a democratic set-up?
- Would the Muslims consider themselves bound by the Constitution of India in case it clashes with the teachings of the Quran?
- Is Islam ready to accept and implement 'rule of law' in the modern sense of the term?
- Would the Islamic states like to abide by international laws and the resolutions of the UN?

Often, such questions motivate a Muslim mind to be liberal and tolerant. A Muslim living in the 21st century and having faith in democracy and rule of law thinks, feels and behaves differently from others:

1. Often he believes that there is an all-pervading Energy, Creativity or Almighty Power which can do, create or operate everything in the universe. He need not (i) speak or reveal his message in person or through some messenger, holy man or God; (ii) write some scriptures, codes or holy book/s; (iii) there is no need to do so for some particular tribe or community at some specific time and place; and (iv) declare that his message is the last and final one. God is impersonal energy which lives in all, both animate and inanimate.
2. If God is God, as experienced, seen or felt by some persons, He can never favour or go against the existence of some community, its practices, beliefs and rituals. He cannot ask his believers to eliminate idolaters, and ask his followers, on the other hand, to worship and kiss some supposedly God sent 'pious stone', and

collect for pilgrimage at some particular place, Mecca or Sangam as all places are sacred being creations of God or nature.

3. If a man as a man feels that he keeps alive because of a small fraction of that all-pervading and all-creating Almighty exists within him, like that of any other human beings, he finds no right with him to kill, harm or injure any other man. Even when he does not believe in the existence of that Creator or Energy, he has no moral right to kill or use force against any other man even when that man is an idolater, infidel or non-believer. If that man himself reaches death, he would be killed or finished by Creativity or God himself.

   However, for dealing with the problems of crimes like violence, oppression, exploitation etc. and welfare of men and women, states over and above every other form of organization and religions have emerged as sovereign entities during the last several hundred years. They have developed an impartial and effective system of governance and compliance to it is obligatory for all. If someone, on any ground, commits violence, kills or hurts another person, he would be treated as 'criminal' and punished by the state concerned.

4. If someone feels solace ad seeks inspiration out of saying prayers to Creativity, it should be done without hurting or disturbing others for others might also be doing the same for them. As Creativity, Energy or Almighty is present everywhere, there is no need to say prayer at a particular time, place or by conducting it under the directives of some specific person, or only in some formally prescribed manner. As it can be conducted subjectively in many ways, modes and places, every man can adjust oneself with the demands of modern living. As God or Creativity does not need prayer for Himself from anyone, it cannot be imposed or made compulsory by a man for another man. God does not require any kind of protection or respect from man in form of building temples, mosques, churches, gurudwaras, monasteries or other fortifications for him. No war can be fought for or against him. He already has His governance over man and creation. No particular rule has to be established in his name. Creativity does not allow anyone to be his guardian or protector or supporter.

5. As God has created both man and woman (and other creatures), and left them free to live as they like and think over. As such, there is no room for domination of man over woman, and vice versa. He has no concern whether man has one or more than one wife, woman puts on 'burqua' or any particular dress or are divorced at will of her husband. However, it is against the universally accepted principle of equality of man and woman, if the latter are forced to live below dignity, exploited or punished for their being a woman. All such, inequalities are ultimately 'man-made' and can be easily done away with.[2]

While adopting liberalism, he can still remain a Muslim. For this he has to keep himself away from certain prescriptions and directions given in the Holy Quran. He may continue to pay respect and have faith in all the basic tenets of Islam, but can not act on all injunctions of the holy book. In view of emergence of entities like State, democracy, rule of law, peaceful co-existence and nationism, he does not feel any necessity individually to fight oppression, oppose non-believers and eliminate idolaters. He virtually gives up his religion-directed right to use force or violence, and believes that the state is rightly doing this job for them. In a democratic set-up there are various ways and means to ventilate his grievances and get redress through various agencies and institutions. He believes that Islam is the religion of peace. He does not find Islam to be the last, final and best of all hitherto existing religions. No religion should ask the devotees to bring the rest of mankind to its fold. Such Muslims enjoy happiness, peace and harmony by practising only the humanitarian teachings of the Holy Quran. They also have enough respect for other religions and their religious practices. Their behaviour is also reciprocated by the followers of other religions also. In effect, all happen to live with peace and harmony. In this process, they happen to come closer and get acquainted with other cultures, languages and traditions. They begin to reside fearlessly in the mixed colonies and grow a sense of brotherhood. Their cooperation with them further strengthens when they happen to live together in such manner for a long time.

Such liberal Muslims get respect and affinity by living among the non-Muslims. They even display allegiance and spirit of sacrifice in defending the land and people of their country of birth and residence. In this manner, they identify their interests with the people as a whole. Thus, as part of a nation, they do not have to be treated merely as a minority or groups of guests and strangers living at the mercy of the majority. In a multicultural society, communities following different religions live together peacefully on the condition that they willingly like to put all of their outward activities and areas under the common control and discipline of the state. There can be no objection if they keep their faith confined to themselves, but practising it is left subordinate to supremacy of law.

However, such liberal Muslims have to face a typical dilemma. If they conform to the liberal principles, they are not considered as true believers and are liable to be punished here and after. Their religious and political leaders look down upon them.[3] They are treated as non-Muslims and can be punished in terms of Islamic directives. Every Muslim is authorized to punish such non-conforming Muslims. Islam does not and can not accept so-called 'liberal' Muslims as true believers. It respects only Islamic Muslims as Muslims who should be willing to bring the rest of mankind under the Islamic fold.

Notes

1. See, Chapter 18, "Wretched Conditions of the Terrorists"
2. See, Chapter 16, "Muslims as Peaceful Citizens"
3. See, Chapter 17, "Liberals Stand Ineffective"

15

Liberals Stand Ineffective

Simply by making outright declarations, a religion does not appear to be 'peaceful'. The conduct of its followers makes it peaceful or violent. In order to be treated as 'peaceful', it has to conform to the laws, traditions and moral rules of the prevailing society. As state exists to maintain law and order, administer justice and realize welfare of the people, nobody is permitted to take law in one's own hands, even if it is ordained by one's religion or some ideology to do so. Democratic governments provide ample means and methods to bring about socio-political and economic change. These methods remain available equally to all citizens and are considered constitutional, legitimate and peaceful. Therefore, there is no room in a democratic state for the exercise of force or violence by any individual, group or organization. Over and above the states, there is the United Nations Organization (UNO) to maintain peace and implement international law and justice, particularly world peace. The international community does not permit to use force on any mundane or religious ground whatever it may be. Neglect of these compulsory institutions paves path of violent terrorism. Liberal interpreters of Islam claim to uproot terrorism without these institutions? In effect, they provide support to terrorism.

Liberal Interpretation of Islam

Most of the recently known terrorists claim to establish victory of the Holy Quran and Islam by eliminating their enemies through violent 'jihad' (terrorism). But a majority of the Muslim liberal and peace-loving scholars declare that Islam is a 'religion of peace' and has no concern with violent jihad or Laden's terrorism.

Some of them are coming forward with the version of their real and liberal interpretation of Islam. Jihad simply means to try for doing some good. Maulana Wahiduddin Khan, in his article entitled 'Islam Says Peace is One of God's Names' points out that, "That so-called Islamic fundamentalism, if judged by its result, is the greatest crime of its kind against humanity. Anything or anyone can be eliminated, but what is impossible to eliminate is the hatred produced a sacred ideology." The target of a Muslim fundamentalism is the elimination of his supposed enemy: "Not until this end is achieved will it ever be down."[2]

Maulana Saud Alam Qasmi says that "Islam was the first religion in the world to introduce stringent punishment for those who practised terrorism."[3] But he puts several preconditions: (i) We should seek guidance only from the Holy Quran. (ii) One can be considered 'terrorist' only by the verdict of an honestly constituted court. (iii) Islam always stands for the oppressed and has always opposed those who incite violence without justification. (iv) One can kill a person in retaliation of murder and/or if he spreads mischief in the land, otherwise "it would be as if he killed all mankind, and if anyone saved a life, it would be as if he saved the life of all mankind (chapter 6, verse 32)." Osama bin Laden found him ordained by the Holy Quran to target even the citizens who being the taxpayers of a particular tyrannical government were potential combatants. Maintaining crusades and martyrdom justified, he further adds that along with 'peace' Islam stands for 'justice' also. Every righteous person has been given the duty to 'oppose' injustice and oppression to anyone anywhere. But it is difficult to stand for a particular value in a clear-cut manner, as what should one 'fight' for: Larger freedom or tolerable injustice or tolerable inequality? Thus, they pave the way to go on 'fighting' for ever.

As a corollary, a Muslim can live and follow his tenets only when he lives in a community without having a state or nation.

However, if he is compelled to live in a state, or a nation or a community different from a Shariat or Quran-ruled entity, he stands at war with it. He can be at peace only in a society of Islam. In a Muslim state too, which is not run according to the tenets of Islam, he finds himself at war with it. From this point of view, a state, where there are persons belonging to Islam or Islam-like religion, unless it is run in accordance with the injunctions issued by that religion, they are bound to consider themselves at war with the prevailing dispensation. They may keep patience or show forbearance till some favourable opportunity arrives to transform that polity into the version of their religion.[4]

Iqbal A. Ansari reiterates that Islam is a religion of peace. But, he accepts that historical-institutional Islam has waged wars and the doctrinal position of the Koran does not support absolute pacifism. The Koran validates use of force for self-defence when people are subjected to extreme persecution to the extent that they cannot practise freely their religion and have been forced to flee their homes. Force is legitimized for liberating a people who have been oppressed and tyrannized beyond endurance: "In cases of lawful use of force, it is ordained by the Shariat that force will be used when all other methods of redressal of wrong have been exhausted. The Shariat also requires that during the conduct of hostilities, human rights shall not be violated and that protection will be ensured to non-combatants and civilians. Accordingly, only indiscriminate use of force causing destruction to civilian life and property is a crime against humanity under Islam."[5] Therefore, he rejects Laden's view that citizens being taxpayers are potential combatants, can also be targeted. Defending the right to use of force for a just war, he quotes the UN Charter (1945), the humanitarian laws of war codified under the Four Geneva Conventions (1949) and Mahatma Gandhi allowing the Indian Army to march into Jammu & Kashmir to fight the raiders there in October 1947. About the Koranic directive to Muslims to kill 'kafirs' (non-believers), he points out that the term includes only particular group of people who drive Muslims out of their homes and who are bent on annihilating Islam. It excludes those non-Muslims who do not persecute them. However, the believer wields the weapon of killing and treat all others kafirs. He exemplifies that the Koran and the life of the Prophet enjoin on every righteous person the duty to oppose injustice, and oppression to anyone anywhere.

With this type of interpretation and explanation of Islamic teachings, the liberals declare that Islam stands for peace and there is no room for fanaticism, fundamentalism and terrorism, especially launched and organized by Al Qaeda and similar outfits. People and governments have pinned high hopes in their declarations.

Liberals in Majority

On the basis of their claims, declarations and writings, the world community expects that they would come forward and organize to defend and protect the fair name of Islam, also take all steps to stop the terrorists from committing heinous crimes. They would expose to the people in what way, why, with what motives and wherefrom these religious fundamentalists and terrorists derive their understanding and the plan of action. As they appear to be in majority, the religious people look to them to stand for the correct interpretation and explanation of the religious books and provide leadership to the world of Islam.

When the liberal scholars and clerics of Islam would do so, the Muslim world can accept their version and refuse to cooperate with the fanatic supporters of jihad (terrorism).They can muster courage to come out in open and prevail upon the supporters and executioners of extremist interpretation. But these liberal interpreters of religion do not do so and they have little impact on the fundamentalists and terrorists. In fact, only a few sections of Muslims accept their leadership. The majority of non-Muslims and their leaders expect too much from them and do not realize their difficulties and problems. In fact, on account of their conviction, conservative affiliation and outmoded thinking, the liberals remain unable to oppose terrorism and provide real relief to the afflicted world.

Inability of the Liberal Muslims

Liberals main difficulty is that they all are, at heart, blind followers of Islam. They have absolute faith in the teachings of the Quran and the Shariat. Even if they like, they cannot change themselves.

No state, nation or world body can claim to stand over and above it. Therefore, the liberals cannot bring any law, constitution or right against the desires and directives of the holy books. A Muslim in terms of the Holy Quran can live and follow his tenets only when he lives in a community without having a state or nation. However, if he is compelled to live in a state, or a nation or a community, different from his own, he stands at war with it. He can be at peace only in a society of Islam. In a Muslim state, which is not run according to the tenets of Islam, he will find himself at war with it. They tactically can keep patience and show forbearance till the opportune moment arrives to transform that polity or community into the version of their religion. This prompts the believers to operate as extremists, insurgents and rebels. There is no way to advise them to live like good citizens.[6]

The liberals fail to reject jihadis' claims. The terrorists become judge unto themselves and have divine sanction to use force. It depends on their individual understanding, training and education that to what extent they fight for the cause of religion. From simple believers to hardened fanatics, fundamentalists, extremists and terrorists can legitimately claim to commit acts of violence in the name of religion almost everywhere. As supporters of force and violence for religion, they stand along with the terrorists. Everyone has his meaning of these terms. The liberals appear no different from the violent jihadis.

Change in Conditions

Their inability to oppose jihadi terrorism is very much prominent in the field of supremacy of state. Forgetting the role of modern state, they render the non-believers as criminals and fail to apprehend the terrorists. Societies world over have undergone radical change. State has emerged as the supreme, secular and sovereign organization, claiming monopoly of obedience of all citizens. It cannot be subordinated to religion. It stands over and above all individuals, groups and organizations. Positive law is considered superior to all other laws. In the field of international relations, the states are placed next to the United Nations Organizations (UNO)—an effective confederation of 190 states. The UNO too cannot be subordinated to any particular religion.

The modern state does not permit anyone to use of force, except in narrowly defined individual cases of self-defence, even when one is subjected to persecution. A person cannot exercise violence even if he cannot practise his religion freely to his satisfaction. No one can be forced to flee their homes. No state, at least a democracy, legitimises the use of force by individuals and groups even for liberating themselves from oppression and tyranny. It does not allow the use of force even when all other methods of redressal of wrong have been exhausted despite their religions permitting them to do so. Modern law does not permit kafirs to drive Muslims out of their homes or to annihilating Islam as well as allow the Muslims to kill or coerce the kafirs. All rights to exercise force and award punishment have been taken over by the state. Taking orders, rights and directions from an agency other than the state for using force opens the way to terrorism. During those non-state days, Islam and its followers could stand for the oppressed and oppose those who incited violence without justification, or with justification, but now all these obligations are performed by the state alone. After the emergence of state, the individual has yielded all his rights, obtained by nature or God to it. They included right to exercise force in self-defence or retaliation, protection of kith and kin, defending places of worship, performance of religious rites etc. Earlier, he himself was asked by the Holy Book to do all of them. He was authorized to seek justice and undo injustice. Most of these functions are now performed by the democratically elected representatives of the people. Democracy provides ample opportunities, means and methods to redress their grievances. All citizens are granted basic rights to grow their personalities on their self-chosen lines. Now, none is allowed to take law into one's own hands.[7]

They are unable to understand the phenomenon that most of the Muslims in India and other states are living peacefully as law-abiding citizens in these countries. It is because of their express or tacit acceptance of status of the state as the compulsory and legitimate organization over and above everything else including religion. They are accustomed to obey law and act on the norms of the society. It means they do not feel any necessity to act on injunctions of the Holy Book to fight oppression or oppose non-believers. They have virtually given up their religion-directed right to use force or violence, and left its exercise in the hands of the state. Perhaps they also realize that neglect of state, democratic set-up etc. results only in indirect support to terrorism, chaos and jungle raj. They have neither wish nor power to restrain the violent jihadis from causing havoc to the lives of the people. However, they appear convinced on the futility of using terrorism as the weapon of religion. They have finally handed over this task too to the state.

Ineffective Liberals

Because of their innate commitment to the religious fundamentals, the liberals remain unable to isolate them from jihadi terrorism and eschew their indirect support to terrorists. When they know that modern state does not permit anyone to use force, even when one is subjected to persecution or cannot practise his religion.

Thus, the outcome of so-called liberal interpretations of jihad has largely been to justify the use of violence by the individual believers on old lines. This results in permitting the continuation of terrorism and breaking of civil laws. The believers in the hands of these liberal scholars are destined to lead a life of criminals and insurgents. These liberals fruitlessly continue to permit jihad when it is no more possible to do so. As they can be declared as renegade or kafir, they cannot tell the believers that now no individual or organization or community has the right to exercise force and violence. They are unable to inform that the state has taken over all of their earlier functions. Under the universal 'rule of law', now, democracy has evolved means and methods to redress injustice, oppression and exploitation. Anyone using violence stands against the 'rule of law' and the constitution. He can, therefore, be treated as a criminal, rebel or insurgent. If they do so, their fear is right that conservative kazis and mullas would declare them as anti-religion, renegades and Satan (evil). But by neglecting the phenomenon of state, and sticking to their earlier position, they are providing moral and religious support to the jihadi terrorists. However, the plane truth is that they, because of the basic nature of Islam and their affiliation to it, cannot go in a different direction.

Notes

1. The International Convention on the Suppression of Acts of Nuclear Terrorism, which is a shot in the arm for the global fight against terrorism. Already three other conventions on terrorism exist—the International Convention for the Suppression of Terrorist Bombings, the International Convention for the Suppression of Financing Terrorism,

and the International Convention for the Suppression of Acts of Nuclear Terrorism. The Security Council had already approved Resolution 1373 soon after 9/11 in a bid to legislate wide-ranging measures for combatting terrorism. See *Hindustan Times*, September 17, 2005.

2. *Times of India*, September 25, 2001.
3. Maulana Saud Alam Qasmi, the chief nazim (theologian) of AMU.
4. "Terrorism is a crime in Islam" in *Times of India*, October 17, 2001. Maulana Saud Alam Qasmi, the chief nazim (theologian) of AMU spokes at the congregational prayers on Friday.
5. Iqbal A Ansari, a former Professor of AMU, in his article entitled "Terrorism Cannot Work: Muslims Must Explore Passive Resistance", October 17, 2001.
6. At the interview conducted at the British High Commission in Delhi Blair said: "Terrorism cannot be justified. Every single dispute has been made worse by it", "The roots of extremism go very, very deep. And, the roots are found in the teaching of hatred at a very, very early age." "...they will see any issue to justify what they do. But, actually, the fundamental point about their ideology is a hatred for anyone different from them." See *Hindustan Times*, September 8, 2005.
7. See, infra Chapter 19, "War against Outer and Inner Forms of Terrorism".

16

Muslims as Peaceful Citizens

Islamic terrorism has made Muslims as suspects almost everywhere, particularly in non-Muslim countries. Most of these countries have large Muslim population. As such, they are eager to know which Muslims are not prone to terrorism and wish to live there as peaceful citizens. They are in search of taking steps necessary for protecting their countries from the onslaughts of terrorism. Threat of terrorism is so widespread that even peaceful Muslim countries are worried on the presence of terrorist elements and trying to restrain them. For this purpose, Muslims may be divided into three broad categories: (a) peace-loving, (b) fanatics and, (c) mixed.

It is a fact that most of the Muslims in India and in some other countries belong to (a) peaceful category and have many sub-variations, such as, (i) law-abiding, (ii) violence-eschewing, and (iii) accommodating. The law-abiding citizens render express or tacit acknowledgement to the state as a compulsory and legitimate organization over and above everything else including religion. They are accustomed to obey law and act on the norms of the society.

The violence-eschewing Muslims continue to pay respect and have faith in all the basic tenets of Islam, but do not feel any necessity to act on all injunctions of the Holy Book (Quran), in particular to fight oppression, oppose non-believers and eliminate idolaters. They virtually give up their religion-directed right to use force or violence, and believe that the state is rightly doing this job in their behalf. They feel that the Holy Book also teaches them to live peacefully with followers of other religions if the latter do not deny opportunities to pursue divine injunctions and follow Islam. Even if they are not happy in accommodating with the people of a non-Muslim country, they do not consider it desirable to wait for the opportune moment when they would be able to convert that country into Islamic rule.

The third sub-category of accommodating peace-loving Muslims believe that Islam is the religion of peace only, and dislike the deeds of many fanatic Muslim conquerors and invaders committed in the medieval past, and recently by the Taliban rulers in Afghanistan. They reject ends and means of the militants and terrorists. But left to themselves, they have neither will nor power to restrain the violent jihadis from causing havoc to the lives of the innocent people. Thus, they appear convinced on the futility of using terrorism as the weapon of religion. They hand over the task of dealing with terrorism to the state.

The (b) category of fanatics includes fundamentalists, militants and terrorists. There are hundreds of terrorist organizations which have been indulging in killing of the innocent people in various parts of the world. They think that they are fighting against the non-Muslims (*kafirs*) to realize the rule of Allah. The fanatics find many clear directives in their books of religion which ask them to execute them without entertaining any doubt, unconditionally, and to the fullest possible extent. They remain ready to exercise force and violence. Islam claims to be the last, final and best of all hitherto existing religions and asks the devotees to bring the rest of mankind to its fold. Some fanatics or diehard followers do so by spreading terror and killing the innocent people, so that others might come under pressure to join their ranks. The perpetrators are assured honour and pleasures by the extremists of the community if left alive, and guaranteed God's grace or right to join heaven if killed in encounter with anti-religion forces. No person from other religions can convince them to deviate or to do otherwise as he is rarely allowed listening to counter-arguments or teachings of other religions leading to eschew the path of violence. As they willingly opt to operate as human bombs and death squads, no threat of law, imprisonment or death penalty can deter them. They kill even their own co-religionists if the latter preach peace or create difficulties in carrying out their bloody mission.[1]

Peace-loving Muslims either withdraw or keep silence. They find it futile to oppose them. Therefore, only use of greater force can prevent or eliminate such jehadi terrorists or diehard criminals. The whole of mankind has come under their deadly threat. As such, the world community, under the leadership of US, after September 11, 2001 attack, has launched war against terrorism. None goes into the intricacies of religion or reasons lying behind terrorism. It is simply killing of innocent people. By the time one ascertains explanation or reasons lying behind their acts of terrorism, and tries to convince them on futility of such violence, they would have killed a few hundred innocent men, women and children more. They can tactically postpone them to gain more favourable opportunity or public opinion. Till they are taught to have been commissioned by God or godmen to kill anti-religion people, they go on committing crimes in the name of religion.[2]

The (c) category mixed Muslims disagree with the fanatics both on their ends and means. If some of them connive at their doings, most of them either maintain distance from them or observe discreet silence. Only a few devoted Muslims support them voluntarily. There are hundreds of Muslims who appear to help them with money, shelter and intelligence. They are forced to do so under threat or pressure exerted by the terrorists. A majority of them are inherently convinced that there would be chaos and bloodshed if terrorism is adopted either as an end or means or both to realise the rule of Islam. In view of the availability of weapons of mass destruction in the hands of these terrorists, they expect the end of the human race itself. The vague idea of 'Ummah' (world community of the Muslims) may not avert this danger. Perhaps, they also realize that neglect of state, democratic set-up etc. would result only in indirect support to terrorism, chaos and jungle raj.

Still they find opportunities to move from (a) to (b) categories and vice versa under pressure or blind faith. To escape from criticism on either side, they like to stay in the (c) category. The number of Muslims in the (b) category is comparative less than (a) and (c). The size of the mixed category is larger than both. It provides a 'to-fro' or grey area in which they can move at their own will to avoid criticism or simply adopt it as a matter of strategy. However, influence or threat of terrorism dominates both (b) and (c), and makes all of them suspect. Therefore, it is necessary that the (a) category Muslims keep themselves away openly and clearly from other (b) and (c), and perform a positive role.

For finding out a pattern of peaceful Muslim citizens, in Indian state, a case study of Rajasthan has been made here.

Muslims in Rajasthan

Unlike some other states of the Indian Union, the Muslim minority of Rajasthan is largely peaceful and active in progress and development of its people. Cases of communal flare up have been few and far between. Spread of jehadi terrorism is minimal. This phenomenon can be dispassionately studied for the benefit of the people of other states. However, this study takes only the post-independence and post-integration phase of Rajasthan into consideration.

Presently, as per 1991 census, there are about 40 lakh Muslims residing in Rajasthan. The total population of Rajasthan is 6 crore, which besides Muslims includes Hindus, Christians, Jains, Sikhs and others. Among other minorities, study of the Muslims is considered more important. Other non-Hindu minorities do not have any history of invasions, aggressions or large-scale conversions in Rajasthan, and always have been living a peaceful manner. Only Muslims, historically, have been related to those events. But, since the fall of the Mughal empire, they have also been living peacefully.[2] Therefore, it is interesting to study in what proportion they have transformed as participants in the democratic set-up of Rajasthan. This change needs serious consideration for the Muslim community of Rajasthan and of other Indian states.

After the Republican Constitution of India came into operation, it can be assumed that Muslims are at par with other citizens of Rajasthan. They can be considered equal with other majority and minority communities in having their own

(a) social set-up and community organization,
(b) economic affairs and livelihood,
(c) equality before law and civic rights, and
(d) lobbying, grouping and organizing politically.

In the context of India in general, and Rajasthan in particular, for peaceful living, there are two important variables or factors—peace with state and peace with religion. Muslims of Rajasthan, according to their creed and behaviour, can be put anywhere in between the two—peace and religion. Muslims in varying degrees of conviction are guided by the teachings of the Holy Quran and the Shariah. Their religion ordains particular form of polity, economy, family and society. Therefore, they require different forms and ways of understanding and doing in democracy. It is necessary to know to what extent the Muslims of Rajasthan have accepted themselves to adopt citizenship and live peacefully with other communities. For this purpose, we require a scale of locations approximated between 'peace' and 'religion'.

The Scale

It shoes the path descending from terrorism to Indianism. There can be eighteen locations or situations for a Muslim of Rajasthan to stand between terrorism and Indianism. Some critical and important locations found between terrorism and Indianism are given hereunder:

1. Activism in terrorist organization
2. Proxy for Pakistan and Bangla Desh or any other hostile country
3. Islam as the best, uppermost and the last religion
4. Use of violence for religion
5. Fanaticism and extremism
6. Communalism
7. Blind faith
8. Opposition of other communities and religions
9. Encouraging separatism
10. Respecting law till the establishment of Islamic rule
11. Co-existence of religions and mutual respect
12. Upholding supremacy of the Indian state with religion confined to self
13. Accepting majority in democracy with religion confined to self
14. Active participation as citizen Muslim
15. Separation of religion and politics with religion confined to self
16. Upholding secularism
17. Total Indianism
18. Indianism disowning past for present

Before assigning a location to a member of the Muslim community of Rajasthan, it is important to observe his expression and behaviour carefully. The state is under obligation to watch and supervise the available patterns of thinking, behaving and responding of the people. Do they claim to belong to the past hordes of invaders, killers and rulers the Rajputana princedoms. It has to be seen whether they have reformed and changed themselves, or have kept on their connections and actions practised in the past. Much depends on the types of their mindsets, learning of particular precepts of their religion and making preparation to act accordingly. Such people can be considered as peaceful citizens if they have improved themselves or have made solemn promises to their fellow-citizens to follow the norms of society and laws of the country. In case all or some of them do not show any such inclination, the society or the state in its behalf will have to put them in the proposed categories and also make all preparations to defend and protect the peaceful communities.

All these locations have been put as positions appearing between variables of 'peace' as secular concept and 'religion' as sectarian concept.

As it is difficult to locate a Muslim specifically on a location, all the locations have been broadly divided into seven broad groups, named as, (a) no state jehadi religion; (b) religion without peace with others; (c) all under religion; (d) both peace and religion; (e) peace with religion; (f) peace and peace; and (g) peace as religion. Various locations, for convenience of classification in the seven-group scale of "Religion and Peace", have been put in the following manner:

(a) No State Jehadi Religion:
   1. Activism in terrorist organization
   2. Proxy for Pakistan and Bangla Desh or any other hostile country

(b) Religion without Peace with Others:
   3. Islam as the best, uppermost and the last religion
   4. Use of violence for religion
   5. Fanaticism and extremism

(c) All under Religion:
   6. Communalism
   7. Blind faith
   8. Opposition of other communities and religions
   9. Encouraging separatism

(d) Both Peace and Religion:
   10. Respecting law till the establishment of Islamic rule
   11. Co-existence of religions and mutual respect

12. Upholding supremacy of the Indian state with religion confined to self

(e) Peace with Religion:

13. Accepting majority in democracy with religion confined to self
14. Active participation as citizen Muslim

(f) Peace and Peace:

15. Separation of religion and politics with religion confined to self
16. Upholding secularism

(g) Peace as Religion:

17. Total Indianism
18. Indianism disowning past for present

The scale can be useful in studying the Muslim minorities living anywhere in India. With certain modifications, the scale can be used in measuring status of other minorities also. On this seven-location scale minorities residing in different regions of a state can also be compared and analyzed on the basis of their pattern of peaceful living. It can be used for studying any one of the seven segments of the Muslim population horizontally found in different states.

Behaviour of Location/Groups

Briefly, it can be stated that groups (a) and (b) mostly include fanatics, fundamentalists, militants, terrorists and extremists. They think that they are fighting against the non-Muslims (*kafirs*) to realize the rule of Allah. The fanatics find many clear directives in their books of religion which ask them to execute them without entertaining any doubt, unconditionally, and to the fullest possible extent. They remain ready to exercise force and violence. The ISI of Pakistan and other terrorist organizations provide training and supply arms and logistics to them. For them Islam claims to be the last, final and best of all hitherto existing religions and asks the devotees to bring the rest of mankind in its fold. At times they do so by spreading terror and killing the innocent people, so that others might come under pressure to join their ranks. The perpetrators are assured honour and pleasures by the extremists of the community if left alive and guaranteed God's grace or right to join heaven if killed in encounter with anti-religion forces. No person from other religions can convince the (c) category Muslims to deviate or to do otherwise as he is rarely willing to listen counter-arguments or teachings of other religions leading to eschew the path of violence. As they willingly opt to operate as human bombs and death squads, no threat of law, imprisonment or death penalty can deter them. They kill even their own co-religionists if the latter preach peace or create difficulties in carrying out their bloody mission. They have an uncompromising attitude towards the members of other communities and religions. However, group (a) Muslims appear to be a microscopic minority in the state of Rajasthan.

Group (c) "All under Religion" actually belongs a kind of mixed category who disagree with the fanatics both on their ends and means. If some of them connive at their doings, most of them either maintain distance from them or observe discreet silence. Only a few devoted Muslims support them voluntarily. There are hundreds of Muslims who appear to help them with money, shelter and intelligence. But they are sometimes forced to do so under threat or pressure exerted by the terrorists. A majority of them are convinced that there would be chaos and bloodshed if terrorism is adopted either as an end or means or both to realize the rule of Islam. In view of the availability of weapons of mass destruction in the hands of these terrorists, they expect the end of the human race itself. The vague idea of 'Ummah' (world community of the Muslims) may not avert this danger. Perhaps they also realize that neglect of state, democratic set-up etc. would result only in indirect support to terrorism, chaos and jungle raj.

Group (d) "Both Peace and Religion" believes in peaceful co-existence and group (e) "Peace with Religion" takes Muslim towards democratic identification. The Muslims of the former group continue to pay respect and have faith in all the basic tenets of Islam, but do not feel any necessity to act on all injunctions of the Holy Book, in particular to fight oppression, oppose non-believers and eliminate idolaters. They have virtually given up their religion-directed right to use force or violence at their own, and believe that the state is rightly doing this job in their behalf. Group (e) believes that in the present democratic set-up there are various ways and means to ventilate their grievances and get redress through various agencies and institutions. Use of violence, under these circumstances, for the cause of religion or otherwise would make them criminals in the eyes of the state. They feel that the Holy Book also teaches them to live peacefully with followers of other religions if the latter do not deny opportunities to pursue divine injunctions and follow Islam. Even if they are not happy in accommodating with the people of a non-Muslim country, they do not consider it desirable to wait for the opportune moment when they would be able to convert that country into Islamic rule. They appear contented with the present state of affairs.

Groups (f) and (g) Muslims firmly believe in superiority of democracy and secularism unmixed with religion. They find that Islam is a religion of peace only, and dislike the deeds of many fanatic Muslim conquerors and invaders committed in the medieval past, and recently by the Taliban rulers in Afghanistan. They reject ends and means of the militants and terrorists. But left to themselves, they have neither will nor power to restrain the violent jihadis from causing havoc to the lives of the innocent people. Thus, they appear convinced on the futility of using terrorism as the weapon of religion. They hand over the task of dealing with terrorism to the state. They feel proud of their Indian identity, and like to disown and disconnect themselves from their historical antecedents. Most of them belong to the upper-middle class levels of Muslim society and hold professional and respectable positions.

Peaceful Muslims in Majority

There is majority of peace-loving Muslims in Rajasthan. Most of the Muslims enjoying happiness, peace and harmony are those who practise humanitarian teachings of the Holy Quran. They also have enough respect for other religions and their religious practices. Their behaviour is also reciprocated by the followers of other religions including the Hindus. They live in peace and harmony with them. In this process, they happen to come closer and get acquainted with their culture, language, traditions etc. They begin to reside fearlessly in the mixed colonies and grow a sense of brotherhood. Their cooperation with them further strengthens when they happen to live together in such manner. Anti-social elements find it very difficult for injecting wedge between the two communities. Members of each community know usually the trouble-shooters and law-breakers, therefore, can promptly act against them in the interest of maintaining communal harmony directly or through other agencies.

Over a period of time, despite rivalry, animosity, battles and wars among the extremists of the two communities, a large number of people have discovered new areas of cooperation, artistic expression, social service, skill and invention. Sometimes, the Muslims have neglected religious restrictions and prohibitions in areas like sculptor, music, dance, business and the like. In socio-economic and religious areas, they have been influenced by each others' customs, traditions, fads and taboos. The Muslims have adopted and borrowed many symbols, styles of marriage, ways of idol worship, and ethos from the Hindus. They are willing to be considered as Indian Muslims or citizen Muslims instead of soldiers of the Holy Quran or followers of Islam.

Still more respect and affinity are earned by the Muslims living among the non-Muslims who, apart from being simply peaceful and accommodative, display allegiance and spirit of sacrifice in defending the land and people of their country of birth and residence. In this manner, they identify their interests with the people as a whole. Thus, they do not have to be treated merely as a minority or groups of guests and strangers living at the mercy of the majority. The majority do not need to feel the burden to provide means of livelihood, special protection or compensate them for their living peacefully or for not adhering strictly to the tenets of Islam. Sometimes, they do more than what is expected of them as compatriots or citizens. Many of them, besides making contributions in the fields of art, literature, crafts and skills, stand by the majority to defend and protect land from aggression, exploitation and treachery.

On the basis of observation of the behaviour of the Muslims of Rajasthan, the Muslim population can be proportionately put into the following groupings:

(a) No State Jehadi Religion	00.15 lakh
(b) Religion without Peace with Others	02.50 lakh
(c) All under Religion	03.50 lakh
(d) Both Peace and Religion	25.00 lakh
(e) Peace with Religion	05.00 lakh
(f) Peace and Peace	03.50 lakh
(g) Peace as Religion	00.35 lakh
Total	**40.00 lakh**

When the major proportion of Muslim population belongs to groups (d), (e), (f), and (g) their participation in the democratic system increases, lessening the events of communal riots. The polity of Rajasthan moves in the direction of peace, progress and development. It also constrains the role of groups (a) and (b). Group (c) swings in between the two. Groups (d), (e), (f) and (g) also come closer to the other majority and minority communities. Politics of five decades in Rajasthan reflects this condition. These groups primarily act on the peaceful and humane commands of the Holy Quran, which are surprisingly common to almost all the religions and faiths of Rajasthan people. There are many faiths or sects of this variety. Most of them have formed part of the common heritage of the Rajasthani people. At times it is difficult to ascertain whether it is a Muslim faith or not. The number of Muslims belonging to groups (a) and (b) is dwindling. Fanatics related to group (a) hardly have courage to appear before the community.

These seven groupings or zones of locations for Muslims living in Rajasthan can, for explanatory purposes, further be associated with factors, conditions, aspirations and goals specially related to them. They can be easily treated as *independent* and *intervening* variables, which empirically point out relationship existing between them. They tell why some of these groupings are affected and influenced by them and behave in a particular manner. Important among these variables are status and form of education, mode of earning livelihood, outside links, interaction with other communities, response of political parties and government and so on.

It has been observed that Muslims of groups (a) and (b) have little or some *madrasa* education, financial, moral and arms support from outside, relations with mafia and muscle men, hateful attitude from caste Hindus and self-serving fanaticism. Muslims of group (c) are mostly 'political' by nature. They try to organize the community on issues of religion, language and culture. Muslims belonging to this category get guidance mostly from political parties in opposition or indulge in separatism or retaliation. Members of groups (d) and (e) equip them with modern education in government or autonomous organizations, socio-economic mobility and political awakening. They gain power on the basis of their organization and constitute the most awakened part of the society. Muslims of groups (f) and (g) take part in and lead regional and national movements, trade unions, labour, youth and people living below poverty line. They make full use of press, media and academia. They often choose subjects for study like science, engineering, law and business and often occupy positions in universities, government and corporate bodies. Thus, the locations groups are connected with specified sets of variables and patterns of living. Three-fourths of the Muslim minority of Rajasthan dominates its one-fourth and does not permit to go too far.

Rajasthan Model of Peaceful Muslims

All together, in this manner, present a "Rajasthan Model of Peace and Religion" or "Rajasthan Model of Peaceful Muslim Minorities". It may have many similarities with the minority patterns available in Madhya Pradesh, Uttar Pradesh, Bihar and Andhra Pradesh. But, the Rajasthan model, more than any other, shows greater cooperation, more harmony and better mutual help among various communities.[3] In this model, Muslim minorities

(a) are more inclined towards liberal teachings of the Holy Quran, Sufism and local customs and ethos prevailing in the region or particular community;
(b) have largely given up their connections and claims with past history of invasions, conversions and dominance;
(c) form only a small proportion of total population of Rajasthan which is spreading over in rural and urban areas of Rajasthan;
(d) are more Rajasthani (Mewari, Marwari, Jaipuri, Tonki, Ajmeri etc.) in habits and lifestyle;
(e) increasingly send their children for getting education in government schools and colleges after passing through *madrasa* seminaries;
(f) consider state as superior to all organizations including party and religion and have faith in law and justice enforced under the Constitution of India;
(g) feel safe and protected in view of fair, peaceful and cooperative treatment received from other major and minor communities;
(h) have been contributing good and able administrators and responsible politicians to the state;
(i) having three fourths of the community belonging to groups (d), (e), (f), and (g) or the 'peaceful zone' are effectively able to control and influence the hostile elements found in groups (a) and (b); and

(j) are in need of greater financial, educational and political support from big communities and the government, both of state and the centre.

This model is merely propositional. It can further be improved and applied to other states, communities and groups.

Notes

1. See, supra, Chapter 13, "Jihad as Terrorism".
2. See, infra, Chapter 21, "Identity and Socialisation of Indian Muslims".
3. Some of the main concepts, location, groups and variables are used in Chapter 22, "Indianisation of Bangladeshis and Migrants living in India".

V

Global Threats to Hindutva

17

Triumph and Defeat of Violent Jihad

Phenomenon of Terrorism (Violent Jihad)

Terrorism is sheer naked, blatant, cruel and inhuman act of killing of innocent people. It is totally against prevailing law, human rights, morality and democracy. It is an advanced stage of extremism, fanaticism and fundamentalism. Blind faith prompts a terrorist to kill others. Terrorists are ruthless killers of the worst type. They embody nothing but evil, hate and revenge. Terrorists are anti-God, anti-man, anti-culture and enemy of the family, state and society. Religion-based terrorists call themselves 'jihadis', 'mujahideens', 'warriors of their religion', 'soldiers of Islam' etc., and not 'terrorists'. They do not allow any other view to prevail. The whole world, particularly the hostile nations, have to abide by them. Their words and actions are the final verdicts upon earth.

Neither terrorism nor fanaticism is new. What is new is the combination of terrorism, fanaticism and the technological capability to wreak vast and inhumane devastation, whether by act of terror or other means. While much of the world has recovered from its 20th century infatuation with extremist political ideologies like Stalinism and fascism, extremism in the name of religion remains a potent threat to our security[1], century and humanity.

Nature of Danger from Terrorism

Families of 600 people killed in the 9/11 attack filed a suit against the Saudi royal family and banks and charities linked to Saudi Arabia and Pakistan, accusing them of financing terrorism. Seeking hundreds of trillions of dollars in damages, the families asserted that terrorists like Osama bin Laden and his Al Qaida network cannot plan, train or act on a massive scale without significant financial power, coordination and backing. The families might stand little chance of collecting any money but they hope the lawsuit will throw light on the financing of terrorism and force governments to act against it. Among the defendants there are three Saudi princes, seven banks and eight charitable groups. Some of the charitable groups named in the lawsuit include the International Islamic Relief Organization, the Muslim World League, the SAAR Foundation and the World Assembly of Muslim Youth.[2]

Terrorist Organizations

The ringleader of Al Qaida, a deadliest terrorist organization having over sixty branches and links with two hundred similar organizations, Osama bin Laden claimed the right of Islam over Pakistan's nuclear bombs, which he claimed to have financed, and supported it.

The terrorist underworld includes Al Qaida, Hamas, Hezbollah, Islamic Jihad, Jaish-e-Mohammad in remote jungles, deserts and in the centres of large cities. In his annual report to the US President the Secretary of Defense Rumsfeld attributed the emergence and growth of Jaish-e-Mohammad and other terrorist outfits to the conditions prevailing in some states, including some with nuclear weapons where there are no capable or responsible governments. The wide areas of Asia, Africa and the Western Hemisphere are fertile grounds for non-state actors to engage in terrorism, acquisition of NMC (nuclear, biological and chemical) weapons, illegal trafficking, or other illicit activities across state borders. He perceived inability of some states to govern their societies, safeguard their military armaments and prevent their territories from serving as sanctuary to terrorists and criminal organizations. Number of such terrorist organizations has been growing continuously.

Objectives and Preparations

So much so that the umbrella terrorist organization Al Qaida under the mastermind leadership of Osama bin Laden, in the name of religion (Islam), gained complete control over the rebel state of the Talibans in Afghanistan, and within no time began to decide the fate of many other democratic and non-democratic countries. Laden established not only several training camps to prepare terrorists but also began to export it for conducting terrorist operations at the time and place of his choice. Its daredevil colossus terrorist attack appeared all of a sudden on September 11 in the heartland of the USA on the WTO (World Trade Centre) and the Pentagon. After suffering heavily from it, the US immediately realized gravity of this global and organized threat from terrorism and took decision forthwith to fight against it by use of greater and technologically advanced form of force. The US was immediately at war with the Talibans in order to eliminate Laden and his Al Qaida camps. Terrorism in Afghanistan was largely a creation of Pakistan. It is unfortunate that America has been compelled to seek help Pakistan to eradicate terrorism, the product of Pakistan and the Al Qaida. The US herself had helped Pakistan to organize the Talibans to eliminate Soviet occupation of Afghanistan at that time.

In the 7,000-page guide titled *Encyclopaedia of Jehad* provides an insight into how terrorists from Osama bin Laden's Al Qaida network operate.[3] Laden has found him ordained by the Holy Quran to target even the citizens who being the taxpayers of a particular tyrannical government are potential combatants. Maintaining crusades and martyrdom justified, he further adds that along with 'peace' Islam stands for 'justice' also.

The Taliban leader Mullah Mohammad Omar, before the fall of Afghanistan to the world coalition, had vowed that his forces would emerge victorious from a long guerrilla war if his country was attacked by the United States. The US and her allies would meet the same fate as the communists. Their leader bin Laden had determined to fight the holy war by spreading terrorism and use all means. He claims Islamic rights over Pakistan's nuclear bombs. Laden has been working to pile up more nuclear weapons as well as chemical and biological weapons. His intended targets reportedly are the US, Britain and Israel. He maintains that there are two parties to the conflict: the world of Christianity, which is allied with Jews and Zionism, led by the United States, Britain and Israel, and the other "is the Islamic world".

The CNN had broadcast excerpts of 64 videotapes obtained in Afghanistan that show Al Qaida members testing poisonous gas and chemical weapons.[4] The SIMI (Students Islamic Movement of India) has "a plan to reconstruct human life in all its aspects in accordance with divine guidance revealed to through Allah's messenger, in order to achieving Allah's pleasure".[5] It had asked the then India's Home Minister, L.K. Advani to embrace Islam and openly stood in favour of terrorism of Laden and Al Qaida. Its leaders declared: "The Quran is our Constitution. If the Indian Constitution clashes with the Quran, we are not bound by the constitution."[6] General Musharraf of Pakistan in his earlier speech had also made it clear that he was yielding to the US demand to join the coalition only in the same spirit in which the Holy Prophet made tactical compromises with his enemies to bide his time to vanquish them later.

Cause, Utility and Effect

Human bombs have no face. That doubles up its power as a bomb. The individuals operating as human bombs have no fear. Just they have an obsession that drives them through hell (this world), in search of heaven. The birth of contemporary suicide terrorism began from October 23, 1983 when Muslim extremists drove into the barracks of the US and the French contingents of the multinational peace-keeping force in Beirut and detonated bombs with no intention of escaping. Ramadan Salah, Secretary General of the Palestinian Islamic Jehad states: "Our enemy possesses the most sophisticated weapons in the world and its army is trained to a very high standard. We have nothing with which to repel killing and thuggery against us except the weapon of martyrdom. It is easy and costs us only our lives.....Human bombs cannot be defeated, not even by nuclear bombs."

After profiling more than 50 Muslim suicide bombers, serving in the Hezbollah, Hamas and the Palestinian Islamic Jihad, Ariel Merari, Tel Aviv University psychologist concluded there is no single psychological or demographic profile of suicide terrorists. "Intense struggles produce several types of people with the potential willingness to sacrifice themselves for a cause. Their motives range from religion, patriotism, hatred of the enemy to a profound sense of victimization." A BBC report states that suicide bombers are typically unmarried men in their late teens and 20s. They act on the belief that they will go straight to paradise after the deed is over. Recruits are picked from mosques, schools and religious institutions and are reassured that their families will be looked after.[7]

Justification of Use of Force

Nature of Islam

Most of contemporary jihad and terrorism is related with Islam, which is a product or creation of a non-state and non-nation society. Therefore, the basic position of a Muslim is that he has little regard for a state or nation. He can be at peace only in a society of Islam. If he is compelled to live in a state, or a nation or a community different from his own, he stands at war with it. Even in a Muslim state, which is not run according to the tenets of Islam, still he may feel at war with it. He may keep patience and show forbearance till the opportune moment arrives to transform that polity into the version of their religion.

Unfortunately, they do not have a permanent and lasting solution which lies in the separation of religion from religious fundamentalism. That remedy may never be implemented. As the terrorists commit violence considering it be their religious duty, even if it goes against national and international laws, there remains no way left except prompt and effective use of force. They cannot be discouraged, stopped or disabled except by quick and effective use of force.[8]

Weakness of Democracy

A large number of countries have had been suffering from terrorism for long. But they did not fight against it because either they lacked courage or they could not understand and decide the difference between religion-related fundamentalism and religion proper.

Terrorism had been playing havoc in so many countries for the last several years. Hardly any serious attention could be paid to it. Countries like India continued to wait in spite of having all information and sources to deal with it. The lengthy procedure and complicated laws in India and elsewhere required more and more evidences as proofs. At international level, it was much more difficult in view of absence of extradition treaties, sovereignty of states, administrative capability and lack of cooperation from governments. The terrorists know all these weaknesses of national and international communities.

Ineffectiveness of UNO and World System

The UN resolutions passed in 1999 and 2000 called for freezing of bank accounts and assets of 146 Talibans officials, 10 Arabs including Osama bin Laden, and three Afghan entities. No action was taken by the member-states. For years the 189 members of the United Nations have wrangled over a critical question: Who is a terrorist? According to the UN's chief lawyer, Hans Corell, the problem is one differentiating between terrorism and the rights to self-determination and combat foreign occupation. Kofi Annan, the UN Secretary General had also pleaded for its precise and legal definition before.

This confusion has inflicted the understanding and working of almost all national and international Human Rights Commissions. They tend to render indirect encouragement to terrorism when they instead of opposing and accusing absconding killers indict the law and order agencies for their actions while investigating the incidents and apprehending the criminals. They became indirect tools in the hands of the terrorists, fundamentalists and insurgents when they instead of chasing and accusing killers indicted the law and order agencies for their actions against these criminals, and for the investigation into the incidents from the inflicted and aggrieved parties.

There is hardly any international judicial system on terrorism. Antonio Cassese, Professor of Law at Florence University, Paris and the first president of the International Crimes Tribunal for the ex-Yugoslavia writes in the *European Journal of International Law* that the impact of the attacks on legal thinking has been 'shattering'. Although the effort to combat terrorism is embodied in several treaties and two UN resolutions adopted in the wake of September 11, there is no world tribunal currently empowered to try terrorist cases. Some said they could be brought before the International Criminal Court (ICC) However, US and other officials have expressed reservations. Allen Pellet, member and former chairperson of the UN International Law Commission, called shortly after

September 11 for work to be speeded up on a framework UN treaty and new ICC statutes to deal with terrorism. Years of negotiations on a comprehensive treaty have bogged down over issues such as what to include as a terrorist act. Marc Cogen, Professor of International Law at Belgium's Ghent University, urged efforts to reach consensus on a definition of global terrorism and to establish a central clearing house to designate offenders.

The UN Security Council approved a resolution requiring all 189 member-nations to deny money, support and sanctuary to terrorists. This legally binding resolution was adopted unanimously. It was introduced and approved in just over 24 hours. It invokes Articles 7 of the UN Charter that makes its provision enforceable, but stops short of providing for mandatory sanctions against those who violate it. However, it does express the Council determination to take all necessary steps to ensure its full implementation. It expands the role of the world body and seeks cooperation of member-states to combat the scourge but does not talk about unilateral retaliatory action that the US intended to take against perpetrators of the terrorism against it. However, it did not define terrorism, which is an important element as some of the states are seeking to differentiate between terrorism and freedom struggle.

Helplessness of India

Similar terrorist camps have already been operating in the state of Jammu & Kashmir of India for the last two decades. They are being supported and guided by the ISI of Pakistan. The ISI had also been operating in Afghanistan to establish the Talibans government and also organizing the terrorist camps there.

India's offering of full cooperation to the efforts of President George W. Bush of the USA in his goal to fight against terrorism was right. It had also the support of the political parties and the country as a whole. The US had done what India could not do for the last 15 years: neither had India wanted to fight, nor was wanting to fight, nor could fight. India chose to remain status quoist. So far India has not taken any strong action against the terrorists for she feared that (a) there would be uprising among large sections of the Muslims in favour of Pakistan latter considering it an attack on the state of their brethren who created it after a long struggle; (b) a good number among 15 crores of Muslims would become a security problem for India; (c) the Islamic world outside India would turn hostile; (d) in such crisis, none of the superpower would be supporting India's cause; and (e) such an action would be risky for India's being militarily weak and dependent upon others for almost every commodity with unfriendly neighbours on all sides. In view of these reasons, India preferred to wait, and stand by the USA.[9] It is a fact which India perhaps under the circumstances cannot face is that religion-born terrorism within no time becomes so fierce that only a superpower like the United States of America that too under a very strong leadership can boldly face. But, India's total dependence on USA and her allies to protect India from terrorists may leave her to live in a world of dream, agony and repentance. India has to look into her problem with her eyes and mind. As the Prime Minister in his address to the nation had rightly pointed out that in our country the roots of terrorism lay in religious fundamentalism (RF). To us, both, religious fundamentalism (RF) and terrorism (T) are closely related and depend on each other. But, the world community (USA and others) considers only terrorism as menace and often stands neutral or apathetic on RF (religious fundamentalism). Accordingly, to them, fight against T (Terrorism) does not automatically mean fight against RF (Religious Fundamentalism). Unless this is made clear and we are able to convince all concerned, the present US remedy of massive retaliation even after passing of the resolution on anti-terrorism by the Security Council of the UN (September 29, 2001) would prove to be short-lived and demonstrative, and terrorism would continue to erupt as before.

Therefore, it is very urgent and important that Indian leaders, scholars and media men effectively make it clear to the USA, European nations and others that the root cause is religious fundamentalism (RF) and for them fight against RF is much more basic and central. India should exhort the world community to make efforts to fight against terrorism based on religious fundamentalism (RF), and not merely against terrorism (T). It is the RF (religion-related fundamentalism), which is the real enemy of culture, civilization, democracy and freedom and humanity. Terrorism is merely a by-product, a symptom and outcome of religious fundamentalism (RF).[10]

Steps Taken by the USA

The US has been taking steps broadly in three directions.

A New Kind of War

It has been realized that fight against terrorism is a special kind of 'war'. It would be longer, multifaceted, more fierce and complicated. It is not 'merely terrorism' as such. It is intermixed with religious fundamentalism and mostly exercised by non-state organizations spread over the world.

Fight against terrorism must be treated not only as proxy war but 'war'. There are two ways to fight terrorism. Firstly, it has to meet by force, if possible, before its occurrence, otherwise after it. The second way provides long-term solution. It requires separation of religion from religious fundamentalism. In place of religion one may have absolute faith in some ideology. Separating religion from religious fundamentalism or fanaticism is still much more difficult. This separation has to be defined, supervised, enacted and properly implemented. Conducting war against terrorism and apprehending the terrorists, both before and after they commit the crime of terrorism, cannot be possible under the ordinary common laws. Its process is slow, dilatory, costly and ineffective. By the time the case is decided the terrorist may commit several fresh terrorist acts. After a few years of judicial proceedings, one terrorist might be sentenced to death. But before that happens, he would have killed hundreds of innocent men, women and children. Ordinary law entails so many loopholes which are fully exploited by the terrorist links. September 11 terrorized the American mind and changed the country for ever. [11]

But the US took a bold and a very wise and just decision. President Bush promised to get Osama bin Laden "dead or alive" and asked all other governments that "either you are with us or with the terrorists". On January 30, 2002 President Bush warned governments which are "timid in the face of terror" that the US will "act" should they fail. "Some governments will be timid in the face of terror. And make no mistake: If they do not act, America will," he said in his first state of the union address to a joint session of Congress.[12] Thus, the US action in Afghanistan and elsewhere has established the super-power's right to intervene anywhere. The apparent mandate is to crack down on terror and impose moderate democratic values everywhere.

Inside Steps

Conducting war against terrorism and apprehending the terrorists cannot be possible under the ordinary common laws. Prevention and containing terrorism involves all sorts of pain and injury to the innocent people. It is the necessary price, which has to be paid for lack of vigilance about keeping watch over all overt and covert activities of the terrorists and terrorists-in-making. Both war against terrorism and implementation of ordinary laws and human rights cannot go together. Containment of terrorism demands less or more sacrifice of rights, conveniences and privileges.[13]

The American counterpart of India's POTO makes for a more imaginative acronym USA-PATRIOT (Uniting and Strengthening America by Providing Appropriate Tools Required to Intercept and Obstruct Terrorism). The USA-PATRIOT Act has threatening implications, particularly for the millions of aliens for whom America has long been the only land of opportunity. It permits the Attorney General not only to incarcerate non-citizens (including lawful permanent residents) on a mere a suspicion, but to deny them re-admission should they be found engaging in speech protected by the First Amendment. Since then, President Bush has further expanded executive power in a way that severely curtails the American notion of freedom. Henceforth, foreigners accused of terrorism will be tried in military tribunals, while the administration can legitimately track down and question thousands of immigrants as well as monitor conversations between the detainees and their lawyers.[14]

Next Steps

Going far beyond the Anti-Ballistic Missiles Treaty of 1972, and the CTBT, USA has moved forward in the direction of NMD (National Missiles Defence) system. In fact, Musharraf had to surrender to a non-negotiable US ultimatum. His speech of January 12, 2002 was in response to the second ultimatum delivered to him through British Prime Minister Tony Blair. The speech was the beginning of the long road to reform on which Pakistan had to embark to move away from a social culture, which had nurtured terrorism and extremist politics. It had been made clear that the Americans were going to stay and clean up Pakistan. Bush had also signed bin Laden's death warrant and explicitly instructed CIA to eliminate Osama bin Laden and his Al Qaida network.[15]

Colin L. Powell, Secretary of State, during his military career, was among the most forceful in insisting that the US should never again fight "a half-hearted half-war". While he paid visit to Pakistan (October 16, 2001), he praised Musharraf for his "bold and courageous" stand to join the anti-terrorism coalition. Powell called on Pakistan to do something about the system of fundamentalist religious schools, called 'madrasas' that have served as breeding grounds for militant anti-Americanism and support for the Taliban. Musharraf responded by pledging "long-term actions to check these extremist views".[16] Bush reached China to attend the APEC (Asia-Pacific Economic Cooperation) on 18th October and got firm commitment of Chinese President Jiang Zemin. "There is a firm commitment by this government to cooperate in intelligence matters and to help interdict financing of terrorist organizations." Alarmed by Osama's links with Pak Nuclear scientists, viz., Sultan Bashiruddin Mahmood, Mirza Yousaf and Chaudhury Abdul Majid, the US had compelled Pakistan in 1998 to remove Dr. Sultan Nasiruddin Mahmood just after 1998 nuclear tests for his pro-Taliban connections. Osama has persistently tried to lay his hands on a nuclear device and said it is religious duty to pursue such a course.

In her new security structure the US is making efforts under the mantle of fighting global terrorism supported by countries the world over. This reorganization has led to a hegemonic coalition, changes in national security laws and the creation of national security states. Since September 11 attacks, the US has taken the task of fighting terrorism, which it has depicted as an enemy without a fixed face or location but with a global presence. This has given the US and its allies the right to access all place at all times and by any means. Most countries have endorsed this kind of action. The US has been able to establish new bases in Uzbekistan, Tajikistan, Afghanistan and Pakistan.

Under the Bush doctrine, the US has openly declared Iraq, Iran and North Korea as 'rogue' states. It has begun to intervene in several local and bilateral conflicts that threaten regional insecurity. The most critical of these have been India and Pakistan, Philippines against the Abu Sayaff insurgents, Nepal against the Maoist insurgency and others.

Impact on the Muslim World

The most obvious changes of the US use of force have taken in Pakistan, but similar changes are happening in the Muslim world. The US success was unexpectedly swift and total. In Muslim countries, anti-US demonstrations disappeared, and the demand for Osama T-shirts collapsed. Al Qaida and the Taliban are no longer touted as Islamic heroes battling the infidels. In Kuwait, after the Taliban debacle, everything has changed. The Kuwaiti government has banned scores of fundamentalist institutions, and stopped dubious outfits from collecting money supposedly for charity, but actually to create 'madrassas' preaching religious hate. In Yemen and Somalia safe haven of terrorists are declining sharply in number and safety. Earlier US attempts to retaliate were either futile (as with President Clinton's bombing of camps in Afghanistan) or stupid (like mistakenly bombing a pharmaceutical factory in Sudan). But 9/11 ended American waffling, and provoked it to declare open war on terrorism. Earlier Osama had got away because the US was reluctant to go into full battle. Pakistan, Syria and Libya have, in the past, supported terrorist organizations. They will doubtless continue to support nationalist terrorists presumably seeking the liberation of a particular territory, like Palestine or Kashmir. The US overlooks this provided these governments crack down on transnational terrorists, who attack distant countries out of ideological religious fervour. The distinction between nationalist and transnational terrorism has not explicitly been made by US policy makers, but it is being followed tacitly in practice.

Pakistan has long tried to straddle both sides of the fence, using militant Islam or its purposes in Afghanistan and Kashmir, yet claiming to be fundamentally secular and modern, and hence a naturally ally of the West. But action by US following 9/11 has forced Pakistan to choose. It has chosen with some understandable ambiguity, to take the secular route.[17] Pro-mullah elements in the Pakistani army have been sidelined. No longer can Pakistan openly allow madrassas to preach religious hatred, and act as training grounds for transnational terrorists. These madrassas had as many as 35,000 foreign students from other Muslim countries, all posing a threat not just to the US or India, but to secular Muslim governments everywhere.[18] However, real change in the Muslim world has to come from within and cannot be imposed by US might. But, the US changed the internal dynamics in Muslim countries by strengthening secular forces and weakening the mullahs. Its firmness on terrorism has achieved this.[19]

Charge of Imperialism

US policies against terror have been charged as a new form of imperialism. This allows 'well-governed' western nations to impose order and stability on the world. It regards active intervention sometimes necessary. This intervention has already been exercised in Bosnia, Kosovo, East Timor and Afghanistan. Apparently, these countries have opted for a reduction in their sovereignty which appears to be a self-invited imposition. Mr. Blair of UK tries to bring in righteous moral favour to George Bush's aggressive pursuit of US right to military intervention anywhere in the world. Richard Haas, Director of Policy Planning and Colin Powell said: "Sovereignty entails obligations. One is not to massacre your own people. Another is not to support terrorism in any way. If a government fails to meet these obligations, then it forfeits some of the normal advantages of sovereignty, including the right to be left alone inside your own territory." This appears to be startling implications for national sovereignty of countries. But this entails lessening of the need of maintaining a massive military machine and nuclear arsenal. If they are assured of a 'protective' armour the country concerned can divert some of the stupendous resources from defence and nuclear deterrence to food, shelter, health, education and infrastructure for survival in a competitive world.[20] Now, President Bush accepts that "the US has long maintained the option to pre-emptive actions to counter a sufficient threat to our national security". He declared that to forestall or prevent hostile acts by adversaries, the US would not use force in all cases to pre-empt emerging threats, nor should nations use pre-emption as a pretext for aggression. Yet, in an age where the enemies of civilization openly and actively seek the world's most destructive technologies, the US would not remain idle while dangers gather. He gave a clear warning to the adversaries of the US that it would not hesitate to launch preventive wars to bring about regime changes in countries which have the potential to develop terrorist groups and can threaten long-term US interests and security. This doctrine, no doubt, violates the UN Charter principle of non-interference in domestic affairs of nations. But such interventions have been carried out by the US in the past. The only difference is, having achieved the status of sole superpower the US now openly, declared its intention.[21] President George W. Bush said that ending tyranny and spreading freedom around the world is only a long-term goal of US that requires "the commitment of generations".[22]

USA has found in Islamic terrorism a credible adversary. One can say more pernicious one than communism ever was. Today, Islamic terrorism has found its foothold in Great Britain,[23] South and Central Asia and threatens US interests, but it also provides an opportunity to consolidate its position ahead of its competitors in another emerging and largely untapped market. Now, everybody is aware of the danger of nuclear weaponry falling into the hands of terrorists, particularly Islamic terrorists like Osama bin Laden. These Islamic terrorists have a divine mission to finish all non-believers, and so-called enemies of Islam. They prepare themselves in form of human bombs or suicide attackers. Their main motivation comes from religious fundamentalism culminating in form of jihad (terrorism).[24] Therefore, America was overcautious in Iraq. President Bush, in his speech to the General Assembly, said that the Security Council had been "right to demand that Iraq destroy its illegal weapons and prove that it had done so" and "right to vow serious consequences if Iraq refused to comply". The US, he said, had not only unseated Saddam Hussein but also defended "the credibility of the UN".[25] Soon after the end of the ultimatum, Iraq was attacked on March 21, 2003, and Saddam Hussein removed. President Bush announced on May 1, 2003 the end of major combat operations in Iraq. By conventional measures, the war in Iraq has been over for weeks. But, the US ultimate goal was not just to topple Hussein but to stabilize the country and instal a friendly government. President Bush appointed L. Paul Bremer III, a retired diplomat and counter-terrorism expert on May 6, 2003 in charge of rebuilding Iraq's government and infrastructure. America had taken a sledgehammer to swat a fly. Its victory had served its primary purpose of warning other 'rogue' states in the region like Syria and Iran and perhaps even Saudi Arabia. War with Iraq could have been averted if it was disarmed credibly on demand from the Security Council. After the attack was over and Saddam Hussein removed in 2003, it has been found that Iraq did not possess nuclear weapons or have preparation to make them. Intelligence (CIA) reports given to the President were found wrong or inadequate. President Bush himself has publicly admitted this and has owned its responsibility. However, it does not mean that US should have stopped till Iraq made nuclear weapons and declared it to the world community.

Iraq officially now has a new constitution by majority. The Shia party—the United Iraqi Alliance—took about 59 per cent of the votes from 89 per cent of ballot boxes counted in Baghdad.[26]

Time and again, with reference to Iran, Bush declared that the US and its allies will not tolerate the construction of nuclear weapon in Iran. US also accused Iran repeatedly evading inspections and violating its commitments at a meeting of the world's nuclear watchdog agency. US also has problem now with Korea and Iran.

Iran has started work on construction of a heavy water reactor and says that it will be used only for peaceful purposes but which could also produce plutonium for a nuclear bomb. Bush has supported using diplomacy to halt Iran's nuclear programme, and UN Security Council sanctions would other diplomatic efforts fail. If diplomacy fails "all options are on the table. The use of force is the last option for any President. We have used force in the past to secure our country." Iranian President Mahmoud Ahmadinejad's recently called for Israel to be "wiped off the map" has, not surprisingly elicited a strong reaction from the international community, with even the UN Security Council condemning it. Observers were appalled at a head of state making such irresponsible remarks about another UN member-state.[27] The head of the UN nuclear monitoring agency IAEA Mohamed El Baradei has thrown its weight behind a proposal that calls for Iran to move its uranium enrichment programme to Russia and plans to carry the details with him to Tehran within days.[28]

Iran removed UN seals at its Natanz uranium enrichment plant and resumed nuclear fuel research drawing sharp western criticism. But there is no immediate threat of punitive action. Iran wants a civilian energy programme to satisfy its booming demand for electricity. Condolezza Rice commented that Iran has crossed all limits, and the matter should be sent to the Security Council by the members of the International Nuclear Watchdog. The head of the UN nuclear monitoring agency IAEA Mohamed El Baradei also said that it is not yet confirmed that Iran's Natanz uranium enrichment plant is only for civil purposes. Recently, Tehran has proposed talks, but America and the European Union have rejected its proposal, considering it an excuse to avoid consideration by the Security Council.[29]

The US had warned North Korea many times against nuclear 'blackmail'. North Korea removed the last UN monitoring equipment at a nuclear fuel fabrication plant taking another step towards the production of weapons grade plutonium. Pyongyang has also issued threats, including one to "destroy the earth" if the US resorted to nuclear war against it.[30]

Now, North Korea has promised to give up its nuclear weapons in exchange for pledges of aid and security, the first major breakthrough in more than two years of deadlock over the crisis. It has agreed for the IAEA inspections and join NPT, but in lieu of help from South Korea, America, Japan, Russia and China in areas of oil, energy etc.[31]

In this way, US is ready to nuke WMD rogues. UK plans to create army of robo-soldiers by 2008 which would be an integrated fighting system.

Evaluation

Thus, there are few leaders like George W. Bush who are able to anticipate big dangers in time and make appropriate plan to avert them. The goal of the terrorists is to secure the victory of certain narrowly conceived religio-sectarian goals against the values of multiculturalism, democracy and globalization. While Al Qaida and its associates are fighting the war on an ideological plane, there is no sign of any ideological content in the anti terrorist campaign of US. As long as Washington persists with this attitude and does not. engage the hearts and minds of the Islamic populations in terms of its integration with global values, there will always be fresh recruits for Al Qaida and other terrorist organizations.

Washington's approach has been one of short term expediency. While not rejecting such short-term steps as part of the strategy of attrition in the war against terrorism, it is necessary to have a cost benefit analysis of such short-term expediencies against the long-term goals of fighting against the values and mindsets that generate terrorist.[32] Most of the countries foolishly cry when a big danger inflicts them severely. Making weapons of mass destruction or nuclear weapons is one of such dangers. They often forget that nuclear threat does not grant time even to cry and call on the world community, including UN, to help them in distress. In the present context, there are countries having extremist, jihadi and fundamentalist motivations to destroy in part or full some other nations and communities. When the leadership of such countries acquires or is likely to acquire nuclear weapons and missile technology, it is going to target its enemy at any moment, and can cause immense mass destruction. Any such country even without the actual use of nuclear weapons can threaten the other to surrender to its biddings. That devilish state usually does not accept any trustworthy and dependable control mechanism settled by the world community or UN. Later on, after the development of nuclear weapons by a particular terror prone nation, it is difficult to stop or restrain it. It continues to make plans to eliminate or harm nations hostile to it. Even advanced nuclear nations start feeling helplessness and futility in trying to stop it. To avoid loss of millions of human lives, even nuclear weapon states may find themselves reluctant to use its nukes against such newly nuclearized states. Therefore, one clear, single and solitary solution of this type of life death problem is to attack and destroy such potentially nuclear power states like Iraq, Iran and others.

Peace-loving nations apparently forget that by the time, the US or the UN gathers proofs and facts to convince such unwilling countries to take action, the potential nuclear power states would transform into nuclear weapon states. To press and wait for more convincing proofs simply amounts to granting them more time to tap sources to accomplish their goal and go beyond the control and reach of the world community. The latter is structurally unable to take a prompt and concerted action in such matter.

However, pitiable as well as painful is the attitude of some other countries who want to escape the nuclear death simply by showing neutrality or keeping away from the actual sight of the conflict. The

US, including India, has not paid any attention to the problem of Islamic terrorism reaching very close to nuclear know-how in Pakistan. India has drawn attention of the US and the Nuclear Watchdog.[33] Few can imagine, Pakistan by enlarging its nuclear capabilities further, with or without the help of US or China or North Korea, dissatisfied with any bargain from them or under the pressure of jehadi elements of its army, can make even USA the first victim of her nuclear onslaught. Pakistan is the only Islamic state having nuclear weapon with long range missiles to carry them. Already there are thousands of Americans, civil and military, in Pakistan. They can be made hostage, as did Iran two decades ago. In that eventuality, all Muslim countries, supported by country-made terrorists, would like to support Pakistan's act.

The US is able to defend itself all alone.[34] But, the rest of the countries depend ultimately upon the support of the US for their survival. Values of freedom, democracy, human rights and dignity of the individual go with power, safety and leadership of the US or US like group of nuclear capable countries. Without US help, no nation can protect itself against a nuclear attack from a jehadi state. Terrorists know well if the US is finished there would not be any difficulty in dealing with the rest. For the maintenance of world peace and save the globe from extinction, it is time that the civilized nations accept vis-à-vis Jehadi Terrorism the leadership of the US or the UN at least in the field of stopping proliferation and making of nuclear weapons and stopping them from going into the hands of terrorist states, nations and organizations. It would be for the sake of their own survival.

After Iraq, Libya and North Korea and others, more dangerous source of nuclear terrorism is Pakistan. Through Pakistan it can percolate to leadership of other Islamic terrorist organizations and ultimately form an Islamic bloc of nuclear terrorism against the rest.

Russian President Putin has anticipated that Pak weapons are global liability. Its weapons of mass destruction (WMD) could fall into the hands of "bandits and terrorists".[35]

By then they would be in a position to bargain with any organization, community or state as well as bleed the latter to death. Stopgap arrangement like promise to keep it as deterrent or wait for the doomsday or compromise may end in disaster. Therefore, an urgent and desirable action would be:

(i) to finish nuclear weaponry of this epi-centre of terrorism and other terrorism prone countries;
(ii) to develop a foolproof safety system at world level;
(iii) to launch an effective pre emptive strike system;
(iv) to prohibit all direct and indirect teaching, preaching, training, education, publication and funding activities pertaining to terrorism; and
(v) to compel such states by applying effective sanctions to dismantle organizations and institutions aiming to spread terrorism in any form.

Even the US would have to think twice in depending upon Pakistan for its own safety and protection from the jihadis.

It is said that Al Qaida people have access to crude nuclear bombs. George Tenet, former CIA Director, finds father of Pakistani nuclear bomb A.Q. Khan is at least as dangerous as Osama-bin-Laden. In the light of the CIA warning of Al Qaida's readiness to use 'dirty bomb' against the US, Khera has suggested that the US must investigate the full extent of Pakistan's role in nuclear proliferation. A.Q. Khan had been running a private company for the dissemination of nuclear weapons' know how blueprints, technology and equipment, as he did with Libya and Iran.[36]

India has insisted that steps, which are being taken against Iran to implement NPT provisions, should also be applied to A.Q. Khan's network situated in Pakistan. It is a fit case for the consideration of International Atomic Energy Agency (IAEA).[37]

Notes

1. Before September 11, the UK already had strong anti-terrorist legislation. The Terrorist Act 2000 delivered a modern, permanent UK-wide counter-terrorism framework which applied the definition of terrorism to international terrorism, as well as terrorism connected with Northern Ireland. UK had banned some 23 terrorist organisations many months before the events of September 11. The list included Al Qaida, Jaish-e-Mohammed and Lashkar-e-Taiba. Jack Straw, Foreign Secretary, UK, *Times of India*, February 27, 2002.
2. *Times of India*, August, 2002.

3. It is unique manual for Islamic terrorists detailing every aspect of how to fight a guerrilla war. It contains 11 volumes and is circulated both in book form and on CD-Rom to terrorist instructors. It is dedicated to bin Laden and Abdullah Azzam, a charismatic preacher who was a formative influence on the Saudi terrorist. It distils the experience of 10 years of guerrilla fighting against the Russians in Afghanistan and draws on stolen CIA and special services' hand-books. Sources of biological material include a list of countries that produce anthrax and a training camp in Pakistan where toxins are manufactured. The encyclopaedia was found in 1999 in the home of Khalil Deek when he was arrested in connection with an alleged plot to bomb Jordan's main airport in the capital, Amman, on the eve of the millennium. Each of the 10 volumes of the main encyclopaedia carries a picture showing a belt-fed machine gun standing in a window next to a copy of the Quran. It requires that the mujaheed should be young, so that he can start the mission 10 years before the start of the jehad.
4. *Times of India*, August 20, 2002.
5. It was banned by Government of India under the Unlawful Activities (Prevention) Act, 1967 on September 28, 2001.
6. *Times of India*, September 30, 2001.
7. An MSN survey tells that 47 per cent of suicide bombers have an academic education, 83 per cent are single and 64 per cent are between the ages of 18-23. One Islamic jehad school taught the boys the benefits of becoming suicide bombers. Boys in between 12-15 are told to draw pictures of themselves with explosives strapped to their bodies. "We are teaching the children that suicide bombing is the only thing that makes the enemy very frightened. Furthermore, we are teaching them we have the right to do so." The reward of suicide terrorism, according to a teacher, is: "A place in heaven where the martyrs will be greeted by 70 virgins."—Nikhat Kazmi, "How to handle human bombs" in *Times of India*, October 7, 2001.
8. Former US ambassador Robert D. Blackwill said, "Those who murder innocents for political motives and who seek to bring down the very pillars of our democracy—in New York, in Washington, at the Assembly in Srinagar, at the Parliament in New Delhi, and presently every day in J&K, are terrorists. These murderers are not missunderstood idealists. They are not disadvantaged dissidents. They are not religious perfectionists. And they are not freedom fighters." *Hindustan Times*, July 18, 2003.
9. In a Seminar on "Role of Media in Terrorism" held in Jammu on 25th September, 2001, it was told that India should not lean on the US to fight terrorism in its territory. Farooq Abdullah, then the Chief Minister of

Jammu & Kashmir, exhorted that 'India has to fight its own war on terrorism and cannot depend on the US to do it for us.' *Times of India*, September 26, 2001. It was highlighted that India had a long experience of fighting terrorism and had succeeded in controlling it in Punjab without any outside help.

10. This religion born terrorism within no time becomes so fierce that only a Super Power like the United States of America that too under a very strong leadership as that of President George W. Bush can take action against it. That too, perhaps, only after experiencing its worst attack on invincible minarets of Power and Freedom. For details, see, his *Address to the American Congress* on September 25, 2001.
11. Over 6,000 persons were killed at one stretch and property worth billions of dollars was destroyed with prestige of the US knocked down for ever.
12. *Times of India*, February 7, 2002.
13. The US created the Department of Homeland Security charging with protecting the country from terrorist attacks. It will takes over the Cost Guard, Secret Services, Border Patrol and Federal Emergency Management Agency. It has about 1,70,000 employees and an annual budget of $ 38 billion. The legislation exempts this new institution from the Freedom of Information Act which provides for declassification of secret government documents after 30 years. It has been considered as the most extensive reorganization of the federal government since the 1940s. The President stated that it provides for intelligence analysis and infrastructure protection, strengthening the borders, improving the use of science and technology to counter weapons of mass destruction, and enhancing preparedness and response capabilities. J.C. Watts declared, "This is a victory for the future of America."
14. *Times of India*, November 24, 2001.
15. *Times of India*, October 22, 2001.
16. *Times of India*, October 18, 2001.
17. President General Pervez Musharraf's address to the Nation, January 12, 2002.
18. Jeffrey Goldberg, *The Education of a Holy Warrior* (In a Pakistani religious school called the Haqqania madrasa, Osama bin Laden is a hero, the Taliban's leaders are famous alums and the next generation of mujahedeen is being militantly groomed.), op.cit.
19. Swaminathan S. Anklesaria Aiyar Swaminomics, "How 9/11 changed Muslim World", *Times of India*, January 6, 2002.
20. Shastri Ramachandran, "New Imperialism", *Times of India*, July 17, 2002.
21. K Subrahmanyam, "Regime Changes emption Ingrained in US Policy", *Times of India*, October 7, 2002.

22. *Hindustan Times*, January 29, 2005.
23. Terror godfather got UK dole: Abu Qatada, a radical Islamic cleric, known the godfather of world terrorism, who was granted asylum and for years drew a monthly £1000 benefit from the British Government was named as be directly involved in inspiring the September 11, 2001 attacks in the US. He is a Palestinian whose real name is Omar Mahamood Abu Omar. *Hindustan Times*, May 22, 2003; London was attacked twice in 2005 by the terrorists.
24. Bin Laden aide Ayman al-Zawahri tells Muslims to wage war against US, Jews: "Carry arms against your enemies, the Americans and Jews....Attack the missions of the United States, United Kingdom, Australia and Norway and their interests, companies and employees". Dubai, May 21 tapes, in *Hindustan Times*, May 22, 2003.
25. *Hindustan Times*, September 25, 2003.
26. *Hindustan Times*, December 21, 2005.
27. *Hindustan Times*, October 31, 2005.
28. An Iranian exile group called on the UN's atomic watchdog to inspect an extensive network of tunnels which it say the Islamic Republic has built to conceal a clandestine nuclear weapons programme. *Hindustan Times*, December 21, 2005.
29. *Rajasthan Patrika*, January 19, 2006.
30. *Hindustan Times*, December 25, 2000.
31. *Hindustan Times*, September 20, 2005.
32. K Subrahmanyam, "Engage Liberal Islamists—Capture Hearts in War on Terror", *Times of India*, December 3, 2002.
33. India's Foreign Secretary Shyam Saran said that there was a new global consensus on non proliferation and India was willing "to be a part of this consensus". But Saran underlined that one of the dragons India would pursue was A.Q. Khan and if Iran was the dock so should be Pakistan. Export standards that go beyond the NPT must include both recipient and supplier states. *Hindustan Times*, October 25, 2005.
34. US suffers three disabilities: (i) It does not have a forceful ideology to the engine of Islamic Jehad out of use; (ii) it lacks the will to fight to finish; and (iii) some US citizens are liking to join Islamic Jehad. See, Anonymous (Scheuer), Imperial Hubris: Why the West is losing the War on Terror, Barssey Inc, 2005; Here is also an American road to jehad. The US News and World Report reveals that in the 1990s and between 1000 and 2000 US citizens left the country to join up to jehad. Since 1989, some 400 recruits have left the US and Canada to be trained in Pakistan and Afghanistan alone. *Times of India*, June 15, 2002.

35. *Times of India*, December 2, 2002; and, also, Jessica Stem, an American scholar met a number of key leaders of the jehad who insisted that the US was assessing the Pakistani army wrongly. "The army is now Islamic and was committed to the Madrasas. Pakistan is a mix of nationalism and religion. Its army backs and organises terrorist acts believe that it is a weapon to keep a more powerful Hindu India at bay." Manoj Joshi, "War without an end", *Hindustan Times*, November 1, 2005.
36. *Hindustan Times*, 25, 2004, P.N. Khera, "Weapons of Choice", *Hindustan Times*, November 30, 2004.
37. *Rashtradoot*, November 25, 2005.

18

Wretched Conditions of the Terrorists

Today, a terrorist is the most dreaded, hated and cursed person on earth. No nation in the world is willing to tolerate his existence within its boundaries. The army and security forces of all countries have standing orders to shoot him at sight.[1] Ordinary citizens begin to tremble and cry at his very presence. All consider such treatment with him as appropriate to his doings. Instead of being considered as man, he is treated merely as a sacrificial goat.

However, all this also makes him a creature of pity and compassion. Despite his engagements in the killings of innocent human beings, he is also a man. Therefore, it should be discussed whether there are ways to save a man turned beast. The fact is that here is a man who while killing innocent man, women and children remains full of pleasure and enthusiasm maintaining that he is obeying directives or commandments of God.[2] Yet he has not learnt this by birth. In fact, he does not know that he has been trained in a manner that whatever he has been taught has become part of his nature and personality. The agency of his training can be some holy book, some 'guru' (teacher), some party or some ideology including his own self overflowing with hatred and enmity against some person, faith or community. The basic training imparted to him is that whatever he has learnt comes down from God or Fate.[3] But the fact is that all of his doings has been planned by some third party[4] in advance but he remains unaware of such schemes. Surely, some third or fourth party to the conduct of terrorism has put his life at stake for upkeep of its own interest, aspiration and status.

The subject-matter of terrorism as such can be looked at from two main angles—legal-secular, and religion-related or *jihadi.* But, the worst victim is the social and family lives of the terrorists. Hardly anyone has mustered courage to think about and take care of it. The terrorist is all alone, helpless and neglected in this world. This aspect of the life of a terrorist is closely related to both of these angles which kill his personal, family and social life in equal manner.

On the basis of sources, causes and types of perpetrators, terrorism can be of several kinds. But, here, we are mainly concerned with its prevailing form, which has matured from extremism to terrorism via religious fundamentalism. In legal-secular parlance, these killings are named as 'terrorism' while committed at the call of religion they are known as 'jihad'.

The legal-secular view looks at terrorism simply as murder or killing of innocent civilians. Thus, a terrorist is murderer or killer. The term 'terrorism' coming out of the root word 'terror' does not spell out what actually it is. It is sheer naked, blatant, cruel and inhuman act of killing of innocent people. It is totally against law, human rights, morality and democracy. However, it is a fact of life. Nobody can deny its existence. This view has no concern with the purpose, motive, goal or result underlying the acts of terrorism.

The other 'jihadi' or religion-related view finds terrorism directly related with God or holy book. The claimant claims to know his divine wishes to do as such. Accordingly, terrorism is murder with a goal, purpose, motive, plan, vengeance and threat so as to compel the victims to act on the directions given by the terrorists. The US-led coalition in Afghanistan had targeted the terrorists, but the latter and their supporters did not regard themselves 'terrorists'. They considered themselves to be 'jihadis', 'mujahedeens', 'warriors of their religion', 'soldiers of Islam' etc. There are thousands of other persons who finance them to enable them to have all types of weapons, such as conventional, chemical and biological, and the like. Their understanding of the meaning and interpretation of the sacred books, which makes up the basis of their gruesome acts, is that it does not allow any other view to prevail. The whole world, particularly the hostile nations, have to abide by them. Their words and actions are the final verdicts upon earth.[5]

Whatever be the view to look at the operations of terrorism, the conditions of the terrorists appear to remain wretched, utterly helpless and despicable. The persons, leaders or bosses who push them to such plight can be put into categories of (1) fanatics and fundamentalists, (2) liberal interpreters of religion or jihad, and (3) ambitious political leaders and military rulers. It may be analyzed how and why the terrorist stands in the hands of these people.

Fanatics and Fundamentalists

Outwardly, conditions of the terrorists are worst, inhuman and intolerable in the hands of fanatic supporters of jihad. They train the terrorists in various *madarsas*, training camps and institutions to die for the religion while killing non-believers and elements hostile to their religion.[6] Senior leaders are authorized to shoot immediately any hesitant, renegade or disobedient terrorist. The terrorists after joining their camp lose all contact, rights and relations with their families and friends, and have to bank upon the contingent care of the managers of terrorist organizations or of the sponsoring state. The senior bosses hardly grant any opportunity to them to express independent opinion, questioning or doubting directives given to them. No chance is given to them to raise controversy over the statements enshrined in the holy books like the Quran, the Guru Granth Sahab, and the Gita and so on, such as:[7] How and why such revelation appeared on earth? Has God really sent such directions or commandments to perform such heinous acts? What and why did he feel it necessary that killings or crimes should be performed especially by me? How any godman, messenger or representative of God or Avatar can, though he appears a man like him can be the final arbiter of good or evil acts? No jihadi is permitted to seek shelter of a different religion, guru, prophet or preacher. When God has created all human beings, how any guru, prophet or teacher can find 'justice' in the killings of non-believers? What is the guarantee that God would really be pleased with his gruesome deeds? Moreover, the terrorists and their mentors might be acting on directions given by their bosses but why should others accept them? But on the gunpoint not only they have to believe in what they say but also have to execute them in action. Whether one is Muslim or a non-Muslim, they have to accept the Holy Book (Quran) as the last and final words of God. None is allowed to discuss it. One cannot raise any objection to statements made in it.

Liberal Interpreters of Religion

A large number of liberal Muslim scholars and clerics claim that Islam does not teach terrorism, that is, killing of the innocent people. But, they accept that there are divine directives to use force or violence for prescribed purposes. This view also provides no relief to the lives of terrorists.[8]

This group of liberal and peace-loving interpreters of jihad reduces the area of helplessness of the terrorists but fails to mitigate it. They do not agree with extremist interpretations of Islam made by the diehard Islamists and also oppose the killings of innocent persons as jihad. But they do nothing to declare that fanatic interpretations made and taught by the bigots as anti-religion, and take no steps to stop their practice in action. Thus, at their hands also, the terrorists see no way to lead a peaceful, respectable and secure human life. They stand for the exercise of violence and force on many grounds, therefore, as far as terrorists are concerned, either appear as passive onlookers or provide indirect support terrorist violence.[9]

While defending the position of the Holy Quran vis-à-vis use of violence and force and arguing against the acts and understanding of the fanatic jihadis, they leave the terrorists in lurch. These scholars fail to see that now it is no more possible or permissible to use force or violence. By enjoining the believers to do so under the prevailing set up is to ask them to live like criminals or terrorists. These liberal scholars forget that Islam is a product or creation of a non-state and non-nation society. A Muslim in terms of the Holy Quran can live and follow his tenets only when he lives in a community without having a state or nation. However, if he is compelled to live in a state, or a nation or a community different from his own, he stands at war with it. He can be at peace only in a society of Islam. In a Muslim state, which is not run according to the tenets of Islam, he will find himself at war with it. They tactically can keep patience and show forbearance till the opportune moment arrives to transform that polity or community into the version of their religion. Till such moment arrives, they will behave like extremists, insurgents and rebels. Hardly can they be expected to live like good citizens.

But no civilized society can be at peace and security with such people even if they claim and remain committed to their religion, God, divine incarnation, messenger, guru etc. In ascertaining the nature and meaning of justice, oppression, retaliation, jihad and the like, they become judge unto themselves and have divine sanction to use force. It depends on their individual understanding, training and education that to what extent they fight for the cause of religion. From simple believers to hardened fanatics, fundamentalists, extremists and terrorists can legitimately claim to commit acts of violence in the name of religion almost everywhere.

Some zealots often forget that imposition of divine directives on others in the name of God or revealed religion can cause more harm than good as the latter might be already having their own revealed religion. They can even be more committed to their faith. Sometimes, the directives of a religion might be contradictory and opposite to others. Others may also make a similar claim to divinity and finality of their religion. In some cases, divine commandments or godly directives were given to the non-state people and did not envisage boundaries of state, nation or community at the time of their appearance. Followers of such religions, who now live in a particular state or nation or some territorial community do not find it possible to obey or follow all the directives given by their religion. Under the present pattern of international law and prevailing state systems, it is neither possible for them to leave that state nor they are likely to be welcomed by a state of their choice, even if there is predominance of their religion in that state. States as such often find it difficult to accommodate such people.[2]

Thus, the outcome of so-called liberal interpretation of jihad has largely been to justify the use of violence on the direction of others. This results in permitting the continuation of terrorism and breaking of civil laws. The terrorists, if remain alive, at the hands of these liberal scholars are destined to lead a life of criminals.

Ambitious Political Leaders and Military Rulers

The worst plight, disconnected with religion, is inflicted on the terrorists by the ambitious political leaders and military rulers. The latter send them,[10] without any reference to religion, holy book or God, to kill innocent people, set their houses on fire, cause disturbance, spread communal tension and the like. The terrorists are asked to do so at times in the name of freedom or avenge some injustice or in the national interest. A government can manage to despatch them as infiltrators, human bombs, fifth columnists and terrorists. As stated above, their condition is much worse than that of killers belonging to first two categories. At least the latter might console them that they are dying for the cause of God or religion, but these terrorists are treated neither as regular soldiers nor *mujahedeens*. Most often, when, in view of worldwide fight against terrorism, it is not possible to enter into an open, large-scale and all-out war, a smaller government often uses terrorism as a political weapon. In comparison with full-fledged war, it finds it cheaper, more effective and efficient. The government and its army, which sends the terrorists to commit acts of terrorism, when they are killed by the enemy forces, refuses to identify them and claim their dead bodies. The enemy does not treat them as military regulars. To think about the care of the families of these unclaimed slain terrorists is beyond imagination.

It may be pointed out here that this category of ambitious political leaders and military rulers, instead of openly claiming to practice terrorism for political-diplomatic goals, also resorts to the religious or jihadi justification. The poor terrorist till the last breadth of his life does not know that his life has been vainly sacrificed only for realizing political goals and not for religion. In fact, the whole people of that country are kept in dark about the real interests of the rulers.

But one another reality pertaining to terrorists belonging to former two categories is that they too actually make use of these terrorists as their political and diplomatic tool. Earlier, the United States of America, in order to uproot the Soviets from Afghanistan, asked Pakistan to prepare an army of terrorists and gave immense financial and military aid to organize it. Pakistan trained the Talibans in religious fundamentalism and ultimately by using them forced the Soviet occupation army to flee from Afghanistan in 1989. The Taliban government of Afghanistan provided shelter and protection to Osama bin Laden, the topmost terrorist, who organized hundreds of Al Qaida camps to train terrorists to operate world over. Within no time it became a threat to the USA itself. After the September 11,

2001 attack on the World Trade Centre and the Pentagon, the US government felt gravity of the situation and fiercely attacked on Afghanistan again with the help of Pakistan. America eliminated the Talibans and the Al Qaida camps. Since then, America as the leader of the world coalition has been fighting against terrorism throughout the globe.

But, the political use of terrorism, as did the USA and Pakistan in uprooting the Soviets in Afghanistan, continues. This time, despite worldwide war against terrorism, it is being used by Pakistan against India to forcibly occupy the Indian part of Jammu & Kashmir. After four defeats in open wars against India, Pakistan finds terrorism as the most suitable as well as manageable weapon to realize its political goals. It has already provided haven to the thousands of Taliban fighters who fled from Afghanistan there to used against India. Pakistan has been operating over twenty terrorist organizations and training thousands of terrorists under the guidance of the ISI, and sending them as infiltrators, killers, arsonists etc. in different parts of India, particularly Jammu & Kashmir. The terrorists are commandeered to kill innocent persons, political leaders, pilgrims, police and security men, and make all attempt to create communal tension. In encounters with the security and police forces, the terrorists are caught and killed, and their dead bodies along with huge cache of arms and ammunition are publicly displayed to the people. But, nobody comes forward to claim them. This state sponsored terrorism by Pakistan has been captioned as 'freedom struggle'.[11]

Dilemma of the Mentors

It is clear by now that the life and families belonging to all the three categories of the terrorists are utterly pitiable, helpless and hateful, and they find no way to escape from them. But, the conditions of their mentors are no less wretched, heinous and despicable. The first category mentors are so fanatically blind that they with their followers cannot even opine that these killings are executed against both God and humanity. The terrorists cannot even think that the preachers of violence themselves are standing on the other side of religion. Thus, it is totally futile to expect that their mentors can ever work to rescue them from such wretched life. The second category of liberals fruitlessly continue to permit jihad for some specific purposes, but lack courage to tell that no individual or organization or community has the right to exercise force and violence after the state has taken over all such functions taught earlier to be done by the individual believer. Under the universal 'rule of law', now, democracy has evolved means and methods to redress injustice, oppression and exploitation. Under these circumstances, anyone using violence stands against the rule of law and the constitution. His acts are punishable as he is treated as a criminal, rebel or insurgent. Still, these mentors, even if they feel like that, and make declaration accordingly, would be treated as anti-religion, renegades and Satan (evil). Similarly, the political and military leaders belonging to this category would not do anything as they would work only to protect their power, position and vested interests. Under the national and international compulsions, they are unable to launch an open and large-scale war against their enemy. Therefore, the only way to justify their military rule is to make use of terrorism as their only available politico-military weapon. Suffering from acute poverty, illiteracy, unemployment and insecurity, the youngsters fall easy prey to their manoeuvre. Once they start treading on the path of terrorism, they cannot retrace or go back for fear of being shot down by their seniors.

In sum, none of these three categories of mentors are able to provide a happy, secure and honourable life to any terrorist though he commits heinous crimes and dies for the job assigned to them. Adequate relief is hardly available to him or to his family. The existence of his life throughout his brief career remains unknown, uncertain and utterly neglected. As the three categories of mentors prompt the terrorist to carry out his mission broadly on the basis of religion, no person who has some faith in that religion finds himself in a position to oppose even some of his acts and utterances, and suggest some alternative way living. If he dares to do that, he is likely to be declared as 'kafir' or renegade, and can be punished by everyone belonging to that faith. On the other side, from the legal-secular point of view, all that a terrorist does is nothing but murder or killing of human beings. A terrorist is but a murderer and killer. Whatever be the reason, he deserves under law everywhere to be sent to gallows only. This view would like to severely punish his mentors also, if possible, the political and military leaders of the state, which sponsors terrorism as a political weapon.

Notes

1. When 350 terrorists forcibly occupied Holy Qaba in Mecca in 1979, special squads of the Saudi government killed them on spot itself. Israeli PM Ariel Sharon vowed, "We will not give in to terror...Israil will go after those who spilled the blood of its citizens".
2. In a Pakistani religious school called the Haqqania madrassa, Osama bin Laden is a hero, the Taliban's leaders are famous alums and the next generation of mujahedeen is being militantly groomed.
3. Jehadi education is imparted to the terrorists since childhood. Tanveer Jafari, Terrorist Attacks are against Islam, *Rajasthan Patrika*, July 20, 2005.
4. For intermediaries or brokers of religion, see, Chapter 7, "Steps in Four Directions".
5. See, Chapter 13 "Jihad as Terrorism".
6. Besides the case of Salman Rushdie, there is Taslima Nasreen: Bangladesh's exiled feminist writer. Taslima Nasreen's latest novel *Utal Hawa* (Gusty Wind), in a sequel to her early novel *Amar Meybela* (My Childhood) has been banned. The Home Ministry said, it "contains anti-Islam sentiments and statements that could destroy the religious harmony in Bangladesh". Taslima, a physician-turned writer, rose to prominence after the publication of her first novel *Lajja* (Shame) in 1993. A local Muslim fundamentalist group put a price on her head because it blasphemed Islam.
7. See, Chapter 14, "Questions and Culture of Liberal Muslims".
8. ....Fundamentalists have taken over the leadership of 15 crore strong Indian Muslim community. It is simply because of apathy and silence of the liberal Muslim who mutely speak that the Prophet advocated jehad only in self-defence, not for territorial gains." However, they hesitate to take over the role of the Imams-called muftis and qazis who are paid by the state to interpret the Sharia to the common Muslim, With the passage of time, these clerics developed worldly interests. Gurumukh Singh, "Distorted Islam-Liberal Muslims must Speak up", *Times of India*, April 9, 2002.
9. See, Chapter 15, "Liberals Stand Ineffective".
10. At present, 82 Intelligence (Spy) centres of ICI of Pakistan are working. They are 23 in Delhi, 18 in Uttar Pradesh, 13 in Rajasthan, and 17 in Pak occupied Kashmir. There are 99 training camps of terrorists in Bangladesh operating in North-East of India, Col. H.S. Shekhawat, *Rajasthan Patrika*, November 29, 2002.

11. Rana, presenting the Great Jihad Machine of Pakistan, reveals that some 30,000 young Pakistanis have died in Afghanistan and Kashmir, 2,000 sectarian clashes have taken place. There is still a pool of 1.2 million young men (and growing) active in jihadi and religious organizations. According to Rana there are 237 religious organizations in Pakistan, of them 82 are sectarian and 27 participate in politics whereas 104 are jihadis and 18 are tablighi outfits that abjure politics and violence. There are, in addition, more than 6,700 madarssas in Pakistan and PK and this does not include madarssas for reading and writing and memorising the Quoran. In addition there are 12 major welfare organizations. See Mohammed Amir Rana, *Gateway to Terrorism*, London: New Millennium, 2002.

19

War against Terrorism

Everybody in India strongly feels that no attention has been paid by the world community to the inner aspect of terrorism. While the US appears to be unaware of it, countries like India are maintaining purposeful silence.[1] Others dare not come forward for different reasons. The US, UN or any other coalition may continue to bomb terrorists and terrorist training camps in different parts of the world, terrorism would still remain there.

However, elimination of terrorism on wider scale requires cooperation from the whole world community. But, the US would get cooperation from the member-nations only when all forms of terrorism would be planned for targeting.

While every form of terrorism is a threat to human life, freedom and democracy, terrorism related to religion or faith is much more dangerous as it acts, besides the needs and necessities of this world, on the basis of assumed guidance from more enduring and overpowering entities like God, Revelation, Heaven and Grace. Those who are put under the influence of religion consider them as realities and do have total faith in them. A terrorist led and fed on fundamentalism based on religion concerns himself only with the execution of his divine mission, and remains ready to embrace death.[2]

However, to escape from the charge that this war against terrorism is a war against a particular religion, it is necessary that texts and literature of all religions which usually form the basis of training the extremists, fanatics, fundamentalists and terrorists are taken into account, scanned and explained.

Religion, Religion-related and Religious Fundamentalism

In plural and multi-cultural societies, it is necessary to look into the susceptibilities of minorities related to religions. One has to be careful about the use of words 'religion' and 'fundamentalism'. 'Religious fundamentalism' and 'fundamentalism imposed by or connected to religion' are two separate or different categories of thought and action. Often these two words are jointly used in a wrongful and rash manner. Only religion-related fundamentalism can lead to terrorism.

With regard to 'religion' and 'fundamentalism' there can be four positions: (i) vis-à-vis religion when a man stands alone;[3] (ii) none between man and his God;[4] (iii) man and God through an intermediary, interpreter, preacher, priest or guru; (iv) man, God and the state, society or nation with or without intermediary. In first two positions there is no problem. One may have full commitment or faith in religion. As it does not affect anyone one's 'religious' or 'religion-related' fundamentalism, it may not be opposed. There is no problem if 'fundamentalism' is really religious or religion-based. It is commitment or allegiance to one's own sense of particular religion. It is often one-way traffic or monologue. A man or devotee feels that others should follow him and be happy like him. Only in some cases, its practice and adoption may not be allowed on grounds of utility, modernity, controversy and public interest. If it hurts none, nobody can oppose religious fundamentalism. Everybody's own religion calls upon him to have such utmost faith. No person or agency is permitted to stand in between man and his God.

While making religious fundamentalism responsible for terrorism, we should put some adjective, qualifying note or some conditions to it. Fundamentalism, even in the sense of deeper commitment to religion, is harmful when it is used for non-religious purposes. When religion is mixed with fundamentalism or the latter is presented and propagated as religion, the whole edifice of 'pure' or 'original' religion crumbles down. Not only God and man are separated, but both of them are taken over by a person or group, which actually is not concerned with religion. To expose the role of this third person, party or group, it is necessary to separate 'religion' and 'fundamentalism'. These two are mixed by the third person in the terms 'religious' and 'religion-related'. The third person or party makes use of both 'religious' or 'religion-related': putting 'religious' for 'religion-related' and vice-versa. He is away from 'religious' to 'religion-related'. He makes use of 'religion' for 'non-religion' or temporal concerns. This third really non-religious person converts simple followers of religion into fundamentalists and terrorists and brings about the third position which directly relates to 'motivated', 'created', 'artificial', 'imposed' and 'narrow' fundamentalism, which leads the human minds towards extremism, fanaticism, terrorism and violence. It is usually created by the third party standing in between a follower and his God: preachers, trainers, teachers, muftis, qajis, priests, clergy etc. Often these people distort the original meaning and intention of religion. It directly relates and leads to fanaticism and terrorism and makes up the inner form of terrorism. This has to be disallowed.

The fourth position raises the claims and demands of state, society and nation over the excesses of both 'religion-related' and 'religious' fundamentalism. These institutions have power to disallow the claims and demands of religious and religion-related fundamentalism, whether natural or motivated or artificial. Religion relates to faith and often does not recognize boundaries of state, nation, status or ethnicity. It could operate freely when there was no state or nation as such. With the evolution of state, religion has to operate within law and remain subject to the requirements of state and society. Religion-related, even religious fundamentalism, sticking to old position, creates problems by refusing to accept the boundaries of state and society. This is the position of many religions of the world.

In order to fight effectively against the inner or subtle form of terrorism, it is necessary to separate religion from religion-related terrorism as it often tries to give the impression of its being 'religious' fundamentalism.

Separation of Religion from Religion-related Fundamentalism

Obviously, not religion itself, but religion-related fundamentalism is the generator of extremists, fanatics, militants, terrorists etc. Most of people like religion, and want to keep themselves away from religion-connected fundamentalism. Religion involves only creation or relationship between man and his God.

As some believers of the sacred books, considering commandments given therein divine, blindly or zealously follow them. It is necessary to find out whether they contain seeds of non-religion terrorism in those divine statements or not. Some steps in this direction can be taken in the following manner:

Step One, scholars, experts and practitioners of that avowed religion should be requested to sit together to trace out portions, parts, sentences, sayings or statements of the holy books, which the extremists and fundamentalists claim to have authorized them to resort to terrorism for divine goals. They can explain the correct meaning and application of controversial divine directions, which are maligned by the fundamentalists for their cruel ends.

Step Two, another group can collect literature, books, leaflets, newspapers and speeches of the leaders of the fundamentalists and terrorist organizations and compare and contrast them with the original statements of the holy books. It may be especially pointed out where the terrorists go beyond the permissible limits of law, society and government. Such exercise would help them to ascertain criminality of the acts and intentions of the terrorists, their trainers and supporters.

Step Three, but a great difficulty lies in the problem of finding out a suitable and impartial person, group or agency to do the job of separating religion from religious and religion-related fundamentalism. Acceptability of their verdict by the followers concerned would play a crucial role. Perhaps persons having closeness between them or/and their religion may not be able to see the reality lying behind the lines of sacred books. Some of them may be standing against or in favour of a particular religion or its teachings. As such, at world community level, a scholarly body might be constituted by the UN to undertake study of important sacred books and religious education of all important radical religions. That high power body, keeping in view of the principles of democracy, freedom and human rights, would sort out relevant portions and parts of religious books and their teachings at different levels. It will specify the form and extent to which the sacred books and their education, and training or interpretations contravene required laws necessary for the survival of a civilized democratic society.

Step Four, its conclusions may be presented before and discussed by the world body and passed by majority of the General Assembly. It would be the responsibility of an expanded and democratized Security Council to get them implemented through the member-states, various UN organs and organizations including recognized NGOs.

Adoption of an impartial high power body is necessary to disallow prejudice, hostility and slur against a particular religion. It will discourage them from taking recourse to some motivated and hostile interpretation of specific parts, commandments, statements and directives of the sacred books and also of practices and conventions emerging from them.

Compulsions of State and the World System

After separating religion from religion-related or religious fundamentalism, it is necessary to determine the status, role and function of religion in the context of modern state and the world system.[5] The idea here is neither to evaluate a particular religion as good or bad nor to improve or discard it. It merely make attempts to refer to its past and prevailing present context of religion pointing out what portions of a particular religion can now be adopted, that too in original or with modification or by attaching certain conditions. We are not concerned here with the truth or falsehood of the contents of a particular religion but its setting in the present time.

It can be added further that imposition of these directives on others in the name of God or some revealed religion could cause more harm than good as they might be already having their own revealed religion. These directives might be contradictory and oppose each other.

In some cases, divine commandments or godly directives were given to the non-state people, which did not envisage boundaries of state, nation or community. Followers of such religions, who now live in a particular state or nation or some territorial community do not find it possible to obey or follow all the directives given by their religion. Under the present pattern of international law and prevailing state systems, it is neither possible for them to leave that state nor they are likely to be welcomed by a state of their choice, even if there is predominance of their religion in that state. States as such often find it difficult to live with them.

As such, all religions, and religion-related fundamentalists and their institutions have to accept existence and supremacy of the state and the world system (UN). They should be accepted voluntarily with reformulation of their faith, ethos and culture. It would be better, if done earlier.

Oath of Allegiance by Citizens and Residents

Under law, every citizen, formally or tacitly, subscribes to an oath to uphold the supremacy of state over everything else. Only those persons who agree under an oath to obey the laws of the state over and above the divine directives should be permitted to reside and participate in the state activities.[6] If they live in that state and do not subscribe to the laws of the state as such, they tend to fall under the category of aliens, non-citizens, rebels, traitors and terrorists. They are not entitled to safety and protection of the state at par with other citizens.

Persons not subscribing to such oath, may feel free from any control by the state, and resort to acts of fundamentalism, even terrorism. Therefore, in view of prevalence of global terrorism, hardly any state would like to permit them to live, reside, enter and seek any kind of shelter in the state. On safer side, it would be better, if, from time to time, such persons, whether citizens or non-citizens, are asked to vouchsafe their allegiance to that state in clear terms. If they do not do so, their acts and behaviour should be put under state surveillance.

Need of Suitable Politico-administrative Measures

Terrorism can also be eliminated by adopting some preventive politico-administrative measures at national and international levels. If these are carefully taken up, terrorism is likely to disappear gradually. It would find little room to continue and emerge again on the world scene. Some such measures are proposed here:

(i) Individuals, families and groups are allowed entry into a country's territory on the condition of subscribing to on oath that they do not accept, whatever be the source, any commands, directives etc. which claim to stand above law.

(ii) The UN Commission on Human Rights, UN bodies, International Court etc. declare that such commandments, directives etc. and their teaching declared as prone to terrorism shall be illegal and against international law, human rights, democracy and freedom.

(iii) The UN shall grant authority to every democratic state to eliminate such terrorist elements in its self-defence everywhere in every possible manner and direct the rest to support and cooperate with it in such ventures.

(iv) Every state, the UN and other public organizations are entrusted with obligations to bring such pro-terrorist matters to light through the use of all forms of media so that all right-thinking men may act, determine and unite for action against terrorism.

Laws framed in this direction by a state or the world body would prevent, restrict and disallow persons preaching, inciting, training and encouraging to indulge in spreading extremism, fundamentalism and terrorism. Even the local authorities of the states, big and small, would be able to prevent and stop terrorism of all kinds. In this way, all terrorism in-making would be intercepted before it comes into existence. The US-led coalition, so some extent the UN, can provide supervision, monitoring, appropriate action and prevention.

Renovation of Democratic Systems

In the end, it may be submitted that our democracies presently are unaware and unprepared in dealing with the problem of terrorism as such. They are slow, inefficient, dilatory and unresponsive to the call. Democracies lack ideology, organization, and programme and will to withstand terrorism.[7] By the time, the state brings the culprits of terrorism to 'justice', the latter kill another hundreds of innocent persons, and tend to incite other thousand ones to commit similar murders.[8] The conventionally organized armies and law and order agencies of present-day democracies stand unable to cope with rising terrorism. Their weapons (prevention, law and order, judicial procedure, media, elections, education etc.) appear obsolete before the powerful weapon of terrorism. Terrorists do not wait and listen to the democratic arguments. Why then democracy should wait and listen to their arguments in the courts (which they condemn and hate altogether) for long years? The more you wait for them to improve or turn humane, more you lose ground and opportunity to smash their networks. Your wait, tolerance, patience and hospitality merely make them more powerful, difficult to contain and impossible to finish them. Democracy has to formulate an effective ideology and devise means to smash terrorism at the earliest.

Attack on Outer Forms of Terrorism

The direct attack by US-led coalition on the outward or outer form of terrorism has been timely, necessary and decisive. Only such step could have destroyed leadership, training camps, supporting armies and authority of the terrorists. These operations have given the clear message to the terrorists that they have to surrender and give up their ways and means forthwith.[9]

It is expected that the outcome of the present war might create conditions necessary for the success of the next important war against inner, subtle and deeper form of terrorism. But, there are many constraints as well as limitations.

Limitations of Attacks on Outer Form of Terrorism

Regrettably, this war on outer form of terrorism is suffering from several limitations:

(a) The US has been fighting this war almost all alone (except Great Britain and some others) as if no other country suffers from the problem of terrorism.

(b) As 'terrorism' has so far been not defined, it merely means Osama bin Laden, Al Qaida outfits and the Talibans, apparently an exclusive concern of the US attacks. No attempt has been made for ascertaining the common elements or features of various forms of terrorism so that they may be made the basis of law or objective criteria to determine, define and declare particular acts as 'terrorism'.

(c) To escape from the charge of bias or hostility against a particular religion, all forms of terrorism, such as Sunni, Shia, Catholic, Palestinian, Jewish, Maoist, Naxalite, ultra nationalistic and the like, have not been taken into consideration. All should have been in the agenda of the UN and the patterns of action on them decided by it in advance.

(d) An agreed definition of terrorism could make all acts of abetting, training, organizing, justifying and funding terrorism actionable crimes. Laws framed in this direction by a state or the world body could prevent, restrict and disallow persons preaching, inciting, training and encouraging all kinds of extremism, fundamentalism and terrorism. In this way, all terrorisms in-making would be intercepted before they are committed.

(e) The UN has not taken over the responsibility and is not monitoring the progress of the struggle made by the US-led coalition. International agencies, states and their authorities and others may be formally empowered to deal with specific form of terrorism prevailing in specified areas. They can further be authorized to operate through the regional association of states, with provision to report to the Security Council for approval and further action. In crisis situations they may be entrusted with powers to take prompt action. But, no such action has been taken as yet.

Emerging Difficulties

Difficulties in the present fight are already coming out. It turns into hot-pursuit of war among certain countries. Such war cannot be undertaken only by a superpower like the USA, and not by others, particularly when some elements of its own population are involved. Moreover, often the terrorist organizations operating in its own country or outside are supported by governments or some of their elements or certain sections of the people. At international level, no such legitimate machinery has been constituted by the UN, which might perform the desired job of fighting against the terrorists directly. The present US-led coalition has neither been able, despite its success in the eliminating terrorism as a common cause, to define it nor internationalize its military efforts.

In fact, it is very difficult to devise a military mechanism at the UN level for fighting terrorism. If each and every country suffering from the scourge of terrorism begins to follow the US pattern, there could be chaos among nations. Still, there is ample scope for military action by the states or group of states as the far advanced, well organized and fully equipped terrorist organizations do not yield before reconciliation, law, or even the limited might of the individual states. Use of force is to be swift, sure, effective and necessary remedy for such diehard groups of terrorists. But cure by this remedy is likely to prove short-lived, limited, unsustainable and beyond the capacity of undertaking by individual states. End of outer terrorism by force cannot stand for long. Therefore, war against its inner form must also be launched.

War against the Inner Form of Terrorism

Military action against outer terrorism should be supported and supplemented by simultaneous war on inner form of terrorism.[10] The real remedy lies in making long-term efforts by law and through states. It would make up another serious, long-term and sincere war against the inner form of terrorism. Important steps in this direction can be briefly suggested here:

1. Elimination of terrorism on wider scale requires cooperation from the whole world community.
2. But, the US would get cooperation from the member-nations only when all forms of terrorism would be planned for targeting.
3. While every form of terrorism is a threat to human life, freedom and democracy, terrorism related to religion or faith is much more dangerous act. It is committed on the basis of assumed guidance from more enduring and overpowering entities like God, Revelation, Heaven and Grace. This needs to be overturned.
4. A terrorist led and fed on fundamentalism based on religion concerns himself only with the execution of his divine mission, and remains ready to embrace death.
5. In plural and multi-cultural societies, it is necessary to look into the susceptibilities of minorities related to religions. One has to be careful about the use of words like 'religion' and 'fundamentalism'.
6. One may have full commitment or faith in religion. If it does not hurt anyone, one's 'religious' or 'religion-related fundamentalism' may not be opposed. There is no problem if 'fundamentalism' is really religious or religion-based.
7. When we make 'religious fundamentalism' responsible for terrorism, we have to put some adjective, qualifying note or some conditions to it. Often, these two words are jointly used in a wrongful and rash manner. Only religion-related fundamentalism can lead to terrorism.

However, in geopolitical terrorism, both forms mixed up, which makes it much more difficult to tide over.

Contextual Changes and Their Enforcement

The enforcement of the results and consequences of above requires that:

a. After the emergence of the state and the nation, obligations granted by the sacred books to the individuals, should now be handed over to the democratically elected governments at the state level and to the UN[11] at the global level.

b. For individuals it is no more possible to obey or follow all the directives given by the religion which either appeared among the non-state people or did not envisage boundaries of state, nation, or community. There is no way to them except rendering obedience to the state over and above everything else.

c. Under law, every citizen should be asked to subscribe to an oath to uphold the supremacy of state over everything else.

d. Individuals, families and groups are allowed entry into a country's territory on the condition of subscribing to on oath that they do not accept and claim to stand above law.

e. The UN Commission on Human Rights, UN bodies, International Court etc. declare that such commandments, directives etc. and their teaching declared as prone to terrorism is illegal and against International Law and Human Rights.[12]

f. The UN grants authority to every democratic state to eliminate such terrorist elements in self-defence everywhere in every possible manner and directs the rest to support and cooperate with it in such ventures.

g. Laws framed in this direction by a state or the world body and their implementation should prevent, restrict and disallow persons preaching, inciting, training and encouraging to indulge in spreading extremism, fundamentalism and terrorism. In this way, all terrorism in-making would be intercepted before it comes into existence.

Notes

1. Henry Kissinger spoke to Manoj Joshi during the two-day *HT Leadership Initiative Meeting* in New Delhi on the principal threats of the age: There are three fundamental problems: the first is what we call terrorism in the US, but which is really the uprising of radical Islam against the secular world, and against the democratic world, on behalf of re-establishing a sort of Caliphate. That is directed against non-Islamic societies. It is executed by private groups that base themselves on territories of sovereign states and launch their operations from there. The second is the spread of weapons of mass destruction. The third is the shift in the centre of gravity of the world from the Atlantic to Asia, or to the Pacific. The fourth is the consequences of globalization for humanity. *Hindustan Times*, November 9, 2004.
2. Tariq Mehmood, an Al-Badr militant after his arrest in Srinagar declared, "I have no regrets. On the contrary, I am happy since I have come to fight for the path of Allah." married and with two small children he was a registered medical practitioner and a Jamaat-e-Islami activist from Pakistan's Gujarat district. What drives such fanaticism is a special "culture of death" that terrorist group foster. When a militant is killed in Kashmir, there are elaborate funeral rites, complete with the burial of an empty coffin in his village in Pakistan. The parents of the "shaheed" are made to sit on a pedestal and feted by the local elite. Emotional speeches detain the "shaheed's" valour. With emotions at the highest pitch, volunteers are called for, and not surprisingly anywhere between 80-100 youngmen register. *Sunday Times*, Manoj Joshi, May 15, 2005.
3. This Religion (Dharma) in at elute, abstract and subjective sense. It is identical with Consciousness, Creativity, Energy, Knowledge, Spirit, Nature or Existence.
4. This is second, lower, objective, demonstrative, and outward sense of 'religion'. It is objective-subjective religion. A man at this level is 'religious' as he is concerned with his own 'self' and his sense of 'God'.
5. Here the term 'religion' has been used in objective, institutional and sectarian sense. The term 'religion' is narrower than 'Religion'.
6. New British citizens pledge loyalty—The 112,000 people who become British citizens each year will have to pledge loyalty to their new country as part of the their citizenship ceremonies. The citizenship oath and pledge: I, (name). (swear by Almighty God)/(do solemnly and sincerely affirm) that, on becoming a British citizen, I will be faithful and bear true allegiance to Her Majesty Queen Elizabeth II, her heirs and successors according to law. I will give my loyalty to the United Kingdom and respect its rights and freedoms. I will uphold its democratic values. I will

observe its laws faithfully and fulfil my duties and obligations as a British citizen. *Hindustan Times*, July 28, 2003.

7. Renovated ideology of democracy has to be strong and prompt enough to defeat every type of terrorism. About democracy in the Islamic world he said, "I think there are not many examples of democracy developing rapidly in emerging societies and it is a particular problem in Islamic society, in a society in which religion and the secular world are sort of fused and in which there is no distinction between the word of God and the world of state. If you had democratic societies, it would be sort of a brake against radical Islam." Henry Kissinger to Manoj Joshi, *Hindustan Times*, November 9, 2004.
8. The new Chief Justice of India Y.K. Sabharwal has expressly undertaken this responsibility, *Times of India,* November 4, 2005.
9. In this respect, role of US, UK, Russia, Israel and India has so far remained commendable.
10. Laxity of Great Britain is observable for years, the British and other Western governments have followed the enigmatic and inexplicable policy of giving shelter to foreigners whose political or religious followers carried out a campaign—quite often violent and secessionist—in their countries of origin, e.g., Jagjit Singh Chouhan, A.Z. Phizo, and several others. Al Qaida mainly comprised Arabs, but the London attacks were carried out (on July 7, 2005) by British born persons of Pakistani origin and connections. About 80 British Muslims, most of the originally from Pakistan, had joined the Iraqi resistance. Another 3,000 British Muslims had attended Islamic training camps in Pakistan, Afghanistan and Central Asia and then returned home. Also see Manji's book *The Trouble with Islam Today.* See Vikram Sood, "The aliens have landed", *Hindustan Times,* July 28, 2005.

   Mohammad Zia-ul-Haq has observed that foreign Muslim religious leaders who have been residing in Great Britain for the last several decades are misusing mosques for inciting Muslims against that country. They would have either been sentenced to death or put behind bars, had they been living in some other state. Honest Muslims feel ashamed of these persons. Mohammad Zia-ul Haq, "Attempt to save Islam from Extremists", *Rajasthan Patrika*, November 4, 2005; UK imams spared Britishness test: An estimated 85 per cent of the 2000 imams in the UK are foreign-born and have mostly come from Pakistan and West Asia. It was suspected that many radical imams had entered the country and were misleading young Muslims there. (The scrapping of the Britishness test is the second climbdown by the government in a week. The proposal to seal mosques suspected of having extremist links was dropped a few days earlier.) *Hindustan Times*, December 21, 2005.

11. A UN summit marking the 60th anniversary of the United Nations opened with an appeal from Secretary-General Kofi Annan to world leaders to restore confidence in the world body and act together to meet the challenges of the 21st century. "We the heads of state and government owe this to coming generations. We cannot afford to fail. We need to find collective solutions based on the rule of law and for this we need a stronger United Nations," *Hindustan Times*, September 15, 2005.

VI

The Remedy of Hindatva (Indianism)

20

The Path of Hindatva

Owing to the blunders committed repeatedly by the Hindus in the past ages, Bharatvarsha spreading over the whole of the Indian sub-continent has been reduced to the present-day India or Bharat. In the light of that experience, if nothing is learnt, India left over to us would also go out of hands. A good number of regions, communities and classes, though physically appearing within India, do not consider themselves to be 'Indian'.[1] The biggest lesson which can be learnt from the past is that the Hindus, leaving all other engagements, must continue to guard themselves against their open and secret enemies, and eliminate their enmity before it goes beyond control. But, the Hindus have to fight to keep up India as 'Indian'. This fight has to be engaged between 'we' and 'our own people'. It would be virtually a social war. This war has to be fought within our own society and the country as a whole. Its first and main battlefield is the Hindu society itself. This society, as we see, is vivisected, decrepit, spineless, weak, parasitic, actionless, fatalist and other-worldly. As such, it is easily preyed upon, and dragged along. Many a time, witnessing its own plight, or owing to ignorance, various segments of the Hindu society themselves begin to follow others. While so following, after some time, not only the converts forget their roots, but also turn hostile against their earlier legacy and forefathers, and settle scores with them for their faults and atrocities. All this has usually happened solely on account of their predecessors' misguiding generous attitudes and thinking.

Generosity or large heartedness, in the beginning, is liked by all. All accord respect to a generous man, and his actions are warmly welcomed in all directions. Gradually, this generosity begins to mean parting away with one's ideas and activities. When one renounces his old ideas, he automatically is categorized as a 'liberal' or 'generous' man. For a long time, the Hindus could not understand the side-effects of this generosity, praise and welcome accorded to them. They still fail to see the consequences. The Hindus, despite irreparable harm caused to them, like to remain generous for enjoying such praise and appreciation. Some of them are masochists par excellence.

But, the adoption of democracy, in India and elsewhere, has transformed the whole scenario. The Hindus are now realizing the role of number, organization, ideological uniformity and leadership as elements of the strength of a community. Exploiting the generosity of the Hindus, non-Hindus, who were a few thousands in the beginning, have multiplied into big and organized communities of millions. Altogether, these communities are posing challenge to the very existence and strength of the Hindus. With the domination of these communities owing to their large size and influence, all the existential priorities of the Hindus are likely to fall in danger. These are increasing in size and strength while reducing the number of Hindus and their strength by all fair and foul means.[2]

Only a great person like Guru Govind Singh can liberate the Hindus from this plight. Such personality extraordinary in stature can transform the credulous Hindu devotees of multitude of statues into one 'Khalsa' community and grant a vibrant ideology. Fortunately, the Hindus do have an organization of committed social workers in form of the Rashtriya Swayamsevak Sangh (RSS). Other organizations look too weak to come to their rescue. But they lack Chanakya and Chandragupta who by bringing about some ideological revolution may provide goals, programmes and relevance to the Hindus. Surely, such great persons would definitely be opposed by the vested interests, anachronistic sectarian saints and traitors. Under these circumstances, such great task can be taken into hands only by leaders of exceptional courage, ingenuity and will. They would succeed only when they remain steadfast and are not affected by their criticism, opposition, orthodoxy and treachery, and march on the path of success after success. However, this entire venture necessitates an ideologically renovated framework to motivate and guide them. This framework has been necessitated after the failure or partial attainments of Hindu Dharma, Hinduism and Hindutva. It has been conceptualized as Hindatva, Bharatatva or Indianism.

Hindatva, Bharatatva or Indianism

The concept of 'dharma' is one of the most important concepts in Hindu worldview. Its meaning differs slightly from one religious or philosophical tradition to another, but all interpretations share the view that it means something like 'natural order' or 'innate law' or *'rita'* in an individual, society and in the universe.

After Keshav Hedgewar, the second great leader of the RSS, M.S. Golwalkar, defined dharma as the innate and fundamental law of the universe and human nature. According to him, this very law of dharma is the standard for deciding the propriety of behaviour in various situations. He argued that "if we carry this concept of dharma even further, not only the state and the nation, but the nature of entire mankind will have to be considered. In other words, the constitution of a nation cannot be contrary to the natural laws".[3] And he emphasizes that since dharma is the supreme law, their ideal of the state must be 'Dharma Rajya'. The rulers ought to follow those innate laws. That dharma or natural law defines the natural *inhabitants* of Hindustan and the natural *borders* of the country as well as the natural order in the society, popularly known as Dharma Rajya or Rama Rajya.

In 1915 V.D. Savarkar wrote a book called *'Hindutva'*. The book deeply influenced the ideas of the RSS founder Keshav Hedgewar. It was precisely the question of who was a Hindu that Savarkar tried to resolve in Hindutva.[4] He declared that the problem came into being because of the loose and eclectic usage of the terms Hindu, Hinduism and Hindutva. He considered the names applied to India: Aryavarta, Brahmavarta, Dakshinapath, Bharatvarsha and Hindustan. He chose the last one which was, in his reading, the original, authentic and most sacred name of this sacred land.

According to Savarkar, the term 'Hindutva' does not mean only the religion Hinduism; it covers the complete Hindu civilization and history. Hinduism is only a fraction of the civilization called

'Hindutva'. That is why, he used the term 'Hindu' to refer to the collectivity of the people of India—Hindus, Muslims, Christians, Sikhs, Parsees, etc. In the rising nationalist movement at the end of last century there are some examples proving that this kind of 'loose' vocabulary was accepted among different religious groups. For example, the Muslim nationalist leader Sir Syed Ahmad Khan (1817-1898) used the term 'Hindu' to mean "the inhabitants of Hindustan".[5] The most important thing is that 'real' Hindus accept natural and thus right attitudes towards their land. Savarkar emphasizes that "a Hindu means a person who regards this land of Bharatvarsha, from Indus to the seas as his Fatherland as well as his Holyland, that is the cradle land of his religion". Since Savarkar, the RSS leader M.S. Golwalkar has stressed the importance of defining the natural borders of Hindustan. In his most famous book called '*We or our nationhood defined*' (1939) Golwalkar means by India or Hindustan the "lands from sea to sea".[6] In fact, the map on the cover of the book gives the outline of his geographic limitations of India, which stretches from Afghanistan to Burma and also includes Sri Lanka.[7]

Change of Terminology

The first step to fight against the internal infirmities and overpowering the subtle and express attacks of non-Hindus or anti-Hindus forces is to renovate the concept of Hind, Hindu and Hindutva by making them Bharat, Bharatiya and Bharatiyata (or Hindustan, Hindustani and Hindustaniat). Words 'Hind' and 'Hindustan' are already known as Bharat (India).

The three conceptual realities captioned here as Hind, Hindu and Hindutva (हिंद, हिंदू एवं हिंदुत्व) are closely related with each other. In them no religious link is attached. They can also be equated, on the basis of the Constitution of India, with Bharat, Bharatiya and Bharatiyata, or Hindustan, Hindustani or Hindustaniyat.

Outwardly, there are two kinds of inhabitants living in India (हिंद) collectively called as 'Hindus' (हिंदू), now 'Bharatiyas'. They can be grouped in two categories: one, containing people who are called 'Hindu' on the basis of their permanent residence in Hind (हिंद), and, two, who, in addition to their Indian residence, regard themselves 'Hindu' on the basis of following Hindu religion and are

Hindudharmi. Both of them are 'Hindu' for they are residents of 'Hind' irrespective their connection or non-connection with Hinduism.

However, the people of the first category to identify them separate from the followers of Hindu religion related to the second category. Instead of being called as 'Hindus', they may be introduced or identified as Hindavi, Hindee, Hindeeya, Hindustani or Hindakeeya (हिंदवी, हिंदी, हिंदीय, हिंदुस्तानी या हिंदकीय). When they like to stand away from consideration of religion, they can also be easily categorized as 'Hindavi' or 'Indian' or 'Bharatiya' (भारतीय).

Anyone, who regards himself 'Hindu' on the basis of his religion and residence in India, is double Hindu. He is 'follower of Hindu religion' or 'Hinduism ('हिंदू' या 'हिंदू–धर्मी'). He calls himself 'Hindu' for being born in a Hindu family or for voluntary acceptance of Hinduism or for considering himself related to Hindu religion. Hindu religion accepts everyone as 'Hindu' even when one expressly believes or does not believe in upholding Hindu rites and rituals. He himself or the Hindus may largely accept such a person as Hindu. The other is a geographical Hindu. Such a person, if lacks feelings for this land or is away from Hind for a number of years, should be treated 'non-Hindu'. If a person is Hindu by religion but has no feeling for the country, he is geographically a non-Hindu. Only a geographical Hindu is a permanent Hindu. A person born in a Hindu family may not be Hindu. Though the term 'Hindu' (or Hindavi, Hindee, Hindeeya, Hindustani or Hindakeeya) is applied to the person living in Hind or Hindustan (India or Bharat), yet only on merit he can be 'Hindu' (Hindavi, Hindee, Hindeeya, Hindustani or Hindakeeya) on having a deep desire to live here, to defend and develop it and to work for realizing the collective goals of the people of India. In other words, one cannot be 'Hindu' or 'Bharatiya' unless he/she has Hinduness, Hindutva, Bharatiyata or Hindustaniyat. The concept of Hindutva, Bharatiyata or Hindustaniyat, thus, involves connectedness between Hind (India) and his willing residence in India, inculcation of certain merits and displaying some necessary conditions to be residents of India (Hind).

Thus, Hindatva (Indianism) or Hindustaniyat, equated with Bharatiyata, is the generic term for all these merits, properties, likings and goals pertaining to the residents of India. They are synonyms connoting all these attributes. In sum, there are two essential or inseparable elements of Hindatva: (a) residence, and (b) commitment to the land of residence called here as 'nationism'. Both together make up the concept of Hindatva or Indianism.

Thus, the Hindus should now not ask all Indians to have faith in the ideology of Hindutva. They should now not unnecessarily invite opposition from anti-Hindutva Hindus and non-Hindu minorities. They should speak from a higher plane. In terms of the Supreme Court judgment and Hindatva ideology, and declare that all are, whether one agrees or disagrees, Hindus simply on the basis of their birth in this country. One is Hindu *fait accompli* even if one denies it. This is confirmed by the use of words like 'Hind' or 'Hindu' occurring in history, geography, international politics, trade and industry and others. When seen from this point of view, Hindatva cannot be an item of any agenda or Manifesto. In this manner, they should not exhaust energy in compelling others to call themselves as Hindus. In territorial or geographical sense all persons living in India are Hindus. But, because of the use of the term for followers of Hindu Dharma, it may not be acceptable by the non-Hindudharmi Indians. On the other hand, Hindatva is borne by every Indian like his birth-based Indian citizenship if one has residence with commitment. Hindatva can also be equated with some other words like Bharatiyata, Hindustaniyat, Indianism or Indianity.

Hindatva or Bharatiyata or Hindustaniyat connotes:

1. A person's connectedness with territory or land of India as his/her motherland who commits oneself to defend and protect the honour, territorial integrity, independence and sovereignty of the country. He has will to maintain unity and integrity of India. 'Bharat' for him means the territory of India which includes its natural resources, maintenance of healthy ecology and pollution-free environment.[8]
2. One should be rooted in 'nationism'.[9] It is feeling of brotherhood for all Indians, irrespective of caste, colour, religion, language, region and culture. Indian nationism gives more importance to land, and less to religion, culture and language. Hindutva or Hinduism should merge into Indianism conceived in the Constitution of India in such manner that Muslims, Christians, Jains, Buddhists etc. appear part and parcel of the same (see Diagram 1).

Diagram 1
Indianization

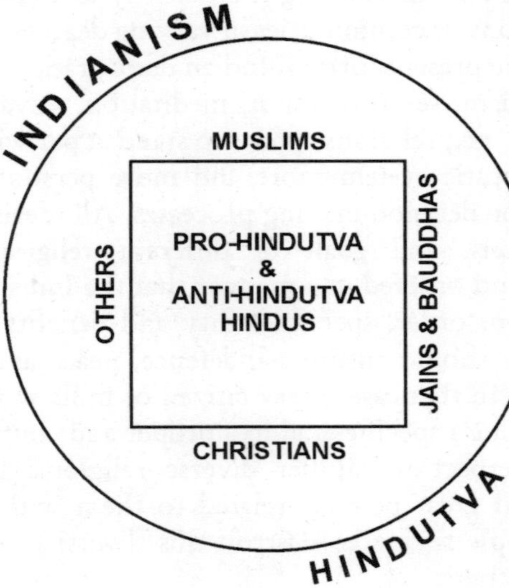

3. Basic Reality, named as God, Almighty, Brahma, Allah etc., permeates both spiritual as well as temporal worlds. Alike spiritualism, the temporal part of God must be prompted to play its role towards the fulfilment of human rights and democracy and appear in form of secularization at different institutional levels. This secularization is the obverse side of spiritualism.
4. Gods and goddesses of Hindus (and of other communities) should be humanized in form of great persons so that their followers in place of merely worshipping the idols and reciting holy verses as praise or bhajans begin to apply their ideals in practical life. The leaders should discourage construction of new temples or place of worship. "Following their great actions rather than worshipping them" would be their new motto. Construction of religious places would be permitted only by the government after it obtains the unanimous decision of the concerned community leaders and law. The government can provide help for having libraries and other audio-visual and electronic machines towards studying gods and goddesses as ideal human beings.

5. From the viewpoint of maintaining the democratic system, all religions should be hierarchically, not at par with each other, placed on merit for running it efficiently and effectively. Only some religions or communities in varying degrees are closer than others to the present form of Indian democratic system. In areas of spiritualism, self-realization, meditation, salvation, absolute knowledge, etc., religions appear to stand at par with each other. In a democratic system more and more persons would share power in the decision-making processes. All ideals, teachings of great persons, and goals of different religions should be organized and ordered in a manner that the Indian society finds coordination, order, specific utility and benefits on practising them. They should ensure self-defence, peace and progress for the society. In that case, every citizen of India would be able to determine one's specific goal in a proper and confident manner. He pays respect to all her diverse religions, languages and cultures and great persons related to them with condition to oppose people trying to destroy this diversity or impose one faith over others.
6. Any person occupying a public position in the present secular set-up, on his showing extremist or fundamentalist connection with a particular religion, caste or sub-caste, language, region or culture, should immediately and automatically be removed from it, and in cases of serious violation of norms awarded punishment of imprisonment or fine or both. 'Dharma' (encompassing religion) being a controversy-creating term should be left to persons and communities at their personal and non-state levels. The people should rise above all other secular and non-secular political parties and pursue 'super-secularism'. It would have to adopt ideology of 'super-secularism'.
7. Their common goal should be to have maximum material, economic, scientific, technological, handicraftual and industrial development with the perspective that its benefits accrue to the people at large in an equitable manner. Amid such development, the individual may, at his own will, realize his this or/and next worldly goals.[10] He enjoys one's rights and duties in a way to realize all-round development of the nation to distribute the gains equitably among all.

8. No person, both man and woman, should be tagged to some particular work, profession, position or status on the basis of one's own birth or caste. He must have the fundamental right and get opportunity to choose his profession, trade and position. He belongs to 'sarvavarni samaj'.[11] It endeavours especially to help the poorest, most deprived, illiterate and backward persons of the society for bringing them at par with others.
9. As labour or work is the most important component of the social organization, the persons and families of hitherto neglected communities, such as SCs, STs and OBCs, women and other very small economically backward minorities, which have depended on labour for centuries, must be given special regard and consideration, by way of reservation, special training and education programmes, loans, subsidies, allotment of houses and lands and the like. The lowliest among them must be given proportionate priority.[12]
10. There should be zealous 'swadeshikaran' of labour and talents to have India's domination world over in the fields of security, trade, industry, science and technology and cultural affairs. Small, rural and local crafts must be granted protection to reduce poverty and unemployment. Excessive domination of the Indian economy by the MNCs (multi-national corporations), owing to LPG (liberalization, privatization and globalization), can be opposed at non-state level by the Gandhian means of boycott, non-cooperation and Indian asceticism as well as intense display of nationalism.
11. Maintaining that government and administration are the pivotal institutions of the Indian political system, they should be made efficient, effective, responsive, tenurial and openly available to all eligible persons. Such steps would lead to actualization of 'rule of law' which alone should determine what directives of religion, morality and tradition could or could not be allowed to be practised in the present set-up.
12. There should be allocation of resources subject to their availability with the state to backward and depressed persons, families, classes and communities in proportion to the extent of their backwardness and need.
13. To eliminate corruption the state would act on the principle of 'escheat'. Property of public servants and persons, who would

have to declare their assets, sources of income, inheritance and obtaining of money or property by chance, would automatically go to the government exchequer when at the end of one's tenure, it is three times larger than their real and lawful income. The services of the Controller and Auditor General of India and the Accountant Generals of the states would be utilized for this purpose. Their verdict, save interpretation of law by the judiciary, would be time-bound and final.

14. The Hindu and each other society should completely denounce and reject casteism in all its forms. It should not be allowed to exist anywhere. However, the people should generate a requisite equilibrium of knowledge, courage, skills of production and exchange and attitude of service in the individual and the society as a whole. No society can make progress if any one of these elements or its variants remains weak or absent. The people as a whole must reorganize themselves on the principle of maintaining this equilibrium within itself. To make recurrence of casteism impossible no one element should be treated as superior to others or considered as the monopoly of one person, group or community.
15. Preparation should be made to meet the attacks launched by opponents and enemies on the Indian socio-political system, updated ideology and programmes. The Indian people, to seek their consent and cooperation, should be made aware of such attempts regularly. They should work for peace, progress and cooperation among the peoples of the comity of the nations by ensuring sovereignty, dignity and freedom of India as a powerful member of the United Nations.

Some modifications around these points can be made for the finalization of the new ideology of Hindatva, which should be expressed in simple, clear and modern terminology. The two main features of this ideology would be (i) totality, and (ii) capacity to respond effectively and promptly to any other pseudo or incomplete ideology. There should be enough room for individual efforts as well as for launching peaceful and gradual reforms and also for ushering radical changes in society and state. This ideology should also spell out the goals, processes, needs and techniques of bringing about such changes, which would always aim at the realization of 'rule of law'. Such steps would discourage the stray elements of the Indian society attempting to join some of terrorist or violent organization or indulge in activities hostile to the country.

This proposed ideology captioned as 'Hindatva' or 'Indianism' would be able to inspire all the citizens of the Indian nation or state to act in the manner of God or Creation. If one does not like to be motivated by God, even doctrines of democracy or humanity can prompt them to act in like manner.

Nationalist organizations like the RSS would work hard towards bringing about more and more territory-based nationalism and consolidation of the Hindus and other communities as Indian nationals. It has not been able to take up and spread refined Hinduism to every nook and corner of India. When there is the Supreme Court judgment that all belong to the Hindutva, which as a 'way of life', it should (i) show the way of leading the modern life of Hindutva; (ii) as all are Hindus now, it should enlist people of different communities, forms of worship, regions and cultures, particularly the Muslims and the Christians, into the fold of RSS or some other broader form of organization; and (iii) open the teaching and training wings of politics, administration, management and warfare for the members of the political side of RSS and other devoted recruits.

Hindatva, in its new form, presently demands leadership of the Dalit Hindus to maintain societal balance.

The upper caste Hindu leaders work with the assumption that they can without caring for the larger interests of the Hindus, go on serving their narrow vested interests till there is majority of the Hindus in India. As the Hindus at large are ignorant, credulous, illiterate and powerless, the upper caste leaders indulge in many undeserving activities with impunity as there is none to control and restrain them whether they are really working for the good of Hindutva or the Hindu community.

Unfortunately, some of these leaders and organizations who claim to serve the cause and protect the interests of the Hindus, Hindutva or Hindu religion, such as BJP, RSS, VHP, SS, Arya Samaj, Ram Krishna Mission and the like, hardly tell specifically what form of Hindutva or Hindu religion do they have in mind and how do they propose to serve and defend it by what means.[13] Often, the ideas they profess to have or ways and means they use to realize them have caused more harm than good to the Hindus. At the most they stand for maintaining the status quo without realizing that this very attempt has been emboldening others to inflict severe damage to Hindutva to the extent of causing its slow disappearance.

Presentation of Hindu Dharma as such is directly related to the superior social and religious status, affluence and livelihood, culture, farsightedness and leadership of the upper caste leaders. It has been causing utmost loss to the Hindu community as a whole, including the lower downtrodden and exploited communities in particular. In order to maintain the Hindu community as a whole, it is now urgent that the latter take over the care, direction and control of the Hindus, and save Hindutva from roots. The Dalits, who have already suffered a lot at the hands of non-Hindu aggressors and rulers as well as the Hindu upper caste leaders, have to be aware that they should come forward to defend the Hindus from being, in this process, reduced to a small minority in India. In that case, the Hindus when reduced to a minority they would have to meet the plight of the Kashmiri Pandits. The Hindu majority then is like to lead life of rootless aliens or stateless persons.

Under the prevailing circumstances, thus, the Hindus as a community should now pin their hopes on the leadership of the Dalits. Only these people have always been remained committed to the dust of this land. However, it may be made clear that the upper classes will never permit the Dalits to take over this leadership of the Hindus in a peaceful and orderly manner. They would continue to rule over and control the fate of the Hindus despite the facts that under their leadership:

(a) non-Hindus in India have grown from a few thousands to over 55 crore;
(b) more than half of the Hindu population had been exploited for several centuries and millions of them were declared as 'untouchables' (*shudras*);
(c) Dalits and Hinduism has been identified with spirituality, toleration, non-violence, asceticism, backwardness and orthodoxy;
(d) almost all non-Hindu religions and communities find the Hindus as easy prey for conversion, and the majority community cut into thousands of segments on permanent bases like religion, language, culture, caste etc. is unable to stand by a democratic system; and
(e) they have produced a community based on casteism, other-worldliness, ritualism, transmigration, *karma* theory etc.,

which hardly allows the Hindus to have a modern state viable enough to withstand all types of terror, inequality and exploitation.

Unless the upper caste leaders surrender their leadership to the Dalits, change in the fate of the rest of the Hindus is difficult to arrive at. Therefore, onwards, the Dalits would have to take over the leadership of the Hindus to realize their humanitarian goals in an effective manner. They have to determine, train up and equip themselves to accomplish this task.

Place of Majority Community

Democracy is regarded as rule by majority. This 'majority' is has to be formed on the basis of opinion. When on some issue the number of persons holding similar opinion increase to more than half of their total number, it is called 'majority'. It is treated as 'minority' when such persons remain less then half of the total adult population. 'Majority' or 'minority' opinions are not permanently attached to some specific communities, religious or cultural groups, castes and the like. When more than half of the total population of a state is permanently attached to these elements it is called 'majority community'. When its members are less than half of the total population, it is treated as 'minority community'. Stability, strength and continuity of democracy in a country demands support of not only of 'opinion majority' (om), but also of a 'majority community' (mc) or a group of many minority-communities forming a kind of 'majority community' (mc). Communities which support the basic values of a political system like unity, progress, defence etc. are necessary to run a democracy. Such communities provide sustenance to a democratic system. In the absence of such 'majority', a democracy cannot function properly.

It is surprising that only minorities as permanent groups belonging to some religion, language and culture find place in the Constitution of India. But it does not recognize any majority community related to religion, language, caste or culture. There are provisions in the Constitution in connection with 'minorities' which tend to move even the majority community towards division and split. During the last 58 years of the Indian Constitution, this tendency of disintegration of the majority community is clearly visible. There is support and protection to minority communities, but no such care has been provided to the majority community. It appears that the Constitution of India gives no recognition to any majority community. It has nowhere been mentioned that if the values, position, culture and institutions of the 'majority community' are threatened or destroyed by minority communities, the state would come to its rescue, i.e., its own existence.

In the absence of neglect of 'majority community' with preference to minority communities, the edifice of the Indian democracy stands shaky having no foundation. Under the prevailing circumstances, now, it is too late to make for such constitutional provisions for the majority community. Nobody would allow making such amendment. Even, the people belonging to the majority community, out of ignorance or otherwise, consider such constitutional amendment as unnecessary and redundant. The sole cause of such opposition is to equate and identify 'majority' with the present 'majority community'. The identification is not always true. But it is an undeniable fact that a democracy survives till it has an active support of the values, culture, aspirations, practices and goals of the majority community. If a democratic polity lacks permanent support from such permanent communities, it can easily be led towards disintegration. This historical experience has often been overlooked by scholars, political leaders and the majority/minority communities of India.

The support of both the majority and minority communities to the values and goals of the Indian democracy is desirable. The Indian democracy cannot be operated either by majority or minority community alone.[14] Both should go along with it. In practice, however, the majority community supporting the democratic values remains responsible to operate it. Still it cannot do so for ever. A democratic system in the long run envelopes all majority and minority communities, and also stands over and above them. It nourishes values larger than that of any one of them. All communities in India can claim to contain some democratic values in them. But it is necessary that the role of majority and its culture is accepted on constitutional basis so as to counter the subversive, discouraging and destabilizing activities of some separatist minorities. It is a fact that so far India's democracy has emerged, operated and survived because of the support of Hindu community. Till yesterday, it has had happened on voluntary basis, but now onwards, in view of its declining influence, special efforts have to be made. However, there are some lags and tags behind the Hindu community and its culture. It would be found that the Hindu community, far more than any other culture, does contain values closer to the Indian political system. It requires, however, further reform and refinement. This has to be done in large proportions. Thus, the Hindu culture remains the mainstay of strength to Indian democracy. Other smaller communities either are status quoists or refuse to change themselves in line with democratic requirements. However, all of them might melt as opinion communities.

State and Justification of Hindatva

However, there is no need of thinking and responding as majority or minority communities. Evolution of state as the collectivity of the whole people has done away with all these old categories. Now, there is rise of the 'supremacy' of 'state' and the 'rule of law' over all others. State supremacy has been universally accepted everywhere including the Muslim countries. In view of such new realities, there is no need of demanding a proper place for the Hindus or the majority community of India. There would also be no need for asking the minorities to earn goodwill of or seek cooperation from the majority community. The state as such seeks cooperation from all majority and minority communities and protects their interests through law. It is also not necessary to request them to amend, change or reinterpret particular statements appearing in their holy books. It is because of the universal acceptance of supremacy of law and constitution. None is permitted to go beyond the ambit of law even if it is directed by God, Prophet, Avatar or Guru. State has been placed over and above all institutions and temporal or divine authorities including religious ones. It operates through execution of dispassionate law. Only state and its agencies, and none else have right to investigate, determine and decide whether an act is crime or not, and punish the guilty. Every citizen in India has been granted fundamental rights. Nobody has any authority to stop a person from doing idol worship or enjoying self-meditation. Every citizen will have to conform all edicts, verdicts or directives of his religion to law.

Followers of a particular religion may be spreading all over the world, and claim themselves to form one 'umma' or community. But, the existing state, in case of 57 Muslim states, keeps the followers of Islam and others divided and separate into political units. No state allows, even if some individuals or groups follow its prevailing or official religion, or permits them to enter or exit without permission. The majority of a state has not been granted any right to inflict harm to person, property, honour, livelihood, business or personal faith even of a small group or community. Nobody in the eye of law can be stopped from constructing temples, mosques, observe own forms of worship or maintain faith. Persons spreading hatred, inciting violence, causing communal rights and the like are punished by the state everywhere. Even the UNO and its various agencies zealously look after the availability of these rights through its collective action. Universal human rights are granted to all men and cannot be violated.[15] The world community has recently constituted the permanent international tribunal to punish war criminals.

Change of Context-Supremacy of State

During the twentieth and twenty-first century the whole scenario has changed. In Islam commandments or godly directives were given to the non-state people. There was no difficulty in following those directives. The Arabic communities did not envisage boundaries of state or nation at the time of the appearance of the Holy Quran. Now, each and every country accepts the principles of sovereignty of state and supremacy of 'rule of law'. In India, being a sovereign state with supremacy of the Constitution, the Muslims cannot act upon the directives which happen to go against law. They are no more bound by the decisions given by the Mullahs and Maulavis. Non-Muslims also are not obliged to follow upon non-legal verdicts. Like Western democracies, India cherishes values of liberty, equality, fraternity, rule of law, justice, etc., which do not permit use of force, violence, terrorism, hostility towards idolaters and the like. It is a secular state, which administers law for the protection and welfare of all. Rule of law applies to all—Muslims, Christians, Hindus and others. Moreover, universal human rights are propagated and ensured by the United Nations and its various agencies. Therefore, all directives, injunctions, teachings, edicts and appeals appearing in the holy books, but not permitted by law, are no more exercisable in the Indian State. Even the Hindus cannot practise, as against law, any other-worldly, spiritual or social inequality. All are expected in the Indian democratic state to create an environment wherein one may pursue his goals without hurting other. Democracy provides ample opportunities, means and methods to redress their grievances. All citizens are granted basic rights to grow their personalities on their self-chosen lines. Now, no person is allowed to take law into one's hands.

Popular Vigil over Communal Riots

Still, there are fundamentalists and religious extremists who from time to time cause communal riots and destroy property, person and honour of the people Every state tries to prevent them. It can do so only by having an efficient, trained and well-equipped police force. It has to operate impartially and in a manner committed to public welfare. However, prevention is better than cure. Such events must be anticipated well in advance. Organization of specialist, reliable and efficient intelligence services can do that. More important than all is the administration of highly trained, experienced and impartial judiciary for the quick disposal of cases. Delay in the disposal of criminal cases is one of the main causes of communal flare-ups.

However, the state would succeed more, if at popular level, the vigilant citizens belonging to the majority community keep an eye over the anti-social activities of their community, and so do the member of the minority communities in respect of their own guilty men. Similarly, the vigilant elements of both majority and minority communities should keep an eye over the fundamentalist elements of the other communities and report useful information to the concerned authorities. Under such meaningful dispensation, there would not be any need to motivate one community to be 'tolerant' and the other to be left untouched for the maintenance of contrived peace. There would not be any need to threaten or indulge in violence to protect one's person, rights, status and honour.

Notes

1. See, 'Indianisation of the People Living in India', Chapter 23.
2. *Rajasthan Patrika*, December 13, 2003: In India, minorities coming from outside like the Jews and the Parsis are negligible. 90 per cent Muslims and

99.9 per cent Christians living in India belong to India. However, in 1881, there were 79.32 per cent Hindus and 21 per cent Muslims in India. In 1991 they respectively became 68.03 and 30 per cent. Christians in 1881 were 0.6, increased to 2.1 per cent in 1991.

3. Golwalkar, Upadhyaya and Tengadi, 1991: 48.
4. In *Hindutva* Savarkar accepted the common argument that the terms 'Hindu' and 'Hindustan' were derived in the distant past from 'Sindhu', which was given by Aryans to the river Indus and, later, to all rivers and seas in the subcontinent.
5. Pandey, Gyanendra (ed.), "Which of Us Are Hindus?. Hindus and Others", *The Question of Identity in India Today*, 1993, New Delhi: Viking, pp. 238-272.
6. Golwalkar, M. S. *Bunch of Thoughts*. Bangalore: Jagarana Prakashana, 1980.
7. Yechury, Sitaram, *What is this Hindu Rashtra? On Golwalkar's Fascistic Ideology and the Saffron Brigade's Practice* 1993, Madras: A Frontline Publication, p. 6
8. Here it is simply reiteration of what the Aryans, Vedicas, Hindus or Indians have been doing from ancient times. See, जननीजन्मभूमिष्च स्वर्गादपि गरीयसी––वाल्मीकि रामायण It is equal to

   or भूमिपूजन that is worship of Bhumi (land) or remembering rivers, mountains etc. at the time of taking bath in गंगे च यमुने गोदावरी सरस्वती नवर्दे सिंधु कावेरी जलेऽस्मिन् सन्निधिम् कुरु। etc.;

   or praise of the capacity of the land of India to turn ordinary human being into gods—गायन्ति ते देवा किल गीतकानि धन्यास्तु ते भारतभूमिभागे।
   स्वर्गापवर्गास्तु पदहेतु भूते भवन्ति भूयः पुरुष सुरत्वात्। or, All the national songs and the national anthem—such as, जनगणमन अधिनायक जय हे, वंदेमातरम etc. The same spirit can be witnessed in Tarana-e-Hind of Allama Iqbal in 1904 'Sare jahan se accha hindoositan hamara'. Worship and praise of motherland is also recited daily in the RSS shakhas:

   Salutations to the Motherland where I was born.
   Salutations to the Hindu Land where I was brought up.
   Salutations to the Land of Dharma for which may my body fall.
   To Her, I salute again and again.
9. The concept of 'nationism' connotes the nature, contents, culture, aspirations, knowledge and achievements of the people of India after independence. It is related to the present and future of the people living in the territory of India. 'Nationalism' is more concerned with the past and desires to formulate its present and future on the basis of distant past. In this, 'nationism' is different from 'nationalism'.

10. See, Introduction, level five in the Table. See, also, A.P.J. Abdul Kalam, *India (2020): A Vision for the New Millennium*, Penguin Books, 1998, 2002.
11. It is a society where all persons belong to all 'varnas'. An individual carries 'varna/s' of his choice and will.
12. In this direction, see, attempts being made by Vasundhara Raje Government of Rajasthan, especially of Gulab Chand Kataria, Home Minister, *Rajasthan Patrika*, October 20, 2005
13. See, 'The Hindu Dharma', pp. 35-52.
14. In order to solve this problem, one has to look into the prompted bogey of 'majoritarianism' of the Hindus. Chapter 8.
15. See Universal Declaration of Human Rights, December 10, 1948.

21

Identity and Socialization of Indian Muslims

In due course of time every country develops some specific features, traits and indicators which make up its 'identity'. People of that country are expected to inculcate those specific features, traits and indicators and carry on that identity to make it a 'nation'.

However, only a few persons possess that identity in full sense of the term. Others might not have that identity at all or might be having only a small part of it. But for the full growth of that country all of its inhabitants should develop that identity to the maximum extent possible. Those who are unable to grow that identity or totally lack it are looked as strangers, aliens, outsiders, intruders or illegal immigrants. They are no more part of that country's society. As few persons are able to grow that identity in natural ways, a country tries to generate that identity in its people by formulating an appropriate 'socialization process'.

'Identity' is primarily a social and cultural status. It is the state of being closely involved with or part of something. It is eligibility of a person to be a member of society and polity. Some of the indicators of identity of a person in India are commitment, work, love, spiritual freedom and understanding. Identity is learnt and attained while living among the people. Identity of the people of a country is formulated by its specific socialization process. Unfortunately, India, even after 58 years of freedom, has not evolved her own socialization process. Some of her people possess it as a result of natural process. But the majority of the people lack it. This country has not evolved its own particular socialization process. She is ignorant of the fact that there is no socialization process to turn out right type of persons as nationals. The existing socialization process is either baneful or inadequate to serve the purpose. In the absence of socialization process it remains uncertain whether the persons living in that country carry its identity or not. The real personality of a country depends on its socialization process, a country may have a name, but cannot have its own identification. The people of this country are largely strangers to each others. A person living in India feels no commitment or allegiance to her society. Only an appropriate socialization process is able to transform the inhabitants of that country into its real human products: as citizens or nationals.

Unfortunately, India is unable to transform her inhabitants as Indians or Bharatiyas. In the absence of an objective socialization process one cannot measure the extent to which a person is Indian or Bharatiya. All persons born in this country, unless they are properly socialized, cannot be treated or considered as 'Indian'. It is generally expected and claimed that those who are born in India would be Indians automatically as birth in a country makes it his or her 'motherland'. However, all do not inculcate that feeling. They may not either entertain that mother feeling or might be considering some other country or land as their sacred motherland or fatherland. Sheer 'residence' or constant contact too does not generate 'Indianness' though it is expected that after a long duration of living in that country produces a feeling of identification with it. But, the intensity and form of this feeling of identification is found to be surprisingly varying. Thus, we might observe that only a few persons are cent per cent Indian. The criterion of being an 'Indian' lies in attaining 'Indianism' or 'Indianness'. On this basis, only half of her population on the basis of its birth in India may be treated imaginatively as Indian. Out of the rest, 20 per cent population could be pseudo-Indian, 10 per cent as non-Indian, and 5 per cent as anti-Indian. The rest may not fall into any category. Some of them may go on changing their categories and try to befool the authorities or people concerned. Only after developing an appropriate measuring scale and applying it properly it can be ascertained that a person or group belongs to a particular category, range or form of 'Indianness'. In the absence of 'Indianness', a person can freely misuse his legal status as 'citizen'. He may be an un-Indian Indian.

Muslims in India

Partition put Indian Muslims in a different category. Muslims under the leadership of Mohammed Ali Jinnah, during the freedom movement, had opposed the goal of 'united free India', and had obtained Pakistan. But all did not migrate to Pakistan. Several crores of Muslims have stayed in India. Pakistan for years had been waiting for India's further dismemberment and had banked upon support of extremist Islamic and communal elements of the Indian Muslims. They became suspect in the eyes of the people. Therefore, it is considered desirable to find out the form and status of allegiance towards India and their identity as Indians. They have been undergoing some form of 'Indianization process', but its pattern is not specifically known. A clear Indianization process would enable the people to know the specific proportions of Muslims passing through various stages of this process. In fact, similar process is necessary for each and every community of India, including the Hindus and others. But, the case of the Muslims is different in view of their association with the demand of Pakistan. Indian Muslims deserve special attention.

Other non-Hindu minorities do not have any history of invasions, aggressions or large-scale conversions, and have been living in a peaceful manner. Only Muslims, historically, have been related to those events. Muslims in varying degrees of their faith and ethos and past history of subjugation of India are guided by the teachings of the Holy Quran and the Shariah. Their religion ordains particular form of polity, economy, family and society. Therefore, they require different forms and ways of understanding and doing in democracy. It is necessary to know to what extent the Muslims adopted Indianism and liked to live peacefully with other communities.[1]

In the Indian context, this type of Indianism is proposed here as Indianization process. Presentation of an Indianization process for the socialization of Muslims of India does not mean that they have to be segregated for this purpose or some non-Muslim agency has to be entrusted with this task. It only means that they form a special category of Indian population, and have to be integrated as Indians.

Millions of them might have already undergone the experience of Indianism. However, it surely aims at transforming the jehadi terrorism of a Muslim into Indianism. Some mid-way Muslims already might be standing closer to Indianism. This Indianization process has several steps, stages, locations or levels. Passing through these stages one can reach the end of Indianism. A desirable form of Indianization process is proposed hereunder.

As this process goes from Islamic terrorism[2] to complete Indianism, it contains 200 points, out of which 100 points display negative or anti-Indian form, and the other 100 points indicate positive face of Indianism. On negative side, a location/stage carries 20 points. But, on positive side, it carries 10 points as the process of 'Indianization' happens to be slow, gradual and incremental.

The proposed Indianization process contains 20 stages or locations as shown below:

	The Indianization Process	*Marking on the Scale*
1.	Fanaticism, violence and terrorism	–100
2.	Proxy for Pakistan and Bangla Desh on the basis of Islamic affinity	–90
3.	Blind, absolute and exclusive faith and behaviour	–80
4.	Communalism—expanding communal interests by all possible means	–70
5.	Encouraging separatism and autonomy	–60
6.	Respecting law till the establishment of Islamic rule	–40
7.	Sectarian residence and family life	–20
8.	Separatist education and livelihood	–00
9.	Participation in local politics	+10
10.	Association, cooperation and sharing community living	+20
11.	Coexistence of religions and mutual respect	+30
12.	Upholding supremacy of the Indian Constitution	+40
13.	Accepting majority rule except in matters of minority rights	+50
14.	Active participation in areas of culture, economy and politics	+60
15.	Separation of religion and politics with religion confined to self	+65
16.	Learning and use of national ethos and language/s	+70
17.	Respecting cultural nationalism	+75
18.	Adoption of Indianism retaining Muslim identity	+80
19.	Indianism disowning past for present and future	+ 90
20.	Readiness to make sacrifice for defence and development of the country	+100

Before assigning a location to a Muslim, it is important to observe his expression and behaviour carefully. The state is under obligation to watch and supervise the available patterns of thinking, behaving and responding. Behaviour of Muslims, who happen to claim to belong to the past hordes of invaders, killers and rulers, has to be observed in particular. It has to be seen whether they have reformed and changed themselves, or have kept on their connections and actions practised in the past. Much depends on the types of their mindsets, learning of particular precepts of their religion and making preparation to act accordingly. Such people can be considered as peaceful citizens if they have improved themselves or have made solemn promises to their fellow citizens to follow the norms of society and laws of the country. In case all or some of them do not show any such inclination, they can be treated as Indianized Muslims reaching that level. All these steps, from 9 to 20, would also serve as a 'scale' to measure the quantum of 'Indianism' attained by them at a particular stage.

It is difficult to put a Muslim specifically on a particular step or location. Therefore, these locations have been broadly divided into seven broad groups, named as, (a) Stateless Jehadis; (b) Supremacy of Religion without Peace with Others; (c) Either Way Mixed Group; (d) Passive Tolerance and Social Outlook or Peace with Religion; (e) Coexistence and Peaceful Living; (f) Acceptance of Cultural Nationalism; and (g) Ideology of Indianism. Various locations, for convenience of classification in the seven group scale of 'Indianization process' have been put in the following manner:

(a) Stateless Jehadis	
1. Fanaticism, violence and terrorism	–100
2. Proxy for Pakistan and Bangla Desh on the basis of Islamic affinity	–90
3. Blind, absolute and exclusive faith and behaviour	–80
(b) Supremacy of Religion without Peace with Others	
4. Communalism – expanding communal interests by all possible means	–70
5. Encouraging separatism and autonomy	–60
(c) Either Way Mixed Group	
6. Respecting law till the establishment of Islamic rule	–40

Contd...

Contd...

(d) Passive Tolerance and Social Outlook	
7. Sectarian residence and family life	–20
8. Separatist education and livelihood	–00
9. Participation in local politics	+10
10. Association, cooperation and sharing community living	+20
(e) Coexistence and Peaceful Living	
11. Coexistence of religions and mutual respect	+30
12. Upholding supremacy of the Indian Constitution	+40
13. Accepting majority rule inclusive of minority rights	+50
14. Active participation in areas of culture, economy and politics	+60
(f) Acceptance of Cultural Nationalism	
15. Separation of religion and politics with religion confined to self	+65
16. Learning and use of national ethos and language/s	+70
17. Respecting cultural nationalism	+75
18. Adoption of Indianism retaining Muslim identity	+80
(g) Ideology of Indianism	
19. Indianism disowning past for present and future	+90
20. Readiness to make sacrifice for defence and development of country	+100

The scale can be useful in studying the Muslim minorities living in India as a whole and anywhere in the states of India. With certain modifications, the scale can be used in measuring status of other minorities also. On this seven location groups scale, minorities residing in different regions of a state can also be compared and analyzed on the basis of their pattern of living. It can be used for studying any one of the seven segments of the Muslim population horizontally found in different Indian states.

Meaning of Locations Groups on the Scale of Indianization Process

Muslims belonging to group (a) mostly include fanatics, fundamentalists, militants, terrorists and extremists. They are about 2 lakh spread over in the entire country. They think that they are fighting against the non-Muslims (*kafirs*) to realise the rule of Allah. The fanatics find many clear directives in their books of religion which ask them to execute them without entertaining any doubt, unconditionally, and to the fullest possible extent. The only remedy is either they change their hearts at will or the security and the police forces capture, control and kill them in encounters. Group (b) Muslims stand with group (a) at the level of faith. They do not want peace with any other religion. They indulge in separatism and communalism and actively engage in riots, arson, rape, conversion and other crimes. They constantly work for the dismemberment of India often in collusion with elements of Pakistan. Their number is over 55 lakh preferably belonging to Sunni sect.

Group (c) Muslims, about 5 crore, actually belong a kind of mixed category who disagree with the fanatics both on their ends and means. If some of them connive at their doings, most of them either maintain distance from them or observe discreet silence. Only a few devoted Muslims support them voluntarily. There are hundreds of Muslims who appear to help them with money, shelter and intelligence. But, they are sometimes forced to do so under threat or pressure exerted by the terrorists. A majority of them are convinced that there would be chaos and bloodshed if terrorism is adopted either as an end or means or both to realise the rule of Islam. In view of the availability of weapons of mass destruction in the hands of these terrorists, they expect the end of the human race itself. The vague idea of 'Ummah' (world community of the Muslims) may not avert this danger. Perhaps, they also realize that neglect of state, democratic set-up etc. would result only in indirect support to terrorism, chaos and jungle raj. Still they find opportunities to move from (a) to (b) and (c) categories under pressure or blind faith. To save from criticism on either side, they like to stay in the (c) category. It provides a 'to fro' or grey area in which they can move at their own will to avoid criticism or as a matter of strategy. However, influence or threat of terrorism dominates both (b) and (c), and this situation makes all of them suspect. Therefore, it is necessary that the (c) category Muslims keep themselves away openly and clearly from (b) and perform positive role.

Group (d) is connected with the transitional stage of Indianization. They constitute about 4 crore, who do not join groups (a), (b) and even (c). They keep themselves away from them and are busy with their routine affairs. They continue to pay respect and have faith in all the basic tenets of Islam, but do not feel any necessity to act on all injunctions of the Holy Book (Quran), in particular to fight oppression, oppose non-believers and eliminate idolaters. They have virtually given up their religion directed right to use force or violence at their own, and believe that the state is rightly doing this job in their behalf. They find that in the present democratic set up there are various ways and means to ventilate their grievances and get redress through various agencies and institutions. Use of violence, under these circumstances for the cause of religion or otherwise would make them criminals in the eyes of the state. They feel that the Holy Book also teaches them to live peacefully with followers of other religions if the latter do not deny opportunities to pursue divine injunctions and follow Islam. Even if they are not happy in accommodating with the people of a non-Muslim country, they do not consider it desirable to wait for the opportune moment when they would be able to convert that country into Islamic rule. They appear contented with the present state of affairs.

Members of the group (d) are equipped with modern education working in government or autonomous organizations, and having socio-economic mobility and political awakening. They gain power on the basis of their organization and constitute the most awakened part of the society. Muslims of groups (f) and (g) take part in and lead regional and national movements, trade unions, labour, youth and people living below poverty line. They make full use of press, media and academia. They often choose subjects for study like science, engineering, law and business and often occupy positions in universities, government and corporate bodies.

Most of the group (e) Muslims enjoying happiness, peace and harmony are those who practise humanitarian teachings of the Holy Quran. They are about 4 crore who have enough respect for other religions and their religious practices. Their behaviour is also reciprocated by the followers of other religions including the Hindus, and live with peace and harmony with them. In this process, they happen to come closer and get acquainted with their culture, language, traditions etc. They begin to reside fearlessly in the mixed colonies and grow a sense of brotherhood. Their cooperation with them further strengthens when they happen to live together in such manner. Anti-social elements find it very difficult for injecting wedge between the two communities. Members of each community know usually the trouble shooters and law breakers, therefore, can promptly act against them in the interest of maintaining communal harmony directly or through other agencies.

Over a period of time, a large number of Muslims have discovered new areas of cooperation, artistic expression, social service, skill and invention. Sometimes, the Muslims have neglected religious restrictions and prohibitions in areas like sculptor, music, dance, business and the like. In socio-economic and religious areas, they have been influenced by each others' customs, traditions, fads and taboos. The Muslims have adopted and borrowed many symbols, styles of marriage, ways of idol worship, and ethos from the Hindus. They are willing to be considered as Indian Muslims or citizen Muslims.[3]

Group (f) Muslims firmly believe in superiority of democracy and secularism unmixed with religion. About 5 crore Muslims say that Islam is a religion of peace only, and dislike the deeds of fanatic Muslim conquerors and invaders of the medieval past, and at the time of partition of India. They reject ends and means of the militants and terrorists. But left to themselves, they have neither will nor power to restrain the violent jihadis from causing havoc to the lives of the innocent people. Thus, they appear convinced on the futility of using terrorism as the weapon of religion. They hand over the task of dealing with terrorism to the state. They feel proud of their Indian identity, and like to disown and disconnect themselves from their historical antecedents.

Group (g) goes further by living among the non-Muslims, who, besides being simply peaceful and accommodative, displays allegiance and spirit of sacrifice in defending the land and people of their country of birth and residence. They constitute about 1 crore. In this manner, they identify their interests with the people as a whole. Thus, they do not have to be treated merely as a minority or groups of guests and strangers living at the mercy of the majority. Sometimes, they do more than what is expected of them as compatriots or citizens. Many of them besides making contributions in the fields of art, literature, crafts and skills, stand by the majority to defend and protect land from aggression, exploitation and treachery. This is 'Indianism'.[4]

Notes

1. Islamic terrorism has further made Muslims as suspects almost everywhere particularly in non-Muslim countries. Many countries have large Muslim population. As such, they are eager to know what Muslims are not prone to terrorism and wish to live there as peaceful citizens. They are in search of taking steps necessary for protecting their countries from the onslaughts of terrorism. Threat of terrorism is so widespread that even peaceful Muslim countries are worried on the presence of terrorist elements and trying to restrain them.
2. See, Delhi City's worst terror attacks on October 29, 2005 which killed 57, injured 153 just before Diwali, *Hindustan Times*, October 30, 2005. Terror in Bangalore. Again, there terrorists barged into an auditorium, where some of the country's best brains gathered for an international science conference, and opened indiscriminate fire on the delegates killing retired IIT, Delhi Professor M.C. Puri on the spot. Puri, an Emeritus Professor of Mathematics who had won several awards for his work on the subject had gone to Bangalore to attend the conference. *Hindustan Times*, December 29, 2005.
3. G. Parthasarthy in "Time to move on, and ahead" *Hindustan Times*, October 5, 2003.
4. On the basis of observation of the behaviour of the Muslims of India, the Muslim population can be proportionately put into these groupings:

(a)	Stateless Jihadis	03.00 lakh
(b)	Supremacy of Religion without Peace with Others	55.00 lakh
(c)	Either Way Mixed Group	200.00 lakh
(d)	Passive Tolerance and Social Outlook	400.00 lakh
(e)	Coexistence and Peaceful Living	400.00 lakh
(f)	Acceptance of Cultural Living	300.00 lakh
(g)	Ideology of Indianism	100.00 lakh
	Total	1458.00 lakh

22

Indianization of Bangladeshis and Other Migrants Living in India

India has been facing the problem of Bangladeshis and other outsiders now living in India for a longtime. They have come over here in millions, and are still pouring in. Unless this problem is solved properly, India may have to face dismemberment as Pakistan had undergone in her early seventies and Sri Lanka has been facing it today. This problem has to be taken up on long-term basis.

Identity and Citizenship

It is proposed to solve this problem on the basis of proper understanding of the concepts of 'citizenship' and 'identity', and relating them through a proper socialization process. Citizenship and identity are two social realities of political life. They are also two important aspects of the personality of a man or woman living in a country. Citizenship is legal and political whereas identity is primarily a social and cultural status. Most of the people mistakenly take them together as one and the same. Identity is eligibility. It is a condition precedent to citizenship. Thus, they are related to each other and are interdependent, but not identical. By identifying citizenship with identity the people of developing countries like India are doing great harm to them. Attainment of identity must be a means to realize the end of citizenship. Granting citizenship is the job of state whereas generating identity is the award of society and voluntary organizations on attainment of Indianism to persons concerned.

Identity is "the state of being closely involved with or part of something".[1] It is eligibility of a person to be a member of particular society and polity. Some of the indicators of identity of a person in India are: commitment, work, love, spiritual freedom and understanding. Identity is learnt and attained while living among the people. Ideally, a person should have both citizenship and identity. But, there are persons who have citizenship without identity and have identity without citizenship. Often, there are citizens without having identity and some have identity without having citizenship. Identity should be a condition precedent to grant citizenship, not vice versa. Form and grant of 'citizenship' is determined by law. But it should not be granted to a person simply on the basis of his or her birth in the country. It should be given to a person only after the confirmation of one's having Indianism or Indianity.

Identity of the people of a country is formulated by its specific 'socialization process'.[2] In the absence of socialization process, it remains uncertain whether the persons living in that country carry its identity or not. As stated in the last chapter, only an appropriate socialization process is able to transform the inhabitants of that country into its real human products as citizens or nationals. This is much more necessary in case of outsiders and illegal immigrants living in India.

Bangladeshis and Other Illegal Immigrants

Today, there are millions of Bangladeshis and other illegal immigrants living in India. Most of them neither are born here nor have attained Indianism. They have not gone through the much needed socialization process. Their inflow continues. They have illegally entered this country and have been living here for the last several years.

According to an Intelligence Bureau document presented at the 38th Conference of Directors-General of Police, the number of illegal immigrants from Bangladesh settled in India is over 15 million and the influx of Bangladeshi nationals continues unabated. It presented figures as 80 lakh in West Bengal, 50 lakh in Assam, 4.75 lakh in Bihar, 3.75 lakh in Tripura, 4 lakh in Delhi and 80,000 in Nagaland. They are also in Mizoram and other Indian states like Rajasthan and Punjab. This influx has significantly changed the politico-economic, social and demographic character of the border states of India. The document spelled out the dangers to India's security, their linkages to terrorist elements in Bangladesh and other movements in India.[3]

Ousting Impossible

Despite immigration laws and government's determination to oust Bangladeshis from India, the task appears almost impossible. Sooner or later they are likely to become, under present or future national and international laws, naturalized citizens, i.e., as alien citizens. But those provisions would make them legalized citizens but not 'Indianized' citizens. In other words, they would live here as citizens without Indianism or without earning goodwill or identity of the country. The goal here is not to encourage illegal immigration from neighbouring countries on massive scale and to obstruct the execution of laws to prosecute them to oust from the country. Till that legality of granting citizenship to them happens to take place, they can be put for some years under observation, trial and education and considered as non-citizen Indians.[4] During this period, a sense of commonality, unity and allegiance can grow in them. The country after their transformation would grow stronger and greater in the comity of nations.[5] Therefore, the only way appearing feasible to solve this problem is to socialize them and educate them as Indians over a period of time. In other words, the Bangladeshis and other illegal immigrants (collectively named here as 'Bangladeshis') have to be transformed into Indians or Bharatiyas. They have to be brought closer to Indianism. For this the country should adopt or evolve a 'process of Indianization' for them. It would socialize them into Indianism or Indianness. After going through this process of Indianization or *Bharatiyakaran* they would identify their interests with India's interests, particularly in areas of sovereignty, defence, culture and development. When they commit themselves alike India-born residents to this pattern of Indianization or *Bharatiyata*, they should not be treated as outsiders, intruders, foreigners or illegal immigrants. They would be treated as Indians or naturalized Indians in a gradual manner or in degrees when they attain some satisfactory pattern of Indianism. This pattern grows gradually and can be of several types, levels, forms and stages. Their ultimate goal would be to attain Indianism or Indianity, which can be indicated by capability, commitment and culture found in a person.

To a large extent, the process of transformation appears voluntary, natural and evolutionary. But, in view of India's past history of foreign domination, deceit, dismemberment and secession, it has to be monitored by the Indian society or nationalistic organizations preferably by some pro-India Muslim body or the RSS, VHP, Shiv Sena and Arya Samaj and the like. Some national political parties can also bear this responsibility. Similarly, a group of the Indianized Bangladeshis also can do this job.

Conditions of Bangladeshis in India

As stated earlier, there are over one and a half crore Bangladeshis in India. They have been living mostly in north-eastern states, West Bengal, Assam, Bihar, Uttar Pradesh, Delhi and Rajasthan. Over half of them are Hindus, and the rest are Muslims and Christians. Muslims and Christians have settled mostly in north-eastern states and West Bengal, while the majority of Hindu Bangladeshis are residing in different parts of India.

Most of them belong to the composite culture of Bangladesh and speak Bengali language. All incoming Bangladeshis are poverty-stricken and move in search of livelihood, employment and small jobs. The Hindu Bangladeshis run out of their country under pressure of extremist elements of Muslims, insecurity and discrimination. The Muslim Bangladeshis go in search of better avenues, religious linkages and political motives to create areas of Muslim domination in Indian states. As they belong to the lower strata of society, they are unaware of their forefathers' deeds of invasions, aggressions or large-scale conversions. Presently, they have been living here in a peaceful manner. Cases of communal flare up have been few and far between. Spread of jehadi terrorism among them is minimal. But, in India, they do not enjoy equality before law and civic rights, and are not politically organized. However, they enjoy certain fundamental rights under the Constitution of India or the Human Rights Charter. All these features form the basis of their transformation from illegal immigrants to Indianized residents of India. To realize this goal, a 'socialization process' or 'Indianization process' has been proposed here.[6] It can also be used as a scale to measure the extent of their socialization during various stages of their stay in India.

Scale of Socialization Process

There are three important variables that can make up a provisional scale of transformation for the Bangladeshi. These are: (a) capability, (b) commitment, and (c) culture. These variables are further classified into sub-variables shown as locations or steps of the socialization scale. A Bangladeshi stands somewhere on the scale of these variables. There can be many locations on which a Bangladeshi can be put on the scale of transformation. These locations also constitute the stages, levels or steps of the proposed socialization process. As the goal of this socialization process is 'Indianization' of the outsiders or strangers, it can also be called as 'Indianization process'. Passing through them one is supposed to attain the goal of Indianism or *Bharatiyata*. The proposed steps or locations are mentioned hereunder:

1. Illegal entry in any one of the states in India
2. Residence and earning livelihood
3. Use of local language and adoption of social taboos and traditions
4. Association, cooperation and sharing community living
5. Participation in local politics
6. Continuation and maintenance of relations in Bangladesh—normal or abnormal
7. Encouraging harmony/separatism
8. Respecting law till the establishment of own rule
9. Coexistence of religions and mutual respect
10. Upholding supremacy of the Indian State with religion confined to self
11. Accepting majority rule in India inclusive of respect to other minorities
12. Active participation in culture

13. Adoption of India as motherland
14. Respecting cultural nationalism
15. Acquisition of education, public employment and civic rights
16. Indianism as faith or ideology
17. Indianism freed from past
18. Readiness to work for the defence and development of India

If we exclude steps 6th and 7th, it would remain a 16-point scale. Those who reach these locations and operate from there do not move onwards.

Method of Fixing Location on the Scale of Socialization

As it is difficult to locate a Bangladeshi specifically on a particular location, the locations have been further divided into some broad stages. Each stage contains several steps or locations. Advancement on each step carries 10 marks for the purpose of quantification. It also indicates total number of years tentatively required to pass through that stage. The scale consists of five stages as under:

(a) Stage of Introduction and contact-seeking economic livelihood and security
(b) Stage of making adjustment
(c) Stage of assimilation/confrontation
(d) Stage of adoption
(e) Stage of citizenship

Various locations shown in the scale of transformation can be put under these stages in the Table 1.

Thus, the scale can be useful for measuring the quantum of transformation of Bangladeshis living anywhere in India. Each step has been allocated 5 or 10 marks. Progress towards stage-wise gradual transformation has also been earmarked in terms of duration and shown on the scale. Their location can help the concerned organizations to take steps for speeding up their transformation, if in positive direction, and for thwarting it if it goes in the reverse direction. With certain modifications, the scale can be used in measuring status of transformation of Bangladeshis in different states or in areas of one particular region.

Table 1

Location of Groups on the Scale of Socialization

Stages with Steps Duration in	*Percentage of Approximate*		
	immigrants	*marks*	*years*
(a) Stage of Introduction and Contact-seeking Economic Livelihood and Security	34%	20	4
1. Illegal entry in any one of the states in India		10	
2. Residence and earning livelihood		10	
(b) Stage of Making Adjustment	33%	30	6
3. Use of local language and adoption of social taboos and traditions		10	
4. Association, cooperation and sharing community living		10	
5. Participation in local politics	10		
(c) Stage of Assimilation/Confrontation	10%/3%	20/-20	4/8
6. Continuation and maintenance of relations in Bangladesh—normal/abnormal		+ – 5	
7. Encouraging unity/separatism		+ – 5	
8. Respecting law/the establishment of own rule		+ – 5	
9. Co-existence of religions and mutual respect/communalism		+ – 5	
(d) Stage of Adoption	13%	50	15
10. Upholding supremacy of the Indian State		10	
11. Accepting majority rule in India with respect to other minorities		10	
12. Active participation in culture		10	
13. Adoption of India as motherland		10	
14. Respecting cultural nationalism		10	
(d) Stage of Acquiring Full Indianism	7%	40	12
15. Acquisition of education, public employment and civic rights		10	
16. Total Indianism as faith or ideology		10	
17. Indianism freed from past		10	
18. Readiness to work for the defence and development of India		10	
Total marks		160	
Marks stopping while at steps 6th and 7th		20+30=5 0-20=30	

Quantification of Socialization

At the first (a) *stage of introduction and contact by seeking economic livelihood and security*, all the Bangladeshis, barring the Islamic fundamentalists and extremists, despatched by the terrorist organizations, make entry into India in illegal ways. They come either in collusion with border police or security guards or surreptitiously at their own risk. They usually come to India in search of seeking livelihood or security of life and honour. At this stage, about four years are passed in doing menial jobs, domestic service and the like. In this process, they easily gain acceptability of the local people. Owing to their illegal entry and low social status, hand-to-mouth living and constant fear of the police, they have to provide cheapest labour. After completing about four years, they enter (b) *stage of making adjustment* where they learn the local language/dialect, begin to understand the local traditions, do's and don't of social life, and start mixing up with neighbourhood at ground levels. They associate with the people in other non-economic activities and find some small space in community life. They make adjustment with others regarding their social activities, marriage, birth and death ceremonies, and other socio-religious affairs. Some of them, at informal levels, start participating in local politics. This stage involves another six years obtaining 10 marks for each stage.

The third (c) stage takes them towards either *assimilation/ confrontation*. Assimilation, in case of Hindu and pro-India Muslim Bangladeshis, occurs with their acceptance of the socio-economic contours of the Indian political system. They take about four years to know and understand it and can pick 20 marks.

During the process of their adjustment in Indian states, they pay respect and have faith in all the basic tenets of Islam, but do not feel any necessity to act on all injunctions of the Holy Book (Quran), in particular to fight oppression, oppose non-believers and eliminate idolaters. A Bangladeshi Muslim in India believes that in the present democratic set-up there are various ways and means to ventilate their grievances and get redress through various agencies and institutions. They feel that the Holy Book also teaches them to live peacefully with followers of other religions. They dislike the deeds of Islamic Muslim conquerors and invaders of the medieval past. In this process, they happen to come closer and get acquainted with each others' culture, language, traditions etc. Both Hindu and Muslim Bangladeshis begin to reside fearlessly in the mixed colonies and grow a sense of brotherhood.

The Muslim Bangladeshis when supported by the extremist and fundamental elements of Indian Muslims or financed by anti-India organizations of Bangladesh take about long 8 to 10 years in making adjustment with the neighbouring people and understanding realities. If they continue to indulge in (a) maintaining abnormal relations with Bangladesh, (b) support separatism for establishing their own rule in India or in collusion with similar elements, and (c) spread communalism, they lose 5 marks for each step. If they do not do so and go in a reverse anti-India direction, 20 marks out of the marks obtained earlier so far would be deducted so as to ascertain their quantum of socialization. In fact, such persons cannot improve or move onwards. In such cases the authorities would suspect them and take steps to oust them from India through courts.

At the fourth (d) *stage of adoption*, the Bangladeshis finally conclude that the Indian communities (not the state) have finally accepted their existence, living and working. It involves a total period of 15 years and 10 marks for each step. Firstly, he learns to regard the Indian State as superior to everything else in worldly matters. He keeps all his religious matters like faith, soul, mind or heart close to his self. Secondly, he begins to respect and accept rule of majority. He can express his dissent within the limits of law and in a peaceful manner. He also stands in favour of values and goals underlying the Indian political system. While making search for these values and goals, a Bangladeshi comes closer to nature, features and form of Indian culture. On the fourth count his acculturization takes him to the idea of India as his or her motherland. Lastly, his concept of India as his motherland motivates him to adopt and understand 'cultural nationalism' growing in India for the last several centuries. Culturalism connotes a sense of granting supremacy to Indianism. Their own cultures remain there but they stand next to this Indianism. Indianism is neither multi-culturalism nor inter-culturalism for them.

At the fifth and final (e) *stage of acquiring Indianism* a Bangladeshi is to be taught to equip himself with better education to gain more respectable job in public or private employment. In this matter, he would be able to enrol himself as employee of some business, craft or industrial concern. All this leads to enjoy civil rights granted to all persons under the Indian Constitution. Indianism means here identification of their self with the interests of Indian State. His Indianism after living for 24 years in India is expected to be freed from the close connections with their own country. They develop an understanding that they would not gain anything by returning back to Bangladesh. At the final stage of their socialization, a Bangladeshi is likely to learn to make personal sacrifices for the development and defence of their adopted country, i.e., India. This stage is likely to take another 12 year with 10 marks for each step. Thus, a Bangladeshi would have approximately of 41 years of socialization in India. Realization of Indianism qualifies him for granting naturalized citizenship by the state after completing all formalities and verifying realities at the official level. The Indian State is granting citizenship to the Pakistani citizens who had crossed over to Western Rajasthan during and after Indo-Pak wars of 1965 and 1971.[4] After the grant of 'citizenship', the Indianized Bangladeshis can be called as 'Bangindians' or 'Bangbharatiyas'. They may be deprived of that status of having 'identity' or 'citizenship' if they happen to lack or lose their Indianism. Such reverted persons may be called as Bangladeshi immigrants or Banglimmigrants or Bangimmigrants. Such persons could be treated as 'Bangladeshis under Observation'. Illegal immigrants remain 'illigrants' or 'illimigrants'.

Prevailing Situation (2005)

The socialization process proposed here is not totally new. It has been already operating for the last several years. But, its nature, form, scope and impact are not known. It has not been formally accepted anywhere. A mindless neglect towards the problem of Bangladeshis and other illegal immigrants continues.

However, tentative figures pertaining to these people can be presented as under:

(a)	Total number of Bangladeshis and other illegal migrants (approximately)	1 crore 50 lakh
(b)	Bangladeshis under the stage of introduction, contact and adjustment	50 lakh
(c)	Bangladeshis under the stage of assimilation	50 lakh
(d)	Bangladeshis under the stage of confrontation	20 lakh
(e)	Bangladeshis under the stage of adoption	20 lakh
(f)	Bangladeshis under the stage of acquiring citizenship	10 lakh

So far, this process is going on almost on a voluntary basis and actual figures are not available. The process of Indianization of the Bangladeshis must be administered by some voluntary agency or organization at the earliest. This can be done till they remain illegal migrants and are under pressure of seeking livelihood and security. Every step should be properly supervised and given further boost toward Indianization. Launching of the mechanism of socialization for maintaining India's unity and integrity and to save the Bangladeshis from falling prey to anti-social elements, disorder, crime and communalism is very necessary. As they are living here at the cost of limited resources of the Indian State, they have to be trained and educated in a much wanting form of Indianism. However these efforts should not mean as inviting more and more Bangladeshis and other outsiders in the Indian territory. The whole problem of coming over of the Bangladeshis in India, in fact, is the result of failure of proper border management by the state governments. But it can be amicably settled by adopting the proposed socialization process. In case, the Bangladeshis living here fail to Indianize within a prescribed period, the state should prosecute them and oust from the Indian territory even if they have passed through first two stages.

Let us understand, about two crore Bangladeshis and others are there in-waiting to enter the Indian territory to settle down anywhere in India.

Notes

1. For 'identity', see, back, Chapter 21, 'Identity and Socialisation of Indian Muslims'.

2. *Hindustan Times*, November 7, 2003.
3. Manoj Joshi writes that India needs an effective policy to tackle the Nepal, Bangladesh crises. When Begum Khalida Zia, widow of Zia-ur Rehman, became prime minister in 1991, the Islamic forces consolidated their influence. They faced some check in the 1996-2000 period when Begum Hasina Wajed ruled, but in the 2000 elections, the BNP capitalized on the failures of Begum Hasina and won a massive victory, gaining 191 seats, while its ally getting another 17 in the 300-strong Parliament. "A Tale of two countries"–*Hindustan Times*. February 10, 2005; Khalida has always been denying that there is any illegal migration of the Bangladeshis to India.
4. A similar treatment has been given by the government of India and the state government to the migrants coming from Pakistan for granting Indian citizenship.
5. This attitude can be witnessed in granting Indian citizenship to NRIs (Non-Resident Indians) by Prime Minister of India at Hyderabad on January 7, 2006. About 2.50 crore NRIs are living in 110 countries.

23

Indianization of the People Living in India

In due course of time every country develops some specific features, traits and indicators which make up its 'identity'.[1] People of that country are expected to inculcate those specific features, traits and indicators and carry on that identity to make it a 'nation'. In the context of India, this identity is named as 'Indianity'.

Concept of 'Indianity'

We are concerned with the phenomenon or reality of Indianity. It is the inner and real aspect of the personality of an Indian. Indianness reflects his outward personality. Indianism is an ideology of being a true Indian. The goal of both Indianness and Indianism is attainment of Indianity.

In the term 'Indianity' we include all the people of India—Hindus, Muslims, Christians, Sikhs etc. To make the concept comprehensive, we have to print out all negative and positive attributes. Indianity likes to exclude certain negative attributes and include all the positive attributes. They respectively make up its minus and plus attributes.

In view of this difficulty, the concept of 'Indianity' has been elaborated here as a cluster of 27 attributes or variables:

(1) extra-territorial links and affinity; (2) resort to violence (jihad) on divine directions; (3) blind, absolute and exclusive faith and behaviour; (4) encouraging separatism and anti-national autonomy; (5) communalism—expanding communal interests by all possible means; (6) belief in casteism and ethnicity; (7) gender discrimination; (8) corruption and donations; (9) working for religious conversions; (10) preference to other-worldliness; (11) residence and family life; (12) religion confined to self; (13) working for worldly affairs; (14) faith in and equality to all essential organs of society; (15) co-existence of religions and mutual respect; (16) cooperation and sharing in community living; (17) learning and use of regional and national languages; (18) secular education, science and technology; (19) earning livelihood and payment of taxes; (20) deference to law and preference to peace; (21) supremacy to state over all units and institutions; (22) accepting majority rule and democracy inclusive of minorities; (23) participation in culture, economy and politics; (24) upholding cultural nationalism; (25) Indianism as faith or ideology; (26) responsibility to work for the defence and development of India; and (27) world peace and security of big and small nations. Out of them, there are 10 negative and 17 positive variables.

Role of Negative Attributes

The negative variables tend to destroy, harm, nullify and neutralize the impact of positive variables. They are less in number and are upheld by less number of persons, but their capacity to cause harm is immense. Therefore, a large number of people having positive attainments are required to face their destructive power. In fact, the persons who have first four negative traits are basically unfit to be considered as Indians. They are anti-state, anti-nation, anti-law and anti-man. They use name of God or religion to indulge in violence and evil. Most of them are Islamic terrorists and militants. It is observable that first three carry more weight than any one of the positive variables. Even one of them has the power to negate the very concept 'Indianism'. For example, extra-territorial links and affinity (1) condemns the very existence of the Indian State and makes him totally unfit to be treated as Indian. Resort to violence (jihad) on divine directions (2) rejects all security and law and order agencies of the Indian government. So are the extremists vowed to blind, absolute and exclusive faith and behaviour (3) who like Al Qaida jihadis commit every type of inhuman act for the good of their life here or in heaven. Below the third level, these elements freely indulge in bloodshed, riots, rebellion and work for the dismemberment of the Indian State.

On negative side, orthodox Hindus also do not lag behind. Standing against fundamental rights, they indulge in casteism and communalism, by resorting to gender discrimination, they downgrade womanhood. In a way, plight of India in the past and present is the direct result of these evils which have been prevalent for the last several hundred years. Despite clear prohibition by the Constitution, stringent laws passed and court verdicts given from time to time diehards of the Hindus society, in the name of religion and tradition, continue to prolong and act on these evils. Under the cover of religion, they make corruption sacrosanct by claiming it as their earning from past good acts. Collecting donations has long been regarded as the sacred profession of the saints and Brahmins. Most of the Christian missionaries in the name of service to the poor and the downtrodden run the vocation of religious conversion creating wedge between the natives and their countrymen. The vast majority of the Hindus by teaching the path of other-worldliness as real one render all out support to these enemies of man. Positive view of Indianity is unable to go along with them. In fact, the first five elements can be suitably dealt with only by armed or security forces, or by well-trained retaliating volunteers. Offenders relating to categories five, six, seven and eight are to be dealt with stringent laws and effective and efficient law and order agencies. Categories nine and ten require strong and convincing force of media, press and public opinion. Right type of Indianity demands a crushing defeat for all of them.[2]

Role of Positive Attributes

But, the strength of Indianity really depends on sustenance of positive values. In all, they are 17. They altogether reflect cent per cent Indianity, Indianness, *Hindustaniyat* or *Bharatiyata*. Total value of these variables is 660. On a scale of measurement, if one acquires 330 marks, a person has 50 per cent Indianity. A person obtaining 165 marks has 25 per cent Indianity whereas 295 marks make him 46 per cent Indian. However, it must be reminded that relationship with even one negative variable, say encouraging separatism and supporting anti-national demand for autonomy (4) reduces the attainments of 50 per cent Indianity, putting him at mere 95 valuations. A person indulging in gender discrimination (7) is a poor and pitiable man, standing a little above 25 per cent, would further degrade him to (165-50) 115. However, in operational terms, one cannot stand with even 25 per cent Indianity if he stands close to any one of the first nine items of negative variables. It may be pointed out that positive variables are usually overturned or nullified by destructive elements, activities, programmes and vicious ideas, particularly first five. They deny and destroy the very existence of religion, society and state. The rest are socially harmful and can undergo transformation in due course of time. The negative variables are less in number, merely ten, but their overall impact or brunt is more than the weight of the normal positive variables.

On positive side of the scale of Indianity, it is not necessary that a person obtains values of all variables at one stretch. One might get them one by one. However, fuller form of Indianity requires that one should invariably have them all together. Hundred per cent Indianity is an 'ideal type'. Variables even on positive side do not have equal value. Faith in and equality to all essential organs of society (14) or supremacy to state over all units and institutions (21) are allotted values of 60 and 70 which are higher than all others. Religion confined to self (2) and learning and use of national language/s (17) have 20 each. It means variables having higher values are elemental to Indianity. Even a few of them when untouched by negative values can entitle one to Indianity. But it is a fact of life that a man at some time standing on the front line of Indianity can as a result of his own limitations and weaknesses go down much below from his earlier position. Similarly, none is destined to remain downgrade for ever. Persons grown in higher positive values when in majority make up power of a nation. Obtaining variables on positive scale is evolutionary and gradual in nature. After making great efforts, a man can jump over only three or four steps. He or she has to maintain each attainment in a constant manner. Reaching the higher stages does not rid of them from earlier ones. Higher the reach of a person on variables greater is the content and quality of his Indianity.

Inculcation of Positive Attributes

Let us examine how some active persons incorporate positive variables during their lives. Accordingly, a person obtains value of 10 if he is born in Indian territory and leads a family-like life (11). These starting situations provide base for the growth of required traits of a citizen. The polity wants that one must be considerate towards worldly affairs and problems (13) and his religious faith should remain confined to his self (12). Outward expression and activities pertaining to religion are subject to the control and regulation of the community, society and the state. Such kind of attitude and understanding enables the people to confront evils perpetrated by the negative factors. For the sake of one's own religious or metaphysical moorings one should not work for an exclusive or segregated society consisting only of saints or soldiers or rich people. In a complete society, there should be persons pursuing different jobs, vocations and professions which have to be paid equal respect (14).

India is a multi-lingual, multi-religious and multi-cultural society. As such, all should believe in coexistence of religions and render respect to them (15). Languages, cultures and religions are almost born with man who remains emotionally attached to them. With this background, one should extend cooperation with others and actively participate in the community living (16). To communicate with larger number of people it is necessary to learn and use regional and national languages (17). Indianity requires lingua franca. Sticking to one specific language/dialect, restrains a person to a confined world. To lead an honourable life in society and develop one's capacities and abilities, one has to undergo education, and learn besides arts and literature, science and technology (18). He must be an earning member always eager to pay taxes (19). Tax evaders, in fact, belong to the group of negative elements. People living in a moderate society, must comply with laws and stand by peace (20). Persons causing disruption, breakdown, disorder, riots and various forms of violence are treated as criminals. A society sustains only when its members regard the state as superior to all other units, institutions and organizations (21). No political party, religion, ideology, nationality, caste or group, language or interest must be considered over and above the state. This is possible only when the political system is run democratically on the principle of majority rule which includes looking after the interests of the minorities (22). Citizens must be able to run government in a democratic fashion and supervise administration to make the latter transparent, responsive and answerable.

They must be active participants in the common culture and economy of the country, and discourage every kind of concentration of wealth or monopoly over knowledge and values (23). An active member of a good polity is expected to be the representative of its 'cultural nationalism' (24). Liberal form of nationalism adds to the strength, unity and integrity of a state. Cultural nationalism invites contribution from all segments of society. All these elements from 11 to 27 when adopted in a progressive manner appear in form of 'Indianism' or 'Indianity'. Their culmination in a man living in India is 'Indianity' (25). It can be a matter of faith for some while others may take it up as their ideology. For a true Indian, mere verbal or hypocritical support is not enough. It calls upon all true Indians to own responsibility, personally and collectively, to work for the defence and development of India (26). However, it would never be pursued at the expense of world peace and security of big and small nations (27).

It may be accepted that putting of values on these variables is an utterly difficult job. At one time, mutual respect to religions (15) may be more important than mere residence and family life (11). Likewise, upholding the ideology of Indianism (25) is no less important and urgent than maintenance of world peace and security (27). Still, in the context of India as a developing country and prevailing economic world order, some such variables have to be granted more weight than others. Their weight can be changed in view of different scenario. It is never meant that a variable assigned less value is less important or unimportant for all time to come. Under the given circumstances, total value of these variables making Indianism as a concrete reality stays at the total of 660. But, it can go higher or lower when the situation demands. All these variables and their values are being presented in Table 1.

However, mere elaboration of the concept of Indianity is not enough. It simply enables us to understand and acquaint ourselves with Indianity, On the basis of scale of Indianity one can know to what extent one is on positive or negative side of India. Persons adopting negative side virtually give up all claims to be treated as Indian. But, the presence of positive variables merely indicates the quantum of Indianity found in a person. On the basis of value put on these variables one can know the extent of his Indianness.

Table 1

Variables of Indianity and Its Scale

	Variables underlying the scale of Indianity	*Proposed*
	Negative Variables	
1.	Extra-territorial links and Affinity	–150
2.	Resort to violence (jihad) on divine directions	–140
3.	Blind, absolute and exclusive faith and behaviour	–80
4.	Encouraging separatism and anti-national autonomy	–70
5.	Communalism—expanding communal interests by all possible means	–50
6.	Belief in casteism and ethnicity	–40
7.	Gender discrimination	–50
8.	Corruption and donations	–30
9.	Working for religious conversions	–20
10.	Preference to other-worldliness	–10
	Total of values for assignment of negative variables	700
	Positive Variables	
11.	Residence and family life	+ 10
12.	Religion confined to self	+ 20
13.	Working for worldly affairs	+40
14.	Faith in and equality to all essential organs of society	+ 60
15.	Co-existence of religions and mutual respect	+ 40
16.	Cooperation and sharing in community living	+ 30
17.	Learning and use of regional and national language/s	+ 20
18.	Secular education, science and technology	+ 30
19.	Earning livelihood and payment of taxes	+ 50
20.	Deference to law and preference to peace	+ 40
21.	Supremacy to state over all units and Institutions	+ 70
22.	Accepting majority rule and democracy inclusive of minorities	+ 50
23.	Participation in culture, economy and politics	+ 40
24.	Upholding cultural nationalism	+ 50
25.	Indianism as faith or ideology	+ 30
26.	Responsibility to work for the defence and development of India	+ 50
27.	World peace and security of big and small nations	+ 30
	Total of value assignment to positive variables	+660

Unfortunately, India has remained unable to transform the majority of her inhabitants as Indians or *Bharatiyas*. They are considered Indians simply on the basis of their long physical presence and living in this country. Only a small proportion of its population can be taken as Indian or *Bharatiya* in the true sense of the term in the absence of a scale of socialization process one cannot measure the extent to which a person is Indian or *Bharatiya*. All persons born in this country, unless they are properly socialized, cannot be treated or considered as 'Indian'. It is generally expected and claimed that those who are born in India would be Indians automatically as birth in a country makes it his or her 'motherland'. However, all do not inculcate that feeling. Only after developing an appropriate measuring scale and applying it properly it can be ascertained that a person or group belongs to a particular category, range or form of 'Indianness'. In the absence of 'Indianness', a person can freely misuse his legal status as 'citizen'. He may be an un-Indian Indian.

Indianization Process for the People of India

Keeping the positive variables of Indianity in view, a common form of Indianization process can easily be proposed here. After the Constitution of India came into operation, it can be assumed that persons born and living in India are in several respects at par with each other. However, to become a full-fledged Indian, they must grow 'Indianity' in them. The full form of Indianity demands an elaborate pattern of Indianization process. This process contains 23 steps. It proposes a time-bound scheme of inculcating a learning of 17 positive attributes as 23 steps. Each step reflects one particular merit or variable. The variables or steps assigned to them are given under:

1. Birth and residence in any one of the states in India
2. Family and social system
3. Education and socialization of norm and values
4. Religion confined to self
5. Association, cooperation and participation in community living
6. Learning and use of national language/s and media
7. Deference to law with preference to peace
8. Coexistence of religions and mutual respect
9. Faith in and equality to all essential organs of society
10. Participation in culture and festivals

11. Accepting majority rule with respect to minorities in India
12. Livelihood-public or private employment and payment of taxes
13. Participation in social service and political parties
14. Gender equality
15. Working for worldly welfare and social justice
16. Interaction with press and media
17. Upholding supremacy of the Indian State
18. Respecting cultural nationalism
19. Adoption of India as motherland
20. Indianism as faith or ideology
21. Readiness to work for the defense and development of India
22. Global and liberal orientation
23. World peace and regional cooperation

These steps or variables of the Indianization process also form a scale. On the basis of attainment of the attributes by crossing over these steps, a person's position can be located on this scale. It would show where does an Indian stand on the scale of Indianity.

Location on the Scale of Indianization Process

As it is difficult to locate a person on a particular location or step out of 23, these locations have been further divided into some broad stages. Each stage contains several steps or locations. Advancement on each step is assigned some marks for the purpose of quantification. Total number of years tentatively required to pass through that stage has also been suggested here.

The steps or locations of the scale of Indianization process have been put under these stages with duration to pass through that stage in the manner as shown in Table 2.

However, there is a stage of 'deviation, fight and change' which has been separately discussed here.

Thus, the scale can be useful for measuring the quantum of transformation of people living anywhere in India. Each step has been allocated 5 or 10 marks. Progress towards stage-wise gradual transformation has also been earmarked in terms of duration and shown on the scale. Their location can help the concerned agencies and organizations to take steps for speeding up their Indianization.

Table 2
Location of Groups in Indianization Process

Approximate stages with steps with no. of years required to pass through them		*Approximate quantum of Indianization expressed in terms of marks*
(a) Stage of Existence (duration: whole life)		10
1.	Birth and residence in any one of the states in India whole life	5
2.	Family and social system whole life	5
(b) Stage of Voluntary Socialization (duration: 10 years)		30
3.	Education and socialization of norm and values	5
4.	Religion confined to self	5
5.	Association, cooperation and sharing community living	5
6.	Learning and use of regional and national language/s	10
7.	Deference to law with preference to peace	5
(c) Stage of Coexistence (duration: 20 years)		40
8.	Coexistence of religions and mutual respect	10
9.	Faith in and equality to all essential organs of society	10
10.	Participation in culture and festivals	5
11.	Accepting majority rule with respect to minorities in India	10
(d) Stage of Active Participation duration (duration: 20 years)		50
12.	Livelihood-public or private employment and payment of taxes	10
13.	Participation in social service and political parties	10
14.	Interaction with press and media	10
15.	Gender equality	10
16.	Working for worldly welfare and social justice	10
(e) Stage of Indianism duration (duration: 15 years)		60
17.	Upholding supremacy of the Indian State	20
18.	Respecting cultural nationalism	10
19.	Adoption of India as motherland	10
20.	Indianism as faith or ideology	10
21.	Readiness to work for the defence and development of India	10
(f) Stage of Expectations of 21st century (duration: 5 years)		10
22.	Global orientation	5
21.	World peace and regional cooperation	5
Total Values		200

Stages of Indianization Process

As this stage, we are concerned here with persons living in India since birth. Therefore, at the first **(a) Stage of Existence,** we find them residing in India since birth. Everyone of them is born in some family and grows as a member of some caste or community. The latter are enmeshed with them in some form of religion or sect. All live at that level. Those who remain below poverty line hardly are able to rise above this stage. About 10 per cent of the people are 'Indian' only in territorial sense. At **(b) Stage of Voluntary Socialization,** the persons residing in India are able to get some kind of voluntary socialization in educational institutions, workplaces, big or small peer groups, and in various forms of associations. Besides their own mother tongue, they learn the local language/dialect and one of the regional or national languages, and act on the local traditions, do's and don'ts of social life, and start mixing up with neighbourhood at ground levels. They associate with the people in other non-economic activities and find some small space in community life. They make adjustment with others regarding their social activities, marriage, birth and death rites and other socio-religious occasions. Some of them, at informal levels, start participating in local politics. As they tend to obey laws and authorities, they usually stand in favour of peace. Socialization at this stage takes about 20 years.

The third **(c) Stage of Coexistence** takes them closer to other communities. In view of their past experience, most of the persons belonging to various religions and sects learn to co-exist and live together, and see other's faith, practices and forms of worship with similar respect. At this level, the impact of Hindu religion appears predominant. It permits all paths to seek God or Truth. Under the prevailing system of governance, they accept principle of majority rule. It includes the consideration to the interests of minorities also. They begin to believe that in the present democratic Indian set-up there are various ways and means to ventilate their grievances and get redress through various agencies and institutions. Both of them accept the socio-economic contours of the Indian political system. These persons begin to understand the role and importance of various jobs, professions, vocations and forms of earnings. They pay respect to all of them. They also happen to come closer and get acquainted with each other's culture, language, traditions etc. Hindus, Muslims and others reside fearlessly in the mixed colonies and grow a sense of brotherhood. It requires about 20 years to pass through this stage.

The fourth **(d) Stage of Active Participation** mostly relates to the people engaged in some public or private employment. These people believe in paying taxes. Such people take part in social service and elections and political parties. They are in touch with press and media. They also learn to discard gender discrimination. They work hard for worldly welfare and pursue social justice. At the fifth **(e) Stage of Indianism** a person begins to belong to the category of 'political community' who regards the Indian State as superior to everything else in worldly matters. Following the nature, features and form underlying the values of the Indian political system, they find themselves closer to Indian culture. Such acculturization takes him to the idea of India as his or her motherland. The idea of India as motherland motivates them to adopt and understand land-oriented 'cultural nationalism' growing in India for the last several centuries. Culturalism connotes here granting supremacy to Indianism. They consider their own cultures standing next to Indianism. In this way, they reach at the end of the process of Indianization or Indianism. Indianism here means identification of a person's self with the interests of Indian State. His Indianism leads him to make personal sacrifices for the development and defence of adopted country. Now, at the last **(f) Stage of Future Expectations,** at least some of the Indians begin to realize that the world is moving fast towards liberalization, privatization and globalization (LPG). All economies are coming at the common counter of WTO, World Bank, IMF and others. Old barriers upheld by the individual nation-states are breaking down. World peace directed by the UN is a common concern. Some of the leaders, managers, producers, elite, information technologists and the like are reaching that stage.

Stage of Deviation, Fight and Change

After the first stage of existence, along with the second stage of voluntary socialization there may prevail an unwanted stage of deviation, fight and change. It includes attributes given on p. 364 of negative Indianity, from one to ten. All of them have been discussed earlier.[3]

Evaluating Indianity in India

After analyzing the concept of Indianity and formulating a scale to measure it, it is possible for us to identify how many persons out of the total population of India are either on positive or negative side of the scale. People on the negative side can also be divided in groups. These groups may be related to different steps. These steps are shown in brackets. Presently, on the basis of secondary resources, in India, there are 2 lakh jihadi terrorists (1-3), 50 lakh anti-Indians (4-5), and 3 crore social destructionists (6-10). There can be several from low to higher levels of negative Indianity. As the social destructionists can be socialized satisfactorily in due course of time, the real threat remains only from 52 lakh persons.

In the same manner, persons inculcating positive variables (17) of Indianity can also be divided on the basis of values given to them. Within each variable, there can be of several levels—very good, good, average, below average, rejectables etc. The total of values of all variable is 660. Accordingly, there can be out of 660, of values obtained in a soldier 600, ordinary teacher 450, average leader 400, business man 300 and a corrupt clerk 120.

'Indianity' is comparatively a stable concept. Indianization is a continuously changing dynamic process. Indians can be shown standing at a particular stage shown on the scale of the Indianization process. As stated earlier, there are six stages of the positive Indianization:

(a) Stage of Existence
(b) Stage of Voluntary Socialization
(c) Stage of Co-existence
(d) Stage of Active Participation
(e) Stage of Indianism
(f) Stage of Expectations of 21st Century

Proportion of population relating to the negative Indianism has to be deducted from the total population which comes about 105-2=103 crore. This part of negative Indianity cannot be included in the category of Indians. Persons belonging to that category are inflicting greater harm to the cause of India. Contemporary notion of Indianism found in the population pursuing positive form of Indianity can be indicated. It can be put in various stages on the basis of their Indianization. However, it should be kept in mind that a part of population can be put at more than one stage, e.g., some people belonging to (c) stage of coexistence may also be found in (d) stage of active participation and also in (e) stage of Indianization. A percentage of population shown in one particular stage cannot be exclusive. The whole population can be shown in terms of percentage. Position of members of various religions can also be shown in terms of percentages at various stages of the scale of Indianization process.

Position of Indianization of population of India—general and religion-wise—has been shown in Table 3.

Table 3

Approximate Condition of Indianization of the People living in India (2004)

Population/Religion & Stages	*General (103 crores)*	*Hindu (80 crores)*	*Muslim (12 crores)*	*Sikhs (4 crores)*	*Christians (4 crores)*	*Jains/ Buddhists etc. (2+1 crores)*
(a) Stage of Existence	10	10	40	5	5	1
(b) Stage of Voluntary Socialization	70	20	40	10	5	3
(c) Stage of Coexistence	50	20	10	30	30	30
(d) Stage of Active Participation	30	10	10	30	30	50
(e) Stage of Indianization	15	10	5	30	10	30
(f) Stage of Expectations of 21st Century	5	10	0.5	25	20	30

As shown above, percentages of total number of inhabitants living in India in general category presently appears at various stages of Indianization Process in the Table 4.

Table 4

Stages of Indianization Process

Stage	*Level*	*Present % of population*
(a) Stage of Existence	VI	10%
(b) Stage of Voluntary Socialization	V	70%
(c) Stage of Coexistence	IV	50%
(d) Stage of Active Participation	III	30%
(e) Stage of Indianism	II	15%
(f) Stage of Future Expectations	I	5%
(g) Stage of Deviation, Fight and Change (first three steps only)	Nil	1%

It may be important to point out that this Indianization process has so far been operating on voluntary basis. As such, about 40 per cent of the population is in a *dormant* condition from the viewpoint of Indianity. About 40 per cent is *neutral*. Its *active* or *participating* part of population is not more than 17 per cent. The rest are anti-Indian nor non-Indian. Unless its over 90 per cent part is equipped with Indianity, India cannot expect to be a strong and viable first-rate nation.[4] This task, it may be suggested, of Indianization of the people must be taken by some high powered agency or corporate body. The latter would keep watch and organize each and every step/stage of the Indianization process in direct or indirect manner.

Notes

1. Samuel P. Huntington, *Who Are We? America's Great Debate*, Penguin, 2004; and Arun Shourie, *Harvesting Our Souls: Missionaries, Their Design, Their Claims*, Delhi: ASA, 2000.
2. In 'Identity', See back Chapter 21, "Identity and Socialization of Indian Muslims".
3. Supra, p. 359.
4. See, infra, Chapter 25, "Challenges of Globalization to Indian (Hindatva) Democracy".

VII

Indian Democracy and Globalization

24

State and Democracy in the SAARC Countries

The theory and efficacious mechanism of liberal democracy has been evolved by the West as a complete piece. But hardly any scholar from East or West has pointed out whether the developing countries, irrespective of their different levels of modernization, should take up their model of democracy at one stretch or there are certain stages or partial formulations of democracy which they should adhere to. When some of them attempted to adopt in toto, or even substantially, they have experienced great difficulties, even faced failures. In particular, the countries of South Asia are passing through this experimental stage of democracy, playing trial and error. They have not found any readymade solution for their problems. One of the main goals of this paper is to determine the location of a polity on the path of growth of democracy and also assess its impact on their governance, and ability to face forces of globalization.[1]

In these countries, governance is an outcome of interaction between state and democracy. All these countries have had state in some form. Democracy in some form has been introduced by the state. For a while both interact with each other. In the beginning state generates democracy and opens more and more avenues for it. Later on, democracy begins to reorient and widen the scope of state. At the highest level of this interactive development, democracy turns into an independent force and runs and operates all the affairs of the state. But, the process, as it happened in Pakistan in October 1999 and in Nepal June 2002 and 2005, may also move in reverse direction. However, a democracy may also have to face unprecedented forces like globalization,[2] terrorism and the like and may get changed or damaged in the encounter. It can deal with them successfully if it is mature and viable.

In the present context of international terrorism, the liberals believe that democracies do not fight wars with one another. But, the democratic peace theories do not claim that democracies are less war-prone than non-democracies. Most of the nation-states have reconciled to the fact that there is no alternative (TINA) to liberalism and democracy. Two arguments are often advanced: one, democratic states evolve political culture of arriving decisions through consensus and compromise, and, two, democratic political culture exercises institutional constraints on decision-making. Of the 416 wars between sovereign states recorded between 1816-1980 only 12 were fought between democracies.[3] The growth of democracies gained momentum after the end of World War II when many of the Third World countries also embraced democratic form of polity. Apart from adopting democratic set-up, now, they have to face the dominating phenomenon of globalization. It operates in the realm of politics, culture, economics and security. Democratic peace is considered closely related to political globalization, but deep tension exists between globalization and democracies. When the state's monopoly over its national economy reduces, its power to provide social security diminishes. "As governments fail to deliver on promises, the gap between them and the people widens, producing a large 'democratic deficit' in the process."[4] It transforms into neurotic celebration of the past. Religious fundamentalism and the resort to ethnicism are its usual manifestations.[5] Now, 'governance' has taken place of simple economic liberalization. In the latest phase of globalization, a new basis for categorization of the states is appearing—"pre-modern, modern and post-modern states".[6] Most of the countries of South Asia belong to first two categories.[7] The present analysis intends to enable scholars to make an estimate of the capacity of the South Asian polities to deal with the force of globalization.

Diagram 1
Ideal Type of Liberal Democracy

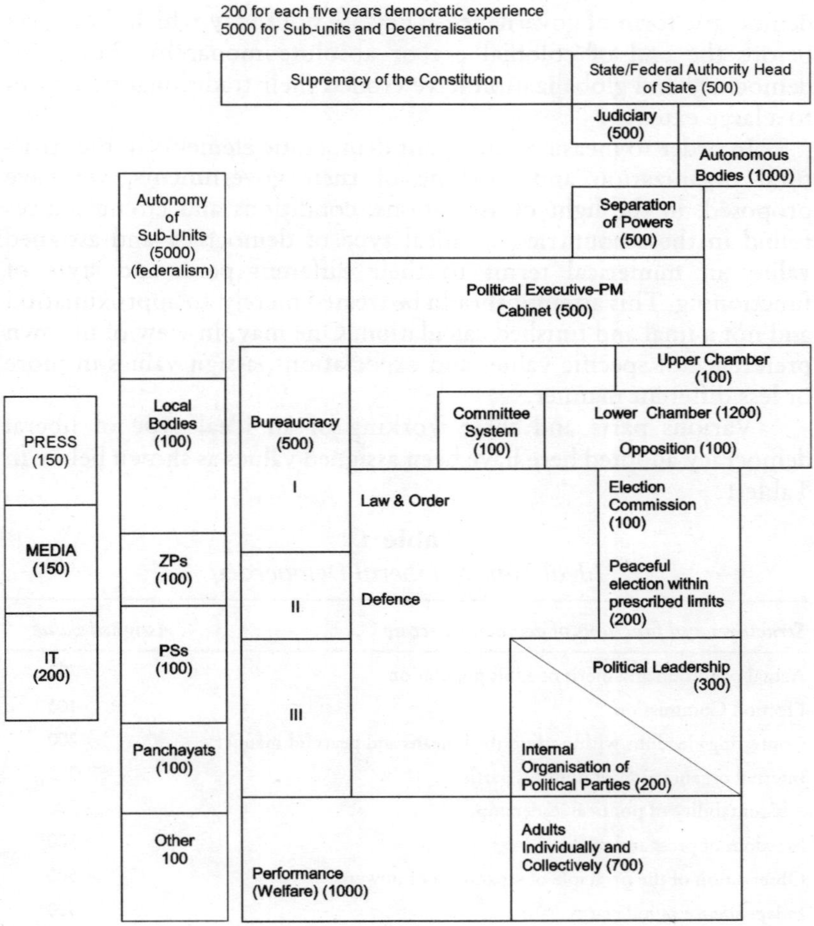

Guidelines

In this direction, we have firstly taken into account the main parts and important processes of an ideal type of a working democracy (see Diagram 1) acceptable to almost all scholars and political leaders. There is a visible trend in all the SAARC countries to move towards a democratic form of governance. They are not today which they were before the end of colonial era or absolute monarchy. Forces of democracy and globalization have eroded their traditional structures to a large extent.

In order to measure important democratic elements in the structural organization and working of their governments, we have proposed, in the light of aspirations, conditions and circumstances found in these countries, an ideal type of democracy and assigned values in numerical terms to their different parts and style of functioning. This attempt should be treated merely an approximation and not a final and finished calculation. One may, in view of his own preference of specific values and expectations, assign values in more or less different manner.

Various parts and their working of an ideal type of liberal democracy adopted here have been assigned values as shown below in Table 1.

Table 1

Ideal Type of Liberal Democracy

Structures and functions of democratic set-up	*Assigned value*
Actual condition and merit of adult population	700
Election Commission	100
Contesting elections within prescribed means and peaceful manner	200
Internal organization of political parties	200
Accountability of political leadership	300
Freedom of press and media	500
Observation of the principle of separation of powers	500
Independence of judiciary	500
Head of state/federal authority	500
Legislature	1500
Lower chamber	1200
Opposition	100

Contd...

Contd...

Committee system	100
Upper chamber	100
Bureaucracy (Grade I, II and III)	500
Autonomous bodies and decentralization	1000
Political executive, cabinet and PM	500
Maximum or total of evaluation of the polity in the present form	7000
Add 200 for each five years of democratic experience of a polity	
Add 5,000 for sub-unit autonomy in case of its being a Federation	

It has been our experience that the quality of democratic structures adopted by these countries and their working is lower than the levels of ideal type of democracies. They have been evaluated individually, and attainments have been compared with each other. This has been done keeping only their preceding and present term in view. We are not directly concerned with their past phase or probable form in future.

These values have been further elaborated. Each item has been given five grades, e.g., for an assignment having value of 50, has been divided 10 each, that is a=50, b=40, c=30, d=20 and e=10. Other assignments may be calculated accordingly. Each structure and functioning of the polity has further been detailed in the manner given below in Table 2:

Table 2

Detailed Distribution of Values for the Items (Structures and Functioning) of Democracy

1.	People – Total Value	700
	It consists of the individual with his collectivity individual, his health, intelligence, character, personality and impression	50
	Traits of collectivity	50
	Political awareness and exercise of franchise	50
	Integration of basic values in society	50
	Fundamental rights in practice	50
	Literacy level	50
	Affinity towards religion, creative-negative	50

Contd...

Contd...

	Employment	100
	Deference towards law and authorities	50
	Social equality – women, depressed classes and others	100
	Others	100
2.	Election Commission and Peaceful Contest within Limits – Total Value	300
	Independence	50
	Impartiality	50
	Efficiency and regularity	50
	Peaceful and within limits contest	150
3.	Leadership and Political Parties – Total Value	500
	Political leadership – personality, its representativeness, culture, cohesion, values and accountability 50 each	300
	Political parties – plurality and internal democracy 50, resources 50, change in top leadership 50, status and working conditions of party members 50	200
4.	Freedom of Press, Media and Hi-tech Information – Total Value	500
	Freedom of press, national, regional and local	150
	TV and radio	150
	Internet, telephones etc.	200
5.	Separation of Powers – Total Value	500
	Presidential system – Executive 200, Legislature 150, Judiciary 150	
	Parliamentary – Executive and Legislature 400, Judiciary 100	
6.	Independence of Judiciary – Total Value	500
	Length and complexity of judicial process	100
	Cost and time	100
	Knowledge and expertise of judges	100
	Confidence and satisfaction of people	100
	Integrity and independence	100
7.	Head of State/Federal Authority – Total Value	500
8.	Organization and Working of Parliament – Total Value	1500
	Distribution of powers between the two Chambers	100
	Lower chamber-vote base	200
	Representativeness	200
	Deliberations	200
	Control over the executive	200
	Political leadership and accountability	500
	Control over bureaucracy	100

Contd...

Contd...

9.	Permanent Bureaucracy – Total Value	500
	Neutrality	100
	Expertise	100
	Responsibility	100
	Integrity	100
	Subordination	100
10.	Autonomous Bodies and Decentralization – Total Value	1000
	Autonomous bodies of education	100
	Accounts and audit	100
	Planning	100
	Distribution of finance	100
	Civil services	100
	Decentralization of powers among local bodies	100
	Panchayati Raj institutions	300
	Higher institutions of learning	100
11.	Political Executive, Cabinet and Prime Minister (President) – Total Value	500
	Effectiveness of leadership	200
	Experience, knowledge and training	100
	Control over bureaucracy	100
	Accountability	100

Performance total value 1,000 (not to be calculated in the evaluation of democracy).

Total marks 1,000 can have five gradations: I between 1,000 to 750, II 750-500, III 500-300, IV 300-150, and V below 150.

If a country has experience of running a democracy for a term of five years, it would have proportionately 200 marks for such each term.

If a country has federal polity on constitutional basis, it would have another maximum of 5,000 marks in addition to 7,000. Maximum marks can be divided as from point 1 to 17 in addition. Evaluation of the structures or functioning of non-federal or unitarian parts of polities of South Asia during the preceding and present period (2001-2002) has been tentatively shown in Table 3. The presentation reflects their interactive relationship between state and democracy.

Table 3

Comparative Valuation of Democracy in SAARC Countries

S. No.	*Items of Democracy with Maximum Value*		*India*	*Pakistan*	*Bangla Desh*	*Nepal*	*Sri Lanka*	*Bhutan*	*Maldives*
1	People	700	300	150	200	200	300	100	100
2	Election Commission, peaceful election within prescribed limits	300	250	50	250	200	250	50	25
3	Leadership & Political Parties	500	300	150	300	300	300	100	50
4	Freedom of Press, Media & Information Technology	500	500	400	400	400	400	200	100
5	Separation of Powers	500	300	200	100	300	300	200	100
6	Independence of Judiciary	500	400	300	400	250	400	150	100
7	Head of State/Federal Authority	500	300	150	400	300	400	100	50
8	Organization & Working of Parliament	1500	800	200	600	400	700	300	100
9	Permanent Bureaucracy	500	300	300	250	200	250	150	150
10	Autonomous Bodies & Decentralization	1000	200	100	100	50	100	50	10
11	Political Executive, Cabinet & PM	500	350	100	300	200	300	200	300
	Performance (not to be calculated)	1000	450	200	150	150	250	100	100
	Total	7000	4000	2050	3300	2800	3700	1600	1085

Table 4

Important Constants of SAARC Countries, 2001-2002

S. No.	Name of Country	Population & Crises	Religion (%)	Ethnic Groups (%)	Language (%)	Territory & Natural Resources	Modernization (A B C), Below Poverty Line & Literacy (%)	Military Power I, II, III or IV & Expenditure
1	India (Republic of India)	1,02,99,91,145 poverty, population, terrorism, J&K	Hindu 81.3, Muslim 12, Christians 2.3, Others 2.5	Indo-Aryan 72, Dravidian 25, Others 3	Hindi 40, Bangla 8.2, Telagu 7.8, Marathi 7.3, Tamil 6.2, Urdu 5.1, Gujarati etc.	32,87,593 sq.km.	B 35 62	I (Nuclear) 2.5 of GDP
2	Pakistan (Islamic Republic)	14,46,16,639 jihadi terrorism, democracy	Muslims 97(Sunni 77 Shia 20) Others 3	Panjabi, Sindhi, Baloch, Pathan, Mahajir	Panjabi 48, Sindhi 12 Siraiki 10, Pashtu 8, Urdu 8(official) etc.	8,03,940 sq.km.	B 42 42.7	I (Nuclear) 3.9 of GDP
3	Bangla Desh (Peoples Republic)	12,91,94,224 poverty, natural calamities	Muslim 88.3, Hindu 10.5, Others 1.2	Bengali	Bangla (official)	1,44,000 sq.km.	C 35.6 38.1	III 1.8 of GDP

Contd...

Contd...

4	Nepal (Kingdom of Nepal)	2,47,02,119 poverty, inflation, terrorism, democracy	Hindu 90, Buddhist 5, Muslim 3, Others 2	Newars, Indian Tibetan, Gurungs, Magars, Tamangs, Bhotias, Sherpas, Rais	Nepali (official) and 20 others	1,40,800 sq.km.	C 42 27.5	IV .9 of GDP
5	Sri Lanka (Democratic Socialist Rep)	1,94,08,635 ethnic war, religious fundamentalism	Buddhist 70m, Hindu 15, Christstain 8, Muslim 7	Singhali 74, Tamil 18, Mors 7	Singhali74, (official), Tamil (official), Others 8	65,610 sq.km.	C 22 93.2	III 3 of GDP
6	Bhutan (Kingdom of Bhutan)	20,49,412 poverty, Nepali refugees, democracy	Lamaist Buddhist 75, Hindu 25, Theocracy	Bhote 50, Nepalese 35, Others 7	Dzongkaha (official)	47,000 sq.km.	NA NA	V 4.2 of GDP
7	Maldives (Rep. of Maldives)	3,10,764 low level of sea, no defense	Sunni Muslims	Indian and Singhalese, Arab	South Indian languages	300 sq. km.	Nil Unemployment nil	Nil Security service

Afghanistan has been included as its eight member in its 13th conference. It has area: 6,52,225 sq. km., population: 2.60 crore, language: Pashto, Dari, Religion: Islam, Life: 46 years, Exports: fruits, wool, opium

However, this numerical analysis keeps constants of each country in mind. These constants are shown in Table 5.

Analysis

Each polity is conceptually a complex whole of 'state' (power structure) and 'democracy' (human dynamics) and constants. Constants form parameters of interaction operating amid these two variables—state and democracy.

There is a struggle between force of state (thesis) and the elements of democracy (anti-thesis) generating an outcome (synthesis) of performance. This struggle goes on until democracy wins over the divisive and coercive elements of the state, and establishes its supremacy. If the elements of democracy remain weak and disunited, the state (monarch, dictator or military ruler) overpowers and restrains democracy. State and its structures serve the vested interests of rulers and work for their stability or supremacy of might over the people.

A state covering some distance on the path of democracy may remain static or go ahead after sometime as it has happened respectively in Bhutan and Nepal. Democracy may engage in run-and-return operation as it has been occurring in Nepal. It may work at the lower levels of democracy and rest there like the Maldivian polity. There are democracies of Sri Lanka and Bangla Desh which went ahead of 'state', and had moved in the direction of liberal mode of democracy, but are wavering under their own unbearable burden of democratic forces.[8]

Comparison of Capacities for Democracy

Comparative valuation of the items of democracy in the governance of SAARC countries makes an attempt to analyze all the important variables of these polities. One can explain the differences among the same items of values on the basis of marks in general and five grades allotted to the items of individual polities. Performance level of each SAARC country has been examined on the basis of marking of their values under 11 major heads (see Table 2). Accordingly, the valuation of the democratic elements interacting with state structures in the governance of these countries has been shown here. This has been done in view of the constants, such as size, number of people or ethnicity etc. of the individual polities. Each SAARC country out of maximum of 7,000 marks allotted to an ideal type of liberal democracy has tentatively obtained following evaluation:

Table 5
Evaluation of SAARC Politics

Name of Polity	*Evaluation*
India	4000 (57.14%)
Sri Lanka	3700 (52.85%)
Bangla Desh	3300 (47.14%)
Nepal	2800 (40.00%)
Pakistan	2050 (29.28%)
Bhutan	1600 (22.85%)
Maldives	1085 (15.5%)

In the total calculation or summing up of the values of individual countries, their performance or achievement, i.e., systemic output has been kept separate.

If a state remains static and does not cooperate with democracy, it is likely to produce an another state or states, as it happened in Pakistan in 1972 and now is happening in Sri Lanka. If a state evolves into a democracy and the latter does not serve the people or fulfils their aspirations, it would return to state for seeking law and order as it has been happening in Nepal.

In the context of SAARC countries, when a polity crosses the capacity range of 50 per cent, it does not mean that it has given up its state structure. Both may go along with and pull together as India has demonstrated all these years. However, a populist democracy may shatter its state structure. In that situation, out of prevailing chaos or turmoil more than one state, as it happened in erstwhile Pakistan in 1972, may emerge. Several factors can contribute to its dismemberment, such as fundamentalism, ethnicity, terror, globalization etc. Without reinforcing and supporting structures of 'state' and 'democracy', a polity is likely to remain unable to face the forces of terror and globalization. Polities having either weak 'state' or populist 'democracy' easily succumb to them. There is no escape route.

Therefore, the remedies for the growing polities of SAARC region are available in different ways. In case they have weak state, they should stand closer to a polity having strong state. If they have strong state but weak democracy, they should follow and learn experience of a strong democracy. However, a major polity having both strong state and viable democracy must defend itself from the onslaught of globalization or terror.

Threat of Globalization

Except India, hardly any other polity in South Asia is able to face the avalanche of globalization. It requires a strong democratic state. Globalization tends to weaken both state and democracy. It tends to isolate governance from them. Globalization governs and controls weak polities through IMF, WB, WTO and MNCs. Market, an instrument of expansion and imperialism, takes over democracy—the instrument of legitimization of political authority and the institutionalization of politics on the principle of welfare and equality. In democracy governance is the exercise of economic, political and administrative authority to manage the country's affairs at all level with the objective to promote social cohesion, integration and well-being of the population. Globalization having emerged from the rich North stands against the spirit of equal social development and welfare state and operates through powerful stateless transnational corporations, which neglect the problems of poverty, unemployment, corruption and the like. The process of globalization, even in India, is dividing the people between the rich and the poor, making the state a capitalist institution. The World Bank's Human Development Report, 2001 shows that 500 million people in the region of South Asia witnessed a decline in real income during the 1990s and the benefits of growth have been confined mostly to segments of the urban educated population. It is being felt that the Indian State is fastly becoming a tool in the hands of business class.

It is now clear that there can be four stages of development of a South Asian polity: (a) state, (b) democracy, (c) both state and democracy, and (d) encounter with globalization. India, despite several difficulties, stands at (d). Sri Lanka is struggling between (c) and (d). Nepal and Bangladesh stand at (b). Pakistan is operating amid (b) and (c).[10] For a long time Bhutan and Maldives are resting between

(a) and (b). Items of values and their gradation displayed with the ideal type of liberal democracy can be helpful in explaining the reasons for their present position. They can also suggest the way to go ahead in right direction. But, a polity operating at whatever stage or location can also go back.

Notes

1. India's Union Cabinet approved an agreement to set up the South Asian Free Trade Area (SAFTA). It is the first step towards evolving a major economic block on the lines of European Union and North American Free Trade Area (NAFTA). It would result into free movement of goods, services and personnel across the SAARC countries. The biggest beneficiaries of the SAFTA would be the least developed countries (LDCs) in the region including Maldives and Bangladesh. The two countries would get unhindered access to Indian markets beginning January 1, 2006. *Hindustan Times*, December 30, 2005.
2. Atul Bharadwaj, 'Man, State and the Myth of Democratic Peace', *Strategic Analysis,* Vol. 26, No. 2, April-June 2002, pp. 305-06.
3. The Politics of Peace, *The Economist*, April 1, 1995, p. 17.
4. Bharadwaj, op. cit.
5. Prem Shanker Jha, *Democracy, Globalisation and War: New Myths to save the West from the rest*, World Affairs, April-June 2001, 5 (2): 34.
6. Samir Amin, "Economic Globalisation and Political Universalism: Conflicting Issues?", in Barbara Harriss-White (eds.), *Globalization and Insecurity: Political, Economic and Physical Challenges*, Palgrave, Oxford, 2002, p. 63; Ian Clark, *Globalization and International Relations Theory*, Oxford, 1999.
7. For example, Nepal, one of the world's poorest countries with an annual per capita income of around $220 and deep pockets of poverty and socio-economic disparity has turned into a good breeding ground for radical groups and their supporters.—Yubaraj Ghimire, "Nepal's agony", *Seminar* 517 Securing South Asia, September, 2002, pp. 48-52; and King Jigme Singye of Bhutan—who famously prefers 'gross national happiness' to gross national product—is trying to end his country's isolation in an globalized world by opting for democracy and modernization. See *Hindustan Times*, December 21, 2005.
8. Mahendra Rajapaksa who won Presidential election in November 2005. Rajapaksa has made it clear that the Tamil demand for a "Tamil

Homeland" in the North East with the right to self-determination and secession was not acceptable to his government. *Hindustan Times*, November 26, 2005.

The United States has warned the warring LTTE that if it returned to war, it would find the cost to be high. *Hindustan Times*, January 12, 2006.

9. The Thirteenth SAARC Conference held in Daaca in November 2005 has decided to made it a Free Trade Area. *Rajasthan Patrika*, November 13, 2005.
10. Pakistan has 25-50 nuclear warheads and India has between 100 and 150. In May 1998, when India and Pakistan conducted nuclear tests, South Asia truly did become, as President Clinton said, 'the most dangerous place in the world.'—Mahnaz Ispahani, "Alternative South Asian futures", *Seminar* 517 Securing South Asia, September 22, 2002.

25

Challenges of Globalization to Indian Democracy

Globalization is a super-transnational force. Global governance is its manifestation as well as management. To succeed in the 21st century there should be a global form of democracy for India. The key elements of Indian democracy may be (a) welfare, (b) participation, (c) representation, (d) equality, (e) freedom, (f) power, (g) wealth, (h) morality/spirituality, or (i) a mix of all or a few other elements of democracy. But, the Hindus of India lag far behind. They fail to appreciate the form, extent and avalanche of globalization and look ahead of it. For this Hindatva has to be oriented properly.

Globalization is the emergence of a complex web of interconnectedness by which our lives are increasingly shaped by events that occur, and decisions that are made, at a great distance from us. It means geographical distance is of declining relevance, and that territorial boundaries of the nation-states are becoming less significant. It is the deepening as well as the broadening of the political process.[1] Anthony Giddens considers it as the intensification of worldwide social relations. Kenichi Ohmae finds it as a 'borderless world'. It is linked to the growth of 'supra-territorial' relations between peoples, where territory matters less because an increasing range of connections have a 'trans-world' or 'trans-border' character. There is a single increasingly integrated and universalized world economy largely operating across state frontiers and also beyond the frontiers of state ideology and state-controlled mechanisms.

Reality of Globalization

Globalization is used to refer to a process, a policy, a marketing strategy, a predicament, and an ideology. But it is not a single process but a complex of processes, often overlapping and interlocking processes, but also, at time, contradictory and oppositional ones. Globalization can be defined as a complex set of distinct but related processes—economic, cultural, social but also political and military—through which social relations have developed global reach and significance. In this sense globalization includes the development of transnational relations of many kinds as well as specifically global forms.[2]

Briefly, globalization stands for (i) cross-border relations or internalization, e.g., movement of goods, investments, people, capital, communications, ideas etc., (ii) removal of regulatory barriers to international trade, travel, financial transfers, transactions and communications, i.e., liberalization; and (iii) increase of trans-border relations making out a 'global village'.

Forms and Contents

Globalization takes many forms: political, economic, cultural, and the like. Political globalization is appearing in erosion of national sovereignty and growing intervention and importance of international organizations and non-state actors. Some of them are: UNO, NATO, European Union (EU), World Bank, International Monetary Fund (IMF), World Trade Organization (WTO), Organization for Economic Cooperation and Development (OECD) and the like. Nation-state is being taken over by inter-governmentalism, supra-nationalism and trans-nationalism.

(1) Political globalization has pronounced neo-liberal or free-market ideological character. They find it as global capitalism which is sure to generate new forms of misery, exploitation and injustice. The Third World critics of globalization feel it as a new method of old colonialists to exploit the developing countries. This neo-colonialism is more dangerous than the earlier one as in this

process the industrialized powers exploit the developing counties without responsibility. To increase profits, the multi-national corporations/enterprises (MNCs/MNEs), employ business process outsourcing (BPO), medical transcription etc. in the developing countries. Emanuel Wallerstein and Samir Amin have observed that globalization favours the developed countries and impoverishes the developing countries. It is defined as the process of enriching the rich and impoverishing the poor. Globalization provokes man's desire for materialistic life and to satisfy these he is instigated to borrow and entraps him in a vicious circle. As a result, inequality between 'core' and 'peripheral' countries increases gradually.

(2) In economic globalization there is a shift from a world of distinct national economies to global economy in which production is internationalized and financial capital flows freely and instantly between countries.

(3) Cultural globalization is the process whereby information, commodities and images that have been produced in one part of the world enter into a global flow that tends to 'flatten out' cultural differences between nations, regions and individuals. It is sometimes seen as a process of McDonaldization.

Thus, globalization is linked to homogenization of cultural, social, economic and political diversities in which all watch the same television programmes, buy the same commodities, eat the same food, and support the same sport and celebrities.

Uni-polar Global System of US Supremacy

After the collapse of bi-polar system, the United States claims that it has won the cold war and being a victor state it has legitimate right to re-shape and re-redesign the post-cold war international scenario. As such, there is the phenomenon of intervention which has become a fact of international life. On the pretext of self-defence or under the garb of issues like human rights, non-proliferation, weapons of mass destruction, intellectual property rights etc., the powerful states are employing the weapon of intervention to serve their interests against powerless states like Serbia, Afghanistan and Iraq. Kofi Annan has already expressed his deep concern against the doctrine of 'pre-emptive military intervention' warning that it could set stage for a 'lawless use of force' neglecting UN and without any credible justification.[3]

Petras and Veltmeyer have dismissed the 'inevitability bogey': The 'inevitability' of globalization is a critical issue. But, a more critical issue, perhaps, is what the discourse on globalization is designed to hide and obfuscate: the form taken by imperialism in the current, increasingly worldwide capitalist system for organizing economic production and society.

The inevitability of globalization and the adjustment or submission of peoples all over the world to free market capitalism depends on the capacity of the dominant and ruling classes to bend people to their will and convince people that their interests are the people's interests, make them see the interests of capital as their own. It also depends on the capacity of these dominant classes and their ideologues to undermine the growing resistance to the model of free market.

In the ultimate analysis globalization is not a global integration by breaking the barriers across and among the nations through a global compact for turning the world into a 'global village'.

It is common knowledge that the UN is often unable to exert an effective influence on global economic and political issues of critical importance. This is due to what may be called as 'democracy deficit', which prevents effective multilateralism—a multilateralism that is based on a democratically evolved global consensus. Therefore, reform and restructuring of the United Nations system can alone provide a crucial link in an expanding chain of efforts to refashion international structures, imbuing them with a greater degree of participatory decision-making, so as to make them more representative of contemporary realities.[4]

The Ugly Face of Globalization

The thesis of Robert Woog and Vladimir Dimitrov is the wider the process of economic globalization, the narrower the circle of those who benefit from it. The free, global market has begun to appear less and less free. Both trade and investment seem to be governed by more and more complicated laws and procedures in favour of monstrously rich economic and financial corporations—the real beneficiaries of the free global market. With the passing of each day, these unaccountable corporations, with unlimited life, size and power, are taking ever-increasing control over national economies—largely to the detriment of the individual consumer, worker, neighbour and citizen. One can find much evidence that corporate-led globalization negatively affects the environment, financial stability, equity, security, food safety, health and cultural diversity of millions of people. Some of the observable facts for India are:

1. The number of the countries classified as the 'most poor' in the world has doubled in the last several years. There is a tendency for the governments in the western 'free' democracy to act as the 'armed' militia for the large financial corporations and banks.

   On a continent where only a minority of the population has electricity, let alone Internet connections, it is difficult not to have considerable sympathy for the sceptics' case, which, in its essence, remains valid.
2. Most international trade is still between the rich countries of Western Europe, North America and Japan, where less than 15 per cent of the world's population is located.[4] Also, while foreign exchange may be highly mobile, land and infrastructure are usually immobile, and even factories are costly to move. Moreover, while there is deregulation in certain areas of economic life, elsewhere, new regulations have been introduced and old ones are rigorously enforced.
3. Patents, copyrights, franchises, business secrets and tariffs shield major western corporations, and the US and European Union agriculture is heavily protected. Further, whilst what Pierre Bourdieu calls the 'left hand' of the state, has been on decline, its 'right hand', which tends to benefit big capital, remains strong (this is notably true of western military might).

Finally, it is governments that are represented at the WTO and the IFIs, and it is governments that have implemented the various neo-liberal policies responsible for promoting globalization (Massey, 2000: 1).

This characterization is underlined when we consider the data on inequality, which reveal increasing divergence, both between and within countries. According to the World Bank, "In 1960 the per capita GDP in the richest 20 countries was 18 times that in the poorest 20 countries. By 1995 this gap had widened to 37 times".

Another study, which compared Western Europe and its 'offshoots' in North America and Australasia with Africa and Asia, showed that the ratio between average income levels in the two regions changed from eleven-to-one in 1950 to twelve-to-one in 1973, and then to sixteen-to-one in 1992 (Moody, 1997: 54). The process was uneven though, and according to Larry Elliot (1999: 16), whereas, in 1960, per capita incomes in Africa were three times higher than in Asia, now, they are less than half as high.

Worldwide, between 1960 and 1995, the gap between the income of the wealthiest 20 per cent of the world's population and the poorest 20 per cent increased from 30: 1 to 82: 1 (Marfleet, 1998: 96). In the next four years up to 1998, the net worth of the world's richest 200 people more than doubled, to reach over $1 trillion, a figure so great that, if they all provided a yearly donation of just 1 per cent of their wealth, it could be possible to provide universal access primary education. The combined assets of the top three—who included Bill Gates—were greater than the combined GNP of the 48 least developed countries (which provided a home for some 600 million people) (UNDP, 1999: 37, 39).

In the US itself, by 1997, the top 1 per cent owned over 40 per cent of all assets, more than 94 per cent of all other Americans combined. The bottom 90 per cent of Americans no longer share in the continued prosperity of America.

Joseph Kruth[5] presents four core issues of the 21st century in the following manner:

1. Environmental Degradation of Life Support Systems
2. The Growing Divide: Increasing Concentration of Wealth and Income
3. The Enormous Growth of Corporate Power
4. Learning to Become Citizens of the 21st Century

Hardly it is possible that individuals may educate themselves about how these financial systems work, who they benefit and how they can be changed? The real state of our society continues to be interpreted to obscure these facts by a media largely owned by corporations benefiting from these policies. Education should develop primarily the ability to discriminate among offered alternatives. Presently, it does not build the capacity to question basic assumptions and think of new alternatives. For this we have to understand the phenomenon of global governance.

Global Governance

Rosenau (1995: 16) notes that global governance consists of "systems of rule at all levels of human activity—from the family to the international organization—in which the pursuit of goals through the exercise of control has trans-national repercussions". According to the Commission on Global Governance (1995), "Governance is the sum of the many ways individuals and institutions, public and private, manage their common affairs. It is a continuing process through which conflicting or diverse interests may be accommodated and cooperative action may be taken. It includes formal institutions and regimes empowered to enforce compliance, as well as informal arrangements that people and institutions either have agreed to or perceive to be in their interest." At the global level, governance has been viewed primarily as inter-governmental relationships, but it must now be understood as also involving non-governmental organizations (NGOs), citizens' movements, multinational corporations, and the global capital market. Interacting with these are global mass media of dramatically enlarged influence.

According to Samuel M. Makinda, the concept of global governance, as distinct from 'good governance', refers to formal and informal sets of arrangements in global politics. It implies that states alone cannot manage global affairs, and therefore it accords roles to international governmental organizations (IGOs), non-governmental organizations (NGOs) and multinational corporations (MNCs).

Taking the concept a step further and perhaps bringing it closer to earth, Finkelstein (1995) defines it as "governing, without sovereign authority, relationships that transcend national frontiers. Global governance is doing internationally what governments do at home."[6]

Globalization evolves its own methods, means and mechanism of global governance. Still global governance is not world government. But is moving towards a form of world government exclusively dominated by G-7. David calls this process as 'transformationalism'.[7]

Key Role of WTO

Global governance related to the key multilateral economic institutions like the IMF, the World Bank and the WTO. The WTO, successor of GATT, divides global governance by means of various trade-related agreements, which are both technical as well as all-compassing general instruments.[8] It varied from TRIPs, TRIMs and agriculture to services, market access and dispute settlements. The World Bank and the IMF charted out a course of action for parties in dispute with each other. It is a remarkable instrument of governance. Corporate power globally is enormous and growing. It is hard to imagine that more than half of the top 100 economies in the world are now private businesses. Corporate power also grows significantly through international treaties. Many people are unaware of the World Trade Organization (WTO), yet it makes decisions which affect the future of everyone. Established in 1994 and located in Geneva, the WTO makes rules and regulations about health, safety and environmental standards worldwide. These standards are often based on industry requests, with little, if any, input from consumers.

The WTO has final authority over all of its decisions, and is more powerful for trade matters than any nation, including the US. All however is not bleak. On the positive side, over 600 non-profit organizations worldwide used the Internet to prevent adoption of one of the most offensive treaties, the Multilateral Agreement on Investment (MAI).

Global governance is a conceptual approach to describe how the world works politically in an era when a focus on the nation-state does not suffice.[9] There is purpose in the global order, and while no actor seems to control the outcomes, there are enough patterns of influence to suggest that some form of management occurs.

Erosion of Sovereignty

State sovereignty is like a living organism; it casts off its meanings as it evolves in response to the demands of global governance. In simple terms, sovereignty can be described as a principle that legitimizes internal political organization and serves as a mechanism for enhancing international order. It is, therefore, linked to both internal and global governance. Alan James makes distinction between three types of sovereignty. The first is external or juridical sovereignty, which is based on the notion that theoretically "the state has over it no other authority than that of international law". The second is internal or empirical sovereignty, which is based on the view that states have the right (and capacity) to control the people, resources and institutions within their territories. The third is individual or popular sovereignty, which is predicated on the claim that all people are entitled to fundamental freedoms and that states exercise control over them only with their consent. Empirical sovereignty and juridical sovereignty accord states rights and responsibilities that other international actors do not have.

The concept of global governance implicitly questions some understandings of sovereignty because it is based on the assumption that states and non-state actors are partners in the management of global affairs. Realists, who claim that states are the most important international actors, would regard global governance as a diminution of sovereignty. The realists' view of sovereignty is that theoretically each state is free to pursue its domestic and external affairs without outside interference. Hence, Hans Morgenthau's definition of sovereignty as "a centralized power that exercised its law-making and law-enforcing authority within a certain territory" appeared. On the other hand, liberals, who subscribe to the view that transnational forces play important roles in world politics, regard global governance as a necessary process of addressing anarchy in the absence of central authority. Liberals believe that sovereignty gives states the right to exercise control within their territories, but that this control is to be exercised with some degree of consent and legitimacy from society. For this reason, liberals associate empirical sovereignty with popular sovereignty. Constructivists, who consider sovereignty to be socially constructed, regard global governance as a part of the social construction and reconstruction of international society. The assumptions that underpin sovereignty date back to the Peace of Westphalia, which inaugurated a new 'international' legal order for Europe. The Westphalian regime, which brought about a break from the previous religious order, is best remembered for making the territorial state the cornerstone of the modern international system. Since then, the development and reinterpretation of sovereignty has closely mirrored the evolution of the state and the prevailing norms of global governance. Sovereignty has undergone various transformations in accordance with the prevailing norms of global governance. Whenever serious crises undermine the legitimizing principles of sovereignty, new norms are negotiated, and these norms often reflect the preferences of the hegemonic states.

Role of the UN

Globalization and global governance will go on with or without the UN. Global governance has so far reflected mainly the interests of western societies, but the UN has the potential to make it truly global. It has the potentiality to ensure that the ideas, norms and rules, which underpin global governance, reflect the diversity of values and interests in the world. The UN needs to work out its programmes in such a way that, wherever possible, racial, gender, cultural and economic inequalities are taken into account.

The UN appears to straddle the borderline between realism and liberalism, and it has lasted this long partly because it has been perceived by both realists and liberals to be in their interest. Realists care about the legitimacy of the UN, but for them this legitimacy is derived from the UN serving as an *instrument* of state interests. A UN without the potentiality to serve as a device through which states use their power to pursue national interests, has little legitimacy for the realists. There is no doubt that various organs of the UN, especially the Security Council, serve as a platform for power politics. What generally concerns Third World states is that most of the power within the UN is held by western countries, which dominate the international system politically, economically, technologically and militarily.

On the issues of democratization and participation, some liberals have argued that the UN has neglected non-state actors for too long. Hence, the increasing calls for the UN to involve the 'global civil society' more deeply in global governance. There is no doubt that a good number of NGOs have achieved phenomenal success in specific issue-areas. However, agreeing on a mechanism for their participation with the UN in global governance is likely to raise difficult questions. NGOs have the capacity to do a great deal, but they have no obligation to do anything. Voluntary organizations are not accountable, even in theory, to those whom they serve. The UN has been an agent of transformation. It has generated numerous ideas on such issues as development, the environment, human rights, women's rights and peacekeeping. In this respect, the UN has become a very important norm-setting organization. As the interests, preferences and identities of member-states are neither fixed nor exogenously given, the UN has participated, however marginally, in influencing the way they are defined and redefined.

However, there is a perception in the Third World that the UN's transformative power has been harnessed by the West and works to the detriment of non-western interests.

The exigencies of global governance in this millennium require the UN to rethink its norms, structures, procedures and practices. If the UN were to make a difference to global governance, it would need to address more seriously the imperative for democratization in its agencies, taking account of growing demands for transparency and popular participation. Greater openness cannot be achieved without creative efforts to recast sovereignty. It is incumbent upon the UN 'managers' to reinterpret the charter to reflect the new global realities. It would be a travesty if the UN Charter were to serve as a hindrance to the evolution of state sovereignty. The interpretive community is to reinterpret the charter consistently.

Programme and Achievements of Global Governance

Global governance refers to transnational networks, institution building, norm entrepreneurship, regime creation and the management of global change. It covers many issues, such as women's rights, human rights, development, democratization, the environment, security and investments. It has worked out some recent achievements, which include the treaty banning landmines, the Kyoto climate convention, the international criminal court, the World Trade Organization, and the 'new generation' UN peace-keeping operations. In a nutshell, global governance describes regimes or systems of rule, embracing both formal and informal regulatory mechanisms. Underlying global governance is tolerance and a willingness to manage differences and reconcile self/other, us/them and inside/outside. This can take place only where there is a common set of values, norms, beliefs, ideas and institutions. As these values evolve, the nature of global governance has necessarily to change. Indeed, global governance "is a broad, dynamic, complex process... that is constantly evolving and responding to changing circumstances". However, it is power that determines whose interests, rules and standards become 'global'. Thus, while global governance requires tolerance and accommodation of conflicting interests across national, racial, class, gender and ethnic boundaries, it is often the preferences of the most powerful actors that are accommodated.

Threat to Nation-States

Both globalization and global governance go together. They are proving threat to the nation-states.

It should be accepted that both of them have made some positive and fruitful contribution to the entire world. But, there is also a great need to be away and remove the evils caused by it. The world has to be safe and livable. They have to be opposed tooth and nail if globalization aims at dismantling nation-states and democracies. Otherwise, let the latter two continue in adjusted forms.

The 'spectre of globalization' haunts the earth. It has raised doubts about the relevance, role and even the need for nation-state at the end of the twentieth century.[10] If the trend continues, there would be neither 'state' nor 'nation' at least in developing countries.

Globalization is undermining democracy. Global governance concentrates economic power in the hands of few individuals. GATT/WTO, IMF, OECD (Organization for Economic Cooperation and Development), World Bank (International Bank for Reconstruction and Development), United Nations Conference on Trade and Development (UNCTD) and other financial institutions manage global political economy. The World Bank, IMF and WTO are expected to work in a coherent manner for it. Every member of the WTO has to accept in its entirety a common set of rules and disciplines covering goods, services and intellectual property. The WTO has legal and institutional foundation for enforcement of its decisions on disputes in the areas of goods, services and the protection of intellectual property rights.[11] Its General Council makes appropriate arrangements for effective cooperation with other inter-governmental organizations that have responsibilities related to the WTO. Other international organizations and agencies mentioned below also operate to regulate the global economy:

1. World Intellectual Property Organization;
2. International Organization for Standardization (IOS);
3. Coadex Alimentarious Commission;
4. International Office of Epizootics; and
5. International Plant Protection Office.

All political power and capacity to decide on behalf of global community is with the western world because of the 'unequal' nature of distribution of economic power among the nation-states, including making of important appointments on these bodies.

Global inequality has become quite acute. Structural inequality of power between the few developed centres of capitalism and a large majority of peripheral developing states has change the whole agenda of contemporary discourse where the very relevance of nation-state as a centre of decision-making for national management has become questionable. This gap has been further widened because of the concentration of finance capital in a 'few capitalist countries'.

Success of a nation-state depended on correct mixing of (a) identity, (b) legitimacy, and (c) security.[12] All of them began to erode during the era of globalization. Both Soviet Union and the US exercised the right of intervention in many sovereign countries. Few members and fewer votes from the developing countries find place on the boards of the IMF and the World Bank. Subscribing to the triad of human rights, free markets and democracy has been put as a condition precedent to them. Owing to expansion the TNCs (transnational corporations) and NGOs (non-governmental organizations) legitimacy of nation-states has lost their former shine. Global business has neutralized national boundaries. A part of power and identity has shifted upwards of the nation-states to the global agencies. About 90 per cent of foreign news and information in the print media is controlled by four news agencies of the North.

However, to counter-balance these trends, Henry Kissinger, the former US Secretary of State has suggested steps to make major progress in the emerging international order by involving all key nations to say to themselves that his is our system. This is not an American system or anybody's system. This is something we participated in creating it and we have an interest in maintaining it.[13]

Democracies and Environment in Danger

Globalization has set people to think about the political institutions, such as state, democracy and civil society. David Held, in search of a supera-national democracy at global level, observes it as a new international order involving the emergence of a global economic system which stretches beyond the control of a single state (even of dominant states), the expansion of network of transnational linkages and communications over the particular states have little influence, and the enormous growth in international organization which can limit the scope for action of most powerful states. The development of a global military order reduces the range of policies available to governments and their citizens. One can witness a crisis of global civilization. It involves a counter-revolution of the powerful against the weak. In much of the Third World the processes of urbanization and economic decline have gone with social chaos, anomie and nihilism.

With weakening inter-state borders, threats to environment are increasing. With the resistance of US and Australia and indifference of Russia and China towards Kyota Protocol (to enformce emission norms for prevention green house effect) and Copenhagen Protocol (to ensure ozone layer protection from chloro-fluoro carbons), the ecosystem is under grave threat. Globalization has led to a new world trade market in environmental waste. The state finds it difficult to balance the trade-off between economic growth and environment preservation. It leaders in theory are accountable to the governed, whereas in practice, they are accountable to market forces, most notably debt structures and structural adjustment programmes. Their major problem is how to make economic revitalization compatible with democratization. The international funding institutions, such as the World Bank, the IMF and the ADB, pressurize the recipient countries for removal of subsidies on even essential sectors like health, education, water, irrigation, agriculture, electricity and free use of public infrastructure such as roads.[14] There is question of quality versus quantity. The fundamental challenge of globalization to the state and governance is to become accountable and responsible to the ruled and also to the global institutions.

Held et al. have proposed an advanced theory of political globalization. Propounding 'transformational' theory, Held believes in the emergence of a world government.[15] As the new global order has apparently escaped the control of democratic institutions located at the national level, the "democracy has to become a transnational affair". He suggests that strategic priority must be given to the key groups, agencies, associations and organizations of international civil society. Their capacity as agencies of democratic control must be extended through an appropriate recasting of territorial boundaries of systems of accountability, representation and regulation and fortified by entrenched transnational bill of social, economic and civil rights.

Challenges to Indian (Hindatva) Democracy

Political leaders like former Prime Minister A.B. Vajpayee and present Prime Minister Manmohan Singh vainly think that there is no inherent contradiction between globalization and national interests or a democratized world order can be realized in near future. These leaders do not know that they cannot face the forces of globalization and global governance with an outmoded political mechanism without radical changes ushering in people's rising expectations and fastly transforming socio-economic system.

Challenges have appeared to the Indian democracy. These challenges would be discussed at two levels: (a) global, and (b) domestic. Steps to counter them would also be proposed against specific challenges.

Any study of the democratic state of India during the 1990s and after is incomplete and inadequate without situating it within the dynamics of globalization. The Indian leaders in 1991 had to opt for the path of capitalist development as the old state-led path had come to grinding halt and the country was involved in serious balance of payments crisis. Since then, the boundaries of the sovereign national-state of India are getting dissolved in the sea of globalization and the ideology of market-led model of development. Indian democracy is becoming subservient to the powerful Western democratic states are passing through a 'superior and subordinate' phase of relationship. To illustrate, on second Pokhran nuclear explosion of May 1998, the western states imposed economic sanctions; on Kargil (May-July, 1999), India had to plead before G7 for the correctness of her stand towards Pakistan. She had to accept ban imposed by Missile Regime Control, US Patent Laws and US Trade Laws and many others. Indian leaders have agreed to stand by US and other global powers as 'junior partner'.[16] Almost all its senior bureaucrats, who had linkages with the World Bank and the IMF, are found to be the main supporters of the New Economic Policy.[17]

Thus, the threat of globalization and global governance is coming from G7 countries. It has to be met against and used by the major and minor communities of Indian population[18], i.e., by the

Hindatva or Indians as a whole. The Hindatva has to operate at two levels: (a) global level, and (b) domestic level.

Meeting Challenges at Global Level

Hindatva would be the present and potential power of whole people, now over one billion. In order to counterpoise US as superpower of the 21st century, India has simply to stand by the UN and defensively equipped with latest war technology and weapons, both nuclear and conventional.[19] With over 8 per cent GDP, it is now world's fourth biggest fast growing economy. It makes up the largest economic market to the West which it can neglect it only at its own peril. Few now doubt that India is the biggest IT power. Some are anxious to include her in the Group 7.[20] With having least intention to make first use of nuclear weapons, it further wields another extraordinary weapon of Gandhian non-violence or 'satyagraha'. India can successfully refuse to cooperate with the MNCs, and use their product and services, thus, can set every exploiting developed nation right, and force it to listen to the saner counselling of India.

Perhaps, few realize the power and role of Indian culture. Only India can save the world from exploitation, decay and extinction under the heavy weight of materialism, machine, cut-throat competition and over-production.[21] In near future, the world economy would be facing ultimate stagnation and standstill. Only India carries the protective shield of spiritualism along with material progress.[22] It stands for the protection of Mother Earth and save it from waste, pollution, destruction of living and non-living world. Use of recycling, renewable source of energy, attention to global warming, restrictions on harmful chemicals etc. remain on its agenda. There is multiculturalism at the root of Hindatva. To have an effective say in the comity of nations, it has rightly been asking veto nations to grant a permanent seat in the Security Council[23], and save the UNO from being rendered as a non-entity or merely a tool in the hands of developed nations.[24]

Meeting Challenges at Domestic Level

India has now fully realized that it cannot meet global challenges in an effective and adequate manner unless it renovates the infrastructure of its democracy and society at home, and improve its operational behaviour. For this, it is moving in the following directions:

1. India has assigned greater role to private sector in almost all areas. However, it has taken special steps to protect and improve its cottage, handicrafts and medium scale industries. It has injected efficiency, thrift, competition in its industry, trade and commerce. This would enable it to stand by the forces of liberalization, privatization and globalization (LPG) and outside MNCs.
2. India is learning that power consists in 'knowledge'.[25] Therefore, it has made education compulsory, granting top priority to science, technology, research and information technology. It has already encouraged learning of English as a widely used world language. Tools and techniques of IT are widely used and bureaucracy is asked to work with e-governance, computers and e-mails. Professionals, experts, engineers, scientists and specialists are welcome everywhere.
3. In order to move towards greater integration of the nation, India has started to take care of its two-thirds of population, mostly consisting of Scheduled Castes and Scheduled Tribes, Other Backward Classes (OBCs), women and BPL families and provide justice, reservations, concessions, social security and other welfare measures to them. This would be done till they remain unable to bear the brunt of globalization and new economic order.
4. India cannot pull on with conventional pattern of it political democracy and pattern of leadership. It has to make its democratic institutions IT-oriented, responsive and accountable with a scheme of obligatory democratization within political parties.[26] It should have adopted gradualism of political experience paving way for the top political leadership to reach through proper channel of Panchayati Raj/Municipal Council to Panchayat Samiti to Zila Parishad to Vidhan Sabha to Parliament. There would be free, fair and clean elections for all the political posts. No room has to be left for the elements of mafia, money and muscle power.
5. As usual secularism permitting plurality of religions, cultures and languages would flourish. It would not be identified with any kind of dharma, supernaturalism, 'sarva dharma samabhava'

(equivalence to all religions) or 'pantha nirpekshta', but used only in positive sense.[27] Religion broadly would not mean mere other-worldliness, ascetism and neglect of essential callings toward others. Reason, science and inquiry would be injected in religion and religious affairs, if necessary, with attempts to revise them at voluntary levels, but respecting fundamental rights and human rights of all persons granted under law and the Constitution.

6. Administration will be transformed into governance by putting political leadership and management and NGOs at the top. Decision-making would be made effective, prompt and appropriate to the problem and available sources. Cells and panels of these units would be coordinated with the people and media at various levels making room for the people's right to information.[28] Accountability and transparency would reduce corruption. IT, e-mail, computers, TVs etc. will be used to bridge over the gap among the people and the state and its agencies. There can be IT referendum on big transactions with the MNCs, WB, IMF, WTO, ADB and other global institutions.
7. In order to realize above goals, India will have to restructure its judiciary, which has been made immune under the Constitution. It has to be restructured in matters of time, cost, distance, procedure, language and people's satisfaction.[29] Justice delayed is justice denied, particularly in developing countries. Globalization would, thus, be made to serve the cause of Hindatva.

Notes

1. B.M. Sharma and Roop Singh Bareth (eds.), *Good Governance, Globalisation and Civil Society*, Jaipur: Rawat Publications, 2004, p. 10.
2. Martin Shaw, "The global revolution and the twenty-first century: from international relations to global politics", in Stephen Chan and Jarrod Wiener, (eds.), *International History and the Twentieth Century*, London: IB Taurus, 1999.
3. Address of Kofi Annan, Secretary-General to General Assembly on September 23, 2003.

4. Quoted by Pantich, L., "Rethinking the Role of the State" in J.H. Mittesiman (ed.), *Globalisation: Critical Reflections*, London: Lynne Rienner, 1996, pp. 83-113.
5. Joseph Kruth, *Entering The Age Of Transformation: Choosing The Destiny of Humanity In The 21st Century*, 1999.
6. Lawrence S. Finkelstein, "What is Global Governance?" *Global Governance* 1, No. 3 (September-December 1995), p. 369.
7. David Held, A. McGrew, D. Gold Blatt, and S. Perraton, *Global Transformation: Politics, Economics and Culture*, 1999.
8. Krueger, Anne (ed.), *The WTO as an International Organisation*, University Press, New York and Oxford, 1998.
9. Vijay Joshi and M.D. Little, *India's Economic Reforms: 1991-2001*, New Delhi: Oxford University Press, 1997.
10. Quoted by Pantich, L., "Rethinking the Role of the State" in J.H. Mittesiman (ed.), *Globalisation: Critical Reflections*, London: Lynne Rienner, 1996, pp. 83-113.
11. The World Trade Organization (WTO) met in Hong Kong and got a promise by rich nations as a result of leadership of G20 led by Indian Minister Mani Shanker Aiyer, followed by G110 to phase out agricultural export subsidies by 2013. The WTO chief Pascal Lamy said, "We are tilting the balance in the WTO firmly and steadily in favour of the developing nations." *Hindustan Times*, December 21, 2005.
12. Pandav Nayak, 'Globalisation and Nation State Today' in Mohan Lal Sharma, *op. cit.*, pp. 315-28.
13. Henry Kissinger spoke to Manoj Joshi during the two-day HT Leadership Initiative Meeting in New Delhi on the principal threats of the age. *Hindustan Times*, November 9, 2004.
14. Aiyer, op.cit.
15. Bryane Michael has deconstructed Held et al. in his article, "Theorising the Politics of Globalization: A Critique" of Held et al. "Transformationalism", *Journal of Economics and Social Research*, 4(2), 3-17; Held, D. et al. *Global Transformations: Politics, Economics and Culture*, 1999.
16. See, Indo-US Nuclear Agreement, August 2005.
17. Arvind Kumar Agrawal, "Globalization: The New Challenges to State and Governance", in B.M. Sharma et al., op. cit., 139-156.
18. After a gap of 12 years, the Centre had constituted a 102-member National Integration Council (NIC) as a forum for effective initiatives and interaction on issues of national concern, to review issues of national integration and to make recommendations thereon. The newly consti-

tuted National Integration Council (NIC) held its first meeting on 31st August, 2005 in Vigyan Bhavan, Delhi after a gap of 13 years. Prime Minister Dr. Manmohan Singh of UPA presided over it. *Hindustan Times*, February 7, 2005.

19. For this India had Indo US Nuclear Agreement in August, 2005. China opposed the July 16, 2005 Indo-US nuclear agreement on the grounds that it is a sell-out to India. The lack of natural uranium makes it impossible for India to even reach the promised 20 gigawatt level by 2020. China has tied up uranium resources from Canada and Australia to ramp up its production of nuclear power to 32 gigawatt by then. *Hindustan Times*, November 7, 2005.
20. The World Watch Institute's State of report of the World 2006 said India and China are positioned to "leapfrog" today's industrial powers and become world leaders in sustainable energy and agriculture within a decade. In line with this trend both should be inducted into G8 club (Group of Eight industrial nations) and International Energy Agency. India should get a permanent seat in the United Nations Security Council. *Hindustan Times*, January 13, 2006.
21. The announcement of the Prime Minister-led 'Trade and Economic Relations Committee' (TERC) is a reflection of new mindset in India. From a defensive, protectionist, isolationist India, standing in one corner, to an India ready, willing and able to engage the world with self-respect, self-confidence and a sense of sell-being, based on competitiveness of the Indian industry and as growing strength in the national economy. Tarun Das, System check, *Hindustan Times*, May 9, 2005.
22. Introduction.
23. The US has signalled that it will not support the quest of India, Japan, Germany and Brazil for permanent seat in the UN Security Council unless they give up their demand for veto power, the New York Times reported on May 15, 2005. *Hindustan Times*, May 16, 2005.
24. In his report Kofi Annan talks of development, security and human rights. Speaking at the India International Centre, New Delhi, on April 28, 2005, he unveiled his latest report the international community—In *Larger Freedom: Towards Development, Security and Human Rights for All*. It says, "No state, no matter how powerful, can be its own efforts alone make itself invulnerable to today's threats. Every state requires the cooperation of other states to make itself secure. It is in very State's interest, accordingly, to cooperate with state to address their most pressing threats, because doing so will maximize the chances of reciprocal cooperation to address its own threat priorities." Lonely crusader, Prem Shanker Jha, *Hindustan Times*, May 6, 2005.

25. Launching the Knowledge Commission, PM Manmohan Singh on August 2, 2005 wanted to bridge over the mismatch between quality standards in India's universities and centres of excellence with the best in the world. It would be headed by technology czar Sam Pitroda. The commission would comprise several eminent academicians and technologists apart from management experts. *Hindustan Times*, August 3, 2005.
26. Cabinet OKs state funding of elections approving a 1200 crore plan for non-cash state funding. EC is likely to ascertain the views of political parties across the spectrum to help force a consensus that will be the basis for implementation of the plan. *Hindustan Times*, December 24, 2005.
27. In the NIC meeting held on 31st August, 2005 in Vigyan Bhavan, Delhi Sita Ram Yechuri of CPM criticized former Prime Minister Atal Bihari Vajpayee for suggesting ekatmata instead of ekta. Ekta assumes diversity whereas ekatmata assumes assimilation. BJP believes in assimilation, not in unity. Also we should not use world 'panth nirpekshta' for secularism but 'dharma nirpekshta'. Panth nirpeksha suggests that only Hinduism is dharma and all other religions are panths. This is not acceptable. Dr. Asghar Ali Engineer, No. 18, September 16-30, 2005, Secular Perspective, Centre for Study of Society and Secularism, Mumbai (India).
28. The Right to Information Bill was passed by the Lok Sabha on May 12, 2005 as a means to fight corruption and inefficiency in the government at various levels—centre, states, panchayats, local bodies, even non-governmental organizations. It marks a major milestone for Indian democracy. *Hindustan Times*, May 13, 2005.
29. The new Chief Justice of India Y.K. (Yogesh Kumar) Sabharwal called for swift punishment to merchants of terror. Trial of cases relating to terrorism should be fast tracked and that judiciary would do its best towards that end. Cases concerning corruption and involving the high and mighty should also be put on the "fast track". He also called for expeditious disposal of cases concerning the old, the infirm and the Scheduled Castes and Scheduled Tribes. *Times of India*, November 4, 2005.

Index